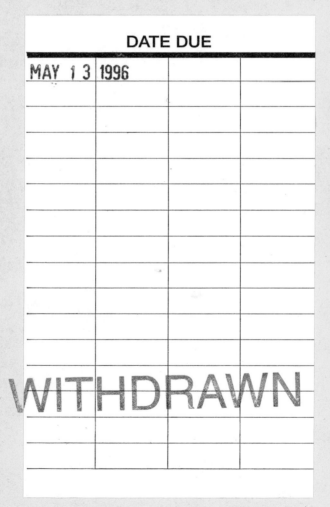

DATE DUE			
MAY 1 3 1996			
WITHDRAWN			

＊　＊　＊　＊　＊　＊　＊　＊

A History of Music and
Dance in Florida,
1565–1865

* * * * * * * *

A HISTORY OF
Music & Dance
in Florida,
1 5 6 5 – 1 8 6 5

Wiley L. Housewright

The University of Alabama Press   Tuscaloosa & London

Copyright © 1991 by
The University of Alabama Press
Tuscaloosa, Alabama 35487–0380
All rights reserved
Manufactured in the United States of America

The paper on which this book is printed meets the minimum
requirements of American National Standard for Information
Science-Permanence of Paper for Printed Library Materials,
ANSI A39.48-1984. ∞

Library of Congress Cataloging-in-Publication Data

Housewright, Wiley L., 1913–
    A history of music and dance in Florida, 1565–1865 /
Wiley L. Housewright.
        p.   cm.
    Includes bibliographical references.
    ISBN 0-8173-0492-4 (alk. paper)
    1. Music—Florida—History and criticism. 2. Dancing—
Florida—History.   I. Title.
    ML200.7.F6H7 1991   90–32563
    780'.9759—dc20   CIP
                            MN

British Library Cataloguing-in-Publication Data available

TO LUCILLA

My friend the reader, to err is human, and no other save God can call himself perfect, and even he, according to the proverb, cannot satisfy everybody. Therefore, if you find anything in this book according not well with your opinion, or some fault of style, I beg of you in your wisdom to endure it all, and not to think me better than one of the authors who is put among the holy books, and who at the end of his work says: That if he has not acquitted himself worthily enough in his history, he should be pardoned; for I submit myself in all things to the correction of those wiser than I.

—Marc Lescarbot, *Histoire de la Nouvelle France*, 1609

To my reader friend: Among all the books giving spiritual and honest pleasure, none gives me more pleasurable entertainment than those dealing with stories about new lands and the conquest of distant and strange lands, among which is the Island of Florida, which has been the latest discovery in the world. Without a doubt it is to be admired over any other place as to singularity and riches because it is full of unknown lands and seas, of strange people, animals and plants; and the spirit is enriched there by the voluptuous delight of novelty, public opinion is formed and instructed with new knowledge, and the uncertainty of things imagined becomes an assurance by beholding with the eye things as marvelous as prodigious land and sea monsters long ago seen and known in that land of Florida.

—Capt. Giles de Pysière, *Discours de l'entreprise et saccagement que les forsaires de l'isle Florida*, 1565

✳ ✳ ✳ ✳ ✳ ✳ ✳ ✳

Contents

＊　＊　＊　＊　＊　＊　＊　＊

Illustrations

✳   ✳   ✳   ✳   ✳   ✳   ✳   ✳

Preface

The reluctance of Florida historians to write on so-
cial or cultural history and the echoing silence of music historians about
the earliest European music made in what is now the United States caused
me to undertake this study. The general historians have given us fine documentation of political, military, and economic life in early Florida. The
music historians of our nation usually write nothing at all of Florida.[1]
They allege that the music of that period and place had no influence on the
music of later years. I do not regard that as adequate reason for remaining
mute on the music events and musical people of our peninsula throughout
history. It is my purpose, then, to document the music that was made in
early Florida history.

The customary sources for music historians are the music scores of composers. The absence of written music among Florida Indians, then, is a
limiting condition of this study. We do have reports of officials, memoirs,
narratives, diaries, and casual observations and vivid epistles of visitors
who commented on the music they heard. We also have information on
the music, the instruments, and the music makers who came with the
settlers of Florida. In later periods newspapers became prime sources, although references to music in these sources are few and widely scattered.
Music was seldom the central event. Usually it was incidental or adjunctive
to religious, political, or diplomatic events. Reports were written in non-
technical language by nonprofessional musicians. Churchmen wrote histories of their denominations without once mentioning a hymn, anthem, or
any form of music in its service, for instance. The settlement of early Florida is one of the best-documented events of sixteenth-century North
America. State archives have preserved valuable documents with references to music. It remains now the task of a musician to document the
occurrence of music in our history and to give contextual definition. The
sources from which the information is drawn have been either unknown
or unused by music historians.

The state is a political unit and is not usually defined as a cohesive cultural unit. The early music of Florida, however, was defined by the distinct national cultures that held political power and whose people populated its land. Its uses were described by military men with political agenda, by religious zealots whose faith led them to martyrdom, and by hardy settlers who brought with them the cultural biases from four or more continents. When reading these reports, one must keep in mind who was writing about his brother-in-law, who was bucking for promotion, and who was a fortune seeker. The stories reveal much about what people saw and heard and their reactions as participants or observers. The cultural differences between ethnic groups through the years may be observed in reports of official agents, enterprising immigrants, and slaves who sang of their yearning for freedom. This, then, is the music heritage of the state, for remnants of it remain in our culture. It is time to blow the dust off some of these songs and tunes, to place them in their historical settings. By knowing them and the traditions from which they have sprung, we will deepen our roots and will understand more about our ancestors and ourselves.

I cannot promise continuity, only samplings or examples. The scenes changed dramatically, as did the cast of characters. The music changed with them. Some of it survived, but much of it did not. No towering Florida figures in music emerged in the period studied, either as composers or as performers. European and American men and women became Floridians by choice. Each of them defined beauty in a way differing from others. Each brought a distinctive repertory. Some sustained music traditions, while others improvised new songs suited to new occasions. Most were amateurs, though a few were professionals.

I have attempted to stand aside as often as possible so that the cast of characters can tell their stories in their own words. To music historians and thousands of us who have immigrated to the state, they are new stories that warrant being told. If the attention of others is engaged, they are invited to read on.

The author of a recent comprehensive history of Florida wrote, "An obvious need is for more studies of the cultural and social history of the people of Florida."[2] This book is a response to that and similar comments by others. In its preparation, I have received assistance from many, and I wish to thank them all.

To the following libraries, I extend my thanks for the use I have made of their collections: British Library, Boston Public Library, Library of Congress, National Archives, New York Public Library, Library Company of Philadelphia, Philadelphia Free Library, Enoch Pratt Library of Baltimore, and Nassau Public Library.

I am equally grateful to the following libraries of Florida, from which I have drawn most of the material of this narrative: Robert M. Strozier and Warren D. Allen libraries of Florida State University, State Library of Florida, Florida Historical Society Library, P. K. Yonge Library of Florida History at the University of Florida, DuPont-Ball Library of Stetson University, Carl S. Swisher Library of Jacksonville University, University of South Florida Library, John C. Pace Library of the University of West Florida, St. Augustine Historical Society Library, Historical St. Augustine Preservation Board Library, Jacksonville Public Library, Daytona Beach Historical Society Library, Miami-Dade Public Library, Pensacola Historical Society and Museum, Tampa-Hillsborough County Public Library, Dr. Peck House in St. Augustine, De Land Public Library, and Monroe County Library.

I am especially grateful for the assistance and advice of the following experts in related studies: the late J. Leitch Wright, Eugene Lyon, William Rogers, Edward Keuchel, Amy Bushnell, Charles W. Arnade, Albert Manucy, Marilyn Gombosi, Robert Smith, and Robert Fichter. Then, I am grateful to June Carland, Sue Boddy, Debora Simpson, Ruth Wenner, Beth Wright, Bruce Frank, and Tim Risher for assistance in preparing the manuscript for the editor, and especially to Kay Hollis.

I am grateful to Carleton Sprague Smith, the first mentor who engaged my interest in American music, and to Robert Glidden, dean of the School of Music at Florida State University. Over the years these men have given generous encouragement and assistance to me and my idea that a chronicle of music in Florida was overdue. I thank, too, my musician-colleagues and students for their continuous good wishes. They are developing the indigenous talent of young Floridians. Someday a book will be written about them.

* * * * * * * *

A History of Music
and Dance in Florida,
1565–1865

1

* * * * * * * *

A Solemn Elevated
State of Mind
Music and the Indians

The large land mass called Florida by sixteenth-century Spaniards extended from the Atlantic coast westward to the Mississippi and northward to the Chesapeake Bay or farther. The peninsula now called Florida was then populated by numerous aboriginal Indians. Among them were the Timucuans and Apalachees in the north, the Ais Indians along the Indian River, Tequestas to the south, and the powerful southwest coast Calusas. Others resided to the north and west. They were described as differing among themselves in appearance from one province to another, though many of their ceremonies were similar. They were an olive color, tall and with painted skins. They were naked except for a strap of fur skins worn by men and a moss-draped garment for the women. Both sexes occasionally wore ear ornaments, headpieces with feathers, pearls, and metal jewelry.

Because they were nonliterate, earliest reports of their music and dance were made by European eye-and-ear witnesses, explorers, official historians, priests, settlers, and visitors. They were non-technical accounts buttressed by drawings or paintings of such artists as Jacques Le Moyne and

KING AND QUEEN IN FLORIDA

Florida Indian king and queen as depicted in a detail of a map by Mercator (1512–92), republished by Jodocus Hondius c. 1609. (Author's private collection; reprinted from Virginiae Item et Floridae)

George Catlin. On the legacy of these documents and oral traditions, historians have written their stories. Remnants of early Florida tribes, even today, attempt to recreate their music and dance based on these sources. In this chapter we recount the uses of music and dance in Indian religious rites, festivals, recreations, and ceremonies. Additional cultural interactions with the Europeans and Americans are narrated in succeeding chapters.

Panfilo de Narváez, a red-bearded one-eyed fleet commander on his way to conquer Florida, was near Trinidad when, on April 12, 1528, he encountered a storm that destroyed sixty of his people and twenty horses. Above the sound of the hurricane he heard a roar of Indian voices and the sound of bells, flutes, native tambourines, and other instruments.[1] To his

INHABITANTS OF FLORIDA, 1683

In his De l'Amérique *series of engravings, Mallet (French, 1630–1706) pictured Florida Indians with tattoos, pearls, and earrings. (Author's private collection; reprinted from Alain Manesson Mallet,* Description de l'Univers)

Hispanic ears the howling music was only a little less welcome than the storm itself. Two days later he dropped anchor in Tampa Bay, and his three-hundred-man entourage began its northward journey to the interior. When they reached Apalache, they were greeted by Indians playing on flutes made of reed.[2] Here they observed an all-night dance and noisy celebration like others they would see as they traveled westward. Percussive patterns were established by hand clapping or by slapping gourds filled with seed or stones. Dancing was ubiquitous, not as recreation or art, but as conjuration or plea for supernatural intercession. Supernatural power came from many sources and was manifest in many ways. Music was interwoven into the structure of that power in customs on both sides of the Atlantic.

On this trip, Cabeza de Vaca, treasurer to Narváez, observed the Indians' therapeutic use of music. He compared customs for treating the sick among the Indians and the Spanish and saw a similarity. Indian cures were brought about by bleeding, blowing breath on the victim, and laying on of hands followed by rejoicing and dancing. The Spanish ritual was to make a sign of the cross, breathe on the subject, and chant a Pater Noster or an Ave Maria.[3] Faith in the healing powers of their own shamans was great, but the Indians could not refuse the additional benefits of Spanish religious rites and music.

Music was also used by the Indians to signal, impress, intimidate, and immortalize. Hernando de Soto, who landed in Florida in May 1539, reported an incident which illustrated these uses. His troops entered the settlement of Ochile, believed to be present-day Ocala, where they were not hospitably received by Vitachuco, one of the ruling chiefs. On each of eight successive days the chief attempted to intimidate the Spaniards by sending to them two or three Indians who blew their raucous best on conch-shell trumpets.[4] The performance was followed by a hail of verbal maledictions and threats to boil half of the foreigners and roast the other half. Vitachuco later decided to do away with his unwelcome visitors by slow poisoning, burying some of them up to their necks, and suspending others from trees as food for the birds. He fantasized that Indian women and children would dance around him singing songs in praise of his clever scheme and that future generations would know of him through these songs. Interpreters informed the Spanish of the plot, and a counterplan was devised which allowed them to escape, but not before they killed over three hundred Indians in battle.

How the Indians composed songs of various tempi and achieved rhythmic precision in a group task was described in an early account of the 1541–42 wanderings of Hernando de Soto in Florida. The narrator was Garcilaso de la Vega, *el Inca*. His colorful descriptions occasionally blended truth with romanticism to achieve a high literary style, yet elements of his story are consistent with both earlier and later reports. Late in the expedition, a fleet of unusually large Indian canoes, each holding twenty-five to thirty warriors and fifty oarsmen, followed the Spanish for two days. Rowing together, they could attain the speed of a horse running at his greatest speed. *El Inca* described how this was achieved.

In order for all to row simultaneously and to rhythm, the Indians compose various songs of different tones, the length and brevity of which depends upon the haste or slowness with which they are moving. In these songs they tell of deeds accomplished in war by their own as well as other commanders, with whose recollection they are incited to battle and triumph. These and similar things they uttered as they rowed to the sound of their songs, at the close of each of which they gave tremendous shouts and outcries.[5]

Another sixteenth-century event illustrated how a powerful Florida Indian chief and his Spanish adversary used music as an instrument of diplomacy. In 1566 Cacique Carlos, ruler of the Calusa, attempted to intimidate the Spanish by a series of stylized ceremonies followed by feasting, singing, dancing, and drinking. The largest of these was a banquet for Pedro Menéndez, leader of the Spanish settlement. It was described by Gonzalo Solís de Meras, brother-in-law of Menéndez and historian of the mission, who was there. "And the day following that on which Cacique Carlos departed from the brigantines, the Adelantado went to dine with him, taking 210 arquebusiers with him and a flag, two fifers and drummers, three trumpeters, one harp, one vihuela de arco, and one psaltery, and a very small dwarf, a great singer and dancer, whom he brought with him."[6] He entered the cacique's house, which was large enough to accommodate two thousand people. The cacique sat on a raised seat in a room with large windows. There he greeted the Adelantado, then his relatives and leaders entered. More than five hundred Indian girls, ages ten to fifteen years, were seated outside the windows in groups of a hundred. Fifty of them sang and stopped, then another fifty began singing, and so on, throughout the evening. "They sang with much order," according to Gonzalo Solís de Meras.

As the meal was being served, Spanish trumpeters played outside the house. Then, during dinner, a few Spanish gentlemen who had good voices sang. The dwarf danced, and instrumentalists played. The Indians were pleased with European music. The cacique ordered the young girls to stop singing, since they knew little and their guests knew much. He asked the Adelantado to have his musicians continue. The Adelantado complied. This was one of the earliest reported examples of cultural genocide related to music in the New World.

Jonathan Dickinson wrote the best-known account of seventeenth-century music among Florida Indians.[7] A Philadelphia Quaker who was shipwrecked off Jupiter Island in 1696, he believed that God's protecting providence had saved him from the "devouring waves of the sea" and the "inhumane cannibals of Florida." He wrote his observations of the latter as he made his northward journey along the Florida east coast. With the Ais Indians he drank the black drink, a tea made by boiling leaves of *Ilex cassine*. The beverage was served from a deep round bowl, large enough to hold about three gallons of liquid. At night the receptacle was covered to become a drum. With rattles, it accompanied singing and dancing. Men prepared for the dance by crying out like madmen or making fearful noises such as the barking of a wolf or dog. They initiated the dance and song and were later joined by young women.

In preparation for battle a three-day war dance was staged. Men painted themselves in hues of red and black and armed themselves with bows and arrows. They erected a large arrowhead painted with red and white stripes and in its midsection carved the thigh, leg, and foot of a man. An old man delivered a howling proclamation, then six chiefs rose. They shook rattles for a half-hour interlude, then the dance began. The violent stamping beat the ground into furrows. The dancers continued until they were faint or sick from their exertion, according to Dickinson.

In the eighteenth century, a similar war dance was practiced by the Indians who lived in western Florida. For over a decade, beginning in 1735, an Englishman lived among them and described their sacred rites.[8] Yo-He-Wah was their deity, and the syllables of his name figured conspicuously throughout the ceremony. In preparation for war these Indians sang their old religious songs. They were accompanied by clay-pot drums covered with thin, wet deerskin tightly drawn and by rattling calabashes. Male

INDIANS CAPTURING SHIPWRECK VICTIMS
*The fierce Tequesta, Jobese, and Ais captured shipwreck victims along the east coast.
Jonathan Dickinson escaped that fate in the eighteenth century and later wrote of
Indian music and dance. This drawing (c. 1707) is an illustration from his* Journal.
(Courtesy Florida State Archives)

dancers moved about in a variety of improvised postures while keeping
time with the drums. They pranced about with wild, quick-sliding steps in
a mock battle exhibition. Women later joined the dance. On their legs
were tied terrapin shells containing pebbles which rattled in percussive
patterns.

On the day following a military victory, scalps were hung by pine twigs
on housetops. Then was sung "the awful death song, with a solemn striking air" occasionally interrupted by shrill war whoops. The leader sang the
syllables of the deity's name at various pitch levels, ending with a shrill
treble sound. The triumphal song followed, then the Indians danced again
in circles around the sacred fire. The patterns of these celebrations were
not unlike those described by other visitors to Florida in the years that
followed. The Englishman wrote of Indian ceremonies in fascinating detail. He told that the Muskogee male Indians painted themselves with

chalky clay and masked their faces with pieces of gourds and hieroglyphic paintings. Their heads shined with oils. Some fixed a pair of young buffalo horns to their heads; others, a tail, behind.[9] While James Adair, author of these descriptions, disapproved of Spanish versions of these religious dances, his own are similar to both the Spanish and French. His history may be trusted on these events. What he saw, he reported with reasonable accuracy. What he imagined to be the Indian ancestry and the meaning of some of the ceremonies should be read with suspicion.

The last of the aboriginal Indians left Florida about 1763, when the early Spaniards moved out. Seminoles and other groups moved in over the next century. The Seminoles were a Muskogean tribe who came from Lower Creek settlements along the Chattahoochee River.

John and William Bartram came to Florida and observed these and other tribes in the southern sector of North America for two years, beginning in 1765. John, a Quaker American naturalist who was botanist to George III, and his son William wrote numerous stories that told of the uses of music among the Indians they met. They wrote that the Seminoles had a great variety of songs, most of which were sung while the Indians danced. They described the instruments played by the Seminoles. Earlier and later visual and verbal documents furnished details of composing, singing, and dancing.

Aside from their own voices, flutes made of cane were the preferred musical instruments of Florida Indians. A drawing of the early woodwind instrument was made by Le Moyne. It is described below in chapter 3. A prototype of the later instrument played by the Seminoles was described as follows:

> The removal of the septums of the cane is like that in other flutes, but the detached piece that forms the whistle head is flush with the tube instead of being in the form of a block or band above the opening. It is tied in place with a buckskin thong, as in the flutes having a wooden block. The flute has four fingerholes spaced about in the usual manner, but its outstanding peculiarity lies in the boring of two holes transversely through the cane at right angles to the sound holes and equally distant from them, the transverse holes occurring between the locations of the fingerholes.[10]

Many Florida visitors or military men were greeted by Indians playing flutes. Three of the early ones were Cabeza de Vaca, Hernando de Soto, and René Laudonnière. Incidents with the Spaniards were recorded in the *Narrative* of Cabeza de Vaca.[11] That of the Frenchmen is in the "Brevis narratio" by cartographer-artist Jacques Le Moyne.[12] The artist also depicted the instrument at the head of a bridal procession.

Drums played a role in setting rhythmic patterns in motion, though they were not as conspicuous in the music of Florida Indians as in some other native North American tribes. Three Seminole types have been reported. A drum with a single head accompanied the green corn dance. A cypress knee drum accompanied the stomp dance. The ball game dance was accompanied by a water drum, a kettle containing water covered with buckskin. This instrument was fastened over the shoulder of the drummer, who also led the dance. The rhythmic function was enhanced by rattles made of gourds, coconut shells, or deer hooves. Small turtle shells were tied around women's legs for the green corn dance, the stomp dance, and the catfish dance.

There were few if any string instruments among most tribes, though in the summer of 1746 a British observer, James Adair, described an eighteenth-century sacred music instrument of very large proportions. It was five feet long, a foot wide at the head of the board. Its eight strings were made of the sinews of a large buffalo. It took men at each end of the bow to produce a tone, which Adair judged to be harsh. Played in the residence of a former Mississippi Nachee Indian, the jarring sound was "sufficient to drive out the devil if he lay anywhere hid in the house," Adair wrote.[13]

The Seminoles used dance for recreation as well as for religion. They had an endless variety of steps, according to William Bartram. They usually preferred slow shuffling, beginning with a toe-to-heel movement of the right foot and alternating with the left. The choreography was illustrated in Bartram's account of a recreational event held on the eve of a ball game. The rally began with an oration by the chief on the benefits of a manly sport and a review of the brilliant victories of the local team, not neglecting to remind all of his own exploits as a youth. The musicians then began to play and sing. Presently young women entered the rotunda singing. They filed into two semicircles, facing the spectators and the musicians, moving slowly. After a while, a company of young men entered with loud shrill whoops. Each carried his racket. They formed semicircles opposite the young women. Then began a series of complex dance movements, each executed with precision. Ranks moved into circles about the central fire. The dance, according to Bartram, was "accompanied with an instantaneous and universal elevation of the voice and a shrill short whoop."[14] In function, this dance and its music was a celebration not unlike that staged by the Cherokees and Choctaws before their ball games. The game of these tribes and the Seminoles was a forerunner to lacrosse. George Catlin described the ball game of the Choctaws both in narrative and in a memorable painting of 1834–35.

A legend of the Seminoles alleged that in the old days, animals talked like people. The alligators, rabbits, and wild turkeys generated their distinctive sounds and rhythmic motion in both songs and dances. When all the people of the earth die, the animals may return, talking like people, singing their songs, and dancing their dances. The respect Indians had for reptiles was illustrated in song and dance for William Hayne Simmons and John Lee Williams when they came to the hills of Tallahassee in 1823 seeking the site for a territorial capital. The rattlesnake song and dance were among those performed for the visitors. Four stakes were placed in an open field, and the singers sang a melancholy but sweet air as they coiled about the stakes in fantastic figures. The song addressed the snakes, requesting them to go into their holes so that they might not be molested by hunters. A sage Indian warned that should anyone touch the stakes, that person would certainly be bitten by a snake on the first hunting excursion.[15] This and other cabalistic songs were part of the religious heritage of the Seminoles. They described the relationship of human beings to nature.

Young men who aspired to the Seminole priesthood were taught music and decorum. They wore white robes. On their head, arm, or hand they carried a stuffed owl as an ensign of wisdom and divination. These bachelors were "distinguished from other people by their taciturnity, grave and solemn countenance, dignified step, and singing to themselves songs or hymns, in a low sweet voice, as they stroll about the town," Bartram observed.[16]

William Bartram and his companions were encamped at Long Pond when they were visited by seven young Seminole men who played and sang recreational music. One was a young prince who was in pursuit of a fellow who had carried off one of his wives or concubines. He declared that he would have the ears of both of them before he returned. After sharing liquor and engaging in conversation, the youths wished the white visitors a cordial good night and retired to their camp. "Having a band of music with them, consisting of a drum, flutes, and a rattle gourd, they entertained us during the night with their music, vocal and instrumental," Bartram reported. "There is a languishing softness and melancholy air in the Indian convivial songs, especially of the amorous class, irresistibly moving, attractive and exquisitely pleasing, especially in these solitary recesses when all nature is silent," Bartram continued.[17]

Another incident elicited a similar commentary by Bartram. The Choctaws were reputed to be expert in music and always brought new songs to annual busks, seasonal tribal meetings. A young Mustee who had learned their repertory attended a great festival and sang a lament. The meaning of the chorus was:

> All men must surely die,
> Though no one knows how soon;
> Yet when the time shall come,
> The event may be joyful.

Bartram responded to the performance by observing: "These doleful songs or elegies have a quick and sensible effect on their passions, and discover a lively affection and sensibility; their countenance now dejected, again, by easy transition, becomes gently elevated, as if in solemn address or supplication, accompanied with a tremulous, sweet, lamentable voice."[18] In a summary statement, he told of the effect of music on the Indians. "The tambour and rattle accompanied by their sweet low voices, produce a pathetic harmony, keeping exact time together, and the countenance of the musician, at proper times, seems to express the solemn elevated state of mind: at that time there seems not only a harmony between him and his instrument, but it instantly touches the feelings of the attentive audience, as the influence of an active and powerful spirit; there is then an united universal sensation of delight and peaceful union of souls throughout the assembly."[19]

Among the religious ceremonies was the black-drink vesper. The drink became associated with other events, but the central rite was described by Bartram. When the chiefs, venerable men, and warriors were assembled, two men entered with large conch shells filled with the black drink. They approached the chief's sofa and rested the shells on tripods. With great solemnity, the syllables *a-hoo-o-jah* and *a-lu-yah* were chanted on two notes, each on a single breath. It was the custom not to remove the drink from one's lips until the singing ceased. The ceremony was followed by a banquet, pipe smoking, and more drinking. Afterward there was music and dancing that continued all night.[20]

Among other essentially religious rituals of the Seminoles were the Green Corn Festival and the Hunting Festival. The June busk was held to give thanks for ample corn to make bread. The autumn event asked for success in the hunts for meat. Both asked for protection from misfortune. In preparation for the Green Corn Festival, streets and houses were cleaned, old clothing discarded, and the body purged. Women cooked comtie and cabbage palm buds in large pots. Ears of fresh corn were laid in the embers to roast. Men hunted deer and bear and skinned them. The chief, in war paint and silver ornaments, opened the ceremony with a brief speech on the significance of the tradition. A sacred bundle of artifacts was opened. Dancers formed a circle around the fire. They chanted a dirgelike song as they began to move, slowly at first, then faster and faster. Presently, exhausted with their singing, yelling, and dancing, they rested and began the feast. The roasted corn was to them "an emblem of future peace and prosperity."[21]

Later descriptions of this ceremony indicated a time extension of four or eight days when subtribes sang a variety of green corn dances. The Cypress Swamp Group sang eight, the Cow Creek Group six, and the Calusas one. There was also a diversity among these three groups in their hunting dance songs. Social dances, which rounded out the festivals, were addressed to alligators, snakes, buffalo, deer, or catfish. Texts of many songs were so ancient that singers no longer knew their meaning, but they survived by repetitions at tribal festivals.

The Seminoles conducted their affairs at public council meetings. Tribal elders met to receive ambassadors, deliver answers to proposals, sing traditional war songs, or commemorate their dead. They also regulated order, peace, and crime. No solemnity or public business was carried on without songs and dances, according to one observer.[22] The chief sang of the remarkable events experienced by the tribe, and others sang in turn.

Council meetings of Indians with Indian agents or military men failed to produce agreements to avert the Seminole Wars, but their principals wrote descriptions of ceremonies enacted before or after the conferences. Two such meetings took place in 1823, one with riffed officer Peter Pelham at Moultree Creek and the other with Gen. Thomas S. Jesup's dragoons. The Indians in their procession were clothed in ceremonial dress. They accompanied their song with a drum and a shrill whoop at the end of each verse. On arrival, the dancers ceased their antic capers. They shook elbows with the officers and touched the heads of their adversaries with a white feather mounted on a stick. They took their seats, smoked calumet, and petitioned for peace.[23] The ritual dance followed. In single file, dancers moved in an ambling gait at a very slow pace. Their singing began with a "monotonous whine," responded to by choruses with differing texts. Counterclockwise they stamped around the fire, with the left hand held to the mouth. The motion accelerated and the chanting grew louder as the melody took up the words *u-han-a-way* or *yo-halin-ah-way-ha*. This common practice among the Seminoles differed from that of the northern Indian tribes described by Theodore Baker in *Über die Musik der nordamerikanischen Wilden*, an 1882 study of Indian music. His conclusion was that "the singers appear to feel no need for crescendo and diminuendo, accelerando and ritardando."[24] The dance leader leaped wildly about and was imitated by others. When the leader was fatigued, he stopped and uttered a shrill whoop, and the dance ceased.[25]

One of the most elaborate council meetings occurred in 1826, when Seminole tribes united under one leader. The man they chose was Tuko-see-mathla (John Hicks). The site for his inauguration was near an Indian agency about two miles from Silver Springs. The Micasukies erected a circular amphitheater fifty feet wide and two hundred feet in diameter which seated about two thousand warriors. About one thousand Indian women remained in the open plain. The ceremony began with the rattlesnake dance. One hundred warriors, dressed in their finest apparel, were led by a Micasuky chief. They entered in single file, holding hands. The chief sang, and the men joined in the chorus. The last man shook a large gourd which represented rattles of the reptile. Slowly they coiled about the fire, singing praises of their chief while beating time with their feet. Then with dignity and grace the dancers uncoiled as they sang a sprightly song. The ceremony lasted about twenty minutes. This was the same dance that the Seminoles had performed in the hills of Tallahassee three years earlier for William Hayne Simmons and John Lee Williams.

The effect of Indian music on American soldiers was reported by several men who served in the nineteenth-century Seminole Wars. Lt. John T. Sprague, aide-de-camp to Maj. Gen. Alexander Macomb of the Eighth Army Infantry, wrote, "They had no music other than their own voices, which made the woods ring with a monotonous but agreeable sound."[26] His assessment a few weeks later, however, changed when he wrote, "This evening they entertained the general with an Indian dance; we soon got tired and left them. Even now, twelve o'clock at night, I hear their hideous shouts and yells, and within view of my tent, I can see men, women and children circling around blazing fire keeping time with their discordant and monotonous tones."[27] By the following evening he recovered his military discipline and sense of duty sufficiently to join the dancing. He wished, he wrote, to convince the Indians that he reposed as much confidence in them as they did in the soldiers. His experience and his reaction were replicated by many brothers in arms.

2

* * * * * * * *

Te Deum Laudamus

Music and the Early Spanish

*Saturday, the eighth of
the said month of
September, day of the
Nativity of Our Lady,
the general landed with
many banners waving
and many trumpets and
other instruments of
military music, and the
booming of many
artillery pieces. . . . I
took a cross and went to
meet them singing the
hymn "Te Deum
Laudamus."*
—Fr. Francisco López
   de Mendoza Grajales,
   1565

The earliest documented European music heard in Florida was the chanting of the Catholic priests who accompanied such Spanish explorers as Ponce de León (1512), Panfilo de Narváez (1528), Cabeza de Vaca (1528), and Hernando de Soto (1539). Excavations and research of Mark F. Boyd, Hale G. Smith, Calvin Jones, and other archaeologists confirm that Hernando de Soto and his company of explorers spent several months on the hilltops and lakeshores of Tallahassee in 1539. Indians from the shores of Lake Jackson to the crest of Myers Park heard and witnessed early enactments of Catholic ritual in Florida in that year.[1]

To place this event in chronological perspective, it is necessary to review developments in New Spain. The precedent for bringing musicians to the New World had been set by Hernando Cortés when he brought six musicians with him to Mexico in 1519 and five others to Honduras in 1524.[2] It was the priests who first taught European music to the Indians. Pedro de Gante taught music in a Mexico City mission school as early as 1527.[3] In nearby Guatitlán, Fr. Juan de Padilla in 1532 taught Indians how to read and write and to sing plainchant and organum. He joined the company of Francisco Vásquez de Coronado in his search for the mythical city of Quivira and traveled to the present states of Arizona, New Mexico, Oklahoma, and Kansas, where he taught until his death in 1542. He is cited as "probably the first European to teach music in America."[4] Cristóbal de Quinones is also cited as the first teacher of European music within the confines of the present United States. He was active in the New Mexico missions from 1598 to 1604.[5]

The Florida candidates for first music teachers came from Santa Cruz in 1559 with the large Tristán de Luna y Arelláno company. Their mission was to settle Ochuse (Pensacola) and Santa Elena (Port Royal, South Carolina). Leading the priests was the first vicar provincial of Florida, a musician-missionary named Fr. Pedro Martín de Feria. With him were four associate priests: Dominic de la Anunciación, Dominic de Salazar, John de Mazuelas, James (Diego) de Santo Domingo, and a lay brother Bartholomew Matéos. It was they who taught the Indians of Ochuse and nearby settlements how to sing the litanies. According to one historian, Fr. Pedro Martín de Feria was "a lover of music and ceremonies of the church. He did not let his episcopal dignity prevent him from personally teaching these to the Indians. The clergy were required to do the same."[6] These priests taught music to the Florida Indians about thirty years after the earliest music missionaries in Mexico City, twenty years after Padilla in the Southwest, and twenty years before the Cristóbal de Quinones mission in New Mexico.

From 1520 to 1577 both the Dominicans and the Jesuits tried and failed to establish missions in Florida, but then Franciscans began arriving. Twelve came in 1587, with Fr. Alonso Reinoso in charge. Among the four who in 1587 sailed in a caravel from La Yaguana to St. Augustine was Fr. Alonso Escobedo, the poet who wrote the epic poem *La Florida*. One who came from the province of Castile in 1595 was Fr. Fernández de Chozas, a Biscayan. With a bodyguard and a translator he traveled to Guale, Quaque, Faluge, Tuma, and Usatipa. Two years later he was commissioned to explore the province of Tama. A thirty-man Indian squadron and intervention of the soldier de Salas were necessary to prevent the Indians from making a leg ornament of the father's scalp. The priest continued his journey toward the coast by way of Yufera and Cancansu, where his sermon was well received by the Indians.

When he returned to San Juan, his home mission, the Indians came out to receive him singing polyphonic songs which he had taught them. Sev-

Te Deum Laudamus

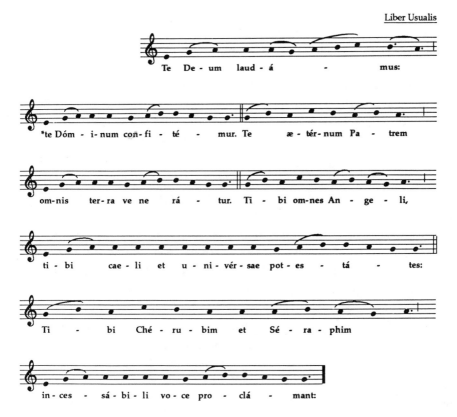

This prayer (We praise thee, O God) was sung by priests on such occasions as safe voyages, battle victories, or visits of bishops. This song of thanksgiving was heard along the chain of missions from St. Augustine to Pensacola. (Reprinted from Liber Usualis, p. 832)

eral historians have reported that these Indians sang to the accompaniment of the organ.[7] Their reports were based on a misunderstanding of music terminology in the poem by Escobedo.

> Hubo por su venida gran contento,
> Cantando a punto de órgano canciones,

Que el Padre Chozas, con su buen talento,
Les daba cada día dos lecciones.
Cuya sonoridad y grave acento
Desterraba del alma las pasiones,
Cuando hacían los indios ejercicio
y cantan una misa era su oficio.[8]

The sense of the poem is that the Indians were happy to have Father Chozas return from Tama, that they sang polyphonic songs which Father Chozas, with his fine talent, had taught them, and that he gave them two lessons each day. This is perhaps the earliest documented instance of Florida Indians singing polyphonic music. Priests of the de Luna expedition and Huguenots of Fort Caroline had taught Indians to sing music of their churches earlier, but Escobedo's was the first reported in these terms: "Cantando a punto de órgano canciones."[9]

Among other missionaries who came to Florida with Fr. Alonso Reinoso in 1595 was Francisco Pareja—linguist, scholar, and musician. He was born in Auñon in the northeastern province of Guadalajara. When he arrived in St. Augustine, he was assigned to Mission San Juan del Puerto on Fort George Island, just north of the St. Johns River, where he was priest of this home mission and nine others for seven years. From his church tower rang a set of ornate bells to summon the Indians to service. The father taught his parishioners to sing High Mass and vespers. From the neighboring villages others came to hear the Salve Regina on Saturdays and stayed overnight to hear the Mass sung on the following morning.[10]

During his thirty-three-year tenure among the Timucua Indians, Francisco Pareja became custodian, head of mission, definitor, and member of provincial council and later served as provincial from 1616 to 1620. But it was for none of these official positions that he is remembered. He became proficient in the Timucuan language and in 1613 wrote a confessional. His are the earliest works that survive in any North American Indian language.[11] This catechism for the Timucuan Indians was written in Florida about 160 years before the first Catholic imprints appeared in Philadelphia, but it was published in Mexico rather than in Florida. It was prepared as an aid for administering the confession by Franciscan priests and is a very early source of information on Timucuan culture and Catholic doctrine of that time. One question in Pareja's *Confesionario* asked, "Because they don't come to dance, have you ordered that some woman be affronted or that penalty be taken to her?" Indian chiefs had authority to order women to dance and to punish them if they did not obey. Another question was equally provocative. "Have you taken a woman out of her house by singing your charms?"[12] Catholic doctrine did not permit Christians to have sexual relations with non-Christians, nor did it allow men to have more than one wife. Indians believed that music had a mystical, irresistible power. Spaniards observed that its power sometimes came into conflict with Catholic doctrine.[13] The confessional questions suggest that the priests attempted to regulate music, dance, and behavior of the Indians.

Sorcerers, diviners, conjurors, and priests served the religious needs of the Timucuan chiefs. They recited spells or prayers as they treated the ill with herbal medicines. Numerous rituals, dances, songs, and prayers invoked bountiful crops or success in hunting. Indians were advised to keep quiet when a woodpecker sang or risk a nosebleed. If one trembled at the song of a bluejay, an important event would occur, or a visitor would come. A singing owl was an evil portent. The priests called Indian superstitions nonsense and attempted to destroy those aspects of Timucuan culture that conflicted with Catholic doctrine. They restricted and in some instances prohibited Indian dances, but their objections appear not to have been to recreational dance as such. There were objections to sexual gestures on occasions, but the strongest disapproval was to the warlike character, the fierceness of the movements, and the explosive emotions generated by the dance. The priests attempted to terminate festivities before they exceeded the Spanish code of decency or incited war. They attended dances for the purpose of monitoring conduct. When the time came, they rang a bell signaling *las ánimas,* that is, sundown, and the end of the celebration.

Before the Spanish arrived, it had been the custom of Indians on special occasions to sing and dance throughout the night or even to continue two or three days. The restrictions of the priests were resisted. The courage, the skill, and the joy of Indian ancestors could not be denied. Only the issue of one wife in perpetuity was resisted more than the freedom to conduct their dances and games on their own terms. The scolding, oppressing, and preaching could not be endured, even with the promise of heaven after this life.

Philip II had ordered kindness toward the Indians, and priests attempted to carry out his wishes while indoctrinating penitents into the

PEDRO MENENDEZ DE AVILES.

Natural de Avilés en Asturias, Comendador de la orden de Santiago, Conquistador de la Florida, nombrado Grál. de la Armada contra Inglaterra. Murió en Santander Aº. 1574. á los 55. de edad.

PEDRO MENÉNDEZ DE AVILÉS

In 1565 this Spanish explorer, leader of the first permanent settlement of Europeans in what is now continental United States, brought with him a chamber orchestra, competent male singers, and a dwarf who danced. To this instrumentation Menéndez de Avilés added French musicians who survived the massacre of Fort Caroline. (Courtesy Library of Congress)

faith. Music was an element in the process. East coast Indians had greeted Pedro Menéndez de Avilés with singing when he arrived. Later, the response of Timucuans to European customs was not uniformly positive. The Calusa accepted European music immediately. They themselves had a strong tradition for music. Their religious ceremonies included processions, singing, and costumes. In the processions they carried carvings of animals or vegetables, and the shamans wore masks. While the ceremonies were similar to those of the Arawak Indians of South America, the format did not differ greatly from that of the Catholics. Yet Fr. Juan Rogel disapproved and ordered them replaced by Christian doctrine and Christian ceremony, just as Chieftain Carlos had ordered aboriginal girls to discontinue singing because he thought the Spanish did it better. The acculturation process continued. Indians of the village of Hotina became converts and valued music only a little less than religion. Menéndez was persuaded to leave with them both a Christian teacher and a trumpeter. Toward the end of the sixteenth century even the intractable, warlike Guale Indians had accepted some of the practices and regulations of the priests. They sang the Ave Maria, the Pater Noster, and the Credo.[14] Yet by 1597 the reprimands and interference of the priests became so oppressive that the Indians of Guale revolted, killing several priests. Among the victims was Fr. Miguel de Auñon, the finest Franciscan singer. The capture or death of other priests was celebrated with incantations and dances.

In the settlement of Florida, not all of the problems were between the priests and Indians. Some were jurisdictional between church and civil authorities, others between Franciscans and Dominicans. Even more urgent than these was the need to confirm many Indians and Spanish of the territory. To perform this duty and arbitrate differences, Bishop Juan de las Cabezas y Altamirano sailed from Cuba into St. Augustine in 1606. The bishop himself was skilled in music. He required performance according to church law, both in his Cuban diocese and in Florida. When later he moved to Guatemala, he took with him a band of Negro musicians from Cuba. In Florida he ordained twenty young men, most of them second-generation Floridians. Among these and those ordained a few years later by Fr. Luís Gerónimo de Oré were the forgotten priests who carried on the music traditions of the church throughout the century. The problem of getting Spanish military men to sing in the choir was only partially resolved when the church gave financial inducement. A longer-lasting resolution was found by those priests who taught Indians to sing the service.

The next bishop who visited Florida observed and reported on the singing of the Mass and processions by the aborigines. He was Fr. Luís Gerónimo de Oré, the Peruvian Franciscan who wrote of his two visits to Florida in *Relación de los mártires que ha habido en las provincias de la Florida (1617–20)*. The father and his three brothers, who were priests, were all skilled at singing plainchant and at organ playing. He visited Spain in 1612 and recruited twenty-one friars, who were sent to Florida. Two years later the commissary general of the Indies sent him to Florida, Cuba, and the province of Santa Elena. As episcopal delegate of the bishop of Cuba in 1616, he returned to Florida for another visitation and to conduct canonical elections.

He was well qualified to report on music of the Florida churches. In earlier years of his ministry, Friar Oré wrote a book of religious verses to be sung by his parishioners in the vernacular Quechua to Peruvian and European tunes.[15] In this book he took a resolute stand that the Indians should learn to sing plainsong and polyphony and to play instruments, since the study of music brought about their conversion. In Florida he visited the provinces and held a provincial chapter. He examined the Indians in Christian doctrine and found that they knew it well. At the convent of San Jose de Zapala in Guale he formed a religious procession and sang the Te Deum Laudamus en route to the church.[16] At the convent of San Buenaventura de Guadaquini, thirty-two leagues north of St. Augustine, he sang the Mass of the Holy Ghost on December 18, 1616. When Fr. Francisco Pareja was elected father provincial, Oré ordered a procession and again sang the Te Deum Laudamus.

As official province visitor, Oré asked the question of priests, "Is there any apparent improvement among the converted Indians?" Fr. Francisco Pareja answered, in part, "They assist at masses of obligation on Sundays and feast days, in which they take part and sing; in some districts they have their confraternities and the procession on Holy Thursday. . . . In the small towns . . . they come together in the community house to teach one another singing and reading."[17]

That the seventeenth-century Spanish were well robed and equipped to observe Catholic ceremonies in the Florida churches is documented by an inventory sent from the St. Augustine father provincial to the king on June 16, 1681. In addition to 47 chalices with silver plates were 71 missals, 92 bells for mass, 238 handbells, numerous silver ornaments, golden ornamental screens, surplices, and 54 silk choir capes of various colors.[18] Several accounts, as early as the sixteenth century, refer to libraries of priests.

Toward the end of the seventeenth century, the Spanish once more attempted to make a permanent settlement in western Florida. On the morning of April 8, 1693, Adm. Don Andrés de Pez and Capt. Juan Jordan sailed a frigate and a sloop into the bay of Santa María de Galve on the northern coast of the Gulf of Mexico. With them was Don Carlos de Siguenza y Gongora, a retired mathematics professor at the University of Mexico. It was he who identified this location as the port of Achusi, sixty leagues from Apalache Bay, discovered by de Soto's men, and the same port where Panfilo de Narváez had landed. The site had been given the name Santa María de Galve when it was occupied by the Tristan de Luna y Arellano colony. After landing, the company sang a Te Deum Laudamus, then organized a procession led by Siguenza y Gongora, who was a lay priest, to the foot of a hastily erected cross. There they knelt and the priest chanted, intoning the Vexilla Regis (Hebrews 9:11–12). Later, on St. Mark's Day (April 25), the first mass was said for the company, and the Spaniards, chanting the Litany of Loreto, again marched in procession to the foot of the cross. On this site Pensacola, the second city of Florida, was founded.[19]

One indication of the maturing of a church, whether a mission or a cathedral congregation, is the sophistication of its service music. The acquisition of an organ has been considered an act of cultural awareness and therefore worthy of notice by music historians. No documentation has been found to establish the date of the installation of the earliest organ in Florida, or the name of the first organist. If the St. Augustine parish church had an organ in 1585, it went up in flames when Sir Francis Drake sacked the city. If other churches or missions had instruments, they may have met with similar misfortune in the Apalache rebellion of 1647, the Timucuan rebellion of 1656, or the attacks of Col. James Moore beginning in 1702. The identity of an organist was firmly documented in 1702, but it is probable that his service in that office began in 1687, or perhaps earlier. He was Don Antonio Ponce de León, and his services to the church spanned at least twenty years.[20] He served the St. Augustine parish church as chief sacristan during many of those years. It is likely that at the same time he improved his competency as an organist. Like many of his associates, he held several positions in the settlement. He was a notary, an attorney, and chief sacristan in 1687. He was appointed official church organist and ecclesiastical visitador of Florida while in Havana (1701?). He

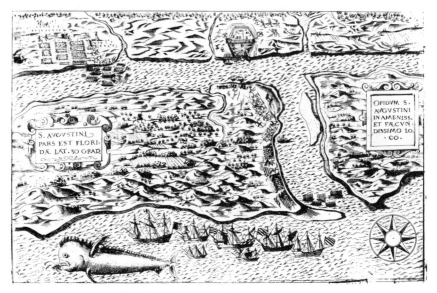

ST. AUGUSTINE 1585—86
This map of St. Augustine shows the Spanish settlement at the time of the English
attack in May 1586. (Courtesy Library of Congress, Florida, no. 16223, 1Q)

returned to St. Augustine on a troop ship sent to oppose Colonel Moore
and his raiders, but it did not arrive until the day after his church and the
organ in it had been destroyed by fire. The irony of the situation was
summed up by historian Amy Bushnell, who wrote, "Don Antonio presented his title as organist notwithstanding and was added to the payroll in
that capacity since, as the royal officials pointed out, it was not his fault
that there was no organ."[21]

To place the chronology of organ acquisition in perspective, it is observed that if Antonio Ponce de León was the earliest organist in Florida,
he was preceded by others in countries as remote as Mexico and Peru. He
or his predecessors, however, were certainly the first in the eastern section
of what was to become the United States. Cristóbal de Quinones, a Franciscan missionary, built the first organ and taught Indians to sing the
church service in New Mexico during his tenure there from 1598 to 1604.[22]
It is unlikely that explorers or earliest settlers of Florida installed organs at
a date as early as 1598. The official historians or others would have commented on the event. That they did have an instrument and a musician to
play it in 1698, and very likely earlier, is significant because the first organ in

a British American colony to be documented dates from 1703 in Pennsylvania. The Johann Gottlieb Klemm and David Tannenberg instruments appeared in the 1720s and 1730s in New York and Pennsylvania. The organ Thomas Brattle gave to his Boston church dates from 1713 and received a cool reception from both the congregation and Cotton Mather. Governor Burnet of New York gave the Dutch Reformed Church its first organ in the 1720s. St. Philip's Church of Charleston imported an English organ in 1728. Organs of the California missions were not installed until the years 1769 to 1823. As in other missions, they enhanced the service rituals. In St. Augustine outdoor processions, dramas and ceremonies, all with music, rounded out the full panoply of ecclesiastical celebrations.

The seed of Spanish drama with music was planted in St. Augustine by the priests who had led religious processions through the city streets. As early as 1607 the governor wrote the Spanish king that Florida Indians had returned to their tribes happy and edified by the religious services and processions they had witnessed during the Holy Season. Funerals held in the church were followed by dramatic processions through the streets by a robed priest and surpliced acolytes with crucifix, candles, and aspersorium.[23] If the deceased were a debtor, religious measures were used to collect money owed by him. "Letters of excommunication were taken out and read in the main churches of both Havana and St. Augustine, and were followed by a solemn procession of parishioners wearing black veils and carrying a cross draped in black, who marched back and forth across town chanting the *Laus Deo* and calling on anyone who was holding anything belonging to the individual, or owing him money, or knowing of someone who did, to declare it or face eternal damnation."[24]

In the early years of the St. Augustine settlement, soldiers and their families who served this military outpost were not affluent enough to support celebrations of the ecclesiastical year. *Cofradías,* or religious brotherhoods, however, were organized, and their activities here, as in Spain, stimulated religious and social life. They were authorized to write and produce plays, with the understanding that taxes of their proceeds were given to support such charities as the poor, hospitals, or schools. Six or seven of these societies were active in St. Augustine.[25] Their activities were under the strict supervision of the church. The dramas of Lope de Vega (1562–1635) and comedies of many lesser writers for the theater were popular in Spain, and it is speculated that they were included in the St. Augustine repertory, though they are not documented by title.

One incident, a disagreement between two priests, does document the production of plays. In 1690 two comedies were prepared for the celebration of Corpus Christi and the week following *(octava)*. The parish priest followed the custom of presenting them at the door of the parish church. Gov. Quiroga y Losada authorized the removal of a portable cross which stood at the church entrance so that the comedies would not be presented at the foot of the cross. As the whole pueblo was about to take their seats to enjoy the comedies, Fr. Pedro de Luna observed the cross leaning against the church wall. In his capacity as commissionary of the Holy Inquisition, he declared the removal of the cross a crime of heresy or apostasy and went out to find the notary and constable of the Holy Office to write up the accusation and order the cross be restored to its customary place. The parish priest was about to sing *las completas* (the compline) before the procession when the confrontation between the two priests erupted and the little town was thrown into an uproar.[26] In his report of the incident, the priest did not tell the Spanish king whether the customary music of the comedies was heard that night or whether, indeed, there was a performance at all. The custom of presenting dramas, however, continued throughout the Spanish regime. In a 1760 report of the governor to the crown, the king was informed that his St. Augustine subjects engaged in *combates* (evening parties or dances), musicales, comedies, and various other diversions.[27]

The fashionable Spanish conquistadores followed the lead of their king in their choice of men and music to bring to the New World. Pedro Menéndez and a music ensemble had escorted Philip II when he went to England to marry Mary Tudor. The Spanish king took ensembles of music with him as he traveled from the Netherlands to Spain. He maintained resident groups including Burgundian, Italian, and Spanish musicians. His noble subjects followed his example by taking with them vocal and instrumental ensembles to the New World. The fifers, drummers, and trumpeters had their military uses as "implements of war." These and other instruments were used also to facilitate diplomacy and enhance social exchange. A long line of Spanish monarchs had supported music in the court and in the church. King Charles V brought his *capilla flamenca* from the Netherlands to Spain in 1516. These singers were a direct-line legacy from the Burgundians and, like them, traveled with the king wherever he went. They were later combined with a chapel choir of Spaniards to form the royal chapel under Philip II.

In addition to the church music of the Netherlands, the legacy of vocal music in Spain was rich. *Cancioneros* of secular songs were filled with *romances* and *villancicos*. The latter also became a popular form for the celebration of Christmas. Among early notable secular composers were Juan del Encina, Ramos de Pareja, and Juan Vásquez. Spanish sacred music composers were well known in Europe: Cristóbal de Morales, Barlotomé Escobedo, Francisco Guerrero, and Tomás Luís de Victoria. In 1585 Ancia reported that Victoria was known "even to the Indies."[28]

As we saw in chapter 1, in 1565 the Spaniard Menéndez brought with him clarine players, trumpeters, fifers, drummers, a harpist, a psaltery player, a vihuela de arco player, four to six gentlemen who had very good voices and could "sing in excellent order," and a dwarf who both sang and danced.[29] Menéndez spared the lives of musicians in the French colony at Fort Caroline and thereby increased his instrumentation to include a fifer, violinist, spinet player, horn (cor) player, three drummers, and four trumpeters.

Because the sound and function of some of these instruments are not in common contemporary practice today, a brief statement about them is appropriate. The harp which Menéndez brought to Florida was undoubtedly the diatonic Spanish instrument of the time which became popular in Mexico and in Central and South America. It was probably well constructed, since several Spanish ordinances required examinations of official *vieloros*, or instrument makers (Seville 1502, Grenada 1528, Mexico City 1568).[30] *Tecla*, or keyboard music of the time, was composed for organ, other keyboard instruments, or harp. Antonio de Cabezón was the most eminent sixteenth-century Spanish organ composer. Other competent performers on and composers for the instrument were to be found throughout Spain.

Instrumental music was written for various combinations of vihuelas and other instruments. Transcriptions and reductions of vocal works were numerous. The most popular forms for instruments were *fantasías, tientos,* and the tablatures of villancicos, romances, and canciones. The vihuela was of particular importance. The instrument brought to Florida by Menéndez, called the vihuela de arco, was a six-course bowed string instrument which was played in the courts of nobility. Solo and ensemble repertory for this instrument was music of remarkable beauty, restraint, and elegance. The plucked vihuela *(de mano* or *de pendola)* later became the *vihuela común,* a transformation of the six-course vihuela to a guitar by removing the outer strings and tuning at a fourth, a third, and a fourth apart. Its repertory was popular music.[31] At least one vihuela was found among the property of deceased private soldiers in St. Augustine. It was a typical instrument of the period.[32] A guitar was listed in the goods of Juan García y Talvarea, another soldier of St. Augustine.[33] Published in tablature was such vihuela music as Diego Pisandor, *Libro de música de vihuela* (Salamanca, 1552), Luís de Milan, *El Maestro* (Valencia, 1536), and works of Luys de Narváez (1538), Alonso Madarra (1546), and Enríquez de Valderrabano (1547), published in Valladolid and Seville. The psaltery (Span. *salterio*) was brought to Spain by the Moors and became a popular instrument throughout that country. Record of its use both in secular and sacred music literature appeared as early as the thirteenth century in *Cantigas de Santa María* of Alfonso el Sabio of Castile, who reigned from 1252 to 1284. Its popularity was waning by the time Menéndez brought it to Florida, but it continued to be useful as a solo instrument or in ensemble or as an accompaniment.

Among the earliest European music heard in Florida, long before the founding of Jamestown or Plymouth, was sixteenth-century Spanish chamber music, keyboard music, and vocal music. The resources, the instruments, and the performers were present, as was a patron. That patron was Pedro Menéndez de Avilés, the Spanish nobleman and military officer who had claimed Florida for Philip II. In 1565 he paid his fifers and drummers six ducats a month, the same pay that corporals received. It was respectable pay, considering the scale. Shipmasters received only nine ducats, quartermasters three, pikemen three, harquebusiers and halberdiers four. The Adelantado brought with his settlement more musicians than authorized by the military table of organization, and it is remarkable that he paid them more than some of his fighting soldiers.

Each company was served by a piper and drummer, whose essential function was signaling. The drummer was used to announce orders when verbal orders could not be heard. A military treatise of the day listed a catalog of orders to be relayed by the drummer. Among them were *recoger* (formation), *adelantar* (forward), *caminar* (march), *volver las caras* (about face), and *parar* (halt). It was recommended that these orders be given by trumpet calls rather than drum beats when more than one company was engaged in battle.[34] Twenty years later, military strategists were still calling on the drum to animate company formations, to give calls. One strategist reasoned that since drummers beat *revile,* they were to be lodged next to the captain's house, where all orders for mustering the men were relayed. The drum major was in charge of issuing orders and teaching the men such drum beats as those for *arma furiosa* (all-out attack) or *retirada presurosa* (quick retreat). Drummers were expected to play calls of every nation and "also things to delight the men," but they were not allowed to be called for target practice or skirmishing except by permission of the sergeant major.[35]

In 1671 the authorized strength of a Spanish company included two drummers and a fifer. The same complement was maintained in 1687, when the size of the company had increased by forty-eight men. An infantry regiment in 1715 paid its drummers nine cuartos daily, the same pay as corporals or assistant squad leaders in a grenadier company. The fusilier company paid eight cuartos daily, a rate midway between the pay of a squad leader and a corporal.[36] In 1768 the drum major of a regiment received 90 reales per month, the first fifer 75, and the second fifer 60. By 1792 the drum major received 120 reales monthly, the same pay as the master armorer. A drummer received 70 reales per month, the same pay as a corporal second class. Drummers for grenadier companies received only 50 reales monthly, and for a fusilier company 45. By 1802 a drum major on the battalion staff was paid 120 reales monthly, the same rate as a fusilier sergeant first class. The three drummers per company were paid 75 reales per month.[37]

In the 1570s, base pay of an officer or soldier on special assignment could be increased by singing in the choir. This practice undoubtedly encouraged men to sing in the services and enhanced the potential of the choir. The funds came from one of the cluster of crown subsidies, this one a bonus *(ventajas)* fund of 1,500 ducats, originally designated for troop commodities, which by the end of the century was liquidated.[38]

Considering the general abuses of government subsidies, it is not surprising that other unauthorized practices were continued throughout the century. The officers of Spanish Florida had four or more slaves in their households at government expense. Treasury officials objected to this practice, but captains bent the intention of official authorization of funds by putting these men on the payroll as drummers, fifers, or flag bearers, though they did not perform the functions of musicians. Then, as now, government funds were not always dispensed for the purposes for which they were intended.

As early as the sixteenth century, tunes and rhythms of the small military bands had spilled over into civilian life in Spain. They served as sources for

La Marcha da Grenaderos

Traditional
Melody from
Toques de Guerra
by Juan Moreno Tejada (1769)

This sixteenth-century march was played by small Spanish bands. It was included in the Madrid edition of Toques de guerra *(1767). (Traditional)*

villancicos composers. Expert organists of the day wrote *battalia* and *missa de battalia* to celebrate victories or even for festivals celebrating the birth of Christ. In 1769 King Carlos III ordered collection and research of Spanish military music. In response, Juan Moreno Tejada of Madrid and Manual de Espinosa, musician of the Capilla Real, produced *Toques de guerra* (Sounds of war). The collection contained pieces from earlier years, including *La marcha de Grenaderos,* which existed in the sixteenth century. Like other ancient tunes and texts, it has undergone several transformations over the years.[39] St. Augustine Spaniards had the musicians and instruments to play this music and to sing its texts. It is probable that it enhanced civilian fiestas and church celebrations.

Commemorations of special occasions were not as frequent in St. Augustine as in Mexico or Peru, but the fifers, drummers, trumpeters, guitarists, and singers joined the Creoles, priests, and government officials in their eighteenth-century rituals. The accession of a king, the marriage of a prince, or the pregnancy of a queen were celebrated. Among these events observed in Florida were the accessions of Philip V, Ferdinand VI, and Charles III. The ceremonies honoring the new Bourbon monarch Philip V were illustrative of the tradition. A large crowd assembled at the *casas reales,* and the governor served drinks, chocolates, and sweets. Dancing and feasting followed. The governor then distributed commemorative silver medals. Among the afternoon diversions were an equestrian parade and horse races. The evening entertainments were several *representaciones* and *loas* (plays and prologues, or interludes). The three-hour performance was attended by the governor, his entourage, and a large number of people. The request for a royal gift brought a meager response from the soldiers, but the revelry of the day celebrated a happy event.[40] Two days of similar events honored the accession of Ferdinand VI to the Spanish throne. In the evenings, there were plays, masquerades, and dancing.

Formal memorials commemorated deaths of Spanish kings Charles II in 1700, Philip V in 1747, and Ferdinand in 1760. These memorial services and the solemn processionals which accompanied them were enhanced by appropriate music of the priests, organists, boy choirs, and musicians of the resident military units. They were memorable occasions not only because they occurred infrequently but because they were ostentatious displays of fealty to Spanish church and state, ties that over the years were to grow more and more tenuous. In these jointly sponsored church and state events, the competition for dominance between curates and governors sometimes led to disagreements that had to be settled by Spanish bishops or kings.

Over a period of years music became the subject of controversy, not between bureaucrats and clergy, but between priests themselves. A 1698 *cedula* of the king had authorized rations and vestments for two acolytes for the parochial church. Duties of the boys were to assist the priest at mass, to sing in the sacristan's choir, and to perform other services for the church. In 1709 Father Acebedo decided that the boys were to serve him exclusively at the altar. The sacristan insisted that the boys should assume their duties as singers and charged the curate with disobeying the cedula of 1698. He appealed to the governor, Francisco de Córcoles y Martínez, who decided that the issue was of such magnitude that he sent the details to Spain, where a decision could be made. Philip V consulted both the Council of the Indies and his own fiscal officer and, after a delay of five years, ordered the curate to allow the boys to sing in the choir as well as serve at the altar. The king offered no advice as to how the boys could do both simultaneously. The curate refused to obey the order, and the boys continued to serve him. At his distance from the king, he probably reasoned that punishment was unlikely. If he did, he was correct. For fifteen years there were no choirboys for the sacristan.

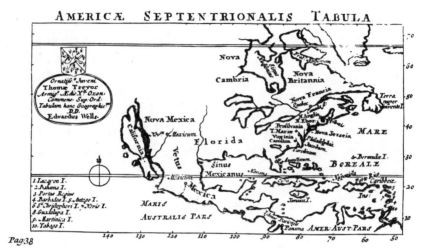

AMERICÆ SEPTENTRIONALIS TABULA

Pag:38

MAP OF NORTH AMERICA, 1738

This map by Edwardus Wells shows Florida extending from the Atlantic Ocean to beyond the Mississippi River. Only New Mexico separates it from the island of California. (Author's private collection)

In 1730, however, the issue was revived by the accountant Francisco Menéndez Marqués, who complained that the choirboys had not sung one amen in the sacristan's choir. This time, the priests took no action. Five years later the problem was resolved by Auxiliary Bishop Buenaventura "by instituting a course in Latin for the boys of the pious families of Saint Augustine and later [installing] them in the sacristan's choir."[41]

While the Spanish governors were attempting to resolve the tempest over small boy singers, they were also attempting to maintain peace and form alliances with the twenty-five or more Indian chieftains of the Lower Creek tribes. Illustrative of their tactics were the festivals arranged by interim governor Juan de Ayala Escobar in 1716 and 1717; which included cannon salutes, parades, gifts, promises of military protection, music, and dancing, all lubricated with ample rum. If the peace was kept, who could say whether it was induced by smoking a pipe or by a Christian impulse growing out of the panoply of the church and the music of the Mass.

In the last years of its two-hundred-year hegemony, Spain had less and less control of that vast expanse from Chesapeake Bay to Tampa called Florida. No gold was found in Florida, but the east coast military had to protect Spanish fleets bringing it from Peru and Mexico. The expense of keeping adequately armed forces was great. Indian revolts made the Spanish intermittently consider abandonment. Creole Franciscans and Spanish friars had feuds. The king and local officers often had differences on policies of political administration. The church bishop and king did not always agree.

From the early years the British had been a threat, with their settlements on Roanoke Island, Jamestown, and later Charleston. Raids of Col. James Moore and Gen. James Edward Oglethorpe had been devastating. There were also disquieting developments of the French in Louisiana. After two hundred years' occupancy, the Spanish holdings were small. Disputes on the definition of a line between English and Spanish claims on the north continued.[42] At the end of the Seven Years' War, the 1763 Treaty of Paris awarded Florida to the British. It gave Havana to Spain, though it had been occupied by the British. Florida, then, became a British colony in 1763 and retained that status for twenty years. After the American Revolution it was to be returned to Spain for a brief span of thirty-seven years. The multicultured legacy left by the British enriched the music culture profoundly and changed the political destiny of the peninsula during the second Spanish hegemony.

3

＊　＊　＊　＊　＊　＊　＊　＊

Distant and Strange Lands

Music and the French

French kings in the sixteenth and seventeenth centuries authorized the exploration and founding of colonies in the New World. In 1523 Francis I sent the Florentine navigator Giovanni de Verazzano to explore the eastern coast of North America from the land then called Florida to Newfoundland. In 1534 he sponsored the exploration of Canada by Capt. Jacques Cartier. While these two explorations gave France tenuous claims to North America, no actual settlement in the New World was attempted until after midcentury. The first of these was in Brazil, and the second in Florida.

Gaspar de Coligny, admiral and adviser to the French king Charles IX, chose two men to head the exploration of Florida in 1562. They were Jean Ribault of Dieppe and René de Laudonnière of Poitou. Most of the group they assembled were French Protestant Huguenots. While on their journey, they and the ship's company daily sang the psalms of David in metrical translations by Clement Marot and musical settings by Claude Goudimel.[1] In June they landed near the mouth of the St. Johns River then sailed northward to present-day Parris Island, where they built Charlesfort,

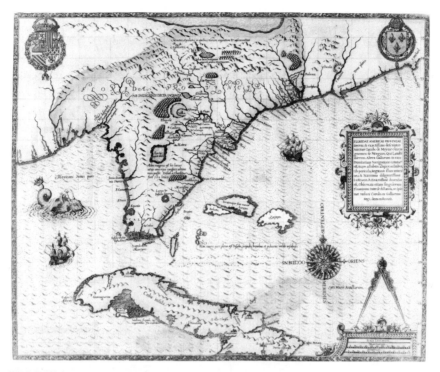

FLORIDA, 1591

French cartographer Jacques Le Moyne prepared this map of the province of Florida. (Courtesy Library of Congress, no. 18478, Lowery Collection no. 78)

a post named for their king. Ribault and his crew returned to France, and a series of misadventures caused the colony to fail.

There was no clergyman on this first voyage, but in accord with the European custom of their religion, the colonists of Charlesfort were called to worship every afternoon. There they continued the music tradition of their sect, the singing of metrical settings of the Psalms. This distinguishing practice of the Huguenots had grown out of recreational psalm singing by French Catholic kings Henry II and Francis I. Calvin had found poets and musicians to set the psalms. The custom of the sect had been described by a visitor to Geneva in 1557. "On the week-days . . . as soon as the first sound of the bell is heard, all shops are closed, . . . and from all sides the people hasten into the nearest meeting-house. There each one draws from his pocket a small book which contains the psalms with notes, and out of full hearts, in the native speech, the congregation sings before and after the sermon. Everyone testifies to me how great consolation and edification is derived from this custom."[2] The Huguenots who came to Florida were faithful to their creed.

Gabriel Gravier, editor of the earliest account of Jean Ribault's first visit, wrote that the settlers sang psalm translations of Clement Marot set to the music of Claude Goudimel.[3] The edition from which they sang might have been any of those by this poet and musician, though it probably dates from no earlier than 1557, when Parisian publishers began bringing out many Goudimel settings. It may have been from the most popular of all editions, published in Paris in 1562.

Timucuans greeted these first Frenchmen as friends, but differences between them and the Europeans were soon apparent. The French reported the religious beliefs and rites of these aborigines, which certainly differed from those of Calvinism. Timucuans worshiped the sun as their deity and sang songs in its honor. Earliest descriptions of their warfare customs and the extended singing-and-dancing celebrations of victory were made by these first French visitors.[4]

One of the most important Indian religious ceremonies was observed soon after the French arrived. On his first exploration, Ribault captured two Indians from the west arm of the Liborne River to take back to the queen of France. When they learned that they were not to return to their tribe, the Indians attempted to buy their freedom by returning gifts the French had given to them. The French gave them back and guarded the men closely. The melancholy warriors then "joined each other in singing softly and sweetly in a way that made us think that they lamented the absence of their friends. They continued singing all night long without stopping."[5] They also continued asking to be returned to their tribe, promising Laudonnière the privilege of seeing their secret ceremonies called Toya if he could comply with their request. They later escaped, and it was left to another Indian cacique to invite the Frenchmen to the secret feast.

Toya was an outdoor religious ceremony observed by Andusta and his tribe. It was celebrated with great solemnity by the Indians but thought by the French to be a primitive joke. Their laughter so provoked the chief that he banned them from the ritual. Only by chance did one man observe it from a discreet distance. The ceremony was directed by a shaman and his assistants. They were thought to have the ability to heal diseases with herbs and could order sacrificial rituals. Indian women cleared a circular

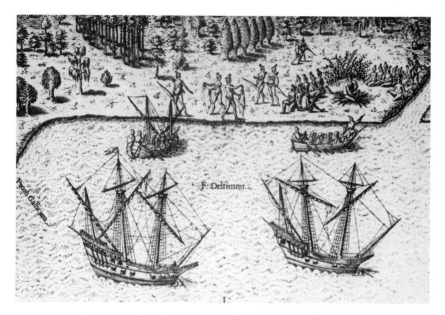

THE FRENCH ARRIVE IN FLORIDA

As the French arrive in Florida, they observe Indians for the first time. (Courtesy Florida State Archives; reprinted from Theodore de Bry, "Brevis narratio eorum quae in Florida Americae provincia Gallis acciderunt" [1591], Le Moyne print no. 1)

plane which the celebrants called the place of Toya. On the morning of the celebration they met at the chief's house, painted and plumed in a variety of colors. Three, painted in distinctive colors, led the others in an orderly procession to the place of Toya. Each Indian carried a small drum in his hand. They entered the center of the circle dancing and "singing in doleful tones." One group sang and was followed by others who answered them. After singing, dancing, and turning three times, they ran swiftly into the woods. The women then began singing and crying in lamentation. They grabbed the arms of the young girls and cut them with sharp clam shells until the blood flowed, then they leaped about crying "He, Toya" three times. Two days later the men who had run into the forest returned and began to dance. Their enthusiasm and gaiety cheered the elder Indian fathers who were too old or feeble to enter the festival. When the dancing was over, the Indians sent for the Frenchmen and asked them to join in a great banquet. The French observed that the Indians ate ravenously, for they had had neither food nor drink for the two days of their absence. One

Frenchman inquired what the Indians did when they were in the woods. He was told that the shaman prayed to Toya and then by magic made Toya appear. When he did, the men spoke to him and demanded strange things of him, so strange that for fear of the shaman, one dared not describe.[6]

Jean Ribault remained in Florida and at Charlesfort long enough to erect stone markers claiming the land for his king and long enough to observe Timucuan life, but soon afterward he returned to France. He left about thirty men, but because of a series of misadventures and disagreements, they abandoned the colony. They built their own ship and attempted to return to Europe, but the vessel was not equal to the task. They were rescued at sea by an English ship's crew. Their time in the New World (from February 1562 to April 1563) must be regarded as an exploration rather than a colonization, but they gave us some of the earliest descriptions of North American Indian music, dance, beliefs, and ceremonies.

In 1564 a company of over three hundred made a second attempt to plant a French settlement, this time under the leadership of René de Laudonnière.[7] They disembarked on a knoll near present-day Jacksonville in June 1564. They called their post Fort Caroline. There they sang their psalms, offered their prayers of thanksgiving, and erected a large bell to call the faithful to religious services. Laudonnière wrote that a few days later at sunrise he commanded a trumpet to be sounded, calling the company together to offer thanks for their "favorable and happie arrival." He continued, "There we sang a thanksgiving to God, beseeching him that it would please him of his grace to continue his accustomed goodnesse toward us his poor servants, and ayde us in all our enterprises, that we might turn to his glory and the advancement of our king. The prayer ended, every man began to take courage."[8] Optimistically, Laudonnière commented that the pastoral setting was so pleasant that melancholy men would be forced to change their humor. Capt. Giles de Pysière, another French maritime officer, called Florida an island of unknown lands, strange people, and sea monsters. He delighted in the novelty.

The French settlers were greeted by a marching band of Indian musicians and warriors who heralded the arrival of Chief Saturiba. Saturiba ruled the large territory between the St. Johns River and Savannah. He had twenty musicians who, according to Jacques Le Moyne, blew hideous discord through pipes of reed. An advance company of 120 warriors came armed with darts, bows and arrows, and clubs. They wore multicolored

RENÉ GOULAINE DE LAUDONNIÈRE

Laudonnière was commander of the 1564 settlement at Fort Caroline, near present-day Jacksonville. (Courtesy Florida State Archives)

feathers, shell necklaces, fish-teeth bracelets, "belts of silver-colored balls, round and oblong, and pearl anklets. Many of the men wore round, flat plates of gold, silver or brass, which hung upon their legs, tinkling like little bells."[9] Two hours later Chief Saturiba appeared, escorted by seven or eight hundred strong, swift, handsome warriors. At the head of the army were fifty youths with javelins and spears. Behind them, next to the chief, "came twenty pipers making the wildest kind of noise, without any harmony or rhythm, each blowing with all his might as if to see who could blow the loudest. Their instruments were thick reeds, like organ pipes or whistles, with only two openings. They blew into the top hole, while the sound came out the other end."[10] If there was singing, it was not mentioned by Jacques Le Moyne. A Theodore de Bry engraving of a Le Moyne drawing shows two men playing large reed pipes hung with oval-shaped metal balls the entire length of the instrument.[11]

The spectacle of the large-scale demonstration by a powerful Indian tribe must have impressed the Frenchmen, just as the beauty of the setting had. The music and the fauna were too exotic to be accepted at once. Aesthetic judgment of Indian music by French gentlemen, however, was based on European models. Reports of lions, unicorns, and flying, man-eating alligators sometimes crossed the line that separated reality from imagination. This company was composed of military men of every rank, including fifty Africans (Moors).[12] French housewives, cartographers, musicians, and others later recalled differing details of their lives as Florida settlers. Interactions with the Indians and the Spanish were reported variously. One subject of reportage, however, was consistent among all who were to write about it: the dominant role of religion and Psalm singing among members of the colony and of the Indians they encountered.

Since salvation, for the Calvinists, included the saving of heathen souls across the sea, the Frenchmen soon began teaching Indians the songs of their faith. Nicholas Le Challeux, a sixty-year-old carpenter among the French colonists, wrote that the Indians sang Psalm 130, "Du fons de ma pensée" (From the depths of my thought), and Psalm 137, "Estans assis aux rives aquatiques de Babylon plorions melancoliques" (Sitting on the banks of the rivers of Babylon, we wept).[13]

In church services, the Indians probably sang the words of Marot to the single-line tune devised by Goudimel, just as the Frenchmen did. The French themselves probably continued a distinguishing practice of their European Calvinist counterparts. At home, for recreation they sang the polyphonic settings of Marot and his successor Thédore Bèze set by

Goudimel and Louis Bourgeois. These settings made free use of the first lines of secular chanson as motto lines, just as Palestrina at about the same time was using quotations from plainchant and other sources for his head motives.[14] Plainsong was also used in this way by Huguenot composers.

The Frenchmen who settled Fort Caroline were gentlemen, artisans, and servants, just as they were in French settlements of Brazil and Canada. Their secular music preferences were undoubtedly as varied as their social classes. Known to be musicians in the colony were a spinet player whose name was not given; Masslin, listed as a violinist and trumpeter; Lt. Jean Mennin, who played the horn (Fr. *cor*); four trumpet players, three from Normandy and Jacques Dulac from Bordeaux; and three drummers, two from Rouen and one named Dronet from Dieppe. One fifer was also from Dieppe. It is possible that other fifers were present to complement the number of known drums.[15] There were instruments, then, available to play the pavanes, basse danses, galliards, and tourdions, and there were both French and Indian women for dancing partners.

The Frenchmen who settled Fort Caroline had a particularly rich music heritage. Besides the Calvinist poets there were such illustrious new lyric poets as Pierre Ronsard. The courtly restraint of Sermisy's homophonic settings of the poems of Clement Marot was matched by the more lively free chanson of Clement Janequin (c. 1490–1562) and Pierre Certon (c. 1510–72). Published in the numerous collections of Pierre Attaignant and Jacques Moderne, these tunes with lively rhythms, sectional construction, and frequent repetition were popular throughout Europe in both vocal and instrumental versions. Among the French at Fort Caroline were musicians to play this music on their violin, spinet, horn, trumpet, and fife. To sing this music and the chansons of their homeland required no more skill than to sing a psalm tune. As Jean Jacques Rousseau defined the chanson a few generations later, it seemed made to comfort homesick young noblemen who were seeking their fortunes abroad or artisans who had memories of youthful romances but little hope for anything more. The chanson to him was "a very short lyric poem generally upon some pleasant subject, to which an air is added so that it can be sung on intimate occasions, as at a table with one's friends, with one's sweetheart, or even when one is alone, in order for a few moments to drive away boredom if one is rich, or to help one to bear misery and labour if one is poor."[16] What music could have been better suited to a young Frenchman so far from Paris?

Titles of secular songs the Florida settlers sang are not recorded, but young gentlemen officers may have joined soldiers and sailors in lively French marching songs or familiar rounds. Jean Memyn, a young lieutenant from La Rochelle, probably knew the chanson de marin "Ce sont les filles de la Rochelle," or its fifteenth-century variant. Sailing men of Brittany and Normandy probably knew sea songs and love songs. Mothers of Fort Caroline possibly crooned "Frère Jacques" and other durable songs to their children. Excepting children of the ill-fated Pensacola settlement of Tristan de Luna in 1559, the French lullabies sung to Fort Caroline children were the earliest from Europe to be heard in Florida. The children of this settlement were born more than twenty years before the birth of Virginia Dare of the Roanoke colony.[17] Transplanting Frenchmen to a new land did not make them forget their homeland, their religion, their lovers, their children, or their songs.

The musical instrument upon which the *joueur d'épinette* played was not described, but it undoubtedly was the earliest spinet in Florida, since it was constructed before 1565. Burgundian and Italian instruments antedate those of France, but Jean Potin, *faiseur d'épinette du roy* (harpsichord maker to the king), is mentioned as early as 1561. Among other French spinet makers of the sixteenth century were Merry Lorillat, Anton Potin, Pierre Lorillart, members of the Dugue family, Yves Mesnage, Claude Denis, and Robert Denis the Younger. Any of these men could have created this first instrument heard on the Florida east coast, or it could have been the work of a maker from Antwerp or Venice. In the absence of documented titles, it can be speculated that the music played came from the published collections of the period. Among them were two collections published in Lyon in tabulature, three of the 1531 Pierre Attaingnant collections, and a Venice publication by Antonio Gardane of 1551. Publishers or arrangers of these dance collections are not named.

Primitive music accompanied many ceremonial events of the Indians. Eyewitness accounts and skillful drawings limn remarkably clear details of the celebrations. The narratives and drawings of Jacques Le Moyne are the richest sources.[18] Three kneeling musicians enhanced the Timucuan ceremony after a victory. One beat a large flat stone, marking time to the spells cast by the shaman. Two others rattled dried gourds filled with stones or seeds. Another ceremony was particularly gruesome. Songs were sung in honor of the chief as a firstborn child was sacrificed in his honor. In another rite just before springtime emerged, Chief Outina and his subjects stuffed the skin of a large stag with harvest roots and decorated it with flowers and fruit. Music and song signaled the beginning of a religious ceremony as the chief and his sorcerer offered prayers to the sun that its bounty would continue.

One of the most elaborate Indian ceremonies occurred when the Timucuan chief decided to take a wife. A procession was formed to escort her to the chief. At the head of the entourage were the musicians, trumpeters blowing bark horns. The instruments were hung with small oval balls of gold, silver, and brass. Their tinkling enriched the variety of instrumental color. The bride-elect was borne on a fur-skin litter canopied with leafy branches and carried by four strong men. Two men walked alongside with large, elaborately decorated fans which shielded her from the sun. Following the bride-elect were the most beautiful girls that could be found. Their bodies were draped with pearls, and each of them carried a basket of fruit. At the end of the procession came the bodyguards carrying their bows and wearing their plumed hats.

The French forces at Fort Caroline were not prepared for the attack by Pedro Menéndez de Avilés. Lord de la Vigne was in charge of the squad of sentinels at the time. Observing the incessant rain, he took pity on his men and allowed them to leave their posts, and he himself retired to his quarters. Laudonnière credited his trumpeter with alerting the Frenchmen by sounding the alarm. Few survived the brutal attack. Clearly, Laudonnière lacked sufficient military force to defend his position. Not more than ten men could bear arms. Others were a cook, four dog trainers, a beermaker, a crossbow maker, two shoemakers, a spinet player, laborers, and women and children. Most of them were slaughtered by the Spanish; the fort was taken and given the name San Mateo. There is disagreement among both the French and Spanish as to the number of survivors. All agree, however, that the musicians were spared and were taken to St. Augustine to play for Menéndez and his settlers.

Ribault and his officer Ottigny were taken in another encounter, since they were away from the fort. Their hands were bound, and they were brutally stabbed and beaten to death. Just before his death Captain Ribault sang the psalm which Nicholas Le Challeux recalled as "Domine, memento mei." The old man's memory may have failed to reproduce the first line exactly, but he must have understood that it was appropriate for his captain to sing Psalm 132, "Memento Domine, David," or "Veuille, Seigneur, estre recors de David et do son tourment" (Lord, remember David, and all his afflictions). In the final verse, the psalmist sings, "His

TIMUCUAN BRIDAL PROCESSION
Musicians lead the retinue escorting a Timucuan bride-elect to her Indian king.
(Courtesy Library of Congress)

---

enemies will I clothe with shame, but upon himself shall his crown flourish." It was a brave valedictory but a decisive defeat.

The expeditions, begun in April 1564, ended with the massacres in September the following year. Those who were not slaughtered left Florida. One of them was René de Laudonnière; another was Jacques Le Moyne, artist and cartographer. Both wrote narratives of their experiences. The musician Jean Memyn, the carpenter Le Challeux, and others gave court depositions at the legal inquiry of the failure of the colony. Spaniards wrote their versions of destruction of the fort, the "heretical bibles and other religious books of their horrid religious sect," and playing cards that obscenely burlesqued the Catholic church. All of these European chroniclers were not alone in their memories. Florida Indians, too, had their own memories. "The simpleminded children of the forest were greatly impressed with the habitual gayety and good nature of the French, and they were especially captivated by the sonorous singing in which the Huguenots perpetually indulged. Long after the breaking of Laudonnière's colony, the European, cruising along the coast, or landing upon the

WEDDING DANCE

Young women dance and sing before the royal bride and groom. Small gold and silver balls attached to their girdles sound in accompaniment as they move. (Courtesy Florida State Archives)

shore, would be saluted with some snatch of a French psalm uncouthly rendered by Indian voices, in strains caught from the Calvinist soldier on patrol, or from the boatman plying his oar on the river."[19]

Confirmation of these reports came a few years later. Dominique de Gorgues raised an expedition of Frenchmen and in 1568 sailed across the Atlantic to avenge the defeat at Fort Caroline. Like his Huguenot predecessors, he ordered the company en route to sing psalms to the glory of God. When they arrived, the Indians greeted them with a noisy marching band and celebrated by leaping and dancing. They believed that their God had sent the French to help them destroy a neighboring tribe.

They sang psalms for the French that they had been taught by early French settlers. Among them were Psalm 43, "Revenge moy, prens la querelle" (Avenge me, take up my cause); Psalm 50, "Le Dieu, le fort, l'éternel parlera" (God, the mighty, the eternal, will speak); and Psalm 91, "Qui en la garde du hat Dieu" (He who dwells in the shelter of the most high God).[20] Charles E. Bennett, a twentieth-century historian of Fort

Caroline, wrote that the Indians also sang for de Gorgues another hymn they learned from the French titled, "Happy is one to be a volunteer for God."[21] This is clearly a reference to the Clement Marot version of Psalm 128, "Bien heureux est quiconques; sert à Dieu volontiers."[22]

Dominique had disembarked to the sound of martial music. When the dancing and whooping had subsided, he distributed gifts among the Indians, and they responded by ordering the Indian women to dance out of respect to the visitors. Saturiba and his Indians were willing partners with the French in their raid of San Mateo, the Spanish name for Fort Caroline. With their help the fort was stormed, and the Spaniards shot or hanged. The Fort Caroline tragedy was avenged. The Indians, jubilant in victory, celebrated in their usual manner with singing and dancing. Dominique de Gorgues and his men returned to France but for political reasons were denied the gratitude or honor of their countrymen. Later, the Spaniards returned and rebuilt San Mateo; France was not willing or able to continue the battle for so dubious a prize as Florida.

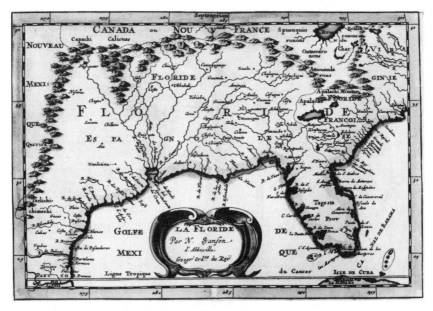

FLORIDA, SEVENTEENTH CENTURY

"La Floride," by French cartographer Nicolas Sanson (1600–1667), indicates locations of Indian tribes and Sanson's concept of French Florida. He shows Spanish Florida extending west to New Mexico and north to Canada, or New France. (Author's private collection)

The French fascination with exotic settings peopled with red Indians did not end with the destruction of Fort Caroline, the death of its martyrs, or the retaliation of Dominique de Gorgues. One example of its continuance is the *opéra-ballet héroïque* "Les Indes galantes" (Love in the Indies), by Jean Phillipe Rameau. The large-scale work has an act set in a Turkish pasha's garden, one in a Peruvian Inca's volcano, and one in a Persian grand park. A fourth act is set among the noble savages of Florida. The work was first produced at the Paris Opera in 1735, and the final act was added a year later. Zima, daughter of the chief, is pursued by Damon, a French officer, and Don Alvar, a Spanish officer, but in the denouement chooses Adario, a native warrior, as her lover. Rameau used no Indian music themes in the work. The Indians of the cast performed no toe-and-heel war circle dances accompanied by whoops and drums. Instead, they executed a Danse du Grand Calumet rondeau with full orchestra. French soldiers and French women dressed as Amazons danced two minuets. In the final scene all were joined by shepherds of the colony to dance a chaconne. They were accompanied by an orchestra featuring trumpets and bagpipes. The French could accept the exotic setting for an art work—but not a trace of the Florida Indian music.

4

✳   ✳   ✳   ✳   ✳   ✳   ✳   ✳

I Long to Hear the Grenadiers March
Music and the British

One of the earliest British explorers to reach Florida shores was Adm. Sir Francis Drake. He and his fleet of twenty ships and pinnaces steered along the Florida coast at dawn on May 28, 1586, when they sighted the Spanish fort of St. Augustine. It was a French musician, a survivor of Fort Caroline, who assured the military success of his mission.

> The lieutenant-general, in a row-skiff, went to reconnoitre it [the Spanish fort]; and though he used all the precaution to prevent being discovered, yet the Spaniards took the alarm and, after discharging some pieces precipitately abandoned the place, imagining the English were approaching to attack them with their whole force. However he returned without knowing that the fort had been deserted, till a French fifer, who had been detained there as a prisoner, coming over in a little boat, and playing the Prince of Orange's March, informed the guard thereof, at the same time offering his service to conduct them over.[1]

The English had landed their own artillery that day and, to the sound of music, displayed six red flags, then moved to the edge of the Matanzas River. The message brought by the fifer encouraged Capt. Christopher Carleill and his men, and the next morning they burned the city of St. Augustine to the ground. "Wilhelmus van Nassouwe" (The Prince of Orange march), national anthem of Holland, was known by the British sailors. It identified the fifer as a French Huguenot rather than a Spanish Catholic. The fifer was Nicholas Bourguignon, who twenty years earlier had survived the attack on Fort Caroline because Pedro Menéndez de Avilés was an *amigo de música* and spared the lives of musicians who could play for his amusement. Once more he was saved from death or imprisonment because he knew an appropriate tune and could play it on his fife. His little heroic deed earned his return passage across the Atlantic aboard a British ship. As for Drake, he continued his northward journey until he sighted an English fortification six degrees beyond Santa Elena, and there rescued Robert Lane and his small colony from the distress of devastating storms and inadequate supply lines. Lane brought back to England tobacco, which became popular among courtiers, and other native fruits and vegetables. Among the latter was one the Indians called macocquer, similar to a calabash or gourd. The Indians removed the meat and seeds, replacing them with stones and attaching a handle. According to Barcia, they played it like a timbrel, "in the fashion the Brazil Indians play their tamarac."[2]

Sixteenth-century English sailors heard fantastic stories of Florida from their Spanish and French counterparts. Riches beyond counting shone in the summer sun, but treasures came only to those who could survive attacks by savages, alligators, hurricanes, or fevers. One of the early entries in the Stationers' Register was "a ballett . . . made by one being greatly impovryshed by the viage prepared to Terra Floryday & c." It was the doggerel of a tipsy English tar in disjointed conversation with a friend.

> Have you not heard of Floryda,
> A country fast bewest
> Where savage pepell planted are
> By nature and by hest,
> Who in the mould, find glysterynge gold
> And yet for tryfels sell?
> Yet all alonge the watere syde,
> Where yt doth eb and flowe
> Are turkeyse founde and where also

Wilhelmus of Nassau

Translation by Jay Williams

Marnix de St. Aldegonde

Wil - hel - mus, Prince of Nas - sau, of old Dutch blood am I;___ My land I'll hold with just - ice un - til the hour I die.__ A__ Prince of Or - ange, free and with - out___ a stain, And loy - al - ty I pledged in sea - son to the Mon - arch of Spain.

This is the tune played by the French fifer Nicholas Bourguignon, who notified a captain of Sir Francis Drake that he and his men could safely land at St. Augustine in 1586. Their response was to burn the city to the ground. (Traditional)

> Do perles in oysteres growe
> And on the land do cedars stand
> Whose beauty doth excell
> With hy! trysky, tryon, go trysky wun
> Not a wallet do well.[3]

It appears that this poor sea dog was one of the early victims of a Florida investment that did not pay off. He returned to Plymouth penniless but was able to write a song about his experience.

One of the earliest English composer-performers to visit Florida was Anthony Aston, alias Mat Medley, composer of *The Fool's Opera; or, The Taste of the Age.* He arrived in Charleston in 1702 and joined the military expedition of English governor James Moore against the Spanish at St. Augustine. He did not describe his role in the pillage of the Franciscan convent, chapel, library, and the parish church, but he did state that he spent fifty-four days in St. Augustine. If the South Carolinians had enter-

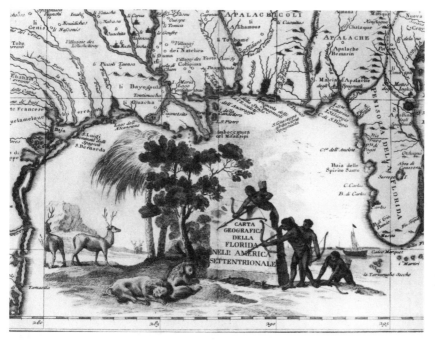

FLORIDA, 1760

This map by Isaac Tirion (Dutch, d. 1769) includes a sketch of Florida flora and fauna and Indians. (Author's private collection)

tainment, Anthony Aston may have assumed the role of actor, musician, or impresario. If he performed these services here, as he had earlier in the Caribbean, St. Augustine rather than Charleston would be the site of the first European-style musical theater within continental limits of present-day United States. Aston returned to England, where he wrote songs for performers at Lincoln's Inn Fields and Covent Garden. In 1743–44 he advertised his "Negro songs" at Goodman's Fields. It is probable that he had heard these songs in St. Augustine, Jamaica, the Bahamas, or Charleston. His songs of this genre, along with the "coon songs" of Charles Dibdin, were forerunners of those sung in American minstrel shows more than a century later.

The British acquired Florida by the Treaty of Paris in 1763 at the termination of the Seven Years' War. The Spanish then began to move out. On January 2, 1764, seven ships with about 350 persons sailed from St. Augustine for Havana. Spanish governor Feliu took his staff. Don Juan Joseph Solana, the parish priest and acting chief sacristan, was in charge

BRITISH COLONIES IN NORTH AMERICA, 1763

In London, Gentleman's Magazine *published this map of the British governments in North America. It includes East and West Florida, the latter extending to the Mississippi River. (Author's private collection)*

of the staffs of the Parochial Church and the Convent of St. Francis. The fifteen volumes of church records from 1594 to 1763, with other valuable property, were placed aboard the ship *Nuestra Señora de la Luz y Santa Barbara.* Holy articles from Apalache were sent aboard the schooner *San Joseph y las Ánimas.* After arrival, on February 6, 1764, Don Pedro Agustín Morel y Santa Cruz, bishop of Santiago, Cuba, and Florida, ordered an inventory that took five weeks to complete. The metal bells and wooden rattles for the Catholic service were stilled. No longer did the faithful Indians sing polyphonic music from the choirbooks, nor the Spanish fathers intone the Latin service.

On August 7, 1763, the English captain Wills, Third Battery of Royal Artillery, sailed from Havana and became commandant of Pensacola. The

GOVERNOR JAMES GRANT

Supper parties, dances, and singing at Masonic club meetings enlivened colonial life of St. Augustine under Col. James Grant, first governor of British East Florida, from 1763 to 1770. (Courtesy Florida State Archives)

Spanish left Pensacola for Vera Cruz on September 3, 1763. Mobile was transferred from the French to Great Britain in October. There Scottish major Farmer and his highlanders lowered the lilies of France and raised the red flag of young Queen Charlotte of England to the music of bagpipes.

British West Florida was no prize assignment for officers of the king's royal regiments. In Pensacola the men found a small settlement of about a hundred huts supplemented by temporary housing of wooden frames covered with palmetto leaves. The military post and stockade left by the Spanish were dilapidated. Elias Dumford, provincial surveyor, was commissioned to plan the city. Communication and transportation were difficult. Goods were shipped through agents from New York, Charleston, Savannah, or English ports. Most of the Spanish had left Pensacola, and only about two thousand French remained when the British took over. During the twenty-year British period about twenty-five thousand people came to settle there. From Connecticut to Georgia, they came from the East; from Mississippi River settlements they came from the West to Pensacola. Some of his countrymen were not sanguine about the future of Florida, but Gov. George Johnstone wrote a letter to the editor of Savannah's leading newspaper extolling the climate, the soil, the bay, and the fishing industry. He wrote that Pensacola was the most pleasant part of the New World and that it would replace New Orleans as the leading commercial port of the Gulf region.[4]

Throughout the years, reports of government agents and eyewitness reports of visitors and settlers appeared in the *Gentleman's Magazine* and in English books. One of the most remarkable public-relations books was that of Capt. Bernard Romans, *A Concise Natural History of East and West Florida,* published in London in 1775. Romans had surveyed West Florida, and his cartography was engraved by Paul Revere. He praised the warm climate and the rich soil. He especially exhorted gentlemen of small fortunes, the middling gentry, and the younger sons of good families to settle in East Florida. The British and their colonists from abroad did come in rather substantial numbers, especially to East Florida. Life revolved around the military government and the military units that supported it.

The earliest British music heard on the peninsula was that of the small military bands parading down the streets of Pensacola and St. Augustine. The initiative for raising a band and paying for it came from the British officers. Musicians were not regularly enlisted men. They were English and

German civilian recruits. The conditions of their contracts were spelled out in Articles of Agreement, devised by William Phillips, lieutenant commandant of the British Artillery in 1762.[5] Five years later they were paid from regimental "noneffective accounts." In 1785 the duke of York enlisted as regular soldiers a band of Hanover musicians to be sent over to England to join his regiment. They played four clarinets, two bassoons, two hautboys, two French horns, one trumpet, and one serpent. That instrumentation varied only a little from the model devised by King Frederick II (the Great), which consisted of pairs of hautboys, clarinets, horns, and bassoons. It was the latter combination, called Harmonie Musik, for which both Mozart and Beethoven wrote. It was also the usual combination of instruments in the bands the British brought to Florida. Variants in instrumentation included trumpets, serpents, flutes, trombones, and drums. Only at about the time the British left Florida were janissary bands becoming popular in England. It is doubtful that Floridians saw acrobatic blackamoors wearing leopard-skin aprons or heard their jingling johnnies, clash pans, timbrels, and drums. They did observe that men of British bands were dressed in the colors of the regiments and distinctive uniforms. The eight musicians who constituted the core unit were required to play violin, violoncello, bass, or flute in addition to the usual paired instrument of the wind band. This flexibility in instrumentation assured regimental officers of music for such social events as dancing or music theatricals. It also provided music instruction for young instrumentalists.

Illustrative of the types of marches played by British bands in Florida is "The Prussian Quick March" in a popular collection of 1775.[6] In duple rhythm, it consists essentially of scale passages and a few broken tonic and dominant chords with ample repetition. It is composed of four-measure phrases with each period repeated. It is in the spirited 6/8 time that was popular with British bands of the period. Other march collections that were widely played by military bands were those issued by the London publishers C. and S. Thompson. One of the best was *A Second Collection of Twenty-Four Favourite Marches,* published in 1771 and scored in seven parts for the usual instrumentation.[7] A collection published six years earlier contained marches from the home counties of British bandsmen who played in Florida. It was James Oswald's *Fifty-Five Marches for the Militia.*

The man who formed a regiment composed largely of provincials in America (known as the Royal American Regiment, then as the Sixtieth Rifles) was Jacques Prevost, member of a French family of distinguished writers, doctors, and military men. His brother Augustin recruited 250 men from Hanover and England who sailed for Florida in 1776 and were stationed in Pensacola and St. Augustine. Augustin Prevost was colonel commandant of the Fourth Battalion in East Florida and was joined in 1777 by Lt. Col. Jean Marc Prevost, another brother, who commanded the three companies of the Second Battalion. The bands of these officers were in residence in Florida and played the simple music of the military ceremonies. Their instrumentation was two clarinets, two oboes, two bassoons, two horns, drums, and other percussion.[8] Antoine François Prevost, a relative, was author of *D'exilés,* the story of Chevalier de Grieux and Manon Lescaut. Based on this novel are operas by Daniel François Esprit Auber, Jules Massenet, Giacomo Puccini, and others.

Military officers and government officials encountered more than their share of misfortune in Florida. Governor Johnstone was recalled in 1767. Brig. Gen. Frederick Haldimand brought happier days, but his lieutenant governor, Monfort Brown, was ousted because he was thought to be a liar and because he fought a duel with Evan Jones, a prominent merchant. The brilliant Swiss general Henri Bouquet died of yellow fever. Gov. John Elliot occupied his post only a month before hanging himself. Governor Chester, Capt. Henry Vignoles, and the Indian superintendent John Stuart drank more than their share of the ample rum ration. General Haldimand fathered a child by his mistress before official orders transferred him to another command. But with the darker side of the British men came also men of character, learning, and leadership. Elias Dumford surveyed and planned the city of Pensacola. Gov. Peter Chester brought stability and growth in his eleven-year tenure. John Fitzpatrick, a merchant, owned a library of English books worth $250. William Dunbar, writer and plantation owner, was an educated Scotsman. Maj. Robert Farmar, who commanded the Thirty-Fourth Regiment in Mobile, was at forty-five a lively man who wrote English verse, entertained generously, and read Montesquieu. Among others who set the social, intellectual, and cultural tone of West Florida were medical doctors John Lorimer and George Brown, military supply contractors Arthur Neil and David Waugh, surveyor-cartographer George Gould, and merchants George Urquhart and Valeno Stephen Cornyn.[9] General Haldiman owned two fiddles but, after several years' service at Pensacola, sold them to Governor Penn of Pennsylvania for $360. In a letter to his shipping agent, the Florida general wrote, "I wish I had more fiddles to sell!"[10]

In 1763 British West Florida was controlled by companies of the Sixteenth and Sixtieth regiments. The territory extended from Pensacola to Baton Rouge and Natchez. When the American Revolution began to materialize in 1776, British governor Peter Chester requested two regiments "to protect his provision ships from molestation by American vessels in the Gulf." The response was not immediate, but in October 1778 General Gage sent two battalions composed of loyalists from Pennsylvania and Maryland and a regiment of German mercenaries from the principality of Waldeck. The English major general John Campbell commanded these soldiers. He thought the provincials would desert if they had the slightest opportunity. He described the Waldeckers as condemned criminals and other species of gaol birds who were ill suited to the mission.[11] On the seventeen-member staff of the Third Waldeck Regiment was a drum major and four musicians. The grenadier company added two fifers and three drummers. Twelve more drummers completed the complement of the four-battalion corps.[12] In the service of the British army, it may be assumed that the simple British marches referred to elsewhere in this account were played for retreat and other military occasions.

The music played by English bands from 1764 to 1784 was written by well-known composers as well as provincial bandmasters. Among the former were Franz Joseph Haydn, Johann Christian Bach, William Crotch, William Shield, Alexander Reinagle, Charles Dibdin, and Karl Friedrich Horn. George Frideric Handel contributed such perennial favorites as "The Dead March" from *Saul*, the march from *Judas Maccabeus*, and the march from *Scipio*. Beginning at midcentury, publishers produced a flow of instruction books and marches.

The best known British march and one of the oldest is "The Grenadiers March," which had its origins in the old cavalier tunes "Sir Edward Noll's Delight" and "Prince Rupert's March." An early version of 1685 was replaced by a 1776 version which became popular in the American Revolution.[13] It was this march that British bands played from Florida to Canada. In 1763 the Royal American Regiment commanding officer, Col. Henri Bouquet, wrote in a letter to Lewis Ourry, "I long to see my native scouts come in with intelligence, but I long more to hear the 'Grenadiers March.'"[14] Colonial bands used it as a signal to advance and for trooping of the colors. It was included in tutors for the fife on both sides of the Atlantic and became a favorite tune in music collections for infantry regiments.[15] The tutors also contained Turkish marches, marches by Handel,

MILITARY MARCH, FIRST BATTALION

This march, published in 1770, was in the repertory of the Sixtieth Regiment band when General Haldimand commanded British troops in Pensacola and St. Augustine. (Courtesy British Library; reprinted from John Reid, A Set of Marches, *pp. 20–21)*

several marches bearing the names of nobility or generals, and special-occasion marches such as "Rogue's March."

Of special interest to Floridians is *A Set of Marches* by R. I. [John Reid], published by R. Bremner in London in 1770.[16] In it are a march for the First Battalion, Sixtieth Regiment (Gen. Frederick Haldimand's), and one for the Second Battalion of the same regiment, commanded by Col. Gabriel Christie. Both of these battalions served in St. Augustine, and it is likely that their bands played these marches dedicated to their command-ing officers. The simple pieces are scored for corni, secondo, primo, and basso, all in the key of C, and they never venture harmonically beyond the I, IV, and V chords. They consist of two eight-measure sections, each repeated. Colonel Christie's march is lively, but General Haldimand's is a

slow march. One military historian stated that the Haldimand and Christie marches must have been composed not earlier than 1778 and not later than 1781.[17] The date of publication assigned by the British Library is 1770, however.

Unlike the Spanish kings, George III never declared that he occupied Florida for the religious purpose of converting Indians. He did not authorize the founding of a string of missions from East to West Florida. Considering the number of people pouring into the area and the intensive advertising to attract even more, the bishop of London made a very small allocation of spiritual leaders for the Floridas. He licensed only nine clergymen, and few of them remained at their posts long enough to accomplish the goals of the Society for the Propagation of the Gospel in Foreign

MILITARY MARCH, SECOND BATTALION

Col. Gabriel Christie commanded the Second Battalion of the Sixtieth Regiment from 1778 to 1783. This march by John Reid was scored for two clarinets, hautboys, horns, and a bassoon and was published by R. Bremner in 1770. This battalion served in St. Augustine. (Courtesy British Library; reprinted from John Reid, A Set of Marches, *pp. 24–25, also in Lewis Butler,* The Annals of the King's Royal Rifle Corps, *vol. 1)*

Parts. Pensacola had no resident Church of England ministers from 1771 to 1780. The Anglican church of New Smyrna, south of St. Augustine, was served by Rectors John Leadbetter and John Kennedy. The situation at St. Augustine was much more stable. Rev. John Forbes served the church there throughout the twenty years' hegemony. It is probable that church services were held by teachers and unlicensed ministers in Apalachee and Pensacola.[18] No church building was erected for the Anglican church either in Pensacola or St. Augustine during the British period.

The British governors were instructed to establish the Anglican church, recognize the authority of the bishop of London, and assure public morality. The sacrament was to be administered according to the rite of the

church, and the Book of Common Prayer was to be read on Sundays and holidays. Parliament promised to make annual grants in support of ministers and schoolmasters. Both of these public servants could be licensed only if they held certificates of orthodoxy from the bishop of London. The salaries were very low, and promises were not kept with respect to housing either for the school children or for the teachers. Services were held in homes or temporary housing. Members of the clergy were among the best-educated colonists. Nathaniel Cotton, for instance, was a graduate of Jesus College, Cambridge University. He was appointed in February 1768 as the second Anglican minister to Pensacola. He received from the bishop of London Bibles, prayer books, testaments, and tracts for members of his congregation. It must be assumed, then, that the format of the religious services conformed to that of the Church of England. The Treaty of Paris, however, guaranteed freedom of religion to the Spanish and French who remained in Florida. Catholic services continued in Mobile in 1768, and their relations with Protestants were described as peaceful. Similar reports of amicable relations were made of Pensacola parishioners after the turn of the century.[19] The largest Catholic community in British Florida was the group of immigrants called Minorcans, who were brought over by Dr. Andrew Turnbull and settled in New Smyrna near St. Augustine.

The asperities of religious life under the Spanish did not continue under the British. While episcopal support and control came from London, a variety of interpretations of regulations and practices were in effect in small churches on both sides of the Atlantic. Only a vigilant rector, a dedicated clerk, talented and faithful parishioners, or a combination thereof could have secured nominally adequate services in Pensacola or St. Augustine. The temporal settings of the services limited the style with which services were presented.

A few inferences may be made about the music of Florida Anglican churches, based on British precedence. In English parish churches of the period, three books of printed music were in common use. The oldest one and the one with greatest longevity was the psalm collection by Sternhold and Hopkins.[20] Another, with rising popularity, was by Tate and Brady.[21] A third was the psalm collection of Isaac Watts, from which Floridians sang well into the nineteenth century.[22] In the decades from 1761 to 1790, these collections were published in a great number of editions and in various sizes. Nicholas Temperley reported the following editions in the British Museum Catalogue of 1971.[23]

	Sternhold and Hopkins	Tate and Brady	Watts
1761–70	30	20	7
1771–80	25	30	10
1781–90	20	22	12

Books were sent from England to Florida from time to time. The Public Records office custom records show a remarkable increase in books imported in the 1770s, and it may be supposed that some of them were small, pocket editions of these collections which settlers and government officials sang from at Sunday services. The Florida firm of Panton and Leslie purveyed six thousand pounds of books (about twelve thousand volumes)

HE man is blest that hath

not bent to wicked rede his eare : nor ledde

his life as sinners doe, nor sate in scorners

chaire, 2. But in the law of God the

Lord, doth set his whole delight : And

in that law doth exercise himselfe both

PSALM I

English colonists of Florida from 1763 to 1783 probably sang from the popular Whole Book of Psalms, *by Sternhold and Hopkins. This is the setting of Psalm 1 from that collection. (Author's private collection; reprinted from 1612 edition)*

from London in 1779. This was an annual total larger than that of any other British colony, excepting only Canada and New York.

Singing in country churches of England in the early 1700s was a credit neither to the literacy nor to the artistry of those who raised their voices. The psalms were read in spoken chant by vicar, clerk, and congregation in some parishes but were sung in others. In small churches, the clerk sang alone. Forsaking the old style and attempting to improve the music component of the services, a few vicars began teaching small groups of young men the skill of psalm singing from the collection of Tate and Brady. Warnings of abuses, both in music and behavior, continued throughout the century, but good reports were also forthcoming. By midcentury several questions on church music continued to be debated. Should the congregation or the choir sing? Should the skill of music reading be encouraged? Was a voice trained for the stage suited to church music? Was it proper to have organs or other instruments in the church? The answers to few of these questions had an impact strong enough to be recorded by historians of the British era in Florida.

It was not unusual for English country choirs to have from one to five or even six instruments to accompany church singing. Regimental bandsmen were in Florida, and regimental officers and their families attended church. The English custom assured a more reliable sense of pitch. The customary instruments were available: bassoons, oboes, flutes, and violoncellos. Their use in Florida church services was probably common practice.

English parochial music style by 1763 had been expanded to include what is now called fuging tunes. Voices were given, one at a time, imitative tunes which entered more or less equidistantly, thus obscuring the text. This treatment often became a refrain following a chordal or familiar-style setting of the text. William Tans'ur's *Royal Melody Complete* (1754–55) provided the model. Englishmen were singing these tunes at the same time the American William Billings went his iconoclastic way with the same idea in New England, spawning several generations of composers of the style. It is not unlikely that the music of Billings had a British echo in Florida. To reconstruct the sound accurately is hazardous, but sources suggest the continuance of old problems: balance, sliding into a designated pitch from a fourth below, gruff sounds in the bass, and a nasal, sharp sound in the tenor. The basically two-part harmony favored root-position triads and treated harmonic relationships of fourth and fifths as consonance. This style produced a sturdy, assured, forthright sound, basic enough to appeal to a man strong enough to cross an ocean seeking his fortune. If it did not succeed altogether, the reasons were not hard to find: apathy, scarcity of spiritual leaders, severity of pioneer life, little religious fervor, the absence of skill in sightreading and singing, or the lack of energy to perform tasks beyond those required to sustain oneself.

To build a bridge between religion and social life, Scottish governor James Grant of St. Augustine installed a chapter of Freemasonry. Chapters of the lodge had been formed among Scottish and English military personnel since 1732. They were designed to raise the moral conduct of the vulgar and licentious soldier and raise his self-respect. Socially, officers and their men who were members could meet as equals. Their purpose was to promote the good and happiness of others. Tunes of "Old Hundredth" and many religious hymns were woven into their traditional ritual. Music was an adjunct to their social life as well. "Fie, Let Us a' to the Wedding" and other ballads served both a ritual and a social purpose. These songs remained popular in Florida well into the nineteenth century. In 1771 Governor Grant declared that St. Augustine was the gayest place in America, that there was nothing but balls, assemblies, and concerts. "We are too inconsiderable to enter into Politics and Faction, and as people have little to do, Novelty has catched, and they are all at present Mason music and dansing mad," he wrote.[24]

For the British who came to Florida, the minuet was the preferred dance. It had been very popular in England throughout the century, especially in court circles. Thompson's music publishing firm brought out annual collections of minuets from 1716 to 1791 in celebration of the king's birthday. A "Coronation Minuet" was written for the coronation ball of George III in 1761 and published by Thompson's firm the following year. These were not the familiar minuet and trios of symphonies by Haydn or Beethoven with key changes, lighter instrumentation, and sometimes spirited movement. They were the earlier form of the slow, stately, and graceful dance. In characteristic triple meter, they consisted of two eight-measure sections, each repeated. The dance steps were based on two-measure units. Writing a minuet was not believed to require great skill. One publisher advertised a "Musical curiousity or Tabular System whereby any person without the least knowledge of music may compose 10,000 different minuets in the most pleasing and correct manner, a real curious and pleasing work."[25] Considering the simplicity of the musical form, one had only to find a tune from an early source or devise one not necessarily of great

EIGHTEENTH-CENTURY COUPLES DANCING THE MINUET

The minuet was the favored dance during the British hegemony. Musicians are seated to the right of the dancers. (Courtesy British Library; reprinted from Thompson's Compleat Collection of Two Hundred Favourite Country Dances, *vol. 1)*

distinction. The naming or dedication was essential in that it supplied an identity to the tune so that it might be called for in honor of the subject. Examples of these works were contained in collections of John and David Rutherford between 1775 and 1780.[26] Most of them were dedicated to members of noble families or to military officers.

Visitors to British Florida observed that minuets were followed by country dances. What kind of dances were they? Can they be reconstructed? What was the music of these dances? The answers to these questions are in such books as *Thompson's Compleat Collection of Two Hundred Favourite Country Dances,* in four volumes.[27] It is observed that the first volume of this collection was printed about three years before the British acquired Florida, and the contents were tunes and dances well known to the British public. Some bore the names of the dance formations, but many others were set to familiar songs. "The Star" and "Cream Pot" are examples of the former, as is "Miss Hamilton's Jigg." Among the latter are "We Have Nothing Else to Do" and "The Bonniest Lass in the World." All are in volume 1. The dance steps were limited to a few, but the variety of figures made by them were many. The tunes were usually eight to sixteen measures in length. Fiddles, bagpipes, or other available instruments were

"CREAM POT" AND "SUKY BIDS ME"

Several British dance collections contained not only the tunes but directions for the
dances. (Courtesy British Library; reprinted from Thompson's Compleat
Collection of Two Hundred Favourite Country Dances, *vol. 1)*

pressed into service. Dance directions in Thompson's collection followed
the music and were specific: "The first couple gallop down," "circle foot it
twice and cast off," "and right hand and left," "back to back," "turn your
partner," "clap five times." These directions and a few of the tunes took
hold in the British colonies of the time and activated dancers in rural
America, where square dancing became a popular recreation.

Military bands played music for the obligatory outdoor parades and
ceremonies, but being "double-handed," they played also for the frequent
social occasions. One music collection published in London in 1760 served
the purposes of both indoor and outdoor functions for military men. It
was titled *Warlike Musick* and consisted of a rich assortment of marches,
dedicated to military units, Kings George I and II, princes, and generals.
Several trumpet tunes, a minuet, and a rigadoon were included for dancing. The collection, labeled as being for German flute, violin, or harpsichord, were scored for melody and figured bass but was easily adapted to
the instrumentation of the military band ensemble.[28] Was this music
played in Pensacola and St. Augustine after the British acquired Florida?
Perhaps, though there is no documentary proof. Yet this and other collec-

March in Scipio

G. F. Handel
Warlike Musick, Book II

Charles Burney observed that this march by G. F. Handel was frequently played on parade by the English king's bodyguards. This version was published in Warlike Musick *in 1760, only a few years before the British claimed Florida. The small British military bands may have played it as they marched through the streets of Pensacola and St. Augustine. (Reprinted from* Warlike Musick, *p. 34; also in Charles Burney,* A General History of Music, *2:734)*

tions of the period deserve comment, since it is upon their content that postulates may be formed as to the music then sounding in Florida coastal towns.

The historian of the King's Royal Rifle Corps stated that the corps had no tradition for choral music.[29] In the sense of an officially approved chorus whose appearances were commanded by the officers, the statement is correct. In the sense of informal singing among the troops, on duty or not, it is not. "The British Grenadiers" was not only the most popular march of the period, it was also the most popular song.

> Some talk of Alexander, and some of Hercules
> Of Hector and Lysander, and such great names as these.
> But of all the world's great heroes,
> There's none that can compare
> With a tow, row, row, row, row, row,
> To the British Grenadiers.[30]

Throughout the century it appeared in collections of instrumental and vocal music. Other songs sung by soldiers and sailors included "Britons Strike Home," "Hearts of Oak," "Rule Britannia," "Tom Bowling," and "Ye Mariners of England." "Ye Mariners" was sung in Florida by several generations of sailors.

> Ye mariners of England!
> That guard our native seas;
> Whose flag has braved a thousand years,
> The battle and the breeze!
> Your glorious standard launch again,
> To match another foe!
> And weep thro' the deep,
> And weep thro' the deep
> And weep thro' the deep,
> While stormy winds do blow.[31]

Charles Dibdin, one of the most popular songwriters of the age, wrote songs in praise of the "New Navy," declaring in one:

> For sailors were born to be handy
> At any job under the sun
> And they say, what a blue jacket won't do,
> Ain't very much worth being done.[32]

Songs were adopted for the following foot regiments that served in Florida: "The Duke of York," for the King's Royal Rifles (Sixtieth Foot); "Meanee Day," for the Cheshire Regiment (Twenty-second Foot); and "Steadily Forward!" for Prince Albert's Somersetshire Light Infantry (Thirteenth Foot). Words of the first of these are by Sergeant Scurfield and Pvt. Philip Clay.

> The Duke of York he was the man,
> He did invent a very good plan:
> He formed a Corps of Riflemen
> To fight for England's glory!
> He dressed them all in jackets of green,
> And placed them where they couldn't be seen,
> And sent them in front, an invisible screen,
> To fight for England's glory.[33]

Aside from patriotic and regimental tunes, Englishmen who came to the British colony of Florida had a remarkably rich heritage of secular songs. Hundreds of collections appeared in eighteenth-century England and Scotland. Handel arias were popular, but Italian opera made way for earthy ballad operas, whose ordinary human (and subhuman) characters replaced mythological heroes, and simple popular tunes were substituted for dramatic melisma. Songs in the collections were sung in the home, on the stage, and in the pleasure gardens of London and environs. Many were exported to the British colonies. They were written by Thomas Arne, James Hook, William Boyce, Henry Carey, Charles Dibdin, and a legion of other composers. They were sung by several generations of Floridians. "Roslin Castle" was a slow love song with words by Richard Hewitt and a tune by James Oswald, chamber composer to His Majesty. It was published in England in 1762 and became popular on both sides of the Atlantic in vocal and instrumental settings.[34] During the American Revolution it became a fife tune favored as a death march at funerals. The American edition was sung in Florida as late as 1821. An equally favored song was "This Cold Flinty Heart," from Michael Arne's opera *Cymon* of 1767. It was published by Eliphalet Mason of Northampton, Massachusetts, in an 1802 songbook and subsequently by other Americans.

> This cold flinty heart it is you who have warm'd
> You waken'd my passions my senses have charm'd

In vain against merit and Cymon I strove
What's life without passion, sweet passion of love.

Especially popular among Floridians who came during the British
hegemony and the years following were the Scottish songs such as those
in James Oswald's *Second Collection of Curious Scots Tunes* of 1770. The music was set in eight- or sixteen-measure phrases, each repeated. It was
scored for melody and figured bass. The harmonic language was diatonic,
with few excursions into closely related keys. There was a variety of tempi
and meter. Many were folk titles that remain in the repertory today:
"Wally, Wally," "Barbara Allen," "The Highland Lassie," "Green Grow the
Grasses," and "The Yellow-Haired Laddie."

The music legacy of early St. Augustine settlers had come from the
Spanish, French, and British, but during the British colonial period other
sources emerged. Gov. James Grant had been in St. Augustine three years
when Dr. Andrew Turnbull, a wealthy Scotsman, was issued a grant for
twenty thousand acres of Florida land. Turnbull arrived in November of
1767 and organized a settlement which he named New Smyrna as a sentimental gesture to his wife's birthplace in Asia Minor. The people of the
colony were called Minorcans because most of them came from that Medi-
terranean island which, now with Majorca and Ibiza, is a favorite summer
resort of northern Europeans but then was suffering from repeated crop
failures and economic depression. Others had been gathered from the
Greek tribes of southern Peloponnesus and the Italian island of Leghorn.
There were almost 1,500 of them, and they had little in common except
religion and birth in a warm climate. Even their religion was not a totally
cohesive force, since the Greeks were from the Eastern Orthodoxy. They
did share the condition of poverty and the reputation for hard work. Religion continued to be a problem, since Turnbull's grant was conditional
that all settlers be Protestant. The Spanish-Catholic background of the
Minorcans meant that they attended Mass and observed many holy days,
but their priest, Father Camps, found it necessary to petition church officials in Cuba to send oils (for baptism and extreme unction) and brevia-
ries of the Divine Office, secretly to avoid trouble with the British.[35]

The Minorcans remembered their ancient heritage throughout hardships and failure of the colony. They continued to teach each growing
generation of children the songs and customs of Minorca. Young Minorcan men strolled the streets of St. Augustine singing *amoroses,* sometimes

inventing bawdy texts to traditional tunes, just as their fathers had done before they crossed the Atlantic. Songs of the church year and children's songs were sung. These songs and the accompanying customs were described by visitors who heard them during the second Spanish period. For that reason, the commentaries on them appear at the beginning of chapter 5.

When the British botanist William Stark came to Florida in 1765, he reported, "The inhabitants [are] of all colours, white, negroes, mulattos, Indians, etc."[36] Fugitive slaves from Georgia and South Carolina had come to the Spanish colony as early as 1726. They were welcomed by the Spanish and by the Lower Creek Indians, with whom they intermarried. Governor Montaino gave some of them their freedom in 1738, and thirty-eight families settled in a community just north of St. Augustine because they had been promised freedom.[37]

The largest number of slaves was brought to Florida during the English occupation, 1763–84, for the purpose of cultivating indigo, rice, and other plantation crops.[38] One of the budget proposals of the West Florida first assembly was "an annual cargo of negroes to be distributed among the inhabitants who were industrious, for the encouragement of agriculture and trade."[39] Georgia and Carolina raiders came across the Florida border and stole slaves from the plantations and the streets. The niceties of legal proceedings were not observed. The British took slaves with them when they left St. Augustine after the American Revolution. African slave trade was prohibited after 1808, but authorities found it difficult to enforce the statutes. A law was passed in 1822, imposing a fine of three hundred dollars for every Negro imported to Florida from countries outside the United States and guaranteeing every imported Negro his or her freedom.[40]

It is curious that the British brought more Negro slaves to Florida than did others yet wrote little about them. Not until the next century were there full-scale British accounts of Negro music and dance on North American plantations. On the other hand, British appear to have found North American Indians quite exotic and therefore recorded many events they observed with the red men. The status of African blacks with British slavers was such that it was difficult for their owners to write about them dispassionately. Language barriers aside, the music of the Negro must have seemed hardly worthy of comment. It was not notated and forwarded to England until it became as exotic as the Indian music had been from the beginning. Many British regarded Africans as slave animals and had little interest in reporting their folklore, songs, and dances. Once Negroes emerged from this subhuman role, they became objects of curiosity. Their music and dance then was seen on the British stage, but some of the music performances were about as faithful to the original as *Aïda* is to authentic Egyptian music. Patronizing parodies served only until indigenous songs sung by black singers were heard.

As sentiment for independence grew among the thirteen British colonies, loyalist refugees streamed into both East and West Florida. By April 1776 the stream became a flood from Charleston, Savannah, and other points north. Florida did not declare war on Great Britain. Like seventeen other British colonies from Nova Scotia and Quebec to Jamaica and Barbados, both Floridas remained loyal to Great Britain throughout the American Revolution. The British navy defended the extensive Florida coastline. The British army protected the white population from blacks, who outnumbered them two to one, and the numerous Indians. The British, though, hired some Indians and blacks to fight for them.

From about five hundred to more than three thousand enlisted men, speaking English, French, and German, were stationed in Florida. It was these men who attempted to relieve the distress of the impoverished refugees. Grants from the government and charity of local residents sustained them. One means of raising money for the loyalists was the production of plays. An example advertised for March 3, 1783, when the George Farquhar comedy *Beau Stratagem* and an afterpiece, "Miss in Her Teens," were produced for the benefit of the refugees.[41] Tickets were priced at five shillings ninepence for the pit, and one shilling for the gallery. While the newspaper of the day did not identify the author of the afterpiece, it was undoubtedly the drama of that title by David Garrick. Certainly it would have been appropriate to sing the Arne ditty of that title at the entr'acte.[42]

One song was sung as a part of the play in act 2, scene 1, by William Fribble, Esq., to Miss Biddy Bellair. Fribble first read the words to his young lady. She laughed in embarrassment and declared that they were very pretty but she did not understand them. Fribble replied: "These light pieces are never so well understood in reading as singing. I have set 'em myself and will endeavor to give 'em to you. —La-la—, I have an abominable cold and can't sing a note; however, the tune's nothing, the manner's all." He then sang:

No ice so hard, so cold as I
Till warm'd and soften'd by your eye;
And now my heart dissolves away
In dreams by night and sighs by day.
No brutal passion fires my breast,
Which loathes the object when possessed;
But one of harmless, gentle kind,
Whose joys are centered—in the mind.
Then take with me love's better part,
His downy wing, but not his dart.[43]

Other plays acted for the benefit of the refugees were *The Tragedy of Zara* by Aaron Hill, *Douglass* by John Home, and *The Oprhan* by Thomas Otway. These dramas with their entr'acte music were well known to audiences in Theatres Royal, Drury Lane, and Covent Garden.

In this loyalist haven, however, there was one jarring musical note. A number of American provincials from colonies to the north had become war prisoners and were sent to St. Augustine for safekeeping. Americans who became prisoners of the British during the Revolution had acute sensibilities both with respect to their honor as gentlemen and their taste in music. When Charleston surrendered to Great Britain in 1779, Josiah Smith, Jr., a member of the South Carolina General Assembly, was sent with other prominent citizens on a prisoners' ship to St. Augustine, where they were in exile for several months. The British soldiers of the Florida port city celebrated the first anniversary of Savannah's surrender by showing the colors at sunrise, offering a twenty-one-gun salute from the castle, and sponsoring a grand dinner and ball that evening. By the following morning the company was "all of them seemingly much heated by liquor." Headed by their commandant and their regimental music, they paraded about the streets between the hours of seven and eight o'clock. When they reached Smith's quarters, they struck up the tune "Yankee Doodle" in derision of the Americans. The tune had been played frequently before at the changing of the guards, and Smith's patience was wearing thin. He demanded an apology for such rude behavior, and the commissary gave oral assurance that no insult was intended. Smith commented that a gentlemanly response would have "declared the repentance of indecent and unprovoked conduct toward strangers, and prisoners on parole."[44] British military bands had played the tune and devised new

THE

ORPHAN:
OR, THE

UNHAPPY MARRIAGE.

A

TRAGEDY.

Written by *THO. OTWAY.*

Qui Pelago credit magno, se fœnore tollit ;
Qui Pugnas & Castra petit, præcingitur Auro ;
Vilis Adulator picto jacet Ebrius Ostro ;
Et qui sollicitat Nuptas, ad præmia peccat :
Sola pruinosis horret Facundia pennis,
Atque inopi lingua desertas invocat Artes.

Petron. Arb. Sat.

LONDON,

Printed by J. DARBY for *M. P.* and sold by A. BET-
TESWORTH in *Pater noster-Row,* R. CALDWELL
in *Newgate-street,* and F. CLAY without *Temple Bar.*
M.DCC.XXVI.

THE ORPHAN

Incidental music and dance enhanced performances of British plays acted for the
benefit of royalists who found refuge in St. Augustine during the American
Revolution. In this tragedy, Castalio sang his advice to lovelorn youths. (Reprinted
from Thomas Otway, The Orphan *[London: J. Darby, 1726], act 4, scene 1)*

lyrics to ridicule the improvised uniforms of American troops. They also
interrupted New England church services with it. By 1779 it had become a
tiresome ploy.

In St. Augustine on July 4, 1781, the Americans shared a common mess
with the loyalists. It was there that some of the prisoner-patriots sang a
new song for the first time. The first lines were:

> God save the thirteen states
> Thirteen United states
> God save them all

Set to tune of "God Save the King," the song "caused great surprise
among their British hosts."[45] This verse is attributed to Thomas Hey-

THOMAS HEYWARD

Three American patriots imprisoned in St. Augustine in 1781 sang "God Save the Thirteen States" at a communal dinner with the British on July 4. Pictured here is Thomas Heyward, one of the trio. All were South Carolinians and signers of the Declaration of Independence. (Courtesy Florida State Archives; reprinted from James Murfin, National Park Service Guide to Historic Places of the American Revolution)

ward. He and fellow singers Edward Rutledge and Arthur Middleton were all signers of the Declaration of Independence.

For the British in Florida the American Revolution had begun in 1775 and lasted until 1785. Over those years Gov. Patrick Tonyn remembered the 1775 music and Eagle Tale dance that the Creek Indians performed in his honor in his early years as governor. He remembered the pleasure gardens of Lt. Gov. John Moultrie's Bella Vista estate overlooking the Matanzas River. He recalled attending dances and plays in 1781. He read doggerel, lampoons, and poetry in the *East Florida Gazette* and observed the Scots St. Andrews Society's annual procession to church, then to Love's Coffee House for refreshment.[46]

Now, in 1784, Florida was returned to Spain. Musketry and artillery fired as the Spanish flag rose over Castillo de San Marco. Father Camps celebrated mass. For a year the British joined the Spanish in keeping law and order, and they brought music and dance into their final civilities by sponsoring a ball for Governor Manuel de Zéspedes and his entourage.

5

✳ ✳ ✳ ✳ ✳ ✳ ✳ ✳

Before the Ending of the Day

Music and the Later Spanish

*They lived here, and died here
They left singing names.*
—Stephen Vincent
Benét

The British had acquired Florida all the way to the Mississippi, including Louisiana, by the 1763 Treaty of Paris at the end of the French and Indian War. Then the Spanish moved out, almost to a man. But twenty years later, now by another Treaty of Paris, the Spanish returned. Unlike the exodus of the Spanish when the British came, there was no mass departure this time.

The Minorcans, Greeks, and Italians who arrived during the British hegemony had moved into St. Augustine and became fishermen, craftsmen, and businessmen. Dr. Turnbull, the large-scale planter, had moved to Charleston, and Dennis Rolle had returned to England, but such prominent property owners and planters as Jesse Fish and Philip Fatio had remained, as had John Leslie, partner in the growing firm of Panton and Leslie. Among the Minorcans was Estevan Benét, ancestor of Steven Vincent Benét, who had arrived in 1771. Petros Drimarachis had opened a school for children, and his house is now pointed out as the oldest wooden schoolhouse in America. While the government was Spanish, the weakened economy and low military strength of that nation could not support full

THE SPANISH IN ST. AUGUSTINE

Artist's concept of Spanish at the port of St. Augustine. Castillo de San Marco is shown in the background. (Courtesy Florida State Archives)

domination of the colony. Spanish officials found it prudent to deal with British traders, who had both domestic and foreign agents. There were multiple problems of poverty, property rights, legal authority, religion, Negro rights, and education which continued throughout their second period in Florida. Perhaps the greatest problem was how to deal with the estimated forty-five thousand Creeks, Cherokees, Choctaws, Chickasaws, and Seminoles. The Spanish left it unresolved, and a series of wars began that continued for about forty years through territorial and statehood days. The government attempted to untangle the complicated property claims and restore substandard buildings. The church took steps to improve education, to build a new edifice, and to revive the spirit of Catholicism.

Fr. Thomas Hassett was chosen to accomplish this mission. From his assignment in Philadelphia, he boarded the Spanish frigate *Santa Anna* for Havana but en route encountered a severe storm in which he lost his books, other personal belongings, and even the king's orders. He requested assistance because of his own misfortune and prepared a specific list of items needed for conducting religious services. He submitted it through the newly appointed governor, Vincente Manuel de Zéspedes, in October 1784, to Bernardo de Gálvez, captain general of West and East Florida. Gálvez was reminded that all the church valuables were sent to Havana when Florida was ceded to Britain in 1763. The new requisition list included a suitable church and residence, main altar and images, capes for the choir, bells to call the devout to worship, and "an organ to solemnize the services." Hassett also asked that both he and his presbyter, Miguel O'Reilly, be given raises in salaries from thirty pesos a month to forty-five pesos, because of the high cost of living. Three Irish priests had accompanied Governor Zéspedes when he arrived from Havana in June 1784. They served in the hospital, the convent, and the barracks. Zespedes brought with him the promise of a forty-thousand-peso subsidy, but typically it was not received for over a year and was clearly inadequate. The awkward Spanish bureaucracy had required subsidies to Florida to flow through the viceroyalty of Mexico, so extended delays were not uncommon.

To Hassett's request, however, must have come an uncharacteristically prompt response. The January 30, 1785, budget for the parochial church in the St. Augustine presidio proposed annual stipends of 700 pesos for the priest, 50 for the principal sacristan, 500 for the organist, 80 each for two acolytes, and 50 for a bell ringer. The priest, sacristan, and organist were required to buy at their own expense the wine, wax, and flour for the Host. Expenses for these items could be recovered by their fees for burials, masses, weddings, and baptisms. A stipend of 350 pesos each was requested for the Franciscan fathers of the convent of Our Father San Francisco. In addition, fathers at the doctrinas (outlying missions) received gifts of food from the Indians. It was mentioned in the budget request that the Dominicans of California were awarded a stipend of 350 pesos and that they got along very well.[1] The request for a subsidy for the organist implies that an organ had been installed in the parochial church by 1784. The organist is not named, nor is there a description of the instrument.

Auxiliary Bishop Cyril de Barcelona, Capuchin father Ignacio Olot, and two pages arrived from Cuba in St. Augustine on July 8, 1788, for an official visitation. The church, cemetery, hospital, and school were inspected. The bishop commanded that the Vespers be sung every Sunday evening and the Salve, a hymn in honor of the Blessed Mother, be sung on all days specified by the diocesan synod.[2] In the spirit of the inquisition, he exhorted members to report abuses or errors of their neighbors. The conduct of the priests did not escape attention. The bishop recalled that the Edicto de Pecados Públicos did not allow priests to dance or play musical instruments at a wedding.[3] There is no record of a priest's being relieved of his duties because of these infractions, though a few were for drunkenness or fornication.

Living in a remote province and on the edge of poverty did not prevent the Spanish people from engaging in occasional large-scale celebrations. Never did these fiestas compare with the elaborate ceremonies of their compatriots in Mexico, but they were important enough to be documented, thus leaving vivid pictures of social life among the earliest settlers. One extended event occurred on December 2–4, 1789, when the aging Governor Zéspedes—then seventy years old—decided to conclude his career in Florida with a celebration of the coronation of Charles IV as king of Spain. The event, he hoped, might tend to absorb the polyglot St. Augustine population into Spanish cultural patterns and loyalty to the new king. Moreover, it might encourage the monarch to look with favor on Zéspedes's son, Vincent Domingo, when the time came for political honors or appointments to be made.[4]

The weather was fine on the bright December afternoon. Windows, balconies, and doorways were hung with brightly colored fabrics, flags, or flowers. The governor's residence was draped with scarlet silk, and in the plaza were portraits of Charles IV and his queen, María Louisa of Parma, canopied and draped with red and white damask and taffeta. Pickets of infantrymen stood at the four corners of the square. At four o'clock the governor appeared on horseback. The leading citizens and military officers joined the *reyes de armas* for a sweep around the square, led by a band in double file to the church for a brief ceremony. When the assembly returned to the square, Lieutenant Zéspedes raised the royal ensign and led cheers for the house of Castile. Artillery resounded from Castillo de San Marcos and from ships in the harbor. Drums rolled, and church bells rang out. The governor then threw to the crowd the silver medals he had ordered struck for the occasion. It was time for the grand parade to begin. The military band set the cadence down Saint George Street to Saint Francis barracks and back toward the river and up Main Street to the governor's residence.

As darkness fell, a typically Spanish general illumination of candles shone throughout the residential districts, and bonfires blazed in the plaza. Clerks from the financial supply offices improvised their versions of Indian-style dances around the flames. On a large stage the Havana regiment gave their premier performance of the Pedro Calderón de la Barca drama *Amigo amante y leal.*

After the parade and *refresco* there were private parties.

Musicians arrived later to provide entertainment for listeners and dancers in a form of social entertainment called a *sarao,* a soirée. Dancing customarily opened with a formal minuet, whose elegant steps were familiar to elite society throughout the continent and European colonies. But as the evening grew cooler and spirits gayer, the violin was replaced by the guitar and livelier contredances occupied the floor. . . . The spirit of revelry was even more animated in St. Augustine's humbler residences, where guests followed the intricate regional dances of Southern Spain, Minorca and the Canary Islands. . . . Boisterous groups of soldiers joined in singing popular songs, improvising a few solo lyrics, while their comrades played cards or dice in the background.[5]

On Sunday morning those who were able attended a high mass sung by Father Hassett. He was assisted by presbyter Fr. Miguel O'Reilly, hospital chaplain Fr. Francisco Traconis, and frail old Fr. Pedro Camps, who had come to New Smyrna with his fellow Minorcans in 1768. The congregation sang the Te Deum at the conclusion of the service.

A final spectacle of the celebration came on December fourth, when six horses drew a large, elaborate float through the town. Aboard it were members of the local carpenters' guild wearing hats with red cockades and carrying torches. At each street corner they paused to give cheers to the new king, and the little knots of citizens standing about responded with cheers of their own. Governor Zéspedes sent notarized reports of the celebration and three commemorative medals to the king and the colonial secretary.

Recurring social events in St. Augustine were on a small scale but continued throughout the second Spanish period and well beyond. One of them, the posey dance, was described by several writers before it became obsolete in the nineteenth century. The women of a family assembled a bower of flowers and candles in their home. One gentleman was presented

a bouquet and named king for the evening. According to an early historian, "These assemblies were always informal, and frequented by all
classes, all meeting on a level; but were conducted with the utmost po-
liteness and decorum, for which the Spanish character is so distinguished.
The graceful Spanish dance, so well suited in its slow and regular movements to the inhabitants of a warm climate, has always retained the preference with the natives of the place, who dance it with that native grace and
elegance of movement which seems easy and natural for everyone, but is
seldom equaled by the Anglo-Saxon."[6]

An English visitor gave a vivid account of the carnival tradition in St.
Augustine in the early nineteenth century.

> I had arrived at a season of general relaxation, on the eve of the car-
> nival, which is celebrated with much gayety in all Catholic countries.
> Masques, dominoes, harlequins, punchinellos, and a great variety of
> grotesque disguises, on horseback, in cars, gigs and on foot, paraded
> the streets with guitars, violins and other instruments; and in the
> evenings, the houses were open to receive masks, and balls were given
> in every direction. I was told that in their better days, when their pay
> was regularly remitted from Havana, these amusements were admira-
> bly conducted, and the rich dresses exhibited on these occasions, were
> not eclipsed by their more fashionable friends in Cuba; but poverty
> had lessened their spirit for enjoyment, as well as the means for pro-
> curing it; enough, however remained to amuse an idle spectator.[7]

One of the most celebrated carnival customs of the Minorcans who
came during the British hegemony was kept on the evening before Easter
Sunday. The young men went from house to house rapping on doors or
shutters. If they received no answering knock, they moved on to another
house. If someone was inside, the young men sang in Mahonese dialect a
traditional hymn in honor of the Virgin. It was a song of many stanzas,
but it was repeated throughout the city. When the religious verses had
been sung, a new stanza was added soliciting a gift of cakes or eggs. The
shutters then were opened, and cheese, cakes, pastry, or eggs were
dropped into a bag carried by one of the serenaders. If the shutters remained closed, a final line of the closing stanza became "No es homo de
compliment." (The general meaning is "He is no perfect gentleman.")
Called the Fromajadas, this is the best-known song and the most-familiar
tradition of the Minorcans. The Jane Quinn editions of the song texts are

in Mahonese, Spanish, and English versions. The music has been transcribed by Howard Manucy and L. Hosmer.

Even with all the ceremonies and dancing, Florida became a pain which the body of Spain was unable to bear. Over the years governors and priests reported the difficulties of governing and the perpetual shortage of provisions for survival. In the final years Spain was less and less able and willing to give financial support and jurisdictional order to a population of numerous ethnic strains. The inability of the Spanish to sustain their sovereignty became apparent. The "manifest destiny" of the American takeover became a reality in 1821, when Florida became one of its territories. More than three hundred years had passed since the first Spaniards had walked in Florida and reported hearing music. Now the Jonathans, the Yankees, the Scots, the settlers from the North and West joined the multiracial, multicultural early settlers and in a few years became a state. The tunes they played and the songs they sang changed over the years, but political fortunes and misfortunes never stilled the impulse to make music in Florida.

6

* * * * * * * *

The Roll of a Drum, the Sound of an Old Song

Music and the Military

Sweet Florida good bye to thee
Thou land of sun and flowers
Where gen'rous hearts and beauty dwell
Amid thy fragrant bowers
St. Rosa's snow-like sands
Are fast fading on my eye
Then take the off'ring of my heart
Sweet Florida, good bye.
—*J. G. Drake, 1835, sailor's song on leaving Pensacola*

In the War of 1812 Pres. James Madison feared that England would land forces in Florida and launch attacks on states to the north. The peninsula was still a Spanish colony, but Spain was believed to be too weak either to rule or to fight. In August 1814 the English did land and began military drills with Negroes and Indians up and down the streets of Pensacola. Andrew Jackson swept into the city in November, and the English retreated to their ships. The Indians and Negroes went fifteen miles up the Apalachee River to Prospect Bluff, where they established a Negro fort. Jackson and his troops went west to Mobile and then to their great victory at the battle of New Orleans. Their triumph occurred two days after the signing of the peace, but it precipitated numerous songs praising Jackson and his men. An English subaltern heard two or three "tolerably full [American] military bands" playing before the battle. He was unhappy at having to hear "Yankee Doodle" played at least six times but patronizingly wrote, "The Yankees are not famous for their good taste in anything, but one or two of the waltzes struck me as being particularly beautiful."[1]

The Seminole Indians lost extensive lands in southwest Georgia by the Treaty of Fort Jackson, which Old Hickory forced upon them in 1814. Their hostile retaliatory raids into Georgia gave Jackson a reason to cross the international boundary into Florida. The conflict developed into the First Seminole War of 1818. American military excursions went out from Fort Scott, Fort Gadsden, and Saint Marks, but it was not until 1821 that Florida was ceded to the United States as a territory. It would be twenty-four more years before she attained the status of statehood. The ceremony transferring Florida opened at seven in the morning of July 17, 1845, when companies of Spanish and American troops entered Pensacola with "a full band of music" and flags flying in the Gulf breeze. After signing the transfer and raising the American flag, the Fourth Infantry band played "The Star Spangled Banner."[2]

By 1834 the government had decided to move the Indians to the West. Citizens had demanded protection from the Indians and black runaway slaves. Indian troubles inhibited mobility on land and sea. Speculators and settlers had their eyes on the rich land of northern and central Florida. A large number of troops were moved into Fort King, Fort Brooke, Fort Drane, Fort Drum, and five or six other forts. Along the east coast were seven or more forts from Fort Marion to Fort Pierce, Fort Lauderdale, and Fort Dallas. To them came also a few seasoned officers and a substantial number of young graduates of West Point who were to get their real taste of war in a conflict for which they were ill prepared. The Florida landscape demanded a new battle strategy. The enemy was scattered and elusive. The life-style was unlike that of the young officers or of the young recruits, who were farmers or laborers from Pennsylvania, New York, Washington, D.C., or South Carolina. The adjustment was even greater for the Irish or English enlisted men, the German Fusiliers and Hamburg Volunteers, and the Polish men who served at Fort Brooke. With the Fourth Regiment Infantry was William Carney, a fifer from Londonderry, Ireland, and Charles T. Heck, a drummer from Lancaster, Pennsylvania.[3] Among the officers were two men who later became presidents of the United States: Andrew Jackson and Zachary Taylor. They served with a remarkable array of other distinguished military men.[4] These debonair officers left memoirs or diaries with vivid descriptions of the setting, the men, and the war. Few enlisted men wrote of their experiences, though some of them did. A few were candid enough to confess that they enlisted because they were inebriated or were in trouble with the law or women.

LASHEE (THE LICKER)

George Catlin made this sketch of Lashee (The Licker), celebrated warrior of the Seminole Wars. (From George Catlin, Drawings of the North American Indians *[Garden City, N.Y.: Doubleday, 1984], p. 159)*

The Second Seminole War, 1836–42, was decisive in destroying Indian power in Florida, but it was costly in manpower and greatly retarded the economic development of the state.

The life-styles of American generals who served in Florida during the Seminole Wars varied greatly, according to their fellow officers. Gen. D. L. Clinch, known as the Spartan General, required only a field tent and a camp stool when he commanded troops. His dress, his food, and his accommodations were those of his men. Gen. Winfield Scott, who was later called "old fuss and feathers," traveled with furniture, a company of musicians, and an entourage that would have rivaled that of the Spanish officers who preceded him.[5] John Bemrose, a medical soldier with Clinch, commented that Scott's wine, furniture, and "a band of choice musicians" were more appropriate to an Indian nabob than "a republic general engaged in warfare with a wild foe in a desert country."[6]

Impressions of Florida recorded by other military men said more about the place than the music. In a collection of personal recollections of the Second Dragoons, a bugler-scout with Capt. Benjamin L. Beall wrote, "Those who have never breathed the balmy air of Florida on the Gulf side, who have never floated on her calm, lullaby waters or heard the low whispering of her tall, majestic pines and palmettoes, can know but little of the real joy of simply existing." In a poem to the dragoons, he is pictured riding in the moonlight, "as he merrily trolls some old-time song." A song "In the Florida War" characterized Captain Beall as a brave and jolly man who sang songs around the campfire all night until reveille sounded the next morning.[7]

> Oh, jolly brave knight was our Benjamin Beall
> In the Florida War;
> As many a jolly bright camp-fire could tell
> In the Florida War.
> Oh! the stories he told that never grow old
> And the songs that he trolled until reveille rolled,
> In the Florida War,
> Made chiefs and subalterns as merry as bold
> In the Florida War.
>
> Who was brave as a lion, yet soft as a child
> In the Florida War?
> Who could swim the Suwannee when waters were wild
> In the Florida War?
> Who could harass Sam Jones till he ached in his bones,
> Rap a redskin whilst laughing, then weep o'er his groans
> In the Florida War?
> Then chant him a requiem in reverent tones,
> In the Florida War?
>
> Who, when shattered and broken, from scoutings and toils,
> In the Florida War?

Could smile at grim death as he felt its cold coils,
    In the Florida War?
Who but valiant old Ben—beau ideal of men,
Who wore gay soldier's togs in the days that we ken,
    In the Florida War?
God rest his old head where his blanket is spread
Far from toil and cold lead
    In the Florida War?[8]

Bartholomew Lynch, a regular army private, was at Fort Brooke in July 1838 when he declared Tampa Bay a perfect Arcadia, a heavenly spot. "I wish," he wrote, "some perfumed cigar smoking, novel writing, city man monkey was here, he could not describe it, he would die of a fit of reality." Lynch had few duties; he had books to read and whiskey at fifty cents a gill.[9] He was amused that mothers and sweethearts at home pictured the soldiers as fighting the Indians, when they, in fact, were at the theater enjoying a program of comic songs, recitations, and an animated Egyptian mummy. With the soldiers was the usual theater mixed audience: aristocratic residents, dragoons, whores, Indians, Negroes, sailors, and marines. "Hurrah, hurrah for the War in Florida," he wrote.[10]

Strongly opinionated Erasmus D. Keyes, an officer with Gen. Winfield Scott at Picolata in 1836, was not content with his assignment in Fort Lauderdale. He liked hearing the waves of the ocean and having the view of Indian River to the west, but then noted:

"It was the abode of serpents, alligators, frogs, foxes, owls, wildcats, and other noisy creatures, whose moans, yelps, and hootings joined with the hum and buzz of the innumerable winged and sharded insects that filled the surrounding atmosphere. There was no cessation nor interlude in the horrid though varied concert. The hum of mosquitos was continuous, the barking of foxes and hooting of owls was nearly so, while the piercing scream and hoarse croak of birds of the night, hitherto unknown to me, were interjected at short intervals to make the hellish fugue complete. The strange noises were not wholly disagreeable, but the army of fleas that invaded my couch kept me awake, and I thought of happier times.[11]

His happier times must have been in military pursuits because his view of other diversions, including the arts, was melancholy. He wrote, "It is

clear to me that no man has lived within the last 100 years who has originated a form of beauty . . . that had not already been equalled and often
excelled. Eloquence and art have long been exhausted developments, and
of music I am not a judge. It is undergoing change and it may be improving."[12]

Not all of the changes needed had anything to do with music directly.
Improvement of the music depended more on army sanitation and health
standards than on the niceties of embouchure adjustments. The band at
the garrison of Fort Reid in 1841 was broken up because of the illness of
many of its members. One musician of this unit was so outraged by his
Florida assignment that he destroyed the music scores of his unit and declared that he would not play another note. This and the decimation of his
ranks caused the commanding officer to request permission to send a
junior officer to New York to recruit musicians. The request was granted,
and Lt. Nathan Darling was sent on the mission.[13]

Because the musicians' presence at drills and regularly scheduled ceremonies was assumed, few military historians have described these routine
duties. Other narratives, some of them by musicians themselves, have
provided the details of what was expected of a bandsman. The duties of the
trumpeter for a company began with the sounding of reveille at daylight,
fatigue a half-hour after, breakfast call at seven, and doctor's call at eight.
Fatigue was played at two in the afternoon, and orderly sergeant's call at
four. Retreat drill was at sundown, and tattoo at nine. Several stable calls
were also necessary for mounted troops.[14] William Drown, a bugler who
took part in twelve battles of the Second Seminole War from 1836 to 1842,
gave a description of his duties at a later date. In his twenty years' service
he had attained the rank of chief bugler, but his duties were no less ar-
duous than those of a recruit. He attended guard mounting at 8:30 in the
morning, saddled up, and rode two miles. He assisted other musicians in
digging a grave and returned at 12:30 P.M. The funeral procession started
thirty minutes later. After the service, he marched to the barracks and
dressed for evening parade. Then he marched to the stable and assisted in
the flogging of a deserter, returned to quarters, ate supper, and wrote in
his journal. His principal duty was to sound the proper calls or signals at
designated times and functions. Some of them were "Boots and Saddles,"
"General," "Disperse," "To Arms," and "To Horse." Trumpeters, fifers,
and drummers transmitted calls and signals, but other music contingents
sometimes assumed duty for parades and other ceremonial occasions.

One instance where musicians were required to participate in disciplin-

The Rogue's March

Traditional

*This march appeared in Bland and Weller's London fife tutor in the 1790s, and a
version of the second theme was notated by the American soldier Abel Shattuck in his
"Sketchbook" during the American Revolution. Its use in a drumming-out ceremony
continued through the Civil War. (Reprinted from Shattuck, "Sketchbook"
[manuscript, Library of Congress])*

ary ceremonies of a unit occurred at Fort Brooke with General Jesup commanding. A ship's captain of a rum smuggler and two members of his crew
were arrested. Their punishment was to be paraded through the military
quarters. A heavy log yoke was placed about their necks, with empty bot-
tles dangling from the ends. "Two drummers and fifers preceding them
[were] striking up the 'Rogue's March,' a party of the guard in their rear
[had] fixed bayonets. The persecuted sailors seem to enjoy the spectacle of
their own degradation more than any other that's looking on," wrote one
observer.[15]

The "Rogue's March" had long been used in the British military services
when public punishment was administered. American military officers
continued the tradition. An English soldier who joined the American
army and served at Fort Pickens, Fort Barrancas, and Fort Monroe reported that some of the men of his unit deliberately deserted and were

drummed out rather than risking being shot up in Texas or Mexico. For them, the Seminole War was a way-stop to the Mexican War. Their punishment was to be flogged fifty lashes with cowhide and to have their heads shaved. The next morning they were marched around the parade ground and about the garrison while the fifer and drummer played the "Rogue's March."

A convivial guardhouse party the night before a battle was the source of a song about another cruel mode of punishment. Corporal Bell, a man from the north part of Ireland serving in the American army, was requested to sing "Bucking and Gagging," a popular song that characterized officers as scheming villains and enlisted men as poor devils. In his broad accent the Irishman responded, "Well, lads, I'll just sing you a verse or two aboot bucking an' gagging, an' then we maun toddle awa' an' tak' a bit sleep, and be ready for our work in the morning." So saying, he commenced, in a good sonorous but subdued voice, to sing the following verses:

> Come, all Yankee soldiers, give ear to my song,
> It is a short ditty, 'twill not keep you long;
> It's of no use to fret on account of our luck,
> We can laugh, drink, and sing yet in spite of the buck.
> > Derry down, etc.
>
> "Sergeant, buck him, and gag him" our officers cry,
> For each trifling offence which they happen to spy;
> Till with bucking and gagging of Dick, Tom, and Bill,
> Faith, the Mexican ranks they have helped to fill.
> > Derry down, etc.
>
> The treatment they give us, as all of us know,
> Is bucking and gagging for whipping the foe;
> They buck us and gag us for malice or spite,
> But they're glad to release us when going to fight.
> > Derry down, etc.
>
> A poor soldier's tied up in the sun or the rain,
> With a gag in his mouth till he's tortured with pain;
> Why I'm bless'd, if the eagle we wear on our flag,
> In its claws shouldn't carry a buck and a gag.
> > Derry down, etc.[16]

The punishment was described by an enlisted man of his unit as follows:

The culprit being seated on the ground, his feet are drawn up to his hams, and his wrists tied firmly in front of his legs; a long stick or broom handle is then inserted between his legs and arms, and going over his arms and under his bent knees, a gag is then placed in his mouth and tied firmly behind his head. In this helpless condition, unable to move hand, foot or tongue, he is left for a series of hours, or even days, according to the humour of his tormenter. This revolting and disgusting punishment is often inflicted at the mere whim of an officer, has long been, and I am sorry to say, still continues a favourite mode of punishment in the American army.[17]

If military men assigned to Florida in the first half of the nineteenth century were massacred by Indians or failed to survive the health hazards, musicians saw them to their final resting place. Gen. Edmund P. Gaines found the remains of the victims of the Dade massacre at the outset of the Second Seminole War and ordered that officers and their men were to be buried side by side. "Then the troops were formed in column of companies; and while the full band of the 4th Regiment at the head of the column played with much solemnity and expression a funeral dirge, the men, with arms reversed and with sad but stern countenances, at a slow pace, marched round the entire ground, and the funeral rites of their bretheren in arms were concluded."[18] The scene was described by Capt. George A. McCall, who was there. But this turned out to be a temporary resting place. The bodies of these men were, with appropriate ceremony, removed to St. Augustine twenty-four years later and reinterred. Even for St. Augustine, this was no usual occasion. The escort was composed of officers of the Eighth Infantry, Third Artillery, and a platoon of Guard of Honor. Musicians in the procession were color guards and bands and field musicians of both units. Local dignitaries included the mayor, aldermen, members of the bar and court, the Masonic fraternity, city guards, and a large procession of townspeople. Services and prayers were conducted by three local ministers and priests. The slow march to plaintive music led the cortege to the cemetery, where bodies of the fallen soldiers were placed in vaults encased by cement shaped into pyramids.[19]

The dignity of one funeral procession was shaken by the unsuitable pairing of two soldiers. John Bemrose, who was one of them, described the event.

GEORGE A. MCCALL

When he was a young lieutenant just out of West Point, George A. McCall was ordered to Florida. He wrote one of the best accounts of early civilian life in Pensacola and of music in military ceremonies during the Seminole Wars. (Courtesy Library of Congress)

ETHAN ALLEN HITCHCOCK

General Hitchcock, in Florida during the Seminole Wars and removal of the Seminoles to the West, wrote that he was too well practiced and had too much music to be an amateur. In addition to the standard repertory, he played music of two manuscript volumes of dance tunes and a few hymn tunes. (Courtesy Library of Congress, no. 16189W)

The procession was imposing, the music solemn. I fear myself and an old Scotch Quartermaster Sergeant had a long slouching gait in marching, which years of drill had not cured. As for myself, not having drilled, I could not march, and the slowness of the tune (the "Dead March" in *Saul*) bothered us sadly. Old Cosmond could keep the beat, but owing to his long stride would slide imperceptibly away from myself and the procession. He was six feet, two inches in height,

The Spanish Dance

Hitchcock Collection

This slow, graceful dance was notated by a young American military officer in Florida during the Seminole Wars. (Courtesy Florida State University Music Library; manuscript in Ethan Allen Hitchcock Collection)

whereas I was as diminutive [Bemrose was five feet, seven inches], and our stations being to walk abreast of each other in front of the corpse, Cosmond would exclaim, "Bless me, keep the step." I would retort, "I cannot without stilts keep pace with your compasses." However, this had an end. We arrived at the church. The priest went through the Catholic ceremonies, and we started for the burial ground.

Bemrose hoped the difficulties were over, but at that moment the band struck up the tune "The Merry Man Home to His Grave." The liveliness of this quickstep invigorated long-limbed Cosmond to even greater strides, with poor Bemrose trotting alongside in comic charade.[20]

Entertainment and recreation with music filled off-duty hours of many army and navy men who came to Florida during the wars of Indian removal. Among the most distinguished men was Col. Ethan Allen Hitchcock. He was both a music performer and a sympathetic observer of the music and dance of the Indians. His performances on the flute appear to have been for his own private enjoyment, as he never referred to playing a concert for an audience. Even on those terms he was a bit apologetic both

Dance Tune

This lively tune with directions for dancers was observed and notated by Ethan Allen
Hitchcock, outstanding flutist of the Seminole War period in Florida. (Courtesy
Florida State University Music Library; manuscript in Ethan Allen Hitchcock
Collection)

about his obsession with playing and the extraordinarily large library of
music he carried with him to assignments over much of America, parts of
Mexico, and the Middle East. A year after his Florida assignment he
counted his bound books of music and found that he had sixty volumes
and enough sheet music for twenty more volumes.[21] It is doubtful that
any American, military or civilian, owned a larger library of flute music at
that time.

Ethan Allen Hitchcock was a graduate of West Point, a grandson of
Ethan Allen, the hero of the American Revolution at Ticonderoga. He

Seminole Indians sang and danced to this music in Florida in the 1830s and 1840s, tunes that are published here for the first time. (Courtesy Florida State University Music Library; manuscript in Ethan Allen Hitchcock Collection)

kept a diary throughout most of his adult life, including the Seminole War years in Florida. Hitchcock was assigned to the Third Regiment and in 1842 reported to headquarters located at Fort Stansbury, twelve miles south of Tallahassee. In December his regiment and two companies of local volunteers marched to the Chattahoochee River, then took a steamer down the Apalachicola to Fort Preston. He effected a friendly peace with Chief Pascofa of the fugitive Creeks. Ten Indians with quills in their hair

Love Song

The First Song in the White Feather Dance

Moderato

Last Song: White Feather Dance

Vivace

came to the camp singing. Presents were exchanged, and a pipe was smoked. On January 8, 1843, at the chief's camp on the Ocklocknee River and in celebration of the peaceful agreement, the Indians lit fires in the woods and danced their farewell to Florida. Officers with Hitchcock joined the dance. Hitchcock had succeeded where three other men had failed in their efforts to remove the Indians.

Few soldiers reported solitary music making during these wars. Some of them were absorbed into local customs and uses of congregate music. Officers sang in the choir of Reverend Axtell's church at Fort Brooke. A daughter of the minister wrote that on a moonlight night the officers also serenaded the garrison "from their piazzas by land, their gondolas by water." A violinist sometimes joined them.[22] The men stationed at St. Augustine took up the social customs of the Spanish and Minorcan inhabitants, including dancing, billiards, and serenading. An English enlisted man wrote, "This last is very much in fashion with Spanish beaus. They are not secret affairs by any means. I have often followed with the crowd in the rear of the party, which would usually consist of half a dozen musicians. After the music had ceased, the lover would slip to the front under the window of his beloved, and gracefully doffing his straw hat, would wish her 'good night,' which would be acknowledged by a plaintive 'buenas noches.'"[23] The songs were Spanish or Minorcan, but young American recruits sang them as their own.

Local customs also included dinner parties where guests sang and dancing followed. One such occasion honored the naval captain of the *Natchez* in Key West. Several wines, including champagne, were introduced and, according to the narrator, "in a short time produced their usual effect. We had several songs, short stories and so forth. Capt. Newton sung several songs very well and some of the other officers also sung well."[24] The party began at three o'clock in the afternoon and did not terminate until half past nine that night. The reporter commented that "nearly all were a little intoxicated and several of them very much so."

Navy men arriving for the campaign of 1836 sang as they approached the bar at St. Augustine. One sang an invitation to his love: "Come o'er the sea, maiden with me." Another, more introspective and perhaps growing old, sang,

> Will you, Ellen, when you hear,
> Of your lover on his bier,
> To his mem're shed a tear—
> Bonnie lassie O![25]

Aboard the *Albatross* en route to Forts Pickens, Barrancas, and Monroe, there was singing and dancing below decks. A free concert on the forecastle elicited comment from a soldier-critic who wrote the editor of the *Albatross* newsletter that while attendance was good and several voices were sweet, he had a suggestion: On rising to sing, every gentleman should state whether the song he was to sing was comic or sentimental. The suggestion was prompted by two singers in the concert. One had attempted sentimental favorites "Alice Grey" and "Oft in the Stilly Night" but had succeeded only in convulsing with laughter his unsophisticated audience. The style of the comic singer of "Nix My Dolly" was termed doleful, lugubrious, funereal. In summary, the letter writer could not resist attributing to Shakespeare his final volley: "To hear by the noise, it sounds like dulcet in contagion."[26]

Soldiers at the various forts had their favorite songs. At Fort Pickens Bob Madden, a foot soldier, sang "Cruiskeen Lawn" and "Cease, Rude Boreas, Blustering Railer."[27] The base surgeon was dubbed "Dr. Brown" because his medical advice resembled that of the doctor in a popular song with that title. The soldiers often sang it in his hearing as he passed through the barracks square.

> He often says, with much elocution
> Hard work, low diet, and resolution
> Are the only things for the constitution.
> Oh! Doctor Brown.[28]

One recruit wrote of the singing in his army unit: "Nigger songs or the broadly humorous, formed the staple of these entertainments, excepting the German portion of the recruits, who, having been taught to sing in their national schools, had acquired a more refined ear, and a taste for music of a rather superior quality. They generally arranged, therefore, a separate party, forming a very pleasing concert among themselves, by singing their national songs; these, when heard a little distance off, had a very beautiful and harmonious effect."[29]

As time wore on, the army soldiers composed a song voicing their impatience with the war.

> And yet 'tis not an endless war,
> As facts will plainly show,
> Having been ended forty times
> In twenty months or so.[30]

Chroniclers of the Seminole Wars make scattered references to bands of the military units. Early in the wars, one soldier was stationed in Fernandina, a small port city on the northeastern coast teeming with vessels bearing Russians, Swedes, French, and Germans. He wrote in a letter to his brother that the troops paraded twice a day. "They have," he wrote, "a band of music which plays every evening until nine o'clock which makes it very pleasant here. . . . The people here play billiards, fiddle and dance on Sunday as much as any other day."[31] He might have added that they also had a Spanish captain who gave a fiesta-banquet followed by a bullfight and dancing.[32] Meanwhile, the Indians occupied a house vacated by refugees, dancing and yelling, feasting and drinking, cutting up the piano and finally setting fire to the whole. The military band only added color to this lively scene. The musicians were paid only sixteen dollars per month, but they had the bonus of serving their country while occasionally relieving the tedium of war for others. They also became part of a heady mixture of social and cultural traditions.

A navy band played for a public dinner honoring members of the commission who recommended Pensacola as a suitable site for a U.S. Navy Yard in 1825. The local newspaper reported, "The company were enlivened and amused by a number of national, patriotic and convivial songs kindly volunteered by several of the company, and the evening passed with the utmost harmony and regularity, and with great satisfaction to all who partook."[33] One of the bands most favorably reported was that of the Second Dragoons under Lieutenant Asheton. A popular song that grew out of their service was "The Dragoon Bold."[34] In his diary, their commanding officer wrote on April 23, 1839, "The band belonging to the Second Dragoons which has contributed so much to our pleasure left today for Baltimore."[35]

Among the final services of military bands in these wars was playing at Indian councils called to bring the conflicts to a close. A council occurred at Fort King on May 18, 1839, in which the Seventh Infantry Regiment band participated. The Indians met with General Macomb, and the peace conference was described by his lieutenant, John T. Sprague. At about four in the afternoon, the garrison band of the Seventh Infantry Regiment and a company of dragoons assembled in full uniforms. Soldiers were stationed at each door with a white flag. In common time, the band led the parade. Sprague wrote: "The band passed through and formed on the other side opposite the General's seat while the dragoons circled around upon the right and left. . . . The Indians were all assembled and looked upon the ceremony with perfect astonishment."[36]

Another occurred when Maj. Gen. Alexander Macomb, commander of the Eighth Army Infantry during the Seminole War of 1839, arrived at

Fort Heillman (Garey's Ferry, Florida) on April 5. Cannon fired a salute, and the Second Dragoon's band played "Hail to the Chief." At the council with the Seminoles which followed at Fort King, the ceremony was so elaborate as to dazzle even those Indians who had seen General Scott's parades. The scene was set the night before the council meeting by lighting the skies with large pinewood bonfires. The following morning the dragoons in full dress uniform escorted the general to the council house, stepping briskly to marches played by the Seventh Infantry band. Lieutenant Sprague wrote that this high ceremony played a crucial role in the agreement that brought the war to an end.[37]

Assessments of the quality of the bands' performances varied a great deal over the years. Henry Summer, a South Carolina lawyer who visited St. Augustine in 1837, wrote that the drummer and fifer of the army regulars marched through the town almost every morning playing martial music. It pleased him "to hear the music of the free floating on the air."[38] A young lieutenant gave his assessment of one unit on December 11, 1837: "Yesterday the Band of Music belonging to the Second Regiment Dragoons arrived from Garey's Ferry and for the last two nights we have been favored with their fine music."[39] A young lady of the city wrote that in 1842 there were two bands, one of Captain Guinn's and the other of Colonel Worth's, playing there. She commented that she had never heard such delightful music.[40] Edward C. Anderson, a young naval officer from Savannah who observed Eighth Infantry companies under Gen. William Jennings North in St. Augustine in 1844, had a candid opinion of both the troops and the music. "They are the best looking American troops I have seen," he wrote, "but from all accounts an insubordinate set of scoundrels." He added that the band drilled every morning but that they were only so-so. If music of the band was not distinguished, one of its members was. Anderson recognized the man later while under Indian attack in Tampa and wrote that this musician deserved knighthood for his valor under fire.[41]

An English writer reported the effect of band music on the troops.

We had an excellent regimental band on board, and in fine weather our officers had it up on deck to play for an hour or two every evening. This practice had a markedly enlivening effect upon the spirits, and must have helped materially to promote health, as it evidently exerted a beneficial influence in promoting a cheerful hilarity and good humour among the men. It was interesting to observe the sudden change from blank and listless apathy to brisk and animated cheerfulness which some well-known and favourite air produced in the countenances of all; the strains of "Auld Lang Syne" calling forth the latent smile on cheeks and lips, and kindling the languid eye of the most melancholy and morose. My friend Nutt, when remarking on this effect one morning, said he could almost believe in the authenticity of the miracles ascribed to the music of Amphion and Orpheus, as he had himself witnessed a most astounding transformation effected in the person of the boatswain of the ship [who] had been so thoroughly soothed by music's magic spell, that he had . . . [begun] talking in the tones, manner and accent of a civilized being.[42]

A navy man enjoyed the band at a social occasion but had doubts of the propriety of parties during wartime. He wrote,

We had the band from the garrison and danced and made merry until nine p.m. There were many pretty girls aboard, very sociable and quite agreeable. . . . Altogether it was a pleasant affair, we had some sweet songs on the guitar and some very quiet little flirtations. I was pleased when they all left and yet then came one of those terrible revulsions to which I am almost invariably subjected after gayety, that calm in the feeling which seems to mock at the pleasures of life and tell us that the levity of today cannot avert the sad realities which may be in store for us.[43]

Music rarely played a major role in the lives of soldiers or sailors in nineteenth-century Florida, but sentimental occasions or loneliness sometimes evoked music to trigger memories or even the philosophical acceptance of their lives. On his birthday, November 8, 1844, naval officer Edward C. Anderson thought of the buoyant enthusiasm of his youth and the great hopes he had as a young naval officer. Then he wrote, "The roll of a drum, the sound of an old song, even the sight of the sea brings back for a moment the thrill which lured me on. . . . There doubtless have been other fools as sanguine and probably will be again to the end of time. Let such be my solace."[44] Just as music consoled this young soldier on the occasion of his birthday, it cheered others who were away from their families on holidays.

Indians were slaughtering settlers of the territory in the late 1830s, and

young navy men were ordered to service along the coast and rivers. As one
company encamped for a respite on Christmas Day, they found scant rations but ample whiskey. The company surgeon remarked that they had in
abundance, however, "a feast of reason and flow of soul." According to
this observer:

> Music too lent its charms to enliven the day; for in Lt. French we had
> a perfect "nightingale in the wilderness" as I once heard him called.
> His powerful and melodious voice with the accompaniment of his
> guitar, frequently having had the effect of charming away ennui, and
> dispelling the most inveterate "azure demons" or Indigoes, that ever
> capered in the brains of mortals. Magruder also occasionally contrib-
> uted his mite on the same instrument and his voice was not disagree-
> able, and always in tune. . . . In fact we abounded in singers. [1st Lt.
> James Lowny] Donaldson and [2d Lt. Arthur Middleton] Rutledge
> sometimes favoured us with the melody of their voices; and when
> piously inclined [Lt. William E.] Aisquith was always on hand for a
> hymn. And when "Cigars and Cogniac" was sung, every man in camp
> disclosed the development of this tune in his cranium; which was
> made known in a most stentorian manner; much to the dismay of the
> sedate owls within hearing, who on such occasions, manifested a
> strong disapprobation, by the most approved manner of hooting.[45]

7

* * * * * * * *

Safety at Home and Respectability Abroad

Music of Patriots, Politicians, and Professors

Although its celebration is confined alone to our own country, yet the day is dawning when the distant and enslaved nations of the earth shall welcome and proclaim it as a day when the sun of liberty first arose to dispel the lowering clouds of ignorance and despotism from the earth.

—Toast to the Fourth of July, Tallahassee, 1839

As Florida became a territory, its citizens assumed the responsibilities of a democracy. Building a framework for government and placing competent bureaucrats in office was a first priority. Meeting spiritual needs came next, then the education of children. Music was an adjunct to all of these efforts, though central to none.

Pres. James Monroe had declared Florida a territory of the United States and appointed Jackson to accept the transfer from Spain in 1821. The exchange took place at a formal ceremony on July 17. Anchored in Pensacola harbor, the USS *Hornet* fired a twenty-one-gun salute and the band played "The Star Spangled Banner" as the American flag was raised. In an old-time tradition of seamen, a song was written, not about this problematic takeover or even for the general himself, but on the heroic role of the *Hornet* in its earlier encounter with England in the War of 1812. Published in the local newspaper, it enriched the catalog of sea-battle songs set to traditional tunes, which had sustained the spirited aggression of early American tars.

Come all you boys, who freedom prize,
And join my song in chorus, O;
John Bull's found out, in this last bout
When Yankees fight they conquer, O.
The HORNET's might, in glorious fight
We've proved upon the Peacock, O;
She spread her sail, and show'd her tail
Which soon our Hornet tickled, O.[1]

Set to the tune "Laurence's Tid Re I," it was sung along with "Constitution and Guerrier," "Ye Tars of Columbia," and other songs of sea victories. General Jackson, never happy with his Florida assignment, made quick work of his administrative duties. In early October he wrote President Monroe that he had met the requirements of his charge and was leaving. In gratitude for his services, the people of Pensacola gave a dinner in his honor. Many toasts were proposed, each followed by music. Among the tunes played were "The President's March," "Decatur and Victory," "The Star Spangled Banner," "Roslin Castle," "Hail to the Chief," and "Come Haste to the Wedding." The last named followed a toast to virtue, fidelity, and woman. There was also a toast to the state of Alabama in recognition of a controversy over where the political boundary should be drawn between it and Florida. It was followed by the tune "I Canna, Winna, Munna, Marry Yet" sung with the words "We Love Her as a Sister, but We Would Not Be Wed."[2]

William Pope DuVal, a man of French Huguenot ancestry, became the first civil governor of the territory of Florida. His singing charmed his friends, but it was used against him in political campaigns. On one occasion a reporter wrote of DuVal, "He has an inexhaustible fund of anecdote full of pith and humor, gathered during the early part of his life. . . . Added to his many other fine qualities he sings an admirable song, and especially when he strikes upon the productions of Bobby Burns. Who has spent an evening in his life-inspiring company and has not heard him sing, 'My Boy Tommy' or recite 'Tam O'Shanter!' It is then that his kind of countenance wears all its sunny hues. His mouth, indicative of comic humor and ready wit, speaks from the very heart, the echoing notes of the music of old Scotia."[3] On another occasion, another reporter wrote that the governor in high spirits sang "A Man's a Man for A' That" and "My Ain Boy Jamie." He sang "with a pathos and tenderness that none but an

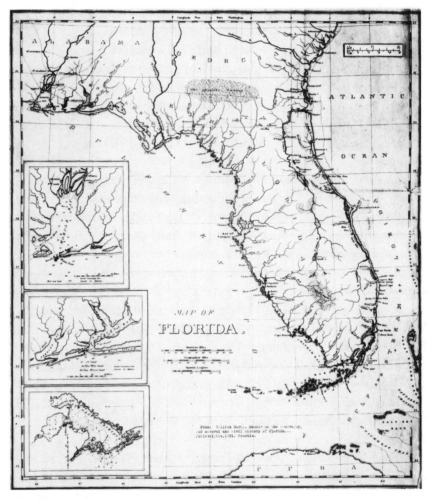

FLORIDA, 1821

Secretary of State John Quincy Adams commissioned Gen. Andrew Jackson as first
territorial governor of Florida in 1821. This is a Darby Tanner map of the territory
on that date. (Courtesy Library of Congress, Florida, no. 16224, 5Q)

honest man, with a heart in the right place could imitate." DuVal's term as
governor ended in 1834, and he ran for the House of Representatives in
1848. He was defeated, in part, because his opponents charged that he was
fit only to amuse a convivial party in a barroom.[4]

The fervor of patriotism in the years following the revolution for American independence was sustained in Florida by annual celebrations on the

Fourth of July. Music was a feature of the ceremony, as were banquets or dances afterward. A sampling of these holiday programs illustrates the music taste of Floridians of that period.

In a newsletter announcement the military men stationed in Pensacola invited all the "respectable citizens" of the town to a Fourth of July celebration in 1823 and prepared a splendid entertainment at Plumb Grove on the Big Bayou. Music was played or sung following each of the numerous toasts.[5] A year later at Fort Brooke in Tampa, a lieutenant read the Declaration of Independence, and an oration followed. At dinner, post officers, citizens, and several chiefs of Florida Indians sat down together. Afterward, artillery fired, people cheered, and toasts were drunk. Patriotic music was played and sung.[6] At Santa Rosa Island in 1827, a member of the company reported that there was no lack of holiday cheer, wine and wit, song and sentiment, harmony and spirit.[7] A year later at Beelersville, the music list grew longer.[8] On the following year at St. Joseph a salute was fired at sunrise, and shipping in port displayed full colors. Citizens of the community celebrated "without distinction of classes or parties with much spirit and enthusiasm." Twenty-seven toasts proposed by captains of the vessels were followed by "huzzas" and music.[9]

The most popular of the patriotic tunes for all of these celebrations were "Washington's March," "President's March," "Star Spangled Banner," "Hail Columbia," "Hail to the Chief," and "Auld Lang Syne." Others are listed in the endnotes of this chapter. Among them were some of the tunes best known and most preferred in America, England, Scotland, and Ireland. To these melodies were sung new lyrics devised by local poets when the birthday of the nation was celebrated.

St. Joseph was a busy port in 1840, but one sailor found time to write an ode for the Fourth of July to be sung to the tune of "Ye Mariners." The author was Jacob B. Moore from the *Brother Jonathan*. The first of six verses in his song was:

> Far o'er the heaving billows,
> By power compelled to roam,
> Fair *Liberty* a refuge sought,
> And here both found a home!
> On every hill her altars blaze,
> In every vale she dwells;
> And her cheer even here,
> All our other gifts excels,

And will, while earth its fruits shall bear;
Or the wave of ocean swells.[10]

The holiday celebration at Apalachicola in 1844 featured a grand ball, horse racing, and gambling. For those who wished to leave town, there was an excursion featuring salt-water bathing, a rich collation, a fine band of music, and plenty of dancing. Those who remained in town formed a procession to the council house to hear an ode, an oration, the Declaration, and prayers. For this service the music was "Before Jehovah's Awful Throne," "America," and "O Give Thanks." Dinner was served at midafternoon. Aside from the thirteen regular toasts, forty-two volunteer toasts were proposed. The newspaper edition reported, "The company adjourned at an early hour, well pleased and in good spirits."[11]

Having achieved official status in the Union, Florida organized political parties and ran elections. Several candidates were said to have been sung into political office in nineteenth-century America. Songs were written to assist in the elections of presidents. Odes, marches, and waltzes were written in honor of military men or others who aspired to election, whether to state or national office. Circulars, broadsides, newspapers, songsters, and political magazines carried the messages to citizens. Authors of the lyrics had few pretensions to literary artistry. They were rhymesters with varying degrees of skill, some gifted, and others only burning with the issues but innocent both of meter and metaphor.

Campaign songs usually reviewed the candidate's career in extravagant detail. They proclaimed his sterling character in the verses and cheered the prospect of his election in the chorus. Political campaigns were taken seriously in Florida. News of political developments in Tallahassee and Washington, then as now, was the grist of every newspaper editor in the state. Opposition to a political candidate generated some of the best satirical songwriting of the age. An early example occurred in 1831.

In the race for Florida delegate to the U.S. House of Representatives, Joseph M. White had won over James Gadsden by the slim majority of eighty-five votes. Citing election irregularities, Gov. William P. DuVal nullified the election. East and West Florida had voted for Democrat White, but Gadsden won Middle Florida by a large plurality. Gadsden, candidate of the Nucleus party, was backed by such prominent men as Richard K. Call, Robert Butler, and William Nuttall, but William Wilson, editor of the *Floridan-Advocate,* favored White. The Nucleus party leaders backed the publication of a competing newspaper, the *Florida Courier.* Altogether, it was a situation guaranteed to generate a partisan satirical song. The need was answered in ten verses set to the tune of "Yankee Doodle," signed *M* by an anonymous author. It ridiculed the governor by suggesting that his head was cracked, just as were the walls of the capitol. The author railed against a proposal to move the capital—a timeworn dependable ploy, especially in Tallahassee. The election was settled when Gadsen refused to pursue his candidacy. White served in the House of Representatives until 1837, when he retired. The lyrics of the first three verses follow:

THE NUCLEUS

In Tallahassee's famous town,
The Nucleus are frisky
And Marvelous wise have lately grown
By drinking of much whisky.
  Yankee Doodle, doodle do
  Yankee Doodle, dandy
  With the nucleus let us go
  And for their work be handy.

The capitol they say is crack'd,
And eke the skull of Billy;
By counting votes his brains were rack'd,
And he is craz'd and silly.
  Chorus

The election then for Delegate
Is null and void, I vow, sir;
For though it seems most profligate,
To this degree we bow, sir.
  Chorus[12]

The eminence of Gov. Richard K. Call on the political scene made him a large target for political opponents and punsters. One songsmith in St. Augustine fired against Call his heaviest satirical volley. He depicted the governor as a protégé of Andrew Jackson (which he was) and a doomsayer, when he correctly predicted a depression. To these, he added the roles of braggart, dubious military leader, bank swindler, and finally, demigod. The scurrilous song was a prime example of yellow journalism, before it had that name. Two of the six verses, sung to the tune "St. Cogniac," illustrate.

> Come on, brother cowards, I'll tip you a song.
> Tho twill bring you up short; twill not last very long;
> Don't twist up your faces, but honorably bawl
> Hosannah and praises to General Call.
>> The Florida citizens, cowards and all
>> Never picked up a jewel like Richard K. Call.
> Great Governor Call, the pet of old Hick
> Says you're panic strick, and will go to old Nick;
> So down on your marrow bones suddenly fall
> And worship the Demi-God, Richard K. Call.
>> *Chorus*[13]

Political demagoguery and protests were countered by an abundant number of songs to be sung in praise of candidates. Beginning with the campaign of Andrew Jackson, nationwide circulation of campaign songs was the custom. Local authors looked up an old familiar tune, adjusted their meter to it, lacquered the candidate's career with their choice hyperbole, added a catchy repeated chorus, then sent it to the local newspaper for publication.

Songs supporting political issues appeared in private collections. In eastern Florida, where sentiment for the abolition of slavery was stronger than in the middle or western sectors, some of them became popular. One family in St. Augustine sang from a copy of *The Republican Campaign Songster,* which was selected and prepared for the Friends of Freedom in the Campaign of Eighteen Fifty-Six. It was in support of Republican J. C. Fremont, the abolitionist, and contained several songs written especially for this publication. Among the antislavery lyrics was a rallying song to be sung to the tune of "The Marseillaise." This and other songs in the collection were the solace of East Floridians who supported the Union, men who did not volunteer for military service in the Confederacy."[14]

In recognition of their duty to educate their children, a public meeting was held in St. Augustine just two months after Florida became a territory. Committees were appointed to propose plans for a public school and a library. Americanization of Indians, Spaniards, and Negroes included provisions for their education. George J. F. Clarke, the native-born lieutenant governor of East Florida, declared that there was no reason why the Indians should be incorrigible, that they deserved aid and instruction from whites. He asserted that all human beings reflected their education and manners. "It is evident," he wrote, "that the only difference in man, laying aside his colour, is the difference in opinion, and that difference in opinion arises from the difference in education." As proof he cited examples of talents, natural and acquired, of Indians of Mexico City in fine arts and belles lettres, of Indian craftsmen of Havana, and of the many workmen in the useful and elegant crafts among the Africans.[15]

Political leaders and parents in West Florida also expressed their sentiment for improving education in the second decade of the nineteenth century. John Lee Williams, a lawyer educated at Hamilton College, came to Pensacola in 1820. He played the flute and was effective in state government. His view of education was, "Good schools are not supported as they ought to be. . . . Science is scarcely thought to be a subject worthy of conversation. Swarms of children are running about the streets, improving rapidly in dissipation and vice."[16] As he moved from western to central to eastern Florida, his influence on this issue continued.[17]

Editors of newspapers played their part by publishing articles supporting the teaching of music and dance in educational institutions. A Dr. Rush was quoted in the Key West newspaper when he defended vocal music on the grounds that it was useful in worship, had a soothing character in domestic life, brought relief in sorrow, and contributed to mental health. He also thought it was an effective preventive against tuberculosis. A Dr. Graham was quoted as declaring that it was a duty to ourselves and our Creator to be cheerful and that this attitude was effectually induced by singing and dancing.[18] Without quoting others, one editor advised his readers that music was for everyone, "the sound and the infirm, the old and the young, the Christian, Jew or pagan."[19] He might have added, the rich and the poor.

Segments of Dr. Graham's *Science of Human Life,* volume 2, were published in the St. Joseph newspaper, encouraging people to sing and dance.

It is infinitely better that people should come together to sing and dance, in healthful exhilaration of their spirits, than that they should come together to eat and drink, or to seek enjoyment in almost any of the social modes of entertainment in civil life. Vocal music ought to be as universal a branch of education as reading and writing; and instrumental music should be almost as extensively cultivated. If I could have my wish, the violin—the best musical instrument invented—should be played in every family in the civilized world. If music, marching and dancing constituted a part of the regular exercises of all our colleges, theological seminars and other literary and scientific institutions, immense benefits would result, not only to those institutions but to society at large.[20]

The education of women was also considered in territorial days. An early St. Augustine Spanish school was racially integrated but admitted no girls. Not everyone agreed that instruction in music, literature, and languages was essential in the preparation of a young lady for marriage. An article by a Boston matron was published in the *East Florida Herald,* in which she averred, "A young lady may excell in speaking French or Italian; may repeat a few passages from a volume of extracts, play like a professor, and sing like a siren. . . . She may dance like Semproaia herself—and yet we shall insist that she may have been very badly educated. . . . For though the arts, which merely embellish life, must claim admiration; yet when a man of sense comes to marry, it is a companion whom he wants and not an artist." This early American adviser to the lovelorn posed the question whether the true end of education was to raise singers, players, painters, women of fashion, and actresses, or women of ideas, principles, and good habits. Her answer was that the good wife would be prepared to "assist [a man] in his affairs, lighten his cares, soothe his sorrows, purify his joys, strengthen his principles and educate his children."[21] Beauty and the arts were assigned no role in preparation for motherhood or the education of children by the Boston matron. In territorial days, Florida parents and schoolmasters disagreed. Instruction in music was not thought to be an essential phase of education, but it was available.

Devising a plan for the education of children had been a problem for Floridians since the time of Spanish occupation, but during territorial days the legislative council encouraged each county to devise means of support for public schools. This and other early public education thrusts, however, were not as successful as those to establish private schools. Music was taught by members of the faculties of these schools and by teachers who opened their own private studios. One of the earliest printed announcements by a music instructor was in 1821 in the *Florida Gazette* (St. Augustine). James Campbell advertised: "The subscriber, late master of the Band of the Eighth Infantry, respectfully informs the citizens of St.

Augustine, that he will remain here during the fall and winter for the purpose of giving instruction in music, if he can obtain a number of students sufficient enough to make it an inducement. His terms are low, and the present is an opportunity which may not occur soon again. Terms— For instruction in violin, guitar, flute and piano, each $3 for 12 lessons in the month; $9 for quarter. For raising a piano—$4, for tuning—$3." Another announcement of the availability of music instruction was made by a Mrs. Weir of St. Augustine in 1829. Mrs. Weir taught pianoforte and guitar.[22]

The Messrs. Scherer and Garner respectfully informed the ladies and gentlemen of Pensacola that on May 6, 1822, they would give a concert and ball in the Spanish Lodge Room on Water Street. This concert was to have been their last in the city, but Scherer must have changed his mind. Two weeks later he announced that he had established residence in Pensacola and was prepared to teach pianoforte and vocal music. His terms were fifty cents per lesson or ten dollars by the month, payable half in advance. He also taught the French language at the rate of six dollars per month. It is probable that Scherer was one of the best performers heard in Florida at this early date. The program he and his colleagues presented in early May was an unusually sophisticated one to present in a frontier town. (It is listed below in chapter 9.) An early reference to the teaching of dance in the territorial period was the announcement in 1829 of Mrs. Hartwig that she would teach individuals or groups during her Pensacola stay. Mrs. Hartwig was a dancer and leading lady with a touring drama repertory company.[23]

Two women tendered their services to the citizens of Pensacola as teachers of music in 1846. Beginning in February, Mrs. Maddox taught pianoforte and guitar at Jenk's Hotel for twenty dollars per quarter.[24] When Mrs. Armstrong arrived in July, she announced that she would teach pianoforte, Spanish guitar, and painting. She came with favorable recommendations from Mobile, Tallahassee, and Quincy. She had taught in Mr. Edmund's Academy and other large and fashionable institutions.[25] A gentleman professor of music who encountered both romance and legal justice in Pensacola that year received an unwelcome report in the local newspaper. He was committed to jail on a breach-of-promise charge, then married the lady for the purpose of getting out of jail, after which, according to the editor, he absquatulated.[26]

The Pensacola Catholic school for boys was conducted in a newly erected church building beginning in 1833. Fr. John Symphorian Gurnand, a newly ordained priest from France, was the permanent pastor and schoolmaster.[27] Then in 1845 a collegiate institute was organized by the Christ Church Episcopal of Pensacola.[28] Neither announced the teaching of music, but this was the beginning of academies in the city where music later was taught.

In the earliest years in Tallahassee, children were taught by governesses or private tutors. As they grew older, they were sent to out-of-state schools and colleges. Some of them were sent to Europe for their formal education. Music was considered to be an ornamental branch of education, along with drawing, painting, and needlepoint. Private schools were opened in private homes, churches, or public facilities when available. Piano and guitar instruction appears to have been generally available.[29] At the Thomas Easton Randolph Female Academy in 1829 in Tallahassee, piano lessons were taught along with French, Spanish, and the histories of Greece, Rome, and England.[30] In 1835 W. H. Orchard, professor of music, announced that he would teach harp, pianoforte, guitar, and flute. He also offered private lessons in vocal music.[31] The professional card of Prof. Hermann Bernrender of Apalachicola appeared in Tallahassee in 1847, when he notified local residents that he wished to remain in their city during the summer to offer instruction in vocal and instrumental music.[32]

A seminary for young ladies opened in Tallahassee on October 23, 1837, with Miss Parrott as instructor. The courses of study included English, modern languages, music, drawing, painting, and fancy needlework. The tuition was from forty to fifty dollars for forty weeks. Miss Parrott had the recommendations of some of the leading citizens of the capital: General Brown, Judge Randall, Gov. R. K. Call, and Colonel Butler. She assured her patrons that every attention would be paid to the mind and manners of the young ladies committed to her charge, as she wished to merit their approbation.[33] In 1843 the Misses Bates School for Girls at Tallahassee offered instruction on the pianoforte at the rate of fifteen dollars for two and one-half months, and guitar instruction for ten dollars for the same period.[34] This venture was so successful that the Misses Bates returned the following year to conduct the Female Academy of Leon, where they taught piano, guitar, French, Latin, Greek, English, and drawing.

When the Leon Academy opened for its spring term on April 17, 1856, Mrs. H. H. Brown was the music teacher.[35] In 1856 John A. Grant was appointed principal of that academy in Tallahassee. His assistant was An-

Texas Waltz

B. R. Lignouski

Polish pianist B. R. Lignouski wrote this waltz for Governor Brown's daughter. It was published in 1847 by W. H. Geib Company of New York. Lignouski was a piano professor at the Leon Academy in 1856. (It appears that he ran into a problem of harmonization in measure 6.) (Courtesy Florida State University Music Library)

drew L. O'Brien. They had operated the Andrew College in Cuthbert, Georgia, and brought several of their colleagues with them to Tallahassee. Among them were B. R. Lignouski, principal of the music department, and Elizabeth Levinus, assistant teacher of music.[36] The press release announcing his appointment stated that Lignouski had taught in many colleges of Georgia and Alabama, that he was well known as among the most accomplished musical professors in the South. That assessment was not shared by Assistant Principal O'Brien, who thought Lignouski a faithless, unprincipled ruffian.

Lignouski wrote the "Texas Waltz" for the pianoforte and respectfully dedicated it to Lizzie (Frances Elizabeth) Brown, the lively eldest daughter of Thomas Brown, governor of Florida from 1849 to 1853. The composition was published in 1847 by W. H. Geib Company, 23 Maiden Lane, New York. The title probably refers to inhabitants in the late 1830s who left Florida for resettlement in Texas because of the devastation of storms and yellow fever.[37] Lignouski also composed a "Tallahassee Waltz" for piano, which was not published but has survived in manuscript form in the private collection of Mrs. John W. Henderson.

Among the earliest documentation of music teaching in a county public school of the state is the response of Madison County officials to an inquiry by the State Board of Trustees of Seminary Lands. The Madison report stated that in 1844, one school taught not only the three Rs but also geography, philosophy, and music.[38] Music instruction was offered at several communities near Tallahassee in the first half of the century. The Chattahoochee Male and Female College opened in January 1840. The course of study for the boys and young men was "similar to that of other schools and colleges in the state, with vocal music and drawing." Both vocal and instrumental music instruction were included in the general fee for academic or collegiate classes. Pianos, harps, and guitars were furnished students as well as books, maps, and chemical apparatus.[39]

Several seminaries and academies were opened in Quincy in the 1840s. The first to announce music instruction was the Quincy Female Seminary, which opened in 1839. Tuition fee for music, piano, and singing with use of an instrument was thirty dollars for the five-month term. Guitar instruction for the same period cost five dollars less, payable in advance.[40] Quincy Male and Female Academies were advertised in Tallahassee in 1843, 1846, and 1851. Piano, singing, and guitar were taught. Mrs. R. E. Ferguson was the music teacher in 1846, and public examinations were held at the end of each year.[41] Among other persons identified as teachers of music were Mrs. Fanny Raney of Apalachicola, R. H. Partridge and Charles H. Stebbins of Monticello, and O. B. Hart of Tampa, who were listed in *The American Musical Directory, 1861*.[42]

John Norton, a Pennsylvanian educated at Amherst College, opened the Henry School House in Walton County in 1848 under the aegis of Presbyterian families. The same denomination later opened the Old Knox Hill Academy. The morning hymns of the school's opening exercises were always led by Mr. Newton, the school principal, until he could train one of the boys for it. The boys said Mr. Newton raised all the hymns to the same tune, "There Is a Happy Land." Undaunted, the principal was so determined to teach rudiments of music and sightsinging that he taught them to all the schoolboys. He is reported to have been the first to introduce "blind notes" in Walton County. This term undoubtedly refers to round notation rather than the shaped-note systems then current in many rural church hymnals.

Mr. Newton was convinced that he should procure a well-qualified music teacher, and he did so in the person of a Dr. Kirkpatrick, who was described as a master of both vocal and instrumental music. Dr. Kirkpatrick set the pitches for school lessons in music reading and vocal exercises with his violin in his weekly evening sessions. The boys especially enjoyed the lively tunes with which he closed the lessons. Dr. Kirkpatrick opened the July Fourth ceremonies by leading the assembly in the singing of "America." Some of the older boys read the Declaration of Independence, wrote and delivered patriotic speeches, and prepared a barbecue. Instrumental music was provided by Washington Polk, an old drummer, and a student fifer.

After girls were allowed to enroll in the school, a young lady piano teacher was engaged to teach them. Mr. Newton insisted that the pupils perform after only five months' instruction, to the dismay of both teacher and students. They were especially apprehensive when it was learned that Mrs. John G. McLean, a professional pianist from Milton, was to be present. The recital of students and teacher, however, "was a revelation to the crowd and accounted for the sale of several more pianos" in the county.

Mr. Newton left the school in 1863 after a controversy with the trustees over their attempt to ban eight or ten volumes he had placed in the library, chief of which was Chambers's *Miscellanies*. He returned in 1866 and resumed his crusade for music among the Scottish settlers of midwestern Florida.[43]

Earliest reports from the East Florida Seminary, located in Ocala, include references to music. Of the seventy students attending in 1854, twelve young ladies were studying music at a cost of $20 tuition each and were paying an instrument-use fee of $2.50 for a five-month period.[44] Vocal and instrumental music was offered in 1860, when the music department tuition was $125 and $132 for the two sessions. The music professor received a salary of $600. Among the equipment purchased was a piano which cost $300. After rigid and protracted examinations by both professor and visiting committees, the vocal and instrumental programs were praised.

In 1856 Florida supported only ninety-seven public schools, with a total of ninety-eight teachers. The combined salaries of these teachers was twenty thousand dollars, an average of a little more than two hundred dollars each. The 185 teachers in 138 private schools fared somewhat better, with an annual total of seventy-five thousand dollars, for an average of four hundred dollars each. As population of the state grew, a state system of public education emerged.[45] Funding was based on average daily attendance, graded courses of study, length of the school day, and length of the school term. Schools within each county were subject to regulation by the county, including the adoption of countywide textbooks. Six or seven subjects were mandated by the state, but lessons in music were provided at the option of each county.

8

* * * * * * * *

Of Thy Indulgence, Love, and Power

Music of the Churches

It will not, perhaps, have escaped the obser-vation of any one of you, that much of the music in vogue is miserable in-deed. Hence the man of piety and principle, of taste and discernment in music, and hence, in-deed, all, who entertain a sense of decency and decorum in devotion, are oftentimes offended with that lifeless and in-sipid, or that frivolous and frolicksome succes-sion and combination of sounds, so frequently in-troduced into churches, where all should be seri-ous, animated and devout.

—*Andrew Law*, The Art of Singing, 1803

Planted early on Florida soil, the Catholic faith grew throughout the territorial and early statehood years, and music continued to be a valued adjunct to its services. The people and the music of the 1822 Catholic congregation in Pensacola were described by a young army lieutenant stationed in that city.

The predominate creed is still the Catholic, and the sole edifice consecrated to the worship of the Deity is a chapel of antique stamp and rusty exterior, on the south side of the "Plaza," as the public square here is called. At this shrine the inhabitants of Pensacola of all denominations are accustomed to assemble to offer up their prayers, and to receive the godly admonitions and the spiritual consolation of the venerable Father Pierre.

On a bright Sabbath morning, standing at the corner of the Plaza, it is interesting to watch the motley multitude of grave and gay, aged and young, wending their way towards the house of worship. There is the elderly Spanish lady, whose thick veil descends in ample folds about her person, followed at a respectful distance by the neatly dressed slave, carrying her chair cushion: the first of these articles being inverted in such a way that the bottom rests on the gay cotton handkerchief with which the girl's head is decorated, and the back descending behind, leaves one hand free for salutation, while the other clasps the cushion. Then come a group of young men, loitering indolently along; these are followed by an old Frenchman, all complaisance, bowing to all he meets. Last of all appears the feminine, black-eyed, naive young Creole, whose air and carriage are as striking and attractive as her dress is simple and modest.

I mingle with the crowd now gathering from all quarters, and slowly converging toward the place of worship: with them I enter the building. The lofty, ill-lighted dome displays little of architectural symmetry: the rough floor of large rugged flag-stones, and the dark walls, altogether give the place an antiquated and gloomy air. It is evidently the product of Spanish art and labor of years long passed.

The service commences. The music of the choir is full and harmonious, and as the solemn strains swell upon the ear, one cannot but feel that the chant of praise, though not embellished by the vigor and efficacy of science, is well suited to rouse the soul to a consciousness of its own high attributes, and to raise the mind to that elevation of thought that fits one for devotion. Who is there that has not experienced at such times a feeling of more than usual seriousness, without being able to say whence it actually comes?—a moment when the heart is opened, and the mind is expanded by an unknown, subtle, and incomprehensible agency."[1]

The singing of the choir and the ecumenical spirit of the sermon at the Pensacola Catholic church were subjects of an editorial in the local newspaper in 1824.

We congratulate our fellow citizens, on the opportunity afforded them, of attending a place of Divine worship every Sabbath; an opportunity which should be considered invaluable by every Christian, and which had heretofore been almost entirely withheld from us.

The Rev. Mr. Maenhaut, the pastor of the Catholic Church of this City, has for a few Sundays past, preached in the French and English alternately; and we understand he intends to continue his labors in this way. We have ourselves attended, and were much gratified; his delivery is mild and interesting, and his sermons moral, persuasive and instructive; and being entirely free from bigotry and sectarian denunciation, and equally inoffensive to all religious denominations, we think that he cannot fail to effect much good.

We have also been highly pleased by the addition of Sacred music to the services, and on that subject, refer our readers to the communication of Handel, hoping that those who now compose the choir will persevere, and that they may be encouraged by being joined by all who have the talents and requirements necessary to render them capable of assisting in so laudable and pleasing employment.[2]

The reference to a Handel communication was to a letter to the editor from a local resident who had signed the composer's name to a pæan of praise to the Catholics and Protestants who "formed a choir for performing vocal and instrumental music in the church." A few weeks later a stranger to the city wrote a letter to the editor commenting on the services he had attended at the Catholic chapel. "The service commenced," he reported, "with appropriate sacred music, both vocal and instrumental; and was executed with great judgement and taste."[3]

While the pious Catholics of St. Augustine continued their religious ceremonies, Protestants had no church in that city as late as 1821. Catholics in this old city had not encountered the prejudice to their sect that was common in northern seaboard states. When opposition did come, it was directed to the excesses of their carnival seasons, rather than to doctrine. The Protestant editor of the local newspaper in 1825 not only refused to participate in the revelry but saw in it a moral threat to the republic. He gave the Spanish, Minorcans, and Italians a history lesson, declaring that the masquerades were originated by Granacci, author of *Rambles in Italy,* before 1543. Then he brought them up-to-date by quoting an American traveler's description of Italian pre-Lenten revels.

Here, once a year at least the meanest artisan might strut the monarch, and dressed in robes of brief authority play frantic tricks, and the kitchen maid, . . . without the intervention of a fairy, be clothed in the twinkling of an eye, in the glittering apparel of Princess. . . .

The masque is no sooner put on than the veil of modesty is laid aside. Women and men abandoning themselves to the intoxication of pleasure, appear to be ready to engage in unexampled feats of libertism. . . . The understanding is subjugated by the power of music, and the voluptuous dances of the waltz and the manfrino, exalt the spirits to that giddy height, which accomplishes the destruction of many a fair Belinda, although encompassed with all her aerial guards.

The evening preceding Lent all assemble at an early hour at the veglione [residence of the oldest or most respected citizen], and the carnival now at its close, collects together the whole population of the place and vanishes in all its splendor. Midnight is no sooner announced, the hall is emptied and the lights extinguished. The bacchanals of pleasure retire from the scene, wearied and exhausted with their long campaign of gaiety, and the first morning of the ensuing Lent hits its pale ray upon many a paler countenance, doomed to expiate the sins of the carnival by all the labours of abstinence and prayer.[4]

Continuing, he advised against introducing masquerades in America, since they threatened to banish virtue. The revelers answered his diatribe by hanging the editor in effigy.

A Methodist minister also deprecated the behavior of St. Augustine Catholics as they celebrated the carnival before Lent. His diary entry for March 1, 1828, was consonant with that of the local newspaper's editor. "On this day, now passed forever, I beheld more of the fruits of popery than I ever expected to see. In the afternoon I saw many lads roaming the streets with curious apparel, and bells hung about them ringing, like a stock of cattle. I saw several men, natives of this place, with hands and faces made as black as Ethiopians. They had on very unusual garments and artificial faces; some dressed in women's clothes. Just before sundown I saw about half a dozen females dancing along the streets before a drum and violin some one was playing. The Catholics call such conduct a masquerade."[5]

Protestant visitors confirmed the use of music in Catholic churches but were puzzled by the ritual. Henry Summer, a South Carolina lawyer, visited Florida in the winter of 1837 and attended the Catholic church in St. Augustine. In his journal entry for March 5, he wrote, "After dinner put letters in the Post Office—and thence went to the Catholic church—heard the full toned organ—beautiful."[6] W. T. Allen, another visitor, described a Palm Sunday service of the Catholic cathedral of St. Augustine on April 4, 1852. He reviewed the music in terms of public exhibition, rather than religious devotion. "Went to the Catholic Church in the forenoon and saw the *performance*—the reading, singing and preaching, etc., was in Latin or Spanish—so that I could not understand much of it. Part of the services were to distribute palm leaves to all who chose to go for them—first went the white men, then white women, next white boys, young and old, next Negro men, next Negro women and children—the boys seemed to enjoy it quite well—all the time of that ceremony, there was chanting by the choir and priests."[7]

If reports of Protestant clergymen are accurate, early Florida residents had not come to the territory for religious reasons. They suffered spiritual as well as economic privations for many years before clergymen arrived to minister to them. According to an Episcopal priest, they were not disposed to place their hard-earned money in support of religion and were "destitute of Christian spirit."[8] In the early years of the century, services were held in private residences, ramshackle public buildings, theaters, and warehouses. By the late 1820s and early 1830s, congregations began erecting buildings where worship services were held. Rural congregations met in brush arbors until they could afford closed shelter. Music indoors or outdoors was reported as a phase of service proceedings.

At about this same time, local newspapers began carrying advertisements of music publications suitable for church services and private devotic.l. For example, the *Quincy Sentinel* of November 6, 1840, advertised for sale *The Boston Handel and Haydn Society Collection of Church Music* and *The Missouri Harmony*. Hymn, motet, and anthem collections were not invariably designed for a specific denomination. There began to appear a few books with hymn verses collected and published in America for a single denomination as early as the late eighteenth century. Then, hymnbooks with tunes favored by one sect or another were published with the denominational designation. Some independent publications were used across denominational lines in both private devotions and church services. From the 1830s to the Civil War, floods of new publications of church music were brought to the state by settlers who had remarkably diverse religious roots. Some of these books remain in private collections, and others have been deposited in libraries of the state. These as well as advertisements in local newspapers are the sources of the narratives that follow.

The earliest Episcopal churches of Florida were Trinity Church of Apalachicola, St. Paul's in Quincy and Key West, St. John's in Warrington, Christ Church in Pensacola, St. Luke's in Marianna, St. John's in Tallahassee and Jacksonville, St. Mary's in Madison, and St. Mark's in Pal-

ST. JOHNS EPISCOPAL CHURCH, TALLAHASSEE

Mary Talbot Whitfield is the St. John's organist in this picture. (Courtesy Florida State Archives)

atka. The early heritage of American Anglican churches had included the English psalm collections of Sternhold and Hopkins and the new version by Tate and Brady. After the American Revolution, some Florida Protestant Episcopal Churches preferred music of the English tradition and continued to use collections from that source. Most, however, sang from *Hymns of the Protestant Episcopal Church,* which at first was appended to the recently devised *Book of Common Prayer* (1789) for Americans. Additional hymns were bound with the prayer book in 1808, the selections being made by William Smith. A new collection, *Hymns of the Protestant Episcopal Church of the United States,* also bound with the prayer book and commonly known as the *Prayer Book Collection,* was published in 1826. It remained in use for thirty-five years. Hymns were added through the years, but a new hymnal for the American church did not appear until 1872.

Two excellent English collections of hymns reached Florida from England soon after publication and were advertised in local newspapers. There can be little doubt that they were used by Protestant Episcopal congregations throughout the territory, and later, the state. They were Reginald Heber's *Hymns Written and adopted to the weekly church service of the year* (1827) and later, *Hymns, ancient and modern* (1860), collected and edited by a committee of high-church clergymen. An American edition of the latter did not appear until 1866, after which it remained in use for many years. An unnamed collection recently published in London was advertised by the Pensacola Bookstore on January 13, 1829. It contained music by Henry Bishop, J. B. Cramer, William Crotch, William Shield, J. W. Callcott, and one member of the Wesley family. The poetry was by Mrs. J. Barley, Mrs. Opie, Rev. H. Milman, J. Montgomery, and R. Southy. A hymn by Mrs. Opie from the collection was quoted:

> There seems a voice in every gale,
> A tongue in every opening flower,
> Which tells, O Lord, the wondrous tale
> Of thy indulgence, love and power.
>
> The birds that rise on quivering winds,
> Appears to hymn their makers praise,
> And all the mingling sounds of spring
> To Thee a general paean raise. . . .[9]

Composers of music for these poems were among the most eminent in England. They were a mixed lot. William Crotch and John Wall Calcott, from Norwich and London, were excellent organists and composers of church music. Henry Bishop and William Shield were better known for their dramatic works, though Bishop did edit an edition of Handel's *Messiah* and wrote an oratorio and a cantata on biblical themes.

Bits of information from scattered sources give hints as to how this music was brought alive. Judge Thomas Douglas, of Connecticut, moved to St. Augustine in 1826 when he was appointed U.S. district attorney for East Florida. As a lay reader of the Episcopal congregation, he was active in assuring suitable music for the new church, which was built between 1829 and 1833. In his autobiography he told how he and the choirmaster went about it.

> Gen. L. Phillips, Esq. who then (and almost ever since) kept a school in St. Augustine, undertook to form a choir, in which he succeeded admirably. I commenced reading the service and a sermon on Trinity Sunday, 1833 and continued to do so for about two years. . . . During all the time that I read the service, we had very fine music. Our choir met every Wednesday evening at the church to practice, and one evening every week, at some private house, generally at mine. Having but few bass voices, I purchased a violoncello to aid that branch of the choir, and everything went along harmoniously while I had charge. But soon after Mr. Brown came, so much fault was found by him and others, but principally by him, that the choir was broken up.[10]

Daniel Brown of the New York diocese was the missionary who relieved Douglas of conducting services.

The early Episcopal churches of Florida were not as insistent on congregational singing as were their evangelical brothers, the Methodists, Presbyterians, and Baptists. They did lead, however, in singing the straightforward, noble music of Anglican parish church choirs and in the installation of organs, bells, and chimes. The music of Samuel Sebastian Wesley and William Crotch was sung by their choristers. Children practiced vocal music at ten o'clock every Sunday morning at the school held in the Pensacola courtroom. The general public was invited to attend.[11]

Christ Church Episcopal Parish of Pensacola was formed in 1827, and a building inspired by Sir Christopher Wren was in use as early as 1838. The organ loft was located at the east end of the church and was reached by stairways on either side of the vestibule. Lucy Barklay, the first child christened in the church, later became its organist and choir director.[12] The

CHRIST CHURCH, PENSACOLA
This photograph shows Christ Church (Episcopal) in Pensacola. (Courtesy Florida State Archives)

church's religious ceremony in observance of July 4, 1835, was reported in the local newspaper. "In the morning a procession formed at Collins Hotel and marched to the Episcopal church, preceded by a band of music. The Rev. Mr. Steele in an eloquent and appropriate prayer, commenced the exercises of the day. . . . The choir of the church was better filled than usual, and several anthems were sung, and performed on the organ with happy effect."[13] The congregation was racially mixed. Several entries in parish records show memberships, marriages, and baptisms of "colored servants" in the years before the Civil War, not uncommon occurrences at that time in churches of most denominations.

Henry Erben, eminent organ builder in New York and Philadelphia, built the first organ for Christ Church in 1844 and another in 1849. The latter had six stops and cost $605. Erben's inventory carries the correct dates for these instruments but erroneously lists a St. Paul's Church as the client.[14]

St. John's Episcopal Church, Tallahassee, was established in 1829. The ladies of the congregation gave $350 toward the purchase of an organ for the church. Henry Erben built the instrument in 1836. The organist was

TRINITY EPISCOPAL CHURCH, APALACHICOLA
This interior photograph shows the tracker organ built for the congregation in 1840 by Henry Erben. Organ recitals and services are now played on the restored instrument. (Courtesy Florida State Archives)

voted a salary of $150 per annum at a vestry meeting of January 9, 1851. A year later he resigned. The rector in 1858 wrote that a salary of $100 had been for some time appropriated for an organist, and several people had earned the money.[15]

Trinity Episcopal Church of Apalachicola was also one of the first Protestant congregations in the state to install a pipe organ. The prefabricated church building was erected in 1838, and an anonymous author of the church history stated that an organ and a bell were installed at that time. The organ builder was Henry Erben, and his inventory list gives 1840 as the correct date. According to a 1976 certificate signed by the vicar, Sydney Ellis, Erben's tracker organ served the congregation until 1920, when it was moved to the balcony for storage. In 1975–76 it was restored by Pennington Pendarvis of Blountstown (Florida) and Atlanta. Erben was the most eminent organ builder in America during his time. He built organs for churches and synagogues across the nation and no less than eight for Florida Episcopal churches: Trinity Episcopal, St. Augustine, 1836 and 1851; St. Johns Episcopal, Tallahassee, 1836; Trinity Episcopal, Apalachicola, 1840; Christ Church, Pensacola, 1844 and 1849; St. Paul's Episcopal, Key West, 1847 and 1852.[16]

The Apalachicola instrument continues in use, now with an electric blower. Its stop list includes open diapason, dulciana, stop'd diapason treble, stop'd diapason bass, gamba, flageolet, principal, and pedal.

It is probable that the Trinity instrument was procured through the initiative of George Field, a layman of the congregation. In his search for a reliable builder, he may have been assisted by the Reverend Charles Jones of the New York Diocese, second rector of Trinity, who was serving that congregation in 1838. He was fortunate in having on his board of incorporators and vestry several directors of the wealthy Apalachicola and Land Company. Among them was Dr. John Gorrie, who in 1850 invented the first machine for making ice. Another distinguished member of the congregation was Dr. Alvin Wentworth, botanist and chapman, who sang in the choir. Aside from the usual church services, Christ Church occasionally sponsored concerts of sacred music. In 1840, for example, Baron de Fleur gave "a finished performance on the organ and piano forte" for the benefit of the church. His was the first reported concert on the Erben instrument.[17]

The choir at Trinity had a problem in 1844 and appealed to the public for resolution by publishing a notice in the local paper. "It is possible that some persons may have in their possession a few copies of Music Books of Handle and Hayden's edition, belonging to the choir of the Trinity church; by returning them, favor will be conferred upon the choir, there being left only one out of a dozen copies."[18] The compilation referred to was the *Boston Handel and Haydn Society's Collection of Sacred Music* by Lowell Mason, first published in 1822. Mason made this collection during the fourteen years he was a bank clerk, choirmaster, and organist in Savannah, Georgia. It was the popularity and profitability of this and subsequent collections that caused Mason to abandon his career as a banker, to return to Boston and, with his sons, establish a music dynasty of publishers, a piano manufacturer, and a pianist-composer of distinction.

Aside from the official hymnal, two collections published in America were used in Florida Episcopal services. The earliest was John Wesley's *Collection of Psalms and Hymns,* published in Charleston in 1738. It remained in use about ninety years. The other was by the American Lowell

Mason, referred to above. This latter publication, used in Episcopal churches of both Apalachicola and Pensacola, went through many editions. It was intended to contribute "something toward the promotion of correct taste, and the improvement of an interesting and a delightful part of public worship."[19] It proposed to do so by making two improvements over earlier collections: first, by providing correct harmony to appropriate melodies, and second, by indicating the precise time, or "actual degree of velocity," of each composition. Use of Maëlzel's recently invented metronome was encouraged. Approval of the old psalm tunes was given, but the compiler responded to public sentiment by including hymns and anthems. Most of the material had English roots, whether in original or altered form. The composers were standard English church stylists: Croft, Boyce, Blow, Callcott, Bishop, Green, Burney, Arne, Purcell, and Arnold. Included, too, were liberal offerings of Haydn, Handel, Mozart, usually extracted from extended works and cast in hymn style.

At about the time Trinity church of Apalachicola was acquiring an organ and its choir singing from America's most popular collection of sacred songs, the Methodist minister at nearby St. Joseph, Florida, was having great difficulty organizing a choir from his racially mixed congregation. On early May 1838 he wrote: "Last night [I] attended a meeting for the purpose of raising a choir in the church to sing. The evening was dark and few attended."[20] In an August 15 diary entry, he confided that fifteen or twenty black members of the congregation attended choir practice, but none of the whites did. The congregation numbered about fourteen whites and sixty-five blacks, according to Haskew. It appeared that blacks had greater interest in singing in the choir than did whites. Yet neither singing nor praying forestalled the tragedies that were to overtake joyful little St. Joseph.[21]

Located on a beautiful Gulf bay, St. Joseph was a growing village. For five seasons in the 1830s, it thrived. Wealthy citizens used it as a resort. There was horse racing for sport, public houses for drinking, theaters for music and plays, and sailors who came from everywhere. While strict churchmen called St. Joseph "the wickedest place in the United States," more liberal historians thought it to be "free from conventionalities and restraints, so gloriously stamped by the Finger of God." It was passengers from an infected ship that brought on the yellow-fever epidemic of 1841. In less than a year a devastating hurricane demolished the little town. While the theater and taverns were rebuilt, by 1843 St. Joseph sank into "an

*In 1844 communicants of Trinity Episcopal Church in Apalachicola sang hymn
settings of English composers from Lowell Mason's popular hymn book. (Reprinted
from Lowell Mason,* Boston Handel and Haydn Society Collection of Church
Music, *p. 95)*

everlasting commercial sleep." The promise of a better life out west beck-
oned, and the sign *GTT* on door after door after door broke up the choirs
and notified passing strangers that the citizens of Sodom and Gomorrah
had Gone To Texas.[22]

Separate churches for black churchmen were rare in early Florida but
became the custom immediately after the Civil War.[23] In 1836 a white

minister reported that frequent inspiriting responses from the Negroes in the gallery enlivened the services.[24] One of the earliest black congregations was that of the Bethel Baptist Institutional Church, Jacksonville, formed in 1838. It was their view that singing created a religious atmosphere which was vital to the full dissemination of the gospel.[25] In Pisgah Methodist Church near Tallahassee, Negroes sang with white members at morning services. They also sang at their own afternoon services.[26] Negro members and their visitors sat in pews with white worshipers, or on front pews, on rear pews, or in balconies reserved for them. Seating patterns were determined by each congregation in the early half of the century. All Florida church histories of the time report congregational singing, but none of the mixed-race congregations report the singing of Negro spirituals. Later reports do confirm the Negroes' preference for the hymns of Watts, doubtless growing out of their attendance at these churches. The racial mix became predominately black in several congregations and remained so for several years. The experience of the Indian Springs church is illustrative of events at midcentury. This church had not had a white majority in over a decade until 1859, when there were thirty-eight whites and thirty-two blacks. The decrease in black membership was due to the withdrawal of several black people in 1858 to found Shiloh Church, the first all-black church in the county.[27] Many Negro parishioners continued to attend historically mixed congregations in such liberal or urban locations as the Church of St. Mary, Star of the Sea, Key West, but others in less benign congregations left to form their own churches.[28]

Methodists came to Florida principally from Virginia, South Carolina, and Georgia, and their churches were established about 1825. Ministers followed them and, true to the tradition of their denomination, made congregational singing an essential element of the worship service. Planting Methodism in Florida was no easy task, but missionaries and itinerant preachers labored there from the early days of the territory. In 1825 Henry P. Cook wrote of his Pensacola mission: "In consequence of the many formidable difficulties which I have had to encounter in prosecuting the objects of this mission, my success has not been as great as I originally anticipated. However, I trust some good has been done." He viewed Pensacola as a place of moral darkness and desolation, yet the pious Protestants of the community were united in promoting the cause of religion. He took no sanguine view of the future. "Wickedness, indeed, abounds with many and the love of some is waxing cold," he wrote.[29]

The minister of the St. Augustine Methodist mission, reporting in the same year, had fifty-one communicants and a more encouraging prospect. A few Spanish and black Catholics presented opportunities for proselytizing. According to the minister, they were charmed by the singing of easy hymns in the vernacular. He wrote, "Our colored members in this place seem very pious. . . . Prejudice and bigotry are on the retreat, and are succeeded by a candid attention to truth."[30]

Tallahassee had no reputation for religious fervor, or even rectitude. Citizens sometimes agreed with a visiting army officer that if there was no law, there could be no sin. Law enforcement officials did belatedly build the city's first jail in 1840, and city ordinances described unacceptable behavior a little more specifically. Yet governmental officials could not claim full credit for the city's improved reputation. Methodist churches were established across the territory, and citing their revivals, the parsons took some credit for the cleanup. One Tallahassee visitor believed that God had intervened by sending a fever to rid Tallahassee of 450 of the worst gamblers and blacklegs. He had to be armed to the teeth to walk down the street just a year before.[31]

The Quincy Methodists, like those of Tallahassee, reported that the galleries were filled with Negro worshipers. They also reported that while all sang, the songbooks were in short supply. The preacher led the singing, lining out the hymns.[32] Camp meetings were held in the 1820s and 1830s, and revivals were held periodically in the 1840s and 1850s. One of the great revivals of Tallahassee occurred in 1842, when seven ministers held all-day meetings for two weeks. The following year Methodists, Presbyterians, and Episcopalians jointly held a nineteen-day revival. Revivals in Quincy also had an ecumenical aspect. For an 1855 revival, all families in town sang the same hymn at precisely seven o'clock one evening.[33]

The Methodists had a proud musical heritage. John Wesley and his brother Charles came to Georgia with James Oglethorpe in 1735. Influenced by Moravians whom he had heard sing both on the voyage and after disembarking, John Wesley decided to prepare a book of hymns for the Church of England. Titled simply *A Collection of Psalms and Hymns*, it was published in Charleston by Lewis Timothy in 1737. A small collection, it and others similar to it which followed were courageous steps toward the goal of a church-music literature that extended beyond psalmody. Controversy over taking this step raged well into the nineteenth century among nonliturgical Protestant sects. Objections centered not so much on the music as on the texts' being prepared by men and women rather than coming from the Bible. After John Wesley returned to England, he sent to friends in America copies of *Psalms and Hymns,* his 1784 collection which he attached to *Sunday Service of the Methodists of North America.* These publications were adopted by the church general conference in Baltimore in 1784. The music collection became the first Methodist hymnal, which was reprinted in 1790. The general conference authorized *A Collection of Hymns for the Use of the Methodist Episcopal Church, principally from the Collection of the Rev. John Wesley,* published in New York in 1821 and revised a year later. A new hymnal was issued in 1849 but was not widely used in Florida.

In the family collections of Methodists who came to Florida was an 1822 New York publication, *The Methodist Harmonist, containing a great variety of tunes collected from the best authors.* It was adapted to all the various meters in the Methodist hymnbook, and the hymn numbers corresponded with those in the hymnal. It was later published as *The Harmonist,* and other editions appeared to 1833.

The Methodist Episcopal Church, South, authorized a hymnbook at its first general conference in 1846. Published in Nashville a year later, it was called *A Collection of Hymns for Public, Social, and Domestic Worship.* A supplement appeared in 1851. These hymnals were used by Florida Methodists and were available in local bookstores. In 1858 the conference authorized an edition of the 1847 collection with music. It was prepared by Lemuel C. Everett, titled *The Wesleyan Hymn and Tune Book,* and issued in 1859.

Oldest of the Florida Methodist churches were those at Amelia Island (1822), Pensacola (1822), and St. Augustine (1823). Trinity Methodist was the first Protestant sect to organize in Tallahassee (1832), but nearby Old Pisgah Methodist had a small congregation from the early 1820s. Moss Hill Methodist Church in Chipley, Washington County, built a log structure in 1857 and there sang their hymns. Madison's Ebenezer Methodist Church had built their log church in the 1840s, but they were not lacking in amenities. An elaborate kerosene lamp chandelier hung from the ceiling. According to T. L. H. Ruykard, a parishioner, "They had singing and an old fashioned pump organ. . . . Georgia Martin Gaston played the organ."[34] The Methodist Conference had ordered congregations to construct plain, inexpensive church buildings. In response, Middlebury Methodists of Clay County decided to forgo installation of stained-glass windows in the 1847 building. Situated among "giant moss festooned oaks, with a background of camellias, hawthorne, azaleas, yellow jasmine and holly," there was little reason to obstruct the view when a better one was framed by the molding of clear glass panes.

Old Pisgah Church was cited as an example of a defender of the faith through the freeze of 1835, the financial panic of 1837, the yellow fever epidemic of 1841, the Indian wars, the Civil War, and reconstruction. Men kept their muskets close by when they attended church services. On Sundays when crowds filled the church, they pulled horses and buggies "under the windows to join in the singing and hear the sermon."[35] In the early years no music instruments were allowed in the church. Given the history of a singing denomination, prohibition of instrumental music could hardly be justified; yet some among the congregation still believed that the devil could lure one to dance by playing hypnotic tunes on his violin. Others had heard old wives' tales that fiddling devils intoxicated people into death dances.

These legends were put to rest by a Professor Folsom, who himself was a violinist, a singer, and a singing-school teacher. By midcentury the church had become a cultural center and, in addition to church services, the site of temperance meetings, political rallies, and lectures. Professor Folsom's contribution did not stop with performing and teaching music. According to the church historian, he gave "the death blow to the prejudices of many Christians against the violin."[36] On August 10, 1854, the professor and his students presented a musical entertainment at the church. Tickets cost fifty cents and benefited the church rather than the performers. The music consisted of "the most fashionable songs, duets, quartettes and church music." It included solos, "Katie Darling" and "The Lord of Creation," as well as a group of temperance songs. A class of small boys and girls performed Charles E. Horn's "Cherry Ripe" and several glees. The recital was well received. The singing school attracted seventy pupils, and even ministers were eager to be taught to play the violin.[37] The church historian failed to report on the moral effect of the temperance songs, but he did comment that the artistic effort was received with great applause.

One Methodist circuit rider, John L. Jerry, remarked on the sobriety of the Florida Territory when he arrived in 1827. "We then had four temperance societies and not one grog-shop," he wrote concerning Monticello. But the Indian Wars brought large numbers of troops who drank, gambled, and used strong language. Religious fervor waned. Nine years later he wrote, "Our temperance officers are now the first to take the bottle, and our old grey-headed Methodists and Baptists [are] drunk, drunk, wallowing in their filth."[38] He was joined by a Baptist minister who observed that moral depravity was a common appendage of the camps of young troops.

The temperance movement fired congregations to hold revivals. The financial panic of 1857 added fuel, as did the imminence of war. Many of the hymns in old and historically important collections were relegated to archives. They were replaced by such militant ones as George J. Webb's setting of "Stand Up, Stand Up for Jesus." The sermons that ministers preached were so lengthy that church members were sometimes unable to remember how they began, but given the time and place, few could forget the singing of Tallahassee's Presbyterian and Methodist choirs and the soft accompaniment of a melodeon. One diarist wrote of them, "I listened to the singing of hymns from two different churches . . . , both singing different hymns, [and it] all together caused a particular sadness to come over me that was almost distressing to me."[39] With the gathering war clouds, there was much to be sad about on that Sunday morning.

King Charles II of England thought that Presbyterian worship was not fit for a gentleman. The English upper classes agreed.[40] One of their objections to the sect was its insistence on congregational singing. When Presbyterians came to America, they brought the *Scottish Psalter of 1650*. The tradition for singing metrical settings of the psalms had served the church well through the numerous editions by Sternhold and Hopkins and Tate and Brady. But when Isaac Watts added hymns to his collection and it was endorsed for the denomination in 1756, a Scottish contingent withdrew from the church. The division was deep. The "old side" favored Old Testament psalmody exclusively. The "new side" allowed references to Christ and the new hymnody. The synod ruled in 1786 that Watts could be used at the discretion of the individual church. The American revision of Watts's *Psalms and Hymns* was sponsored by the general assembly. It was retitled *Psalms of David* and approved in 1802. Committee reports of psalms and tunes revised especially for the Presbyterian church of 1828 and 1829 were rejected. But in 1830 they were accepted, and a year later a new *Psalms and Hymns Adapted to Public Worship* was issued.

Northern American Presbyterians began accepting folk hymns and camp-meeting hymns by the turn of the century, but it was 1825 before most Southern Presbyterians accepted hymns into the church service.[41] A new publication was issued in 1831 as *Psalms and Hymns Adapted to Public Worship*. The final break between the old schoolers and new schoolers came in 1837, but it was six years before old schoolers came out with their revision of the 1831 *Psalms and Tunes*. It bore the title *Psalms and Hymns adapted to social, private, and public worship in the Presbyterian church of the United States of America, 1843*. The hymnbook retained 419 old hymns and added 260 new ones and served for twenty-five years. This collection contained only texts, but in 1852 the first Presbyterian hymnal with music published in the United States appeared. Prepared by Thomas Hastings, it was given the title *The Presbyterian Psalmodist* and was designed to be used with the 1843 *Psalms and Hymns*.[42] Floridians sang from it for many years. Another new publication to win favor with Florida Presbyterians was *Parish Psalmody: A Collection of Psalms and Hymns for Public Worship*, published in Philadelphia in 1850. It contained Watts's metrical psalms and 200 of his hymns. Philip Doddridge and Charles Wesley hymns were included as well as those of John Newton and William Cowper, compilers of the celebrated *Olney Hymns* collection. The first hymnal of the Southern Presbyterian church was commissioned in 1861 but was not published until 1867.

Three early Presbyterian settlers in Florida are remembered for their use of music. One of the earliest was Neill McLendon, formerly from the Isle of Skye and later from Richmond County, North Carolina. He was followed by a sizable colony of Scotsmen in the 1820s. They settled in the Euchee Valley, near Marianna. Their log church was erected in 1828, and a new frame church in 1848. Their Knox Hill Academy opened school every morning by reading a Scripture, singing a hymn, and praying to God. Another musician, Mrs. Elanor Adair White of the Monticello congregation, held similar services for slaves of Casa Bianca Plantation. She led the singing and taught Sunday school classes. Then, Dr. William W. Waddell, a prominent member of the Tallahassee church, was praised for his talent and "his passionate fondness for sacred music."[43]

The Presbyterians in Florida were as strict in their choice of music as they were in their code of behavior. Strong language with little tact characterized not only sermons but also evaluation of members' personal habits. Rachel Jackson, wife of Gen. Andrew Jackson, was an unwavering Presbyterian who lost no time in ridding Pensacola streets of fiddling, dancing, cursing, and gambling seamen. Jacksonville Presbyterians faced similar problems with sailors who frequented Bay Street bars. Promiscuous dancing "was not allowed in amusement halls, social parties and private homes."[44] The position on music was unyielding. Longer than any other denomination, Presbyterians adhered to the tradition of singing the

metrical psalms, their Calvinist heritage filtered through many generations. The Tallahassee choir, on one occasion, had wearied of singing a
traditional hymn tune and dared to enhance the text with a new tune.
Simon Towle, then state comptroller and local choir director, became so
agitated at this aberration that he ran from the audience and stopped them
in midhymn. He then led them back to the monotonous tune, allowing no
variation.[45] One historian reported: "Choirs often upset decorum of the
worship services, trampling on the rights of other segments of the membership. For example, the attention of the Quincy session was called to a
matter which was creating some dissatisfaction in the congregation." The
singers had preempted the gallery which "had been erected for the accom-
modation of the colored population." Protests were made that rights of
the Negroes had been abridged. This incident occurred in 1853.[46]

If one churchman averred that military men had brought sin to Florida
at the beginning of the Indian Wars, others had equally strong claims that
these men and their wives also had a large part in establishing and maintaining the twenty-six Presbyterian churches that had taken root in the
state by 1850. Among them were Col. Robert Butler, who had accepted
Florida from Spain when it became a part of the United States in 1821;
Eliza Clinch, wife of Gen. Duncan L. Clinch; Maj. Robert Gamble, who
fought in the battle of Withlacoochee; and Elias Gould, the editor-mayor
of St. Augustine, who was burned in effigy for disapproving the excesses
of Catholic revelers. Achille Murat, Tallahassee's eccentric French Catholic
nobleman, took a dim view of the formidable American Presbyterians. He
regarded them as overseas cousins of the heretical French Huguenots. "Its
bilious children, rigid disciples of the gloomy Calvin," he wrote, "have
inherited all his gall and venom, and do not scruple to arm the Divinity
with their spirit of vengeance and satanic wickedness."[47] He thought their
doctrine was a preposterous hypocrisy.

After all the years of Indian Wars, Florida then faced the difficult decision of remaining a state in the Union or joining the Confederacy. The
ultimate decision was by no means unanimous. As in other earlier wars,
Florida choristers intoned the psalms and hymns of their faiths, secure that
God would support their cause. Meanwhile, their eyes were set on heaven.
A land of delight, it was visualized as a place where the sun perpetually
shone on green fields and apprehension was replaced with pleasure. A
small comfort against the fear and terror of war, the text of the following

hymn by Isaac Watts was offered to a Presbyterian congregation in Pensacola in 1853 by visiting minister Rev. John J. Sparrow as his favorite hymn.[48]

> There is a land of pure delight,
> Where saints immortal reign;
> Infinite day excludes the night
> and pleasures banish pain.
> (five more verses)[49]

The hymn heritage of Florida Baptists encompassed several editions of Isaac Watts's *Psalms and Hymns,* including American mutants. The earliest popular hymnal by a Baptist was a 1787 collection by Englishman John Rippon designed to accompany Watts's metrical psalms. In 1791 Rippon brought out his *Selection of Psalms and Hymn Tunes from the Best Authors.* New editions of this work appeared until after the middle of the nineteenth century. This book was advertised by a bookseller in Pensacola in 1823.[50] *The Comprehensive Rippon,* a collection containing 1,100 hymns, was not issued until 1844. Lowell Mason heard a congregation lining out hymns from Rippon's collection on his first visit to England. He and many other compilers borrowed freely from this collection.

Several other Baptist collections served Florida congregations. Among them were *Dorsey's Choice,* compiled by William Dorsey in 1820, and *The Dover Selection of Spiritual Songs,* published in Richmond in 1828 by Andrew Broadus. *Lloyd's Hymns* was published without tunes and usually sung to those printed in the *Sacred Harp* collection, which had wide distribution. *The Psalmist,* first published in Boston in 1841, was adopted by the American Baptist Publication Board two years later. It served the denomination well in the northern states, but so many favorite hymns of southerners were omitted that a supplement of them was added. The 1843 edition was edited by Baron Stow and Samuel Francis Smith, author of "My Country 'Tis of Thee."

Among the earliest Baptist ministers in Florida was Joshua Mercer, of Georgia. He came to Florida in 1841 and was a soldier in the Seminole Wars. In East Florida he reported finding "exceedingly wicked sinners" who had "matchless ignorance" of the Bible.[51] Joshua Mercer served thirteen years in Sharon Church, East Florida, and returned to Atlanta in 1853. His brother, Jesse Mercer, had written *The Cluster of Spiritual Songs, Divine*

Florida S.M.

Isaac Watts

Mercer's Cluster Hymn 526
Truman S. Wetmore

From Jesse Mercer's hymnal early Florida Baptists sang this setting of Isaac Watts's warning to sinners. The music is in the fuging-tune tradition and was included in B. F. White's Sacred Harp. *(Reprinted from Jesse Mercer,* The Cluster *[Philadelphia: Thomas Cooperthwaite, 1835], hymn 526)*

Hymns, and Social Poems, published in Augusta, Georgia, in 1817. It was advertised in Tallahassee in 1831 and was especially favored by Baptists.[52] By 1835 it had gone through six editions—the fifth in Baltimore and the sixth in Philadelphia. Mercer also compiled *Church Psalter and Hymn Book,* which was published in 1854. It, too, found its way to Florida.

Florida was for seventy years considered a missionary outpost of Georgia preachers, according to one church historian.[53] The typical country church had no pastor. It was served by an itinerant minister who preached about once a month to each congregation on his circuit. Among the oldest churches of the denomination were Ebenezer Baptist Church, near Monticello. It was established in 1828 with twelve members. Nearby Indian Springs Baptist Church was chartered the following year. The Missionary Baptist Church of Concord, also in Middle Florida, was established in 1841 with sixteen charter members, six of whom were Negro servants. Aenon Baptist Church in Leon County was formed a year later. By 1854 there were forty-one churches affiliated with the Florida Baptist Association. Of the 2,390 members, 1,355 were white. The church records and informal histories of these early congregations are rich in details of financial affairs and church discipline. The essence of church membership was summed up simply by one writer. "Fundamentalism was universal, and even those who were excommunicated from the church were as certain of the existence of heaven and hell as they were of Washington and Tallahassee. An infidel was considered worse than a murderer or hog thief."[54] Hymns were sung at almost every gathering, whether a service or church business meeting, but few titles were listed.[55] Historians did supply titles relating to congregations formed later. In the 1860s in Taylor County, two Baptist and two Methodist congregations sang "Rock of Ages," "Come Humble Sinners in Whose Breast," "There Is a Fountain Filled with Blood," "When I Can Read My Title Clear," and "On Jordan's Stormy Banks I Stand."[56] These hymns were illustrative of evangelical doctrine and musical taste of early Florida settlers.

After midcentury, small groups of Unitarians moved to Florida. Historically, this denomination had enlisted a succession of fine hymn writers to meet its needs. Among them were Oliver Holden and William B. Bradbury. In 1848 Prince Achille Murat had expressed his opinion that Unitarianism would become the dominant religion of the upper classes in America. "Their worship is pure, elegant, and free from all sort of ceremony and superstition," he wrote; "they address themselves solely to the mind's reason, both in the selected hymns they sing, and in their sermons, which are generally moral discourses, possessing real literary merit."[57]

Harriet Beecher Stowe, sister of Rev. Henry Ward Beecher and author of *Uncle Tom's Cabin,* was among the Congregationalists to make Florida their winter home. She would not have received a unanimous welcome before the Civil War, but she prudently waited until 1867 to settle on the St. Johns River. With her, she brought the *Plymouth Collection of Hymns and Tunes,* which had been published two years earlier for her brother's congregation in Brooklyn. Henry Ward Beecher wrote the introduction to the collection, which was a model of clarity and reason. It eschewed partisan differences and supported a position that in hymns, a warmhearted response was more important than a correct harmonic progression. He wrote: "A collection should be made so large and various that everyone may find in it that which he needs. . . . Everyone should have all the liberty and the means of following his own taste. . . . Many hymnbooks have been so fastidiously made, as to not only exclude many hymns, as extravagant, that were not half so extravagant as are the Psalms of David, and as is all true and deep feeling which gives itself free expression; but also those retained have been abused by corrections, so called, and tamed down from their noble fervor and careless freedom, into flat and profitless propriety.[58] A tune which has interested a congregation "ought not to be set aside because it does not follow the reigning fashion, or conform to the whims of technical science. There is such a thing as Pharisaism in music. Tunes may be very faulty in structure, and yet convey a full-hearted current that will sweep out of the way the worthless, heartless trash which has no merit except a literal correctness."[59]

The compilers of this collection gathered hymns from many Christian denominations: Catholics, Moravians, Methodists, and others. Among the others were stalwart composers who had been borrowed from earlier collections and who would again be borrowed from this one: Cowper, the Wesleys, Stennet, Newton, Doddridge, Mrs. Steele, and Watts. To the list was added composers of popular revival melodies which Henry Ward Beecher regarded as excellent. A musical editor for this book was Rev. Charles Beecher, who lived in Florida from 1870 to 1877 and who became Florida's state superintendent of public instruction in 1871. Hymns by Charles Beecher appeared in this publication. They were sung, along with those written by his sister Harriet, by Florida congregations of several denominations.

The acceptance of hymns from all faiths and a great variety of styles to accommodate the taste of all members of the congregation humanized the use of music in the church. It represented a striking change from the prevailing thought at the beginning of the century. It also proposed a solution to the acceptance of music by American composers. New England divines had strong feelings and preferences about music, and some of their ideas were brought to Florida when their church members moved to that state. Samuel Worcester, pastor of Tabernacle Church in Salem, Massachusetts, tackled the issues in an address in 1810. "A very obvious reason for the preference for 'false music' is, that it requires less taste, and less skill, than that which is genuine." He observed that some parishioners preferred the "light and jingling fugues of an [Lewis] Edson or a [Daniel] Read to the sterling compositions of a Handel or a Giardini. . . . All that is captivating in crude and spurious musick strikes the uncultivated ear at once, charms for a while, then palls and disgusts. But music which is genuine requires the exercise of taste and skill, and will please the more, the more and the longer it is familiarized and practised. With good singers a good piece of music will never grow old."[60] He continued by calling attention to the work of native composers and teachers. "We have in our country," he wrote, "a rich supply of good music . . . of these, several excellent selections for the use of our school and choirs have recently been published, and are easily to be obtained. . . . The day must come when the American public will do justice to the meritorious labours and improvements of Mr. [Andrew] Law."[61]

One would find it difficult to refute the principles by which Worcester distinguished "false" and "genuine" music or to disagree with his judgment as to the durability of the composers of "Joy to the World" or "Come, Thou Almighty King." He did, however, underestimate the long-lived appeal of such fuging tunes by Edson and Read as "Bridgewater" and "Sherburne." Their durability, however, was assured more by the singing-school teachers of Florida and other southern states than by the Boston Handel and Haydn Society or the urban choirmasters of New England. The conclusion that our country was well supplied with good music was apt, but it was not based on the dynamic men of the William Billings tradition as one might expect. That Andrew Law deserved public recognition was patently true, though he got his full share only with the publication more than 150 years later of Richard A. Crawford's dissertation on his life and work.[62] It was not Andrew Law's preference for European music or his notation innovation that vitalized the church music of nineteenth-century Florida. In rural sectors it was the rhythmically stirring and harmonically open tunes in collections of Ananias Davisson, William Walker, Joseph Funk, B. F. White, and others. In urbanized areas Isaac Watts held sway until enriched by numerous denominational hymnbooks throughout the state. Whether rural or urban, throughout the nineteenth century, Florida musicians took the final advice of Samuel Worcester to form choirs, singing schools, and associations to improve their skills, cultivate their taste, and raise their spirits. In their best moments, it helped them feel the presence of the Holy Spirit or touch the hand of God.

In the 1830s and 1840s several Florida Protestant churches periodically held "protracted meetings," a series of eight or ten evening services with heavy evangelical overtones. Rev. Dr. Nathan Hoyt described the role of music in a Tallahassee meeting he conducted in 1843. "Humble supplications and grateful songs of praise, as the fruits of recently renewed and joyful hearts, were offered up in the domestic circle by voices and tongues, which, to say the least, were a few weeks before, very differently employed." His own elevation of spirit was noted. "Happier days and nights than some of those recently spent in Tallahassee or brighter manifestations of the love of God to his soul, the writer never anticipates this side of holy heaven."[63]

The euphoria did not extend to Prince Achille Murat. He cynically commented on the moral and social effects of revivals and camp meetings where some of these books were used. He wrote first of a Methodist camp meeting. The meeting ceremony began when a minister "gave out" a psalm, which was sung by the congregation. "In fact," he wrote, "a real camp-meeting is deemed most convenient, on many accounts. It is a point of reunion for all idlers and young people, for those who have bargains to make or conclude, for candidates who are canvassing for election. Each attends to his or her own little private affairs, whether it be to sleep, eat, make love, sell a horse, disparage or elevate a candidate. . . . The *tout ensemble* presents a beautifully romantic appearance, while roaming, amid the umbrageous foliage of the gigantic primitive trees of the forest by moonlight, and hearing in the distance the voice of song in hymns." When the sinner is being converted, he wrote, those within the sheepfold "commence an uproar which may be heard at the distance of miles, crying aloud, singing, praying, weeping or preaching all together."[64]

Prince Murat took no brighter view of revivals. "The apparent object of these *revivals* is to place a new and handsome Bible in all the houses of the place, to mulct the credulous peasants in a certain portion of their hard earned gains in order to circulate it; which you can well imagine, while they forbid them their little harmless recreations, break their fiddles and flutes, dance off the dancing master, extends the countenances of the inhabitants to a foot in length, and gives their complexions a jaundiced appearance."[65]

The social intercourse of youth was enhanced by other musical events that occurred under church sponsorship: the singing school, the all-day singing, and the singing convention. When the crops did not need attention, Floridians walked many miles to fill the social vacuum by attending Sacred Harp sings. But while the social value was present, no singing-school master or members of his class would identify that as the prime purpose.

The singing schools had a long history in our country, dating back to the eighteenth century. They were devised as a means of teaching people how to sight-read music on their own initiative rather than parroting a middleman who would "line out" between phrases while halting the forward motion of the music. As with other movements, numerous devotees devised ingenious methods for learning to sing accurately and musically, even piously. But their English models of theory were not always the best—besides, America had declared political independence, so some of the native-born composers declared their musical independence as well. They preferred to be free of constraints described in Lampe and Tans'ur, their early models. Only later did they discover that if they would not accept the rules of others, they would eventually have to devise their own. The issue of reforms became critical, and controversies developed. The merit of one system over the other was debated with the fervor of a political campaign. In the developing cities, European music models took over church music practices, and the native singing-masters moved to the South and West to sparsely settled communities. They came from New England, through Pennsylvania and the Shenandoah valley of Virginia, to Tennessee, Alabama, Georgia, and Florida. The books they brought with them were filled with selections of British and American tunes, some in three-voice (bass, tenor, counter) arrangements; others were fuging tunes which varied the texture with imitative passages. Folk tunes took their place alongside psalm tunes and hymns and anthems, all set to religious texts.

Compilers of many hymn collections continued to include prefaces that explained the rudiments of music. Given the population of the nation, the number of these books coming off the press was remarkable. Almost all of them cited reasons for adding one more publication to a highly competitive business. One group believed that the tunes in their book had intrinsic excellence because of their antiquity.[66] Another group "deplored the degraded state of church music and would cheerfully contribute all in their power to a reformation of the public taste." They proposed to do so by adding compositions by American composers. Among those selected were works of Timothy Olmsted, John Cole, S. Chandler, Timothy Swan, Daniel Read, Jacob Kimball, Samuel Holyoke, William Billings, and U. K. Hill. These were some of the finest composers of church music in the nation; yet the editors self-consciously apologized for their presence. The tunes were not thought to be destitute of merit—but still were not the best. "There is a levity," they wrote, "in some of our best written American tunes, which renders them odious to serious people; not so much on account of the movement as the character of the compositions." Another group of compilers solved the problems of old versus new, elite versus populist, and American versus European by novel means.[67] About their edition, they wrote, "The valuable foreign musick which is retained and which the public has not ceased to venerate and admire, is still preserved in this collection, secure from the touch of American innovation."[68] They reminded patrons that this collection circulated over portions of the country where refinement of taste and opportunities for improvement were necessarily unequal and that they may have missed some of their church classics. In an effort to raise popular taste, the editors proposed gradually to increase the "genuine and perfect tunes."[69]

One collection that met the needs of West Floridians along the Georgia and Alabama state lines was *The Sacred Harp*, by B. F. White and E. J. King. It was published in Philadelphia in 1844 by T. K. Collins and P. G. Collins and used a four shape-note system. Two singing associations were largely responsible for its dissemination. The first, the Southern Musical Convention, was formed in 1845. It thrived until 1868, when a controversy over the exclusive use of *The Sacred Harp* caused a decline in membership. Another group, the Chattahoochee Musical Convention, was organized in 1851 and had its first meeting a year later. Both of these groups were spawned in central Georgia and moved south and west. The precise date on which Floridians were included has not been determined, but numerous county units of the panhandle region were active by midcentury. The movement reached north central counties a few years later. Reminiscences of participants document the songs they sang. Copies of their collections are now in public and private libraries of the area. Some of the musical ancestors of *The Sacred Harp* are to be found in these same libraries. Many are known to have been gifts of local families. Among them are William Little and William Smith's *Easy Instructor* (1817 edition) and Andrew Law's *Musical Primer* and supplement *Harmonic Companion and Guide to Social Worship* and *The Art of Singing*, including *The Christian Harmony* and *The Musical Magazine*, second number. These editions of Law's publication date from 1800 to 1819. Also included are *The Southern Harmony* of 1835 by William Walker and *Missouri Harmony*, published in Cincinnati in 1835. The seven-shape tradition is represented by *The Christian Minstrel* (1846).

The earliest collection to be published in the South was Ananias Davisson's *Kentucky Harmony,* in Harrisonburg, Virginia, in 1815 or 1816. Like its New England ancestors, it was an oblong book with an introduction to the rudiments of music, followed by the song collection. The "shape-note" system of the book was that used by William Smith and William Little in *The Easy Instructor* (1801), a very long-lived New England collection. The seven syllables of traditional solmizations became the four-syllable *fa, sol, la, mi,* each with a distinctive notehead. Fa was a triangle, sol was round, la was square and mi was diamond shaped. No direct reference has been found as to the use of *Kentucky Harmony* in Florida, but it is the prototype, and probably the direct ancestor, of the collection preferred by the large number of Baptists and other evangelical sects who moved into the agricultural regions of northern and central Florida in the first half of the nineteenth century. These were not the affluent plantation owners but dirt farmers and their families, who scratched a subsistence-level living from the sand and hard clay.

Tunes came from such sources as British psalmody, hymnody, and folk songs, to which were added a liberal assortment of newly devised melodies, some no longer than eight measures, others extended to anthem length by simple rhythmic or melodic imitative devices and called fuging tunes. Their songs were called coarse and their taste uncultivated by urban Americans who were discovering German and Italian music, but they were God's greatest gift to many Floridians, a gift that became more precious with every singing.

The Sacred Harp was not used in regular church services, though a few tunes occur both in it and in denominational hymnals. It was reserved for "sings" and singing schools and, later, for singing conventions.

While the composers and compilers of *The Sacred Harp* never came to terms with the theoretical requirements of European music textbooks, their gapped modal melodies, their pentatonic tunes with unexpected omissions, and their fuging tunes constitute a rich variety of religious music. The individuality and independence of its composers have been strong enough to sustain the tradition. Devising a new method for sightsinging, writing a vast body of religious songs, and devising a new concept of appropriate tone quality in singers were challenges which Floridians, southerners, and Americans met as they sang from these books. An unshakable belief in a literal heaven, deliverance from the uncertainty of life, and the rewards of happiness and riches led compilers to include reassuring texts. Poetic craftsmanship was subservient to the strength of the message.

A countermove to the "deleterious influence of unworthy material" flooding the country was made by Thomas Hastings, Lowell Mason, and several of their associates. The material thought to be unworthy was popular folk hymns, fuging tunes, and revival songs that flooded New England. Later it found its longest traditional residences in the South. The singing schools of Florida and early congregations without regular ministers carried on the tradition of learning and the pleasure of recreation as they sang from these fa-sol-la collections. But Hastings and Mason had as a central purpose the elevation of musical taste. They proposed to furnish materials that matched utility with taste. They aimed for the taste of European gentlemen, and they borrowed liberally from the collections of these men. Earliest of Hastings's collections to reach Florida was *Musica Sacra; or, The Springfield and Utica Collections United,* published in Utica by William Williams in 1818. Following it was the *Manhattan Collection,* published in New York by Daniel Fanshaw in 1842. At least one Tallahassee family sang from another collection prepared by Thomas Hastings for the American Tract Society in 1842. It was called *Sacred Songs for Family and Social Worship* and was published in 1842. Aimed to promote devotional singing of evangelical songs, it contained Lowell Mason's setting of "My Faith Looks Up to Thee" and Cowper's "There Is a Fountain Filled with Blood." It also contained perennial favorites "Rock of Ages," "Blest Be the Tie That Binds," and "Joy to the World."

One other collection was also calculated to elevate public taste, but the signals of the preface and those of the music itself were mixed. The author declared that he was aware of public taste in New England and that he therefore had not filled his book with arrangements from the great masters of music. He rationalized that if he had, few people would have bought the book, and almost nobody would have used it. The book was subtitled *The American Collection,* though there were few American contributors. The standard composers were present: Handel, Haydn, Giardini, Pergolesi, Pleyel, Mozart, and many British luminaries.[70]

The Lowell Mason collections influenced church music taste in Florida and the nation more than those of any other compiler or editor in America in the nineteenth century. Mason collected abundant resources from European sources and was first to publish them in the United States. He attacked the works of his American colleagues. "The *original tunes,* so called

. . . (and their name is legion), can only be explained on the ground of a deplorable state of musical taste and knowledge, or of egotistic vanity and ignorance."[71] One Mason collection, designed for choir performance, contained arrangements and adaptations of music by Handel, Mozart, Schubert, R. Schumann, Michael Haydn, and other European composers. Americans were represented by Lowell Mason, Daniel Read, and William Mason. Another collection by Mason was intended as congregational music, "plain and easy for all classes of people and weak and feeble congregations." English and German repertoire dominated the collection.

Florida churchmen organized ecumenical societies to deal with social problems. Typical of the nonpartisan use of music was the role it played in the temperance issue. In 1835 Charles Joseph Latrobe described the attempts to organize a temperance society as "ludicrous beyond description." When he and Count Pourtales visited Florida in 1833, they stopped at Brown's Hotel in Tallahassee, where there was great excitement over the election of a delegate to Congress, with Call and White as candidates. Political parodies to familiar tunes had been sung during the campaign, and barroom ballads had accompanied election-day tippling. A temperance meeting was held on the evening of Latrobe's visit to the hotel, but since "little was accomplished," many gathered afterward at the bar "to partake of such drinks as mint julip, mint sling, bitters, hail stone, snow storm, appletoddy punch, Tom and Jerry, or egg nog."[72] A special target of the societies was the dawn-to-dusk drinking on American Independence Day. The editor of the *St. Joseph Times* wrote: "The Temperance Societies will be thrown back at least a year. Byron says that a man being reasonable should get drunk, and we anticipate that there will be a great number of reasonable people on that day. . . . We suspect a man's patriotism who profanes his mouth with cold water on the Birthday of our nation. It is Liberty's Carnival."[73]

Whenever temperance organizations sprang up, music was there. Vocal or instrumental, it followed the toasts at ceremonies or banquets. On Independence Day 1842, the Marshall Temperance Society of Salubrity in Quincy organized a procession to a church where they sang hymns and urged reluctant citizens to sign the pledge.[74] Newspapers frequently printed temperance texts to be sung to familiar tunes. Ministers enlisted music in the cause.

Simon Peter Richardson, a Methodist itinerant minister, exceeded all others in music showmanship when he reorganized a temperance society in Key West. He told of it in his autobiography.

I determined to make a raid on the whiskey traffic; but while my church was with me, there were few who felt any interest in total abstinence. I organized the old Washingtonian Pledge, and held a temperance meeting every Friday night, but failed to control and direct the public mind to ensure large results. We had an old bachelor, and he was one of the finest violinists I ever heard play. He was a strong anti-whiskey man. There was another who was a fine flutist. I got these two men to play for me. I then engaged twenty of the girls, the best singers I could find on the island, and sent to New York for about three hundred temperance song books. We opened up a regular temperance opera. This brought out the whole town. When I left there we had over five hundred grown people on the pledge, besides the children's society. We literally fiddled, fluted, and sung the whiskey traffic out of town.[75]

Though local ecumenical efforts had brought churches together on issues of common agreement, other stronger issues had caused churches of America's North and South to draw apart. Denominations were getting hymnals with their own imprimatures, but regional differences strained unanimity in music no less than in religious doctrine or politics. The musical result in some instances was the publication of doctrinaire hymnals on both sides of the Mason and Dixon's Line. In them both were hymns with militaristic, unchristian sentiments. Vilification of the enemy was a theme that outweighed the prayers for peace in many hymns. Congregations north and south sang them with equal fervor, convinced that God was on their side.

9

✳   ✳   ✳   ✳   ✳   ✳   ✳   ✳

Where Gen'rous Hearts and Beauty Dwell

Music in Social Life

This, gentlemen, is the land of my adoption. I have seen many improvements raised up, as by magic, in the bosom of the wilderness. I have seen the members, composing a delightful society, arrive one by one from their distant homes and it would be impossible for me . . . to forget the strong feelings which all this has excited.

—Prince Achille Murat, 1830

In early territorial days, the wealthy and educated people of Pensacola engaged in sporting events and social life as a distinct class. The native-born inhabitants sprang from French, Spanish, and English ancestry and continued to speak the language of their ancestors. The offspring of intermarriages among these three groups were called Creoles. The women were described as having soft, dark eyes, a natural sweetness of expression, and a remarkable natural grace of carriage. The men were described as having "little love of glory and less of enterprise." They were also described as indifferent to everything but pleasure and having no love of knowledge. They were friendly with each other, "hospitable to strangers and not unkind to their slaves."[1]

The cultural life and recreation of the community centered around music drama, concerts, parlor music, and dancing. Traveling professional companies brought plays with music and dance and gave concerts with soloists and orchestras. Balls were a tradition from Spanish times. Local amateurs played and sang music that was popular on both sides of the Atlantic. Officers of ships that put in to the Pensacola Naval Yard often invited local ladies and gentlemen to attend balls aboard their vessels. The chief social events of the year were dances during carnival season, the bouquet ball, and patgoe. A raucous frontier shivaree followed by a dance sometimes celebrated the second marriage of a widower. Dramas with music were especially favored.

The carnival season in Pensacola opened on December 26, the Feast of St. Stephen. It was a time of license and excess, according to one observer, when practical jokes could be played without offending and lack of restraint was no cause for censure. A *bal masqué* opened the 1822 season and was described by one who was there. A Madame Louise outfitted the social set with costumes and masks from New Orleans and sometimes discreetly revealed the disguise to a friend. Music animated dancers to the strains of the fandango, the waltz, or other dances. The gentlemen offered their arms with greetings to the ladies, "Ah, beau masque! Je vous connois." An observer described one couple.

A little, old, grey-haired shrivelled Frenchman led into the [dance] area . . . a young sylph-like shepherdess, and, gracefully and profoundly bowing to her, commenced the fandango. . . . The beauty of this dance consists in assuming the various postures, attitudes and gestures expressive of the feelings the dancer wishes to exhibit towards his partner. The advances of the old gentleman were at first ceremonious, and marked with respectful consideration; they were received by his youthful partner with great assumed timidity and maiden coyness. As the dance progressed, the spirit of both was aroused, and the grey-beard evinced all the impassioned vehemence of a youthful adorer. His tantalizing partner now enticed him by the graceful display of a fairy foot and half the lower limb, or allured him with outstretched arms; and then at the moment he seemed about to clasp her, she would elude his attempts with a skill and agility that were truly surprising.[2]

After the carnival dancers were fatigued, supper was announced, and strangely paired, they began the promenade, "Indian chief with a shepherdess; the monk and the merry-andrew . . . ; an old woman . . . with a boy; and a blanketed squaw . . . by a powdered beau of the past century." The voluptuous widow La Fleur, dressed in a Turkish costume with trousers and turban, was escorted by a gallant Englishman. The music resumed with the playing of a waltz. A young army lieutenant observed: "The whole thing far exceeded my most sanguine expectations. There was certainly a great want of what you would call refinement; but there was a spirit, a warmth of sentiment, perhaps you will say of mundane pleasurableness, that greatly compensated in my opinion for the want of it. . . . Let us . . . justly estimate the enjoyments of the passing hour, assured that the visions of the morrow will be as sadly clogged with earthly reality as are the verities of the passing day."[3]

The bouquet ball was a custom in every town from St. Augustine to New Orleans during the social season. A gentleman was designated king and paid all expenses for the music, the entertainment, and the dinner. Mr. Norton, an English merchant on Pensacola's Palafox Street, was king for the event described in a letter by George A. McCall dated December 1, 1822. "Invitations," he wrote, "were extended to every family where there was a pretty face." Love of the dance broke down any strict distinction of classes. Simplicity and good taste of dress coupled with native grace and dignity of carriage made it difficult to distinguish between classes. McCall stated that appearances were similar, whether proud patrician or "the scarcely less polished plebeian."

The ball was held in the large ballroom of the Hôtel d'Espagne. Mr. Norton had chosen as his queen the sensual widow Madam La Fleur. As the band played a march, the couple made a dramatic entrance. "Mr. Norton moved through the room with measured step and consequential air, bowing right and left in the most grave and condescending manner; while the graceful La Fleur hung languishingly on his arm, and, with the most bewitching smiles, returned the salutations of her numerous friends and admirers." After the promenade, the gentlemen were called to lead their partners to their positions for the dance. "The King and Queen, of course, occupied the most conspicuous position in the dance, on the night of the Spanish contra-dance. The music, measured and slow, commenced; the queen began the figure. She glided through the intricacies of the dance with a light step, to which the movements of her matchless figure (full but not over-grown) conformed with facility and grace. . . . This dance, uniting the beauties of the minuet with those of the waltz, is unrivaled in the fine attitudes and chaste movements its peculiar figures are calculated to exhibit."[4] The Spanish dance was followed by a waltz. Later, supper was announced as the band played a march. The bouquet was then ceremoniously presented to a bachelor Scottish gentleman who was reputed to be rich but penurious.

A social custom called the patgoe was practiced in Pensacola from days of the early settlement. Introduced in twelfth-century Brittany as *La fête du Papegai,* it became the centerpiece of a large-scale event that invariably included singing, feasting, and dancing.[5] The host of one patgoe was a Monsier De la Rue, a French Creole who invited guests to a *déjeuner à la forchette* at his Red Bluff Plantation, situated on a high promontory overlooking Escambia Bay. A bugle call announced the approaching event, and the band played martial airs in the arbor where spectators sat. The carved wooden figure of a chicken cock festooned with ribbons and feathers was mounted on a high flagstaff. Young marksmen tried their skill with rifles. When one dislodged the plumage, supplied by a young lady, she became his partner for the first contradance. After dinner, couples danced to waltzes and lively tunes of the band. Several ladies sang Spanish songs as they crossed the water returning to Pensacola.[6]

In one frontier social custom, fifes and fiddles probably played secondary roles to tin kitchenware and other noisemakers. The Spanish shivaree was a custom of young Pensacolans when a widow or widower was married. In 1822 a mob dressed in outlandish costumes and hideous masks and carrying torches was "accompanied by an instrumental din of unsurpassable grandeur." They were led by two pranksters mounted on their best horses; one was served by an aide-de-camp mounted on a candidate for the soap factory on whose shaved tail was attached a cowbell. Their destination was the house of an old Spaniard who had taken to wife a young Creole. Upon arrival, one member of the Knights of Hymeneal Torch addressed the bridegroom, "Most enviable groom and illustrious Señor, is not more demanded of thee than to provide music and abundant good cheer, and these devoted knights and faithful soldiers will return; in the flashing of a flambeau, each accompanied by his adored fair one, to dance and make merry with thee till Phoebus, god of day, shall warn us to give over. Have I said well, my merry men?" His men responded with yells and "a deafening peal of instrumental music." The Spaniard thundered his rage and slammed the shutters of the window. The noisy revelers paraded the streets and visited every tavern or public house demanding free drinks. Toward morning they returned to the sleepless groom, denouncing his lack of hospitality. The maskers then retreated to the plaza for breakfast and regrouping. They returned to the house, placed it on rollers near the water's edge and once again confronted the groom. Only the tearful intervention of his bride checked the fury of the man and caused him to agree to the entertainment. The leader of the knights congratulated the Spaniard on his bravery and assured him that his men would behave with the utmost propriety. In a few hours all was ready, and the knights reappeared, dressed in their finest black suits. A good band struck up the Spanish contradance, and the Creoles glided through it and the figures of the waltz. "The bride was all smiles. The groom all dignity."[7]

As early as 1822 the waltz became popular among young Pensacolans, although its propriety was still being debated in Pennsylvania and other American states in 1829. A correspondent to the *Philadelphia Advertiser* complained that fashion was striving to influence the introduction of the waltz into the refined society of the city of Philadelphia. He reminded readers that the duke of Saxe Weimar attended a dance in New York where the women danced nothing but French contradances. American ladies, he observed, had so much modesty that they objected to waltzing. The duke, however, did meet with the waltz in the course of his tour. It was at the Quadroon Balls in New Orleans. If he had visited Florida, he could also have observed it in Pensacola, Tallahassee, or St. Augustine.[8] Dancing masters had taught it in these towns since the early days of the decade.

While amateur music-and-theater groups operated in St. Augustine, Pensacola, and Tallahassee, the arrival of professional performers in Florida awaited the improvement of transportation made by steamboats. The Florida coastal towns were served by companies from New York, Cuba, and New Orleans. Overland travel developed later and brought companies on a circuit through Tallahassee, Thomasville, Dothan, Columbus, Montgomery, and Savannah. Announcements of concerts and theatrical offerings appeared in newspapers during the territorial period from 1821 to statehood in 1845. Many productions, however, were announced by circulars distributed about town. Reviews were rare.

The concerts usually featured soloists, small ensembles, and sometimes an orchestra in a great variety of works and media on a single program. Vocal and instrumental solos were interspersed between Haydn or Mozart symphonies. Opus numbers or symphony subtitles were usually omitted, nor was it indicated whether the orchestra played the entire work or a single movement.

An evening at the theater in Pensacola, Apalachicola, Tallahassee, or St. Augustine opened with a main piece. The repertory was chosen usually from classics and lighter works written for the British stage. Since this was a period when the common man was replacing larger-than-life heroic characters on the British stage, the vehicles instantly appealed to the frontiersmen and their families. After the main piece, the orchestra, singers, dancers, magicians, or comedians took over, or a short skit was enacted. Then followed the afterpiece, which was usually a farce or comedy. Songs were often a part of even the most serious dramas. George Farquhar wrote songs for such pieces as his "Recruiting Soldier." Thomas Arne, William Shield, and other composers wrote works of greater musical pretentions which were presented either as musical stage works or in concert form.[9]

A facility for presenting stage and music performances was constructed in Pensacola early in the nineteenth century. Among the French who came from New Orleans to make their home in Pensacola in the early years of the century was Juan Baptiste Casanave. He built the Tivoli Dance Hall in 1805, but its function and its name changed in 1821 when it became the Jackson Commonwealth Theatre. The facility had a capacity of from 200 to 250 and opened its doors on the very day Andrew Jackson accepted the city from the Spanish and became the first territorial governor of Florida, July 18, 1821. The first performances were given by a theatrical company from New Orleans.[10] They included a presentation of a Mr. Hanna, recently of the New Orleans and Western Theatres, in the character of Baron Steinfort in Kotzebue's play *The Stranger.* Shakespeare's comedy *Catherine and Petruchio (The Taming of the Shrew)* was followed by the farce *Animal Magnetism.* The celebrated drama *Castle Spectre* was concluded with the farce *The Spoiled Child.* These last two were enigmatically announced to be for the benefit of "Mr., alias Miss Barrymore."[11]

A dramatic version of *Parsifal* was offered at least twice in Pensacola, the first in 1821. (The Bayreuth premiere of Richard Wagner's opera did not occur until sixty-one years later.) The fourteen-week season closed with a performance for the exclusive benefit of the musicians in the band. It was reported that the musicians received no other compensation for their long and faithful services but that the benefit performance might induce lovers of music to fill the boxes.[12]

The manager of this early company was Andrew Jackson Allen, who was born in New York City in 1788. He made his debut in 1815 at the Albany Theatre, where he sang a Negro ballad. He was one of America's first performers of a song-and-dance routine in blackface. The first Negro dialect song he sang with the 1821 Pensacola company was in a production of *The Battle of Champlain.* In addition to A. J. Allen, two other early players became known nationally: J. M. Scott and Mrs. Price (later Mrs. Stone, still later Mrs. Bannister).

One of the most impressive concert programs in early Florida was given

Pensacola audiences found stage works especially appealing. This example is a dramatic moment from a cantata by John Braham that they heard in 1822 at the Spanish Lodge Room. This piece was published by five American publishers in 1818. (Courtesy Florida State University Music Library)

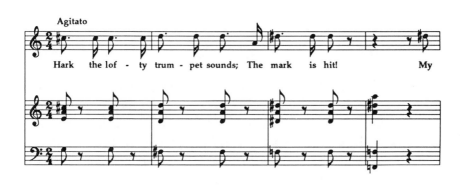

Hark the lof - ty trum - pet sounds; The mark is hit! My

child is free! In - to his fath - ers' arms he bounds, In -

spir'd by love and_____ li- ber- ty. And

etc.

in the Spanish Lodge Room on Water Street, Pensacola, in May 1822. The performers were a Mr. Sherer and a Mr. Garner, a pianist and vocalist. The presence of an orchestra may be presumed, since symphonies by Haydn and Mozart were played, a dance followed the recital, and a performance was given for the benefit of the orchestra. Keyboard works by Hummel, Gelinek, and Dussek were included, as was the popular "Battle of Maringo," by Bernard Viguerie. Two songs were about soldiers and the others were love songs by some of the most eminent song composers of the day. The *William Tell* piece was possibly that by John Braham, the famous British singer. It was published by no fewer than five American publishers in 1818. Tickets could be had at the bookstore, the bars of Messrs. Collins' and Austin's Hotels, and the New York Coffee House.[13] The full program follows:

PART FIRST

Polacca	Hummel
Song—"The Rose on Beauty's Cheek" . . .	Bishop
"The Soldiers Slumbering after War" . .	Whitaker
Rondo	Gelinek
Song—"Thou art all to me, love"	Braham
Symphony	Haydn
Polacca—"No more by sorrow chas'd my heart" . .	Braham

PART SECOND

Battle of Maringo	Viguerie
Song—"On this cold flinty rock"	Braham
"In this cottage my father once dwelt"	
(The celebrated Echo Song, from the Opera of Narensky)	
Symphony	Mozart
Song—"Auld Lang Syne"	
"Dearest Ellen"	Stephenson

PART THIRD

Rondo	Dussek
Song—The Victory—"He was fam'd for deeds of arms"	
"Where shall the lovers rest?"	Clark
Thema, with variations	Piano

Song—"My heart with love is
     beating" . . . . Shield
Symphony . . . . Mozart
The concert will conclude (by particular desire) with the celebrated
cantata of "William Tell," the Swiss patriot.

The passion for stage plays and music had begun early in Pensacola. A
keen observer of social life there in 1822 tells of one public performance of
"la comédie pas de tout intérieur." "Vive la bagatelle! was the motto of the
hour," he reported, "and the winning charm of the Creole's manner

My Heart with Love is Beating

John Braham

*This song by the celebrated tenor John Braham was performed on a program in
Pensacola in 1822. It was a simple love song, but Braham added Italianate melisma,
which the public cheered. (Courtesy Florida State University Music Library)*

wound into the chorus of his song the voices of both the tenacious Briton and the proud Spanish. . . . The principal directors on the occasion were Manuel Ricaneir and Pierre Le Rocher." The name of the French comedy was not given, but it was being well received by the audience when the performance was interrupted by one of those incidents which occurred throughout the theatrical circuit of the time. A drunken Irish tar who had low tolerance for a language he did not understand rose and shouted, "Stage ahoy! I say. What's your play called. I've seen many a better one aboard ship; and it's rather long between drinks here, so I'm off." He then attempted an exit over the heads of the other sailors and their fair quadroon women, but the improvised seating gave way, and calamity ensued. The pile of arms and legs were sorted out, the Irish sailor escaped, and in the words of the observer, "The play was resumed, and played out without further interruption."[14]

John and Eliza Vaughan headed the company that offered a twenty-night season at the Tivoli in 1822. On opening night they presented two of the plays that were popular favorites. Advertisements proclaimed:

For twenty nights only—first night, Saturday Evening, June 22, 1822 will be presented the much admired Tragedy in five acts, called "Douglass," or "The Noble Shepherd."

Between the play and farce, will be sung the comic song of "Nothing at All," by Mr. Carr (His first appearance here).

The evening's entertainment will conclude with the laughable piece in two acts, called "Miss in Her Teens."

Captain Lovet	Mr. Wells
Billy Fribble	Vaughan
Captain Flash	Carr (a singer)
Puff	Frithey
(His first appearance here.)	
Miss Biddy	Mrs. Degrushe
Tag	Vos

Box tickets one dollar, pit 75 cents—places in the boxes can be taken from ten until twelve. Smoking in the theatre is prohibited, as it is considered dangerous. Visitors cannot be admitted behind the scenes. Doors will be opened at seven and curtain rises at 8 o'clock precisely. Nights of performance Tuesdays, Thursdays, and Saturdays.[15]

The Ludlow Company opened the 1828 season with two favorite players who were also talented in music. The leading lady was born in England and played opposite such leading men as Junious Brutus Booth in New York before joining southern and western repertory companies. She was a singer and dancer as well as an actress in both comedy and tragedy. Professionally she never used the names of her first and last husbands, but she did use those of her other three: Hartwig, Tatnall, and Hosack, as well as her maiden name, Pritchard.

The season was announced as follows in the local newspaper:

Theatre

The citizens of Pensacola are now favored with the presence of a small company of Theatrical Performers, which has not been the case before for several years past. On Wednesday Evening the House was opened, with the *Tragedy of Douglass,* and the Farce of the *Day after the Wedding; or, The Wife's First Lesson.* This evening the celebrated Comedy of *Simpson and Co.; or, A New Mode of Banking,* to be followed by the Farce called *Fortune's Frolic; or, The True Use of Riches,* together with other entertainments, will be performed. We trust the company will receive such patronage as may encourage their future visits to Pensacola, with an addition to their present respectable forces.[16]

Two weeks later the newspaper reported that a benefit performance for Mr. Hartwig had been well attended and that Mrs. Hartwig had "acquitted herself to the admiration of the audience." Commended, too, was the leading man, a Mr. Myers, who, after a performance of *Castle Spectre,* gave "an extraordinary exhibition of vocal powers." This event led to several additional evenings of song by Mr. Myers, whose celebrated talent caused him to receive the support and approbation of the theatrical and musical audiences.

The same theatrical company returned to Pensacola on its 1829 tour. The principal performers remained the same, but the repertory changed. They announced:

Will be presented for the first time this season, this evening Tuesday, 17th February, the celebrated laughable Operatical Burlette, called "A Day after the Fair," in which Mr. Rice will appear in Six, and Mrs. Hartwig in Three, different characters.

In the course of which, Mr. Rice and Mrs. Hartwig will each stage a number of celebrated Songs.

To be followed by the laughable Farce of "The Irish Tutor."

Teddy O'Rourke	Mr. Rice
Mary	Mrs. Hartwig

The evening's entertainment to conclude with the laughable Ballette of "The Cobbler's Daughter; or, Old Hunks Outwitted."

Old Hunks	Mr. Hartwig
Crispin (The Cobbler)	Mr. Rice
Fanny	Mrs. Hartwig

In the course of the Ballette
A Comic Dance by Mr. Rice
A Pas Seul, By Mrs. Hartwig, and a Figure Dance by the Characters. For further particulars see bills of the day.[17]

A novelty was announced for the evening of March 13, 1829.

Mr. Saunders,

Most respectfully informs the Ladies and Gentlemen of Pensacola and its vicinity, that his Benefit is fixed for the above Evening; when, he hopes, the Amusements selected for the purpose will insure him a share of Public patronage.

In addition to the usual performance there will be a

THEATRICAL LOTTERY

consisting of the following Prizes; viz. 2 Gold Seals, a Key & Ring; A set of the Casket, for 1828; 12 Barege Handerkerchiefs; 1 dozen Elegant Half Hose; A Dissected Puzzle-Map. Each person purchasing a Ticket will receive a Number, and the Prize drawn to the Number will be awarded, accordingly.

After the performance, there will ascend from the back of the theatre a very LARGE BALLOON, 18 feet high, and 52 in circumference.

The Prizes are deposited for inspection at Mr. Hunt's Bookstore. For the pieces selected for the Evening—see Bills of the Day.[18]

A benefit performance for Mrs. Hart included *London Assurance* as the main piece and the farce *Loan of a Lover*. Mrs. Hart sang and Fanny Hubbard danced before the afterpiece. At Mr. Hart's benefit the troupe performed the romantic drama *Ali Pacha* and a scene from *The Hypocrite* and concluded with the farce *The Rival Soldiers*. Mrs. Hart and Miss Hubbard again sang and danced.

The 1829 company included among its players Thomas Dartmouth Rice. He had played with the Samuel Drake's company in Louisville in 1828 and while there observed the style of a Negro street dancer. His elaboration on this dance and singing the song "Jim Crow" in the drama *The Rifle* (by Solon Robinson) led Rice into a career as a blackface performer of international repute. The minstrel shows in which he rose to fame, however, did not become popular until the 1840s. Pensacola audiences saw him in such comic dance interludes as those in the balletic *The Cobbler's Daughter; or, Old Hunks Outwitted*. It is possible that they saw him perform Negro character dances which emerged in short skits, then enlarged into his larger-scale plays, such as *Bone Squash* and *O Hush! or, The Virginia Cupids*. His Jim Crow routine was described by Hans Nathan, minstrel historian.

> While singing the first four measures of his song ["Jim Crow"], . . . Rice probably moved cautiously along the footlights. In the refrain, however, to clear cut accentuations, he began to dance. How strained, sprawling, and distorted his posture was, and yet how nonchalant—how unusually grotesque with its numerous sharp angles, and yet how natural! . . . [He] wheeled, turned and jumped. In windmill fashion, he rolled his body lazily from one side to the other, . . . of one foot and on the toes of the other . . . on the words "just so" [he] jumped high up and back into his initial position. While doing all this, he rolled his left hand in a half-seductive, half waggishly admonishing manner.[19]

In the first half of the century, repertory companies traveled the circuit from New Orleans to Pensacola, Apalachicola, Tallahassee, Tampa, Key West, and St. Augustine. A few traveled by stagecoach and wagons from Savannah to Dothan, Alabama, and returned by way of Thomasville, Georgia.[20] Transportation was tedious, time consuming, and uncomfortable. However welcome the traveling players and musicians, their rewards were small. The population in Florida cities was not then sufficient to support a sustained season of plays and music. The dining room of Pensacola's Florida House hotel was converted into a theatrical playhouse in 1837 and opened with the Jack Barnes family playing an original tragedy,

Lafitte, written by Charlotte, the sixteen-year-old daughter. Charlotte received favorable reviews of her writing, her acting, and her skill at the piano.[21] She and her parents returned several times in the 1830s and performed to full houses.

Theatrical companies from New Orleans and Mobile came to Pensacola sporadically from the late 1820s through the early 1860s, though in small numbers. The periods 1829–37 and 1843–62 appear to have been particularly lean, yet music was mentioned as a feature or an adjunct to many productions. The orchestra was not always reliable, not to say artistic, nor was the singing dependably on key, but the fiddlers, singers, and dancers were invariably there to keep the attention of the audience between acts and to fill the interval between the main piece and the afterpiece.

In nearby Mobile, Pensacolans could see the rich offerings of the Ludlow Company in the 1820s and even richer fare after Sol Smith entered the scene in the early 1830s. There was stage music for every taste. Among the melodramas of the 1827–28 season was *The Devil's Bridge,* presented at the Theatre Royale on April 23, 1828. Popular, too, were such British operas as *Poor Soldier* (William Shield, Dublin and London, 1783; New York, 1786), presented May 3, 1828, and *No Song No Supper* (Stephen Storace, London, 1790; Philadelphia, 1792), presented at Mobile's Saint Emanuel Street Theatre in 1833. *Rosina,* an opera by Shield, was presented in the 1833–34 season. One of the earliest plays with music by men who had become prominent in American music circles was *Pizarro.* The play was a version of an original work by Kotzebue, rewritten by Richard Brinsley Sheridan. Alexander Reinagle wrote the music in collaboration with Raynor Taylor.[22] Occasionally the playbills announced songs, fancy dance, a concert, a musical mélange, or a grand concert. *Clari* and *William Tell* were staples. Listed in the 1827–28 season was *Don Giovanni,* and in 1833–34 was *The Barber of Seville.* It was not until the 1837–38 season, when Ludlow and Smith were able to bring such stars as Ellen Tree, that the Gulf coast patrons could hear performances of *Cinderella* and *La sonnambula,* starring Mrs. Watson. The grand-opera tradition continued in the 1841–42 season with repeated performances of *La sonnambula* and *Norma.* Among the ladies of the company were the Mrs. Seguin, Richardson, and Brunton. Among the men were Messrs. Manvers, Hodges, Brunton, Seguin, and Archer. Several of these productions were given in Mobile and Pensacola not long after their European premiers. *La sonnambula,* for instance, had its Milan premier in 1831, played in New York in 1835, and did not reach Chicago until 1850, twelve years after the first Mobile performance.

Popularity of these stage works carried over into Pensacola parlors. Agents of Chickering and other domestic manufacturers placed pianos in homes throughout Florida in the two decades before the Civil War. Mothers, daughters, and even some young men studied from local teachers, and a few went to northern schools, where they became proficient in the repertoire of the day.

That repertoire in Pensacola, as in northern states, was composed of fantasies and variations on themes from operas, dance music in both its functional and idealized forms, marches and battle pieces, show pieces by European virtuosi recently transplanted to or visiting in the United States, and a great variety of songs. The standard piano repertory played in Pensacola included works by Mozart and Mendelssohn, Liszt's Grand Galop Chromatique (op. 12), and Chopin's Polonaise in A-flat.

Clearly, the most popular selections were those from operas. A few were faithful transcriptions of marches or other instrumental works; others were arias to be sung with piano accompaniment. Most popular of all, though, were the fantasias and sets of variations on operatic themes. Given the dominance of the French among the population and the proximity to New Orleans, where excellent French opera companies performed, it is not surprising that Pensacola residents played and sang airs from French operas that had been arranged by virtuoso pianists. A few airs and overtures were set as piano duets. From the French repertory they played arrangements of *Le calife de Bagdad* (Boieldieu); *Masaniello, Les diamants de la couronne,* and *Fra Diavolo* (Auber); *Zampa* (Herold); *Robert le diable* and *Les Huguenots* (Meyerbeer); *Faust* (Gounod); and *Hamlet* (Thomas). These works date from 1801 to 1868 and are a rich sampling of French opera of the period. Pensacolans also heard performances of operas produced in New Orleans and in nearby Mobile. Occasionally there were local performances as well. Pensacola musicians purchased some of this music and music from Italian operas in New Orleans from A. E. Blackman, 167 Canal Street. Blackman published a collection entitled "Gems from Favorite Operas" which included those listed here and also those from *La traviata, Il trovatore, Les Vêpres siciliennes, Rose of Costelle, Fille des régiment, Maritani, Le pardon de Ploërmel, Crown Diamonds,* and *Le prophète* during this period. Nearby Mobile publisher J. H. Snow, 102–104 Dauphin Street, sold "Fantaisies sur motifs d'opéras par Ferd. Beyer," twenty pieces from twelve operas, and some of them were in the bound volumes of sheet music played in Pensacola by a local gentleman pianist, Archie C. Yonge. Collections of this and other Pensacola musicians have been preserved at the University of West Florida.

From the Italian repertory, fewer composers were represented, but a larger list of operas served as sources of piano transcriptions and elaborations. Donizetti led the list with offerings from *Lucia di Lammermoor, Lucrezia Borgia, La Favorite, Linda di Chamounix,* and *Don Pasquale.* Bellini was also a favorite with *I Capuleti e i Montecchi, La sonnambula, Norma,* and *I puritani.* Rossini was represented by *Mose in Egitto* and *Guillaume Tell,* and Verdi with *Rigoletto* and *Un ballo in maschera.*

Fantasies on these operas were written by Maurice Strakosch, Henri Herz, Sigismond Thalberg, H. A. Wollenhaupt, Richard Hoffman, and others. They and other midcentury pianists came to the United States from Paris, Vienna, Leipzig, and London. In Europe they had studied with Liszt and other virtuosi of the day. They wrote original pieces as well, which were played in Florida. Two American-born virtuosi wrote opera fantasias but are best known for original pieces. Louis Moreau Gottschalk, a child of Jewish and Creole heritage, native of New Orleans, was the most colorful figure on the concert stage at this time, with the possible exception of Franz Liszt. Gottschalk was represented in the library of Katie B. Sullivan, a Pensacola pianist, by two selections: "The Banjo," based on the sounds of local instrumentalists, and "The Last Hope," his most famous work, an extravagant effusion now best known because its principal thematic material was transformed into the hymn "Holy Spirit, Truth Divine" by Edwin Pond Parker. William Mason, a celebrated Boston and New York composer, performer, and teacher, was included in Archie C. Yonge's repertoire by his popular "Silver Spring," op. 6.

Among numerous sets of variations were those on the Scottish tunes "O Swiftly Glides My Bonny Boat" and "Bonny Doon." The boat song bears one of the earliest copyright dates—1829—of any piece in the collection of Julia A. Cole, who married Julian Yonge. It is a set of five variations and a coda by W. H. W. Darley and was published by George Willig, Jr., of Baltimore. Henri Herz set his on the Irish tune "Tis the Last Rose of Summer," and J. C. Viereck those on the minstrel tune "Miss Lucy Long." The marches from operas *Moses in Egypt* (Rossini) and *Norma* (Bellini) were arranged for pianoforte, and there was a "Turkish March" by J. B. Cramer. From the American scene a march dedicated to the U.S. Marine Corps was composed by an unidentified young lady of Charleston. It was transcribed for piano, as was the "Duke de Reichstadt's Grand March" by Johann Strauss as performed by the Boston Brigade's Band. Tributes to nationally known figures, whether musicians or politicians, were made in fantasies. One was called a "Souvenir d'Ole Bull, Fantaisie sur De Carnavale de Venezia," one of Bull's must successful pieces. Another by Richard Hoffman was titled "Grand Fantaisie on the celebrated air Here's to You Harry Clay." It was first performed by the composer at the anniversary festival on the birthday of Henry Clay, April 12, 1850. Among the novelty pieces for piano was the popular "Battle of Prague" (F. Kotzwara).

Fanny Elssler, Mme. Taglioni, Mme. Duvernay, Mme. Cinti, and the Dodsworths figured conspicuously among the dance-music collections. Elssler's Gran Pas espagnol, "La Gitana," and "La Cracovienne," her famous Gypsy dance, were played. Convernay's "Spanish Cachoucha," Cinti's "Valses brilliantes," and Taglioni's "Caradora Waltz" were included, as was Miss Oceana's so-called Mexican dance, "La jota aragonesa." Gallopades, polkas, schottisches, quadrilles, and Virginia reels were popular and were included in libraries of local pianists.

Few examples of patriotic sentiment are in the collections, the Sigismond Thalberg set of brilliant waltzes titled "Souvenir d'Amérique" being one of the few relating to the United States. Two composed to celebrate the coronation of Queen Victoria were played, one a duet.[23] Quicksteps dedicated to military bands were popular pieces in the 1840s, though there was little difference between those for the New York Light Guard and those for the Boston Light Infantry.

Sheet music was not the only source of songs for Pensacola singers. The local newspaper published song texts frequently. Their richest source in the 1820s was the poems of Thomas Moore. One of the earliest examples was sung to the air "The Rose Tree."

> I'd mourn the hopes that leave me,
> If thy smiles had left me too;
> I'd weep when friends deceive me,
> If thou wert like them untrue.
> But while I've thee before me,

> With heart so warm and eyes so bright,
> No cloud can linger o'er me,
> That smile turns them all to light.[24]

The editor retained the original text here, but in another issue abjured the Moore poetry while retaining the traditional tune.

Another old song began,

> Those evening bells, those evening bells,
> How many a tale their music tells
> Of truth and home and that sweet time
> When last I heard their soothing chime!

It was sung to the national song "The Bells of St. Petersburgh." The Pensacolans knew this tune and retained its lyricism, though they changed the subject of the text.

> Those beautious flowers, those beautious flowers,
> Just freshly kissed by summer showers,
> Now brightly bloom, in rich array,
> As though they ne'er would fade away.[25]

A rollicking Scottish drinking tune, known first as "The Happy Toper" and later as "Willie Brewed a Peck o'Maut," became a favorite song in Pensacola. From the Scottish repertory, aging couples preferred the poignant sentiment of "The Birks of Invermay."

> Think not, dear girl, that withering years,
> Can change the feelings of this heart.
> Nay! Let me calm thy doubts and fears,
> From thee, my faith shall ne'er depart.[26]

Scottish songs were popular throughout Florida. The Whitfield family of Tallahassee owned the four volumes of the G. Thompson *Select Collection of Original Scottish Airs*. From it they sang the songs of Robert Burns, with musical settings by Franz Joseph Haydn.

One tune was so popular that it was set to ten or more issues from 1813 to 1824. Titled *Musette de Nina,* it first appeared in a Philadelphia publication by G. E. Blake, with later arrangements by Benjamin Carr, Charles Gilfert, and Christopher Meineke. The poetry published in Pensacola was the following:

When the silken band that fitted our youth
Is surrendered, by fate's imperious decree,
And the fondest hope of our yearning heart's truth
Shall wither away as a leaf on the tree;
Ah! Tis vain; the heart injured once
May throb till it breaks, but never feel more.[27]

This song was sung by Jenny Lind and other artists later in the century.

A collection of sheet music for Spanish guitar, owned by Julia A. Cole, gives a sampling of the repertory for that instrument both in Pensacola and possibly St. Augustine, since she was a native of the latter. While a few airs were played by the guitar alone, all were provided with words to be sung. Only a few of them have instrumental music sources. Three with copyright dates of 1828 were published by George Willig of Philadelphia: "The Watchman" (arr. T. E. Gubert); "Twilight Dews," a French air (arr. B. F. Peale); and "The Wandering Harper," composed by B. Carr and arranged for guitar by Franklin Peale. These bear the earliest dates of the published guitar music in the collection, though a few many have been written earlier. The Benjamin Carr ballad has as its text an excerpt from the Walter Scott poem *Rokeby*. It was also issued by J. Carr in Baltimore as no. 9 of the publisher's "Musical Miscellany in Occasional Numbers."

Added to these were songs of the Irish, "Believe Me If All Those Endearing Young Charms" (words by Thomas Moore) and the ballad "Kathleen Mavoureen," the Scottish "Flow Gently Sweet Afton" (words by Robert Burns), and the ever-present songs called Swiss, Tyrol, or Alpine, which swept the country in the 1830s and 1840s. Popularized by touring family singers from Switzerland, they combined nostalgia and the yodel. The novelty appealed to Florida families no less than to those of Maine or Massachusetts. Maria Malibran, one of the greatest singers of the age, wrote a Tyrolean song sung in Pensacola, "There Is No Home like My Own." W. J. Wetmore wrote another, "My Mountain Home." T. J. Strawinsky arranged "Oh! Take Me Back to Switzerland" for guitar, and Emil Hurbrugger arranged "A Swiss Air." L. Meigmen arranged an Alpine March which was published as no. 62 of *The Euterpeiad*. A series of Tyrolean and Hungarian waltzes arranged as instrumental solos for guitar is in the Cole bound collection. Songs written in America by European residents included "Woodman, Spare That Tree" by Henry Russell. Native Americans contributed songs of sentiment and religion: "Look on

JENNY LIND

Jenny Lind and her songs were known throughout Florida, as they were elsewhere in the nation. The Swedish author Fredrika Bremer visited Florida, where she read newspaper accounts of the talented singer and discussed Lind's vocal merits with the Frenchmen who awaited her appearance in new Orleans. (Courtesy Florida State University Music Library)

the Bright Side" and "Mary of the Glen" (George T. Root) and "Take Me Home to Die" (I. B. Woodbury). From the minstrel shows came Stephen Foster's "Old Folks at Home" and "Poor Robin's Growing Old" from Wood's Minstrels. "Wood Up" was an American novelty referring to the taking on of wood for fuel on steamboats. It was popular enough to be included in a piano collection arranged by J. Holloway with the subtitle *Mississippi Quickstep* and in the guitar collection arranged by Blanchor and published by G. E. Blake of Philadelphia.

Pensacolans sang some of the art songs that have remained in the repertory into the twentieth century, if one is to judge from the surviving sheet collections. Franz Schubert's "Serenade," Franz Abt's "Schlaf wohl, du süsser Engel du" (Dear angel! Sleep thee well), op. 213, and Robert Franz's "Er ist gekommen" (Fondly he sought me) are three songs that did continue in the active repertory. The collections have fewer arias or vocal ensemble selections than might be expected from a public that attended music drama performances and that was awash in piano elaborations on a great number of operatic themes played in the home. Arias from operas by Auber, Donizetti, Herold, Bellini, and Balfe appear but not with the frequency of the ballads and popular songs.

Henry Russell provided the richest song literature for West Florida, as he did for other settlements of the young nation in the 1830s and 1840s. Russell was a British baritone who came to Rochester, New York, as a young organist for the First Presbyterian Church, but he soon established himself as an appealing singer and most of all as a composer of songs that were sung throughout the land. Pensacolans sang his two hit songs of 1838, "A Life on the Ocean Wave" and "The Ivy Green." After 1841 they sang his "Our Native Song," subtitled "A National Refrain." "Woodman, Spare That Tree," his most famous song, appeared with guitar accompaniment. These songs sustained Russell's popularity, even after he returned to England. Pensacolans sang them and his sentimental ballads "Return to Me Again" and "The Mother Who Hath a Child at Sea."

The words of Thomas Moore's poems were perennial favorites of parlor singers. Most favored was, here as elsewhere, "Oft in the Stilly Night," a longing for boyhood days, remembering the happiness of youth before one was aware of the threat of death. "Rose of the Desert" and "If I Speak to Thee in Friendship's Name" were sung with accompaniment by guitar or piano. From Moore's *Sacred Melodies* was "There's Nothing True but Heaven," set to music by the blind American organist-composer Oliver

Shaw. Two ballads represented the Irish heritage and their strong attachment to their mother country: "Erin Weeps Forsaken," words by Wordsworth and music by J. G. Maeder; and "Lament of the Irish Immigrant," by William R. Dempster. A copy of the latter carried the notation: "Portraying the feelings of an Irish peasant previous to his leaving home, calling up the scenes of his youth under the painful reflection of having buried his wife and child, and what his feelings will be in America." Dempster's talent was equally available to the Scottish when he set a C. H. Waterman ballad, "I Canna Lv'e Him Less." An even more popular song was Robert Burns's poem "Highland Mary," arranged by S. Nelson.

Talented young sailors stationed at the naval base composed and performed music while in Pensacola. Among the most gifted was James C. Drake, who wrote lyrics for his songs that were first sung in Florida and later published in Philadelphia and Baltimore.

John Hill Hewitt, later to be called the bard of the Confederacy, was represented by three songs, all composed in the 1830s and 1840s. "The Mountain Bugle" and "The Alpine Horn" were based on keyed bugle calls, a favored compositional device of Hewitt. These songs were published in Baltimore and New York, and the former became one of Hewitt's most popular. Published also in Baltimore, but undated, was a ballad poem by Hewitt set to music by W. C. Peters, "Sing and Remember Me." Three very popular British songwriters are represented by "Beautiful Venice" (Joseph Knight), "They Have Given Thee to Another" (Henry R. Bishop), and "The Blighted Flower" (M. W. Balfe). Bishop's famous "Oh No, We Never Mention Her" appears both in a vocal edition and in a set of piano variations.

The music of popular touring groups of singers was included in family libraries. The Hutchinson family was represented by "The Old Granite State," "The Grave of Bonaparte," and "The Humbug'd Husband." In the first number Judson, Abby, John, and Asa Hutchinson tell the story of the family of thirteen sons and daughters. They sing their names and declare themselves to be Yankee teetotalers all, for liberty, against oppression, and for emancipation and equal rights. The Rainer Family, the Swiss singing group, was known through the celebrated "The Alpine Horn" ("The Sailor Boy's Carol").

Comic songs relieved the heavy sentiment of some of the parlor ballads. Written by George Washington Eggleso, one was dedicated to and sung by Miss Julia W. Pomeroy of New York, with the greatest demonstrations of approbation on the occasion of her debut at the Apollo Saloon in 1843. It was titled "I've No Heart for the Men." The text declared:

No [six times], I never will marry,
I'd rather live single by far
For in men you can find but deceivers
And some very wicked there are
I am at present so happy,
I know such thing as allow,

Sweet Florida Good Bye

J. G. Drake

Sweet Flor - i - da good bye to thee, Thou land of sun and flow ers._____ Where gen' - rous hearts, and

Composer, poet, actor, and lawyer James C. Drake wrote songs of sentiment and the sea that were published in Philadelphia and Baltimore between 1825 and 1850. This one was written while he was a sailor at Pensacola naval base. (Courtesy Library of Congress)

take the off'-ring of my heart, Sweet Flor - i - da good

bye,_____ Sweet Flor - i - da good bye,_____ Sweet

Flor - i - da good bye.

So why should I e'en with a husband,
Share any part of my joy.

No [six times], I never will marry.
Though wives are so happy they say.
It may be so in the first part
But not through the whole of the play
I know nothing of cupid so pretty
With his wings, fine figure and dart
But I know that he'll be very clever
If he gets any share of my heart.
No [six times].

Author Thomas C. DeLeon, who visited Pensacola, assessed the state of music there and in the South generally at the beginning of the Civil War.

In art and his twin sister, music, the South displayed taste and progress truly remarkable in view of the absorbing nature of her duties. Like all inhabitants of semitropical climes, there had ever been shown by her people natural love and aptitude for melody. While this natural taste was wholly uncultivated—venting largely in plantation songs of the Negroes—in districts where the music-master was necessarily abroad, it had reached high development in several of the large cities. Few of these were large enough, or wealthy enough, to support good operas, which the wealth of the North frequently lured to itself; but it may be recalled that New Orleans was genuinely enjoying opera, as a necessary of life, long before New York deemed it essential to study bad translations of librettos, in warmly packed congregations of thousands.[28]

He also commented on "considerable latent music among their amateurs; happily not then brought to the surface by the fierce friction of poverty." The cities of Pensacola, Tallahassee, Jacksonville, St. Augustine, and Tampa had populations of less than ten thousand at the outset of the Civil War and thus lacked the resources for large-scale music productions. In each of them, however, were individual performers who had well-developed technique and taste, if one is to judge by the music libraries they left.

Among the distinguished citizens or descendants of illustrious Americans who came to Middle Florida in the first half of the nineteenth century were Francis W. Eppes, Thomas Jefferson's grandson; Catherine Daingerfield Willis, George Washington's great-grandniece; Dr. Thomas Y. Henry, Patrick Henry's grandson; Laura Wirt Randall and Elizabeth Goldsborough, daughters of William Wirt, U.S. attorney general under Presidents James Monroe and John Quincy Adams; and Augustus Brevoort Woodward, the first superior court judge, who was a founder of the University of Michigan and a city planner of both Detroit and Ypsilanti, Michigan.[29]

Social life in Tallahassee during territorial and early statehood days revolved around the large plantations: Waukeenah, home of John Gamble; Lipona (anagram of Napoli), home of Achille Murat; Belmont, home of Thomas Randall; El Destino, home of the Nuttal family; and Casa Bianca, home of Joseph White. Merriment rather than formality was the order of the day. Mrs. "Florida" White, wife of Joseph, was the most beautiful woman, Achille Murat the most interesting eccentric. Horse racing was the most popular sport. Dinners and balls were the usual diversions at plantation homes and at the City Hotel, Florida Hotel, and Washington Hall. Dancing school and concerts were given in the Hall of Representatives in the state capital. Music, formal or folk, was omnipresent.

The style of the English country gentleman and that of the Virginia planter prevailed in Middle Florida during territorial days, and vestiges of it have continued to our own time in the group referred to as the plantation set. Weekend parties or visits were favorite diversions among plantation families. Outdoor recreations such as picnics, horseback riding, and beach parties at the coast were popular, as were tournaments, horse racing, and May Day parties.

The profits from cotton raising brought to plantation owners sufficient money to develop their local social life and travel to centers of recreation and culture. The enrichment and sophistication of their own social resources came first. One historian, writing of the 1840–60 period, commented, "Perhaps no part of Georgia or Carolina presented a more compact, intelligent, and prosperous body of people than middle Florida at this early day."[30]

Sir Walter Scott's Waverly novels and *Ivanhoe* inspired Florida residents to enact ring tournaments in Tallahassee, Quincy, Monticello, Madison, Ocala, Bartow, and Fort Myers in the years between 1840 and 1890. The earliest was organized in Tallahassee, the others after the Civil War. Horsemanship became the essential element of an outdoor/indoor social celebration of gallantry and sentiment in a historical setting. The young knights took their names from the characters in novels and poems by Scott, Spencer, Tennyson, Cervantes, or others. The event opened with an oration on chivalry and a charge to the knights. Then came the contest, announcement of winners, and a crowning ceremony. A fancy costume ball or concert at city hall closed the tournament. Knights arrived at the ball in their tournament costumes. Ladies came as Titania, Undine, Daughter of the Regiment, Folly, Cupid, Diana, or another favorite character. The ball began with a grand procession of knights and ladies, led by the queen of love and beauty. After the promenade, the queen and her knight, from a flower-decked throne, reigned over the ball and a festive dinner.[31] Negro fiddlers and small instrumental combinations furnished music for the well-regulated dances.

Two French gentlemen added a special panache to Tallahassee society: Prince Achille Murat, son of the king of Naples and Napoleon Bonaparte's youngest sister, and Count de Courcy, a French exile who had served Napoleon in Russia. The two men relived the French Revolution at Lipona, Murat's plantation, and there enthusiastically sang the "Marseillaise." Achille Murat was crown prince of Naples. He came to the United States in 1821 at the age of twenty-two and was encouraged by Richard K. Call to settle in Florida. En route, Achille Murat had visited his first cousin Jerome Bonaparte in Baltimore and his uncle Joseph Bonaparte, whose estate, Point Breeze, was on the Delaware River. One of Joseph's neighbors was Thomas Paine, author of *Common Sense* and *The Rights of Man*. Another was Joseph Hopkinson, the Philadelphia who wrote "Hail Columbia." Hopkinson introduced Prince Murat to Peter S. Duponcean, a music patron and native of France.[32] In 1826, after he had arrived in Tallahassee, Murat met and married Catherine Daingerfield Willis Gray, a young Virginia widow. He noted that the people of Florida had been conquered by the Spanish, French, and English and saw that their manners and customs reflected their countries of origin. He saw the people as "temperate, quiet and rather indolent, affectionate and friendly to each other and kind to their slaves." He observed that "dances, card parties, etc. were frequently indulged in, but never to excess." He thought the lively mixture of inhabitants in St. Augustine and Pensacola made those settlers more carefree than those of Tallahassee, who had come from American stock. Yet he believed that he would find Tallahassee's rational society to be

PRINCE ACHILLE MURAT

Achille Murat, crown prince of Naples and nephew of Napoleon Bonaparte, was a leading citizen of Tallahassee in the 1820s. (Courtesy Florida State Archives)

equally congenial. He predicted that in a few years the young capital city would "become a charming place of residence though . . . probably . . . never . . . a place of much commercial importance."[33]

In 1832 Prince Murat's *Esquisse morale et politique des États-Unis* was translated and published as *America and the Americans.*[34] In it the prince described a dilemma of Tallahassee social life and its resolution. In 1825 the town's leading men wished to organize a celebration of George Washington's birthday, and one man proposed a ball. The project was abandoned when it was determined that only three ladies of the town danced. Others must have learned the art during the year, since on the following February 22 the occasion was celebrated in style. The prince himself described the scene.

> The hall is brilliantly lit with tallow candles, while the ladies, however (God bless them), are as well dressed, and as beautiful, as any in New York. The planter had doffed his coarse leather hunting coat and substituted a handsome, fashionable blue dress coat in lieu thereof, which said coat he had worn in other times, and in another land, while perchance gallantly playing the Lothario, or that nondescript, a "gay deceiver." His manners, however, are those of the best society. The want of a Strauss band, and somewhat discordant harmony of the ebony orchestra, add much to the evening's entertainment, and serve to create and keep up dancing, good fellowship, and that true hilarity which springs from the heart—until they come to the determined resolution of not going home "till morning." We will say nothing about champagne headaches, vows, broken promises, hearts, etc.[35]

An editorial in the local newspaper reported that this ball was attended by

> all the beauty of this infant Metropolis, which with the gentlemen comprising the assembly were concentrated from more than half the states of the Union, yet all, with the utmost cordiality and harmony, united in the festive scene. In the mazy dance or the social coterie, all were gay and happy. Among the company we were much gratified to meet with Col. Achilles Murat, who like his illustrious countryman *Lafayette,* has abandoned princely titles and with that suavity of manners peculiar to his nation, mingles in the society of the plain re-

publicans, with as much apparent pleasure as tho' he was an entire stranger to the splendor of an Imperial court.[36]

Whatever the social occasion, it usually ended with a dance. Beginning in 1827, Prince Murat and his lady entertained the neighborhood with a large Christmas party. For a dance at Robert Gamble's Welaunee Plantation, the prince brought his Negro violinist to furnish the music. The Murats and the Richard Keith Calls attended a dinner party at Belmont, the plantation home of Judge and Mrs. Thomas Randall in 1828. The hostess wrote in a letter to her mother that the guests had later "danced, waltzed and looked at books." Douglass Voss sang a song; Laura Randall played her guitar. A Negro-style jig was danced by Edmund Voss, Dr. Lacy, and Mrs. Call.[37]

The imminent departure of Prince Murat and his lady for France in 1830 was the occasion for an elegant ball organized by ten of Tallahassee's most distinguished citizens, including Richard Keith Call, as a way of expressing their esteem. It was held at the Planter's Hotel. The decorations and transparencies made suitable references to those "two events most auspicious to liberty, the American and late French Revolution." The report of the ball was that one "could hardly believe in the reality of what he saw or reconcile the presence of so many sylph-like forms, floating through the mazy dance to the wild and thrilling airs of Castaly." The prince was pleased with his dearly beloved friends and the delightful society and declared that he should never forget the strong feelings which his years in Tallahassee excited. He hoped to return, and he did.[38]

One person who undoubtedly contributed to the success of the social seasons of the 1830s into the 1850s was a Mr. Tarteen who lived at a local hotel and gave dancing lessons there. He was the first to teach the Spanish dance to the young ladies of the community and one of the first to teach the waltz. Mildred and Lizzie Brown, daughters of Thomas Brown, who was governor of Florida from 1849 to 1853, were two of his star pupils. Lizzie wrote, "Waltzing was not allowed in the United States. We danced the Spanish dance and waltz long before it was allowed in America." By the prosperous 1850s, Tallahassee had an academy "for instruction in the elegant art of dancing." The dances that were taught included lancers, quadrilles, caledonias, mazurkas, la gallopade, Spanish dancing, the polka, and the popular waltz.[39] A Mr. Rasimi, from the Academies of London and Paris, announced that he would teach these same dances at a dancing academy he proposed to open on about December 1, 1850. The academy opened at the City Hotel as scheduled. There were classes for juveniles morning and night. Gentlemen were taught in night classes.[40]

Achille Murat was present when the waltz was first introduced on the stage in New York. He thought its reception created an uproar equal to a *musard carnaval bal inferno* in Paris. He wrote, "From the moment of its introduction the waltz was looked upon as most indelicate, and in fact, an outrage on female delicacy. Even preachers denounced in public the circumstance of a man who was neither lover nor husband, encircling the waist, and whirling a lady about in his arms, as an heinous sin and an abomination. . . . They had yet to learn and admire and appreciate the gracefulness and voluptuous ease of a Taglioni, Cerito and Fanny Elssler."[41]

Members of the legislature spent most of the winter in Tallahassee. They came from all parts of the state and brought their wives, daughters, and young men with them. They were welcomed by a grand ball and, as a farewell, reciprocated in kind. Lizzie observed, "It was a gay time then."[42]

At his Lake Jackson home, near Tallahassee, Col. Robert Butler, adjutant to Gen. Andrew Jackson, was host at an annual "feast of roses," a combined garden show, ball, and midnight feast for the plantation set. Fiddlers and banjo players furnished music for reels and breakdowns. "Polly Put the Kettle On" and "Leather Breeches" were favorites. At supper there were toasts and songs. The colonel sang "Jock O'Hazeldean" and "My Boy Tammy," then recited his original poetry. Others followed with their stories and songs.[43]

The dance that climaxed the season of horse racing in Tallahassee was usually held at the City Hotel. The hall was decorated with evergreens, and committee members wore jockey-club badges. Ladies from Virginia, Georgia, and the Carolinas attended. Married or single, they understood that flirtation was allowed. The most popular dance was called Spanish. "The Spanish dance is peculiar to Florida. It is a gliding, swinging movement, particularly adapted to display of graceful action, but as intricate to me in its evolutions, as the labyrinth of Ariadne to her pursuers; but they dance it well here, and it is beautiful," Ellen Call Long wrote. The local newspaper was equally approving, as it had been throughout the decade of the 1830s. "Heigh for the races during the day and hurrah for the concert or ball at night."[44] The Marion course had begun as a recreation for gentlemen but later deteriorated into a public nuisance, a hotbed of vice. With the loss of decency and good order, the races were discontinued.[45]

Fanny Elssler
in the Character of

LA CACHUCHA

ATWILL Publisher 201 Broadway NEWYORK

"LA CACHUCHA"
Prince Achille Murat observed that Americans had to learn to appreciate the grace and voluptuous appeal of Fanny Elssler and other stage dancers. Florida pianists eagerly purchased sheet music of their dances. (Courtesy Florida State University Music Library)

Wirtland, residence of a Jefferson County plantation family, was the site of an alfresco entertainment which began with tea around a bonfire of pine knots, followed by a roasted ox dinner and a full-scale production of Shakespeare's *Merchant of Venice,* with a local cast. The evening ended at about midnight when Miss Catherine Wirt "threw a blue ribbon over her neck, which supported a guitar, and to its accompaniment sang sweetly, 'The stars are in the quiet skies.' Mr. Voss, a widowed sister, and Mrs. Wirt harmonized."[46] Texts of sentimental songs such as these the Wirt family sang were often reprinted in Florida newspapers, just as they were in the *New York Mirror.* Three popular ones of the 1830s appeared in the *Tallahassee Floridian and Advocate:* "The Harper's Song," "The Merry Mountain Horn," and "First Love."

The flowering of the azaleas and dogwood trees in Tallahassee prompted celebrations on the arrival of spring. The tradition of a May Party is believed to have begun in 1833, but the earliest records are for 1838. The party was held annually, excepting wartime hiatus, until the 1960s. In the early years it was held in the evening in the courthouse, or capitol. Later it was enacted on the green under the ancient live oak trees of Lewis Park in the center of town. A colorful early account of the event in a local newspaper is that of the *Floridian* dated May 6, 1848. The reporter was a participant in the event, and the style of his language communicates the sentiment of the day. He averred that there was no essential change in the ceremony from the days of the Tudors and Plantagenets. Vocal and instrumental music enhanced the spectacle of the costumed youth as they stepped through their procession, read their poetry, and danced their dances. The queen's speech was a plea for "the elevation of her sex." She asked for an open field and fair play for the exercise of their talents. When she asked that men rule by sentiment and govern by love, "the whole house rang with acclamations of applause, and resounded in sentiments of devoted loyalty." The queen led off the cotillion with the reporter, "showing that she could spin a waltz and run the gallopade with the same ease and grace that she could rule an empire." Revelers retired to another wing of the capitol for "the richest of viands, creams, curds and strawberries." The party ended at three o'clock in the morning.[47]

In the summertime affluent Tallahasseeans, with their servants, took refuge from the heat at resorts in cooler climates: the Green Briar in White Sulphur Springs, Virginia, and Shock Springs. After the yellow fever epidemic of 1841, Bel Air, a small town three miles south of Tallahassee, became a health resort. Families spent three or four months a year there camping in the pine woods. Bel Air became a social center of "evening rambles, bees, teas, and tableaux-cards, lunch and music." In a poetic description of *Mes amis* at the resort, one young lady was said to have "grown musical lately." Her anonymous critic wrote, "She warbles and quavers like a Sontag or Grisi."[48]

Near Tallahassee was Newport, Florida. On the St. Marks River near the Gulf of Mexico, it also became a resort where society folk gathered to vacation and bathe in the mineral springs in the 1840s. They read in their newspaper of the marriage of Jenny Lind to an English gentleman, but the local social events were reported at greater length and in grander language. The editor was confident "that even the far-famed Saratoga could not exhibit more intellectual graces, or a higher degree of elegant recreation and moral refinement than the events of the Newport week." He wrote that the poetic idea of "a feast of reason and a flow of the soul" had been fully realized by a dance, a promenade, guitar music, and conversation. Three guitarists entertained the company after a dance at the Wakulla Hotel. One of them played "Tink, Tank, Sadi, Listen to Your Spanish Lady, Tink, Tank, Ting." Silvia, "the Ole Bull of Tallahassee," and Tom, "the Manatee Paganini," were the popular violinists of the 1847 season.[49]

One visitor to Tallahassee wrote that there were splendid houses in the city, but he was astonished by what he saw in the country. He was struck by the incongruity of ill-constructed log cabins that were furnished with pianos, sofas, tables, rich sideboards, Turkish rugs, and cut glass. It seemed strange that the church was a windowless log cabin, but the simple weekday dresses of the ladies were replaced by rustling silk, gold watches, and spectacles. The servants who attended the gilt carriages were in livery.[50] If their settlement was remote, it was not devoid of music and other refinements. The point may be illustrated by looking into the musical interests of some of the men and their families who moved into the area.

One man who was destined to become a governor of Florida brought his family to the state to the accompaniment of music. Thomas Brown, disenchanted with his prospects in Virginia, left for Tallahassee in 1826. In 1827 he returned for his wife and six children. They formed a caravan with 20 young men, 144 Negroes, and ample equipment and began the overland trip. It took two months to reach Tallahassee, but the tedium of the leisurely trip was relieved by singing and dancing. Elizabeth ("Lizzie"), daughter of Thomas Brown, recalled, "There were violins, flutes, a French Horn, some fifes, a clarinet and any number of fiddles and this cacophony among the trees and bays must have startled wildlife in the extreme. . . . The sound of the French Horn was very cheery and bright. The mellow horn, I remember we called it."[51]

Among the Middle Florida plantation set, music had been especially woven into the fabric of one family. William Wirt of Baltimore, the family patriarch, was appointed U.S. attorney general by Pres. James Monroe. On special occasions, he told a good story and wrote political satire poetry, but it was music that consistently captivated his attention. He bought a large plantation in Jefferson County, near Tallahassee, which he gave to his children. Elizabeth, his second daughter, married Capt. Louis M. Goldsborough of the navy. On advice of the captain, the attorney general organized a communal settlement on his Florida plantations, a venture that Gov. Richard Keith Call approved. A group of 150 Pennsylvanians, all Protestants from Bavaria, signed a covenant to work the farms for a period of five years. Their children were to stay until they reached the age of twenty-one. They sailed on *The Laurel* from Baltimore, on the regular run to New Orleans. William Wirt devised this plan for the colony:

Their preacher, a Calvinist, will accompany them and is to be the schoolmaster for their children. They will form a fine little village in the settlement, with the gardens in the rear of their dwellings, a broad street between, and a church, schoolhouse and parsonage at one end. . . . Ought we not to have as many German primers and spelling books and psalters, as we have children to be taught? . . . I would suggest the propriety of doing everything for their recreations, that can be done compatibly with industry. I would even promote their festivity and enjoyment. I would ask them to give me a specimen of the rustic waltz of Germany, and encourage music, dancing and all innocent amusements . . . set some of them in their leisure to making Alp horns for your shepherds. . . . With abundance and peace, and the neighborhood of those good simple hearted creatures, with their German hymns and their church and school, their bands of instrumental music of a summer evening, their rosy-cheeked children and laughing faces blessing and blessed by them, I could not close my days more comfortably to myself than surrounded by them and my own family.[52]

Although the German emigrants broke their contracts and the experiment failed, members of the Wirt and Gamble families continued their Florida residency as well as their devotion to music through many generations.

To the western sector of the territory came new towns, new amusements, and music. Indians had been removed from the fertile regions of the rivers named Chattahoochee, Flint, and Apalachicola, and settlers moved in during the decade of the 1820s. A town was yet to be formed, but the site of Apalachicola as a busy port began in 1822 when 266 bales of cotton were shipped from it to New York on the brig *William and Jane.* Shipments increased from 317 bales in 1828 to 51,673 bales in 1836.[53] This growth in wealth and activity attracted migrants who could deal with the isolated existence. Some could not. Those who could were entertained by visiting theatrical companies who presented singers, dancers, and such dramatic fare as *London Assurance, The Loan of a Lover, Ali Pacha, The Hypocrite,* and *Rival Soldiers.*[54] In the quiet summertime, residents played whist and listened to the music of the local Aspaleggi Band serenades.

In the wintertime music was brought to the state by professional circus companies, beginning in 1831 when Dean's Grand Traveling Cosmorama visited Tallahassee. Handbills assured the public that good music would accompany the exhibitions of wild animals, equestrians, and the performer on "a musical organ." In 1833 Sizer's Circus came touting "a whole company of comic songs by the clowns," a comic duet "Polly Hopkins and Tommy Hopkins," sung by Mrs. Sizer and Mr. Gullen, and "a laughable scene of Billy Button's Unfortunate Journey to Brentford." Handbills advertised the appearance in 1834 of the Baltimore Menagerie and Circus. With them was the Baltimore Band of Music, which played waltzes, Scotch airs, duets, marches, and overtures. By 1849 Tallahassee attracted the Stone and McCollum's Leviathan Establishment, which had both a brass band and a string band. When the Spalding and Rogers Circus company paraded down Monroe Street in 1852, it was headed by a cornet band. The Great Southern Show of 1856 offered ballet dances, pantomime, and a comic afterpiece. Grand opera selections were played in 1859 by both the brass and string bands of the Robinson and Lakes Great Southern Menagerie and Circus.[55] Repertoire of these bands was wide enough to appeal to the whole community, but the off-duty behavior of some of the performers caused citizens to doubt the wisdom of return engagements. Yet, professional performers appeared too rarely to be taken for granted. Periodically, the folks decided to take the moral risk.

Among middle Florida residents who wrote of life in early statehood days was Charles A. Hentz, a medical doctor who played both the flute and E-flat alto horn. His principal residences were the Marianna and Quincy areas. Hentz's paternal grandfather emigrated from Koblenz to the United States and attended Harvard College. His maternal grandfather served as U.S. adjutant general in the American Revolution. Dr. Hentz came to Port Jackson, Florida, in 1848. The small settlement near Chattahoochee and Marianna had few diversions, but the young bachelor did attend what he termed a "genuine piney-woods shindig" soon after his arrival. The dancers responded to the fiddle with a Virginia reel, the men fired with whiskey. "It was," he wrote, "an entertainment intolerably distasteful to me."[56] On another occasion he complained of the villainous scraping of a fiddle which kept him awake in the middle of the night.

Much more to his taste was music he heard at Sibly's plantation, near Quincy, as ladies of the household played and sang. There was Eugenia Armistead, who was a professional harpist, billed as the Southern Jenny Lind. Betty Booth sang "Annie Laurie" and "Call Me Pet Names, Dearest." The hostess and her sister Callie struck Charles Hentz as "sweet Musicians." The young doctor also approved of the music at an evening entertainment given for him and his bride in 1854. A Dr. Telfair played the violin, and Henry Horn the violoncello. A few evenings later Hentz played his flute and Jesse Coe the piano while young ladies waltzed around the room. He wrote of the death of Patsy, a Negro servant, and the music in her memory, "The Negroes had the usual exercises of singing and prayer all night over her corpse."[57] The minister prayed that Patsy would walk the streets of the New Jerusalem with a golden harp in her mouth. The harps of angels in heaven to him were Jew's harps, the only kind of harps he had ever seen. In 1865 Professor Odens, a Quincy music teacher, kept his piano in Dr. Hentz's office and the following year opened a teaching studio. In that year, too, Professor Hennsher organized a Quincy brass band. A set of secondhand instruments was bought for twelve to fourteen players. In this ensemble Dr. Hentz played the E-flat horn. The band played in the upper piazza of the old Nathan's house on Saturday afternoons while women and children promenaded around the courthouse square.[58]

Singers who immigrated to Florida brought their own collections of vocal music. They came from from Washington, D.C., Baltimore, Buffalo, Philadelphia, Lexington, Cleveland, and other cities. Bringing their music to Florida was the first step necessary to absorbing both them and their music into the cultural heritage of the state. If they had a regional bias, it rarely showed in their choice of music.

Middle Florida owners of vocal albums preferred songs about love above all other subjects. The awakening of love was celebrated in "I Wonder If She Loves Me" (Samuel Carusi), rejected love in "I'll Hang My Harp on a Willow Tree" (W. Guernsey), and sadness at parting by "Silken Bands" (James Drake). Young ladies, their voices, and their eyes were the song subjects in "Sally in Our Alley" (Henry Carey), "The Voice of Her I Love" (John Perry), and "Blue Eyes" (James Malloy). Numerous other songs praised the beauty of young ladies, some nearby, others in distant lands. Mountains were the setting of many romantic encounters, as F. H. Brown's "Will You Come to My Mountain Home?" In more than one collection were such titles as "Let Us Love One Another" (W. R. Dempster), "They Told Me Not to Love Him" (E. Thomas), and "I Offer Thee This Hand of Mine" (L. T. Chadwick). The entire cycle of a sentimental lifetime was recalled in "She Wore a Wreath of Roses" (J. P. Knight). Couples seemed always to be parting but not wanting to in these songs: "Oh Must We Part Tonight?" (David Lee), "The Parting of the Sailor's Wife" (G. A. Godson), and "Goodby Sweetheart" (J. L. Hatton).

Sentiment lay heavily in lyrics of other songs on a variety of subjects. Mothers were favorite subjects, as "My Mother Dear" (S. Lover) and "Weep No More Sweet Mother" (J. M. Harris). Reminiscences of elderly people, places, and things were popular subjects: "My Boyhood Home" (W. M. Rooke), "The Auld Wife" (W. R. Dempster), "The Old English Gentleman," and "The Old Arm Chair" (H. Russell). Songs about home were popular, too: "Home, My Happy Home" (G. A. Hodson), "The Happy Home" (H. Herz), and "Be Kind to the Loved Ones at Home" (I. B. Woodbury). Pity, especially for children, was the subject of such songs as "The Orphan Ballad Singers" (H. Russell) and "The Blind Flower Girl" and "The Blind Boy" (W. R. Dempster).

A few songs were set in American locations, such as Henry Russell's "Rockaway," but many of them told of faraway places. The Tyrol had a special fascination in such songs as "Tell Me Not of Morning Breaking" (R. Andrews), "Ranz des vaches" (J. Metz), "There's No Home like My Own" (M. Malibran), and "The Blue Alsatian Mountains" (Stephen Adams). The exoticism of the American Indian appealed more to British composers and singers who could glorify the "Indian Hunter" (H. Russell) than to Americans, who still faced the prospect of being scalped—

though Indian maidens were subjects of both British and American songs. Exoticism extended to Hindu mothers, mysterious gypsies, and lunatics, all of whom were song subjects in the bound sheet music collections of Middle Florida.

Many of these songs became known to Floridians who attended out-of-state concerts by an impressive parade of European singers from the 1830s to the 1850s: Anna Bishop, Henry Russell, Maria Malibran, John Braham, Joseph Philip Knight, and Jenny Lind. Lind, who toured under the auspices of P. T. Barnum, sang such ballads as "My Home, My Happy Home" (G. A. Hodson) and "A Ride I Once Was Taking" (F. Kucken) and such operatic contrasts as an aria from *La figlia del reggimento* (G. Donizetti) and the scene and prayer from *Der Freischütz* (C. M. von Weber), all of which were in Florida music collections.

There were no works by native Florida composers among the collections. James Drake of Kentucky, Pennsylvania, and Maryland did write about Florida, composing love songs and ballads while living in Pensacola as a navy man. He is represented in the collections both as lyricist and composer. Among other American song composers having one or more works in the collections were Benjamin Carr, Thomas Bayly, John Hill Hewitt, James Pierpont, Stephen Collins Foster, George F. Root, and I. B. Woodbury. Several British composers who had immigrated to America in the 1830s and later are represented.

The only extended vocal work was the cantata *The May Queen*, with words by Tennyson and music by Dempster. Comic songs from old traditions were "The Nice Young Man," "Il Paddy Whack in Etalia," and "Polly Perkins of Paddington Hill." From the Americans were songs about the misfortune of having a musical family: "The Musical Wife" and "Musical Miseries."

One of the earliest collections, that of Ann Purvis, was formed largely of Scottish dance music. All of it was published in Edinburgh or London, and none bears a copyright date. The material was from the early years of the nineteenth century. The largest segment of the collection included the 106 dances in Nathaniel Gow's *Complete Repository of Original Scots Slow Strathspeys and Dances*. The publication *Clarke's Collection of Famous Airs* included waltzes, rondos, and variations on airs from Ireland, France, and Germany. The M. L. Weaver collection included dance music by Johann Strauss, Theodore Moelling, Maurice Strakosch, and Carl Bergmann, leader of the touring Germania Society. The Mary H. Haynes collection contained quadrilles by Henri Herz. The first collection of Susan Branch included the "Redowa Waltz" by F. Burgmuller, "Woronzow Waltzes" by Joseph Labitzsky, and P. K. Moran's "Saratoga March." Among dance music that received American titles were Louis Antoine Jullien's "Katydid Polka," W. V. Wallace's "World's Fair Polka," and Alfred Jaell's "Belles of Boston" galop. With even deeper American roots were dance transcriptions of the band tune "Wood Up" and the minstrel song "Lucy Long." The Mary H. Haynes collection included five stylized Elssler quadrilles, arranged by Charles Jarvis.

From the piano core literature were Beethoven's Sonata op. 78 and his Romance and Rondo for piano and violoncello, op. 69, in the collection of M. L. Weaver. Evelyn Byrd Cameron's collection had Beethoven's Sonata in C-sharp minor, op. 27, two Chopin nocturnes, and the waltz op. 64, no. 2.

No piano collection of the time was complete without fantasies and variations. Those in these collections are based on thematic material from operas: *Henry the Fourth* (J. P. E. Martini), *Fra Diavolo* (D. F. E. Auber), *Norma* (V. Bellini), *Il trovatore* and *La traviata* (G. Verdi), *Lucia di Lammermoor* (G. Donizetti), *Martha* (F. von Flotow), and *L'étoile du nord* (G. Meyerbeer). Based on national music was Beethoven's variations on "Rule Britannia." Based on popular songs were variations of "Home Sweet Home" and "The Last Rose of Summer" by Sigismond Thalberg, and of "The Mocking Bird" and "Auld Lang Syne" by E. Hoffman.

Descriptive pieces included "The Storm" (Henry Weber), "Whispering Wind" (H. A. Wollenhaupt), and a set of variations on Paganini's "Witches Dance" by W. V. Wallace. Ceremonial occasions were celebrated by pieces such as Charles Dupuis's divertimento "The Restoration of the Bourbons." Public interest in the opening of the American West was present in "Lake Erie Quickstep" (John Willis) and in "Louisville March" and "California March" (William Iucho). The military units and their officers were honored by a steady stream of marches and quicksteps.

The Middle Florida collections were short on standard art music for the piano. The bows to Chopin and Beethoven were hardly more than nods. The greatest number of pieces were for dancing: waltzes, polkas, and quadrilles. Quicksteps and marches were popular among the young military set. The slow old Scottish strathspeys held their own until Johann Strauss swept the field with his irresistible Viennese waltzes. Pianists demonstrated their virtuosity in show pieces about witches, storms, and battles. They recreated the high drama of opera by purloining themes from works that few of them ever saw in complete performance. They played pieces about places that few of them would ever see, but their imagination and skill brought fantasies for all in Monticello, Quincy, and Tallahassee. For a few moments they transported their audiences to faraway places where strange or exciting events kept them in thrall.

Some of the most detailed descriptions of social life among plantation families living near Tallahassee were written by Susan Bradford Eppes in her book *Through Some Eventful Years*. The heavily scented romantic style, the strong southern bias, and even several inaccuracies of fact diminish the value of the document as literature or history but do not lessen its impact as a primary source, written by a young lady who lived in the years of early statehood, the Civil War, and reconstruction. Her information, her attitudes, and her thoughts bring alive the events of the time and humanize them. The details of her comments on music events may be regarded as reliable. Susan Eppes, according to her own account, had less aptitude or skill in music than her sisters, but she did have competent music tutors and a keen sense of observation. Music served her less as an art than as an adjunct to dancing or as entertainment to relieve the tedium of plantation life. She told more about music and attitudes toward music than any other Tallahassee writer in antebellum and Civil War days.

Susan Branch Bradford was born on March 8, 1846, at Pine Hill Plantation, north of Tallahassee. Dr. Edward Bradford, her father, had moved to Leon County from North Carolina. His brother Richard owned nearby Water Oak Plantation; Thomas, another brother, owned Walnut Hill. Susan's mother was Martha Lewis Branch, daughter of John Branch, last territorial governor of Florida, who lived at Live Oak and Waverly plantations. Her father served as North Carolina's governor and U.S. senator as well as secretary of the navy in Andrew Jackson's administration.

Susan and her siblings were educated by a series of governesses. One was particularly noteworthy in music, according to Susan. She was Letitia Hannah Damer, an English lady who came to Pine Hill when Susan was eleven. "She dances beautifully and sings gloriously. . . . I told her how I lived to hear her sing and she said she had studied music for the stage but her people would not hear of it," Susan wrote.[59] "We have a large blackboard on an easel with a musical score, as well as other things. We all study music and the music master comes out from Tallahassee. That gives Miss Damer time to play and sing for us," she continued. Susan regarded her sister Mart as a wonderful performer and cousin Lize as the next best musician. Her sister Mag was a singer. Governess Damer told the girls that she was King George IV's granddaughter by Mrs. Maria Fitzher-bert. Her claim assumed a degree of credibility when at the end of a year a London barrister appeared at Pine Hill and presented papers that con-firmed the allegation of her tutor, according to Susan. Miss Damer was told that she had inherited a great fortune and left for London with the barrister as her escort. Historians have been unable to confirm or deny the romantic story.

The last northern governess at Pine Hill was a gifted musician and a mathematician but had no other requisites for her position. She was Cor-nelia Platt from Rhinebeck, New York, and soon after her arrival in November 1859, she and her charges "scrapped openly." A few days later she admitted that she had taken the position only to ferment discontent among the slaves and to organize them in support of the cause of aboli-tion. If she had chosen her employer with greater care, she might have succeeded in her mission, but the Bradfords did not share Richard Keith Call's benign position on Negro rights. Miss Platt was sacked and escorted to Tallahassee, where she left posthaste for New York.

The affair of Miss Platt might also have taken a different turn if Susan's mother had made the decision. "Mother does not approve of slavery—she would be glad not to own a single slave . . . and wishes to see them all freed and sent to Liberia," wrote Susan. It was a song that Susan sang for her father and his response in 1858 that awakened her to the slavery issue. She sang these lines:

> Oh, perish the heart and the land
> That would mar our motto of
> Many in one.

Her father replied, "'Take care, my baby, you may be calling down con-demnation on your own.' Of course I wanted to know what he meant, for 'E Pluribus Unum' had seemed a beautiful sentiment to me. Then father explained what he meant, [and] for the first time I heard of the strong, deep feeling of dislike and mistrust, which existed between the North and the South. For the first time the dreaded abolitionists took a tangible form."[60]

The issue had been brought to Susan's attention a year earlier by discus-sions of the thirteenth edition of Harriet Beecher Stowe's novel *Uncle*

Tom's Cabin and by a piano tuner at Governor Branch's house, who played the latest hit song about a Negro who went to New York in search of Mrs. Stowe, only to find that she was in England.

> I went to New York City a month or two ago,
> A-huntin' fur dat lady Aunt Harriet Beecher Stowe,
> I seed de abolitions, dey sed she'd gone away,
> Day tole me in de city dere warn't no place to stay.
> Oh, oh, oh, Aunt Harriet Beecher Stowe,
> How could you leab de country an' serve pore Niggah so?

Of the Negro songs reported by Eppes, only one was a spiritual. On summer vacation she heard a North Carolina ferryman sing:

> Jesus wept, and well he might,
> To see the sinner take his flight.[61]

Incendiary lyrics of the songs and poetry from both northern and southern sources stirred Susan's passion, but she did not view the struggle as a religious war. She was a partisan southerner and was apprehensive as the boys from neighboring plantations marched away singing "The Girl I Left behind Me."[62] The declaration of war was a blow to her patriotism, but she believed none of the lies of both sides of the slavery question. In Tallahassee on the July Fourth before Florida seceded from the Union, Susan attended the customary celebration of her country's birth. Her brother Amos paraded with the Governor's Guards. Her pride in him and in the country's flag caused her to write:

> [The guards] have handsome blue uniforms and a brass band to play for them to march. It is a cavalry company and all have fine horses; it is needless to say they make a splendid appearance. The color-bearer carried a large silk flag and I was so proud of "The Star Spangled Banner." Francis Scott Key, who wrote that beautiful song, was a friend of Grandpa's [John Branch] and sent him one of the very first copies ever printed; it is bound in Mother's music book, and she is so proud of it. Today when the company paraded, the band played "Hail Columbia" first but the crowd clamored for "The Star Spangled Banner," showing which they loved best. After the parade there was a picnic dinner and a dance on a platform built for the occasion.[63]

Social occasions with music were not rare in the affluent 1850s, when cotton brought fortunes to the planters. There was music and dancing at sister Mag's wedding, as well as a dress imported from Paris and ample champagne. In a poem titled "Christmas Eve at Pine Hill Plantation," Susan described the music festivities for that holiday.

> Mother's music fills the air,
> Perfect in time and measure,
> The floors are cleared and everything
> Awaits the dancer's pleasure;
> The boys all seek their partners
> When the rhythmic sounds they hear,
> Each couple turn with one accord
> And dance to the tune of "The Forked Deer."
>
> Both "North" and "South Carolina"
> Are danced with Christmas glee,
> Then "Molly, Put the Kettle on
> And We'll All Take Tea;"
> "Fisher's Hornpipe" speeds our steps,
> Which makes it very handy
> To execute some brilliant stunts
> For "Yankee Doodle Dandy."
>
> Then come quadrilles, as stately
> As Grandmother's minuet'
> Next, like a crowd of children,
> We merrily dance the "Coquette."
> Tired, we stop for supper—
> So many good things to eat—
> But time is short, and most of us find
> We have little wings on our feet.
>
> Waltzing is not in favor here,
> Yet a venturesome lad and lassie
> Are circling smoothly around the room,
> To the strains of "Tallahassee."
> Mother's fingers again touch the keys,
> "Sir Roger de Coverley" rules the hour
> Young and old stand up on the floor,

BLIND TOM

Thomas Green Wiggins (Blind Tom), a celebrated Negro pianist, played several concerts in Tallahassee and Jacksonville. His repertory included works by Beethoven, Bach, and Mendelssohn, as well as fantasies on opera themes and his own compositions. His battle pieces were especially popular. (Courtesy Florida State Archives)

Moved by the music's compelling power,
For who of us all fatigue could feel
When Mother played the "Virginia Reel"?[64]

House parties with Negro servitors to take care of the guests were frequent. There was usually ample room to accommodate them in the main and guest houses. Dancing followed by conversation and informal singing was the usual entertainment. In the early years the music was sentimental love songs. In the years of the Civil War, the dances were for the soldiers from Camp Randolph, a military camp near Goodwood Plantation in Tallahassee. Bands played and Susan grew emotional when a Captain Oliver sang "Maryland, My Maryland."[65]

Blind Tom, a savant-syndrome Negro pianist, attracted most attention among visiting professional musicians. His 1864 performance of his own recreation of "The Battle of Manassas" Susan thought was stunning. One of the most moving concerts by local talent, assisted by others from Quincy and Monticello, was held in the capitol for the benefit of the Martha Reid Hospital in Richmond on April 6, 1864. Susan wrote of it: "Sister Mart was one of the star performers and there were a score of others. . . . Several gentlemen with fine voices offered their services and we had fine music, both vocal and instrumental. They sang operatic selections; they sang soft, plaintive Confederate songs; they sang the old-world ballads that everybody loves and they sang patriotic songs and wound up with 'Dixie,' sung by the entire assembly and followed by cheers so heartfelt as almost to shake the foundations of Florida's Capitol."[66]

Ellen Call Long, another Florida author, chronicled events of the same period. She chose a fictional form to tell of antebellum plantation life, but her characters were real. Some of her early episodes were reconstructed from fireside conversations with her father, Richard Keith Call, who had been a general in the Seminole Wars and twice governor of Florida. She was able to describe the New Orleans opera scene from her own experience, since she spent time in that city as a young girl with her grandparents. She returned to Tallahassee in 1843, a girl of seventeen who had lived for a time in Nashville and attended schools in Baltimore and Philadelphia. A year later she was married to a local lawyer and continued to live an active social life until she expired at the age of eighty in 1905. Even her fictional account gave her the chance to defend her father's position in strong support of staying in the Union while popular support was for secession. She also supported unpopular positions on race relations is-

Oliver Gallop

Thomas Green Wiggins

Recitals by Thomas Green Wiggins (Blind Tom), Negro piano prodigy, were applauded in Tallahassee and Jacksonville. "Oliver Gallop" was published in 1860 by P. H. Oliver and was Wiggins's first published composition. (Courtesy Florida State University Music Library)

sues. For these reasons, her book *Florida Breezes* was not commonly approved. The writing style, too, must be described as matter-of-fact, occasionally relieved by lively observations on events, social problems, political issues, and the human condition. Ellen Long was at the center of life among the plantation set for the last fifty years of the century. She was also a keen observer of life among the poor—the poverty-stricken settlers, the farmers, and the Negroes. She is one of few Floridians who wrote of these people in these years.

Among her own social set, dinner parties followed by dancing were the favorite recreations. Plantation families continued the customs of provincial Virginia society. As mint juleps enlivened the company, laughter and conversation gave way to toasts, "sentimental, patriotic and humorous," and then songs. Ellen observed the difference between entertainments at her father's plantation and that of Col. Robert Butler's, where the taste was egalitarian. According to Ellen, the colonel had been Andrew Jackson's adjutant at the battle of New Orleans and had acquired the general's respect for the common man and for his music. At one party at the colonel's mansion, a guest remarked, "That's good music, and none of your Italian stuff; give me 'Polly put the kettle on,' or 'Leather Breeches,' for a good 'break down.' Them fiddlers and the banjo, particular, were raised on this here plantation."[67] There was considerable economic and social distance between the well-to-do planter and the dirt farmers, but when it came to dance music, that distance closed. The banquet balls and feast of roses were better-organized affairs, and decorum was more strictly observed than at country hoedowns, but the folk-music repertory was essentially the same for both. English ancestors had set the precedent by dancing country dances and singing popular Scottish songs. Floridians continued the traditions at informal picnics and at dances. On two occasions the country fiddler was "old Fred," and the settings were old St. Marks and old St. Luis fort.[68]

For those who were tired of dancing or who objected to it on religious grounds, there was music, song, euchre, and whist. In the pages of Ellen Long's novel, a young major sang Thomas Moore's "O, 'Tis Sweet to Think," and an unnamed man sang "Alice Grey." Gov. William P. Duval sang "Highland Mary." On an afternoon at Springwood Plantation, "finally the conversation yielded to song, a guitar accompaniment directing a moving concert," just as on many similar occasions.[69]

On two occasions, Ellen Call Long attended annual sugar-boiling parties, which were usually attended by young people from the neighborhood and from nearby towns. Sugarcane was cut in mid-November, ground, then boiled until it became either syrup or sugar. During the grinding and boiling stages, neighbors gathered to drink the plain cane juice or the fermented juice called buck. The customary entertainment was play-party games and the singing of traditional songs. One of the oldest of the game-songs was:

> King William was King David's [or James's] Son:
> From the royal race he sprung
> Wore a star upon his breast
> That was called the star of rest.
>
> Go choose to the east; go choose to the west;
> Choose the one that you love best.
> If he's not here to take his part,
> Choose the next one to your heart.
>
> Down on this carpet you must kneel,
> As sure as the grass grows in the field.
> Salute your bride and kiss her sweet;
> Then you can rise upon your feet.[70]

King William was King James' Son

Traditional
Trans. by Leonard Deutsch
Folksongs of Florida

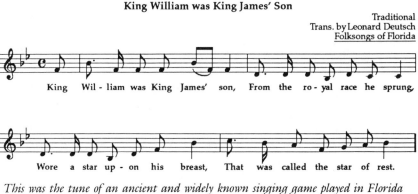

King Wil-liam was King James' son, From the ro-yal race he sprung,

Wore a star up-on his breast, That was called the star of rest.

This was the tune of an ancient and widely known singing game played in Florida well into the twentieth century. Singers did not always remember who was King William's father, but they seldom forgot the third verse, which was rewarded with a kiss. (Reprinted, by permission, from Alton C. Morris, Folksongs of Florida, *p. 222)*

Another popular tune with these young people are "Coffee Grows on White Oak Trees."

Music was placed in the service of Gen. Richard Keith Call when he held a political rally for Floridians "whose heart beat time to the music of the Union." It was an emotional final formal attempt to prevent Florida from withdrawing from the Union. There were eloquent speeches and solemn warnings, according to Ellen Long. "Twenty-three young and beautiful girls, representing the sisterhood of the States, made a pretty feature of the entertainment, and the loveliness and simplicity of dress well illustrated the purity of our country. They sang for the last time our national songs, 'Hail Columbia' and the 'Star Spangled Banner,' but we could sing no more and we hung our harps."[71] Neither words nor music could sort out slavery from the bigger issue of preserving the Union. Southern land would become useless without laborers, but war was declared and continued until the manhood of Florida had been squandered.

Social life in East Florida differed from that of Middle Florida because of its long history and rich cultural mix. In the early years visitors commented on the grace of Spanish dancers. Gen. James Grant wrote of the obsessive interest in dancing when the population was largely British. The

Greeks, Minorcans, Italians, British, and Spanish historically had differing customs and differing music, but a few of both were accepted by the community. Dancing to instrumental music or to songs was a strong tradition not limited to a single group or to a single time of year. Now, near the end of the second Spanish period, an anonymous visitor wrote that dancing continued to be a favorite amusement and balls were frequent.[72] He attended one and wrote, "The elder couples opened it with minuets, succeeded by the younger couples displaying their handsome light figures in Spanish dances.[73]

In 1821, at the beginning of territorial days, the local newspaper reported a splendid military ball. A change in political alignment did not change the taste in recreation.

> On Thursday evening last, a ball was given by the American Officers of this Garrison, and gentlemen now in this place, to the Spanish inhabitants. The old Government House was selected as the most suitable place. A suite of rooms on the second story was most splendidly decorated with the respective flags of the United States and Spain, and entwined with, and partly concealed by wreaths of laurel, vines, etc. with which the walls and ceiling of the room was likewise elegantly festooned—the whole having the effect of almost transporting the spectator, in imagination, to some enchanted grove, and giving the *tout ensemble* the appearance of a fairy scene. A cold collation, etc. was prepared for the gentlemen and the art of the pastry cook and confectioner were put in requisition for the ladies. We think there must have been a hundred ladies and gentlemen present, and a greater display of elegance and beauty on the part of the fair sex, has seldom been witnessed in this, and we may almost add, in any other place of equal population. Among the guests we notice his excellency Governor Coppinger, the Marquis de Fougere, French Consul of Charleston, and mayor of this city and several of the civil and military officers of the late government. Aurora had already gilded the eastern horizon ere the lingering votaries of the dance had retired.[74]

As an enhancement of the local passion, in 1823 a Mr. J. Suter, formerly of Charleston, advertised the cotillion parties would commence on the following Friday, November seventh evening, in the St. Augustine house occupied by Captain Darling. Gentlemen could procure tickets of admittance at the Exchange Coffee House. He announced that he was opening a dancing school with afternoon sessions, and evening, too, if there were sufficient subscribers.[75] Suter had announced earlier that he taught not only fashionable dances but small- and broadsword exercises and divisions of the cut and thrust. Several decades would pass before Florida outlawed dueling. There was no chance that dancing would suffer the same fate.

Jacob Rhett Motte, a Harvard-educated Charleston aristocrat, came to St. Augustine as an army surgeon during the Seminole Wars in 1836–38 and commented on the social scene. "We attended several parties during our short stay," he wrote. "The St. Augustine ladies certainly danced more gracefully, and kept better time than any of my fair country women I ever saw in our more northern cities. It was really delightful to see the lovely Minorcan girls move through their intricate waltz to the music of the violin and tambourine. The Spanish dance seemed deservedly to prevail over all others except the waltz; but it was a very different thing from that which is called the Spanish dance in our northern cities; here all was grace and ease, like the floating of down upon the breath of morning."[76] W. W. Marsh, another observer, agreed with this assessment fifteen years later when, after attending a dance, he wrote, "There were two quite pretty Minorcans there with deep dreamy, languishing eyes, fine form—grace, etc., but not remarkably handsome. They dance to kill and make the champagne fly."[77] William Tecumseh Sherman, as a young lieutenant, before his fame achieved during the Civil War, was stationed at nearby Picolata and came to St. Augustine for diversion. In a letter dated February 15, 1842, he wrote, "The inhabitants [of St. Augustine] still preserve the old ceremonies and festivals of old Spain. Balls, masquerades, etc. are celebrated during the gay season of the carnival (just over), and the most religious observant of Lent in public, whilst in private they can not refrain from dancing and merry making. Indeed, I never saw anything like it— dancing and nothing but dancing, but not such as you see in the north. Such ease and grace I never before beheld."[78]

During carnival season in 1825 the Minorcan ladies of St. Augustine continued their custom of arranging posey dances for eleven nights. The style of the custom was less formal than in Pensacola. A writer for *Knickerbocker Magazine,* a New York monthly magazine, described the setting and the social reasons for the posey dance.

> The *Minorcans,* who, to judge by their dwellings, we should take to be poor and miserable, are, on the contrary, in some cases rich and al-

La Linda

Arr. by Charles Zeuner
St. Augustine Spanish Dances

Many visitors to St. Augustine commented on the grace of the Spanish dances. Some of them composed their own dances and dedicated them to the sloe-eyed señoritas. (Courtesy St. Augustine Historical Society Library; reprinted from Don D. D. G., St. Augustine Spanish Dances, *arr. Charles Zeuner [New York: William Hall and Son, 1849])*

most always happy. From the doors whence we might expect nothing but misery to issue, well-dressed, innocent girls would come, and they are forever dancing. They seem to meet and have balls every night. In the carnival time, especially, (for if they are Catholics) they seem to go mad with mirth. Dancing and masquerading is the order of the day, while this season lasts. They go out into the streets, and enter every house, and turn all the furniture, where they find any, up side down, and do everything but real injury—and then, with all sorts of instruments, not forgetting the tin pan, depart in peace. Thus they keep it up. They have also what they call the *Posey dances,* which we think not so bad, and the trick might not be out of place in Gotham, in dragging many an old bachelor out of his shell of snapping turtle. It is this: Some lady—how the first one is chosen I know not—has a bouquet of flowers with which she dances, and she is considered the queen of the evening; but toward the last, she fixes her eye on some bachelor, and with a great deal of grace and archness offers the flowers. He knows what it means, and that he is bound in all gallantry to accept the gift, and make some other queen for some other evening, which his favorite may appoint. The wherewithal comes from the new king, of course. Thus is the ball kept up, and many are the sly tricks resorted to, to bring wary old rats into the trap. The graver they are, the more sport they make. They make it a point not to have them expensive, and there appears to be no difficulty to find some one always willing to accept the honor—but old bachelors or widowers are most desired. There is a great deal of primitive simplicity and poetry in the manners of these people, with which I was much pleased.[79]

Accounts of the carnival season were left by a London visitor, a local journalist, and a Minnesota Episcopal bishop. The London observer wrote of the street parades: "Masks, dominoes, harlequins, punchinellos, and a great variety of grotesque disguises, on horseback, in cars, gigs and on foot, paraded the streets with guitars, violins and other instruments; and in the evening the houses were open to receive masks, and balls were given in all directions. I was told that in their better days, when their pay was regularly remitted from Havana, these amusements were admirably conducted, and the rich dresses exhibited on these occasions, were not eclipsed by their most fashionable friends in Cuba, but poverty had lessened their spirit for enjoyment, as well as the means for procuring it; enough, however, remained to amuse an idle spectator."[80]

One local newspaper description caught the spirit of the celebration and named the dance figures. "It began about a week before the season of Lent, parties of maskers going out in the evening visiting from house to house. . . . These maskers were headed by a band of music, generally winding up the evening at some particular house where the hostess had gathered a goodly company for dancing with the maskers, the beautiful Spanish dances, now obsolete, with their many figures and slow rhythmic movements." The figures of these dances were "La angelita," "Las gracias," and "Follow My Love." The music of the dances had quaint names: "Buena maloja" (Good hay), "La coscooga" (The firefly), and "La dulci mulatto." "In the two days before Ash Wednesday carnival was at its height. In the day time, floats filled with gaily dressed girls were seen; *Diabolitos* with pointed caps and bells and long whips were running through the streets; men dressed in grotesque costumes in carts and on foot were in evidence everywhere, throwing confetti on all who came their way." Twenty or thirty people were in a carnival party, handsomely costumed.[81]

Masquerading which began during the Christmas holidays and continued until Lent was a new custom to the eyes, the ears, and the dignity of Bishop Henry B. Whipple, who visited St. Augustine in 1843–44. The serial entries in his diary attested to the very active social life of the old city and to the bishop's fascination with the costumed maskers. "These masquers select their own disguises and then visit from house to house acting their several parts. Sometimes the masquers send word to a gentleman that they will dance at his house in the evening and he provides the entertainment and they take their music with them. . . . Every evening there are several parties of these masquers who go from house to house."[82] The bishop's first visitors were three Minorcan girls disguised as old women who danced beautifully. Another group brought along their tambourine and violin and also danced to lively music. On the following evening an ancestor of Stephen Vincent Benét was disguised as a deaf and dumb man and his daughter as a country maid looking for a leap-year husband. They waltzed. Governor Duval then entertained with stories of his experiences. On the following evening three other groups appeared. A hideous Spanish brigand armed with knives, pistols, and a carbine was accompanied by a malicious but beautiful gypsy lady who played the guitar. They closed the masque by singing "The Brigand's Song" in Spanish. On the final evening two parties brought such disguises as a page, a Quaker, a drunkard, a Paul Pry, a Frenchman, a fruit woman, and a Negro who played the banjo. The best-acted part was the man (Mr. Fareira) who was dressed and painted as a Seminole warrior. (This was the era of the Second Seminole War.) He danced a war dance and whooped a war cry.

The bishop made several comments on the credibility and beauty of the disguises. He observed that this amusement was for common people, but he was clearly troubled that elite society of the town could unselfconsciously shelve their dignity and social standing by disguising themselves as Billy Bowlegs or an Indian squaw. He predicted that morality would be improved when this and other old Spanish customs gave way to American tastes and amusements. The Episcopal bishop from Minnesota found the flavor and customs of others equally exotic or sinful or both.[83] He believed that the Catholic church of St. Augustine was not vigilant enough in intervening in the customs of its people. "This is ever the case," he wrote, "with a religion based on the superstition of its people. On the contrary, a pure religion aims at cleansing all the fountains of pleasure as well as to cure the open evils of a community."[84]

Some of the earlier Catholic residents of St. Augustine believed that carnival season originally consisted of dignified, elegant parties and balls. It was the Anglos who later had added rowdy, drunken revels, they wrote. The Protestant Anglos countered that the antics of the maskers were unacceptable on religious grounds. Others objected because Negroes used the carnival as a way of joining social customs of the whites.[85]

The poet William Cullen Bryant visited St. Augustine in 1843 and described the culmination of carnival in the old city. He wrote:

> Some of the old customs which the Minorcans brought with them from their native country are still kept up. On the evening before Easter Sunday, about eleven o'clock, I heard the sound of a serenade in the streets. Going out, I found a party of young men, with instruments of music grouped about the window of one of the dwellings, singing a hymn in honor of the Virgin in the Mahonese dialect. They began, as I was told, with tapping on the shutter. An answering knock within had told them that their visit was welcome, and they immediately began the serenade. If no reply had been heard they would have passed on to another dwelling.[86]

Bryant transcribed and published in Catalan, in the Minorcan dialect, the Easter song "Fromajades" or "Fromajadas," which is still sung in the Minorcan towns of Ferreries, Villa-Carlos (El Castell), Migjorn Gran, and Sant Lluis.[87] The chorus is sometimes called "Deixem lo dol" and may be found with music notation in an island publication listed as *Goigs de Pasqua, Cango' de les formarjades,* "Deixem lo dol." The ending verse is listed as *Despedida.*[88] Bryant believed his version of the song to be the first printed, though he was not expert in the language and used an unskilled copyist. There are differences in his version and that of Jane Quinn, historian of the Florida Minorcans. She gives the texts of additional verses which enlarge the story of the resurrection. Texts of other verses are similar, differing largely in spelling of the dialect. Both versions have the final four lines, but the Quinn version contains an extra verse before them. Quinn gives both Spanish and English translations. Her English translation of the final lines is:

> This house is walled round
> Blessed be he who walled it.
> The owner of this house
> Ought to give us a token,
> Either a cake or a tart,
> We like anything,
> Which comes from this house,
> So say you not no.
> This house is walled round,
> Walled round on four sides.
> The owner of this house
> Is a polite gentleman.

The customary reward for serenaders was a cheese pastry. If none was given, the final line declared the host was no gentleman: "No es homo de compliment."[89] Bryant's version of the Easter song is in Appendix A.

Bishop Whipple's comments on other music that he heard on his trip to the southland were not confined to carnival celebrations. He heard music wherever he went and commented freely both on it and the people who made it—Irishmen, Negroes, military men, civilian voters, and the sinful French. Aboard a ship, about fifty Irishmen in bedtick breeches sang bold songs in free and cheerful voices and danced to the music of an old cracked flute. He heard Negroes on plantations between Savannah and St. Augustine who sang "Lucy Long" and "Jim Crow." Around the wharves in Mobile they sang "Old Dan Tucker" and "Yaller Gals." He wrote of New Orleans black men, "The Negroes on the levee are death on singing." He saw slaves for the first time on this trip and found them a great curiosity. He wrote, "The slaves seem well fed and are generally well clothed. They seem an idle and lazy race of beings and appear happy and contented. . . . The Negro is a bundle of oddities, of strange conceits and singular notions. He sometimes possesses some wit and humor, which is most usually exhibited in his songs. . . . If you did not know it you would never imagine they were slaves."

The bishop vacillated between pity for the slaves' condition and stereotypical unapproving prejudice against their behavior. His judgment of both blacks and whites rested on a strict moral code, which included no violations of the principle that Sunday must be kept a holy day. He did not object to the lively Christmas festivities of the Negroes on General Clinch's plantation on the Satilla River, where tambourine and fiddle provided music for a dance to 1843. He did not disapprove a Negro parade on December 27, when he heard the music of a band composed of "three fiddles, one tenor and one bass drum, two triangles and two tamborines, later augmented by two fifes." He reported the martial music of the Eighth Regiment band, heard early mornings and evenings in St. Augustine. When he visited Gen. William T. Worth there at the close of the Seminole War, he was less approving of the celebration on election day. Members of the winning party "had a glorification in the evening and marched through the streets singing and laughing, their music being diversified by the sound of a cracked tambourine." Music figured conspicuously on the bishop's list of evil pursuits he observed in New Orleans: French opera with ballet dancers, a masquerade ball, organ grinders playing on street corners, a pleasure party on a lake, the Kentucky minstrels, Irish harpers, Negroes singing, a military band on parade, and a fireman's parade with music. At least six of these were also Florida infractions.

Among the pianists and singers whose music was brought to St. Augustine in the first half of the nineteenth century were Maria Fullerton, Margaret Ash, Margaret Webb, Ella Duncan, Lucy Peck, and a Mrs. Smith, possibly Mrs. Hannah Smith, the wife of Josiah Smith and mother of historian and diplomat Buckingham Smith. Volumes of their sheet music collections have been preserved by the St. Augustine Historical Society and the Women's Exchange, administrators of the Dr. Seth

Fromajadas
Minorcan Folk Song

Transcribed by
Howard Manucy
L. Hosmer

Smith Peck House on St. George Street. These collections have served as primary sources of information about the music played, sung, and danced in the Ancient City from 1808 until the Civil War. Another source is a bound collection largely from the eighteenth-century English repertory, which was brought to the St. Johns River area no later than 1835.[90] There is no evidence that the book was brought to Florida by British subjects

who remained after the English hegemony, 1763–83. Its music, however, was popular in England during that period. Its chronological and geographical relationships are noteworthy, since this local source contained numerous songs that may have been known to the English-speaking population of Florida east coast settlers. The songs were certainly known to several generations of English people who settled in Charleston, Bal-

Minorcan youths went from house to house serenading on the eve of Easter by singing and playing the Fromajadas song, a custom they still continue. (Traditional; transcribed by Howard Manucy and L. Hosmer)

timore, Annapolis, Philadelphia, and New York at that time. The first 30 pages of the 190-page collection have been removed. The remaining pages contain songs from operas, ballad operas, pasticci, and plays and selections from popular song collections of the day. Of the sheet music collections examined for this study, this is the oldest.

The oldest music of the collection was composed in the waning years of the seventeenth century by Henry Purcell, thought by many to be England's greatest composer. Twelve songs were from the stage works of Thomas Arne. Three are from his English-style opera *Comus* and four from his Italian-style *Artaxerxes*. Others were from the pasticcio *Love in a Village* and from *Thomas and Sally*. Arne's son was represented by "This Cold Flinty Heart" from *Cymon*, a song that was sung earlier in Richmond by the Virginia Company (1790) and in Charleston by the West and Bignall Company (1798). William Shields's comic operas *Rosina* and *The*

Flitch of Bacon were sources of several comic songs. Six selections by Charles Dibdin were included, though none of them were the sea songs for which he was famed.

From other St. Augustine collections of the period were Scotch and Irish airs, canzonets, ballads, and English songs. Duets and trios were by Samuel Webbe, Mozart, and Haydn. Classic Italian song of the time was represented by a work from the Giovanni Paisiello corpus. Paisiello wrote more than one hundred operas for the courts of Napoleon I, Catherine the Great, Ferdinand IV, Joseph Bonaparte, and Joachim Murat, the king of Naples and father of Prince Achille Murat, who lived in St. Augustine and Tallahassee.

One collection was of music from the 1830s. It contained songs and dance music by American composers, published in America. Three very popular songs were included: "Pense à moi," by James Drake, who began his songwriting career while at the naval station in Pensacola and later continued it in Louisville and Baltimore; "Some Love to Roam o'er the Dark Sea Foam," composed by Henry Russell, the English ballad singer who came to America in the 1830s and lost no time becoming both the most celebrated composer and performer of the genre; and "Near the Lake Where Droops the Willow," a southern refrain composed by Charles E. Horn, then popularized by his wife. A hundred years later it would be revived in solo and choral versions by Aaron Copland. Three love-song ballads were issued by the publisher George Willig, Jr., in Baltimore in the mid-1830s: "They Told Me Not to Love Him," "O Why Hast Thou Taught Me to Love Thee?" and "Tell Him I Love Him Yet." Two-part songs were included. One was a German air "Am I Not Fondly Thy Own?" and the other a church anthem "Strike the Harp in Praise of God," composed by S. Nelson.

The piano music of this collection contained the march from "The Battle of Prague," written by Franz Kotzwara. Judged by musicians as banal in the extreme, the piece became popular on both sides of the Atlantic. Percy A. Scholes wrote of Mark Twain's reaction to hearing the piece played by an American young lady in Lucerne a hundred years after its publication: "She turned on all the horrors of *The Battle of Prague,* that venerable shivaree, and waded chin deep in the blood of the slain."[91] The battle music descriptive of Napoleon Bonaparte's career appealed to collectors. This collection included "Bonaparte's March Crossing the Rhine" and "Bonaparte's Retreat from Moscow." Several marches and quicksteps were included celebrating military units (cadets, cossacks, and the U.S. infantry). The cover page lithographs took as their subjects soldiers, swords, flags, cannon, trumpets, and drums.

The dance music for piano included four waltzes by Mozart, the waltz from Gioacchino Rossini's opera *La cenerentola,* the "Double Sliding Waltz" composed by J. Schell, and "The Hope Waltzes" as performed by the Prague Company. The set was completed with four waltzes by Johann Strauss. Five quadrilles from D. F. E. Auber's opera *Le Dieu et la bayadère* had not only the music score but also directions for dancing each of the sets. "La cachucha," a Spanish national dance in triple time, was arranged by F. Hunten.

In 1808 St. Augustine pianists played sonatas by Ignace Pleyel, Muzio Clementi, Sixtus Bachmann, and Henri Cramer, all in foreign editions. A few years later they played a four-hand version for piano of Franz Joseph Haydn's Symphony no. 12. From the opera repertory they played Rossini's overture to *Tancredi* and variations on "Fra tante angoscie" and "Non piu mesta" from the *La cenerentola.* Margaret Ash, collateral descendant of José Sánchez Ortigasa, lived in St. Augustine beginning in 1814. She played from Carl Maria von Weber's opera *Der Freischütz* the "Echo Waltz," the "Grand March," and the "Hunter's Chorus," all from domestic publishers.

On St. George Street Lucy Peck, daughter of a local medical doctor, played A. Diabelli's transcription of the *Der Freischütz* overture and Francis Adrien Boieldieu's overture to his *Calif of Bagdad,* and gems from Bellini's opera *Norma.* Ella Duncan, ancestor of the Van Campen family, played fantasies on such familiar operas as *Norma, Il trovatore, Oberon, La sonnambula, I puritani,* and *Faust.*

The craze for piano elaborations on opera themes, however, was not as virulent in St. Augustine as in Pensacola, where live performances of opera were more accessible. It did extend throughout the first half of the century, the late years being represented by H. A. Wollenhaupt's "Illustration [Variation] sur 'Le Brindisi' de l'opéra *Lucrezia Borgia,* op. 50." Thematic material was also chosen from other sources; a rondo by T. H. Butler was based on the popular air "Hearts of Oak," published in Edinburgh; one set of variations on "Auld Lang Syne" was by native son D. Ross of Edinburgh. Jean Tatton Latour's variations were on the French tune "La pipe de tabac," and his divertimento was on the well-known tune "The White Cockade"; L. Fischer's variations were on the German melody "Herz! Mein Herz." Then there were variations on "Home, Sweet

Home" and "Believe Me If All Those Endearing Young Charms," both arranged by Thomas Valentine and published in New York.

The songs preserved in sheet-music collections of St. Augustine reflect only a few segments of the national, ethnic, or religious heritage of the Ancient City. English, Irish, Scotch, and American songs dominate extant collections. Rossini, omnipresent in Pensacola collections, is represented in music surviving from St. Augustine by a sole entry, "Tu che accendi questo core," the recitative in *Tancredi* and the aria that follows, "Di tante palpiti." The English composer William Shield is represented by the popular ballad "My Heart with Love Is Beating" (reissue of "The Maid of Lodi") and an air from his opera *Rosina,* "Her Mouth Which a Smile." The latter had been sung in America since the 1780s, and both songs appeared in numerous American collections. From other dramatic productions were the Irish tenor Michael Kelly's "The Wife's Farewell" from *Of Age Tomorrow* and "The Mischievous Bee" from *Time's a Tell-Tale.*

Preference for Scottish tunes or the poetry of Robert Burns was shown in the thirty-six songs of a John Parry collection, in the John Ross setting of "The Heath This Night Must Be My Bed" from Walter Scott's *Lady of the Lake,* and the Robert Burns, "Oh My Love Is like the Red Red Rose" from *Rob Roy.* Three of the most popular songwriters of the day were included: John Braham ("Dulce Domum" from *Out of Place* and the dramatic *William Tell, the Swiss Patriot*), Henry Bishop ("The Dashing White Sergeant," "Home, Sweet Home," "Oh No I'll Never Mention Him," and "Cherry Ripe"), and John Stevenson ("Dearest Ellen," a ballad not quite so popular as his "Minstrel Boy," or "Believe Me If All Those Endearing Young Charms"). One brief, novel vocal selection is bound in the St. Augustine collections. No composer, lyricist, publisher, or a date is listed on the song titled "Crazy Jane." It was thought by Oscar Sonneck, music librarian of the Library of Congress, to have been published before 1800, but later research appears to have established 1800 as the date of the first American issue. The music is by Harriet Abrams, the words by G. M. Lewis. An 1804 edition bears this note: "The following was written in consequence of a lady having in her walks, during a residence in the country, met a poor mad woman, known by the above appellation, at whose appearance the lady was much alarmed." The tune was "Gin Ye Meet a Bonny Lassie." "Crazy Jane" appeared in many editions and collections around the turn of the century.

A humorous song in Lucy Peck's collection was "The Old Maid; or, When I Was a Girl of Eighteen." It was dedicated to an unnamed bachelor.

When I was a girl of eighteen years old
I was scornful as scornful could be
I was taught to expect wit, wisdom and gold,
and nothing less would do for me.

Her first suitor was too poor, the second a navy man with only one leg, the
third a judgmental lawyer, next a dandy who had only a gig; the man from
the South was too old, from the West (Tennessee) was badly dressed.
These were her last, for now she was forty-four, then fifty-three. Her final
advice to young ladies was not to be scornful lest they awake (as she) an
old maid of fifty-three.

The choruses of several songs were arranged for four voices. Among
those designed specifically for group singing are John Parry's *The
Cambrian Minstrel Boy*, dedicated to the noblemen and gentlemen of the
Cambrian Society, a group formed for the purpose of promoting Welsh
literature, poetry, and music. Four members of the Rainer Family (Mar-
garetta, Ellena, Lewis, and Semir) came to the United States in 1839.
They sang the songs of Switzerland in costume and actuated the fashion
for yodel-figured songs that swept the nation in their wake. Their performances are thought to have inspired the Hutchinson and other family
groups to prepare concerts and undertake tours. From the Hutchinson
Family repertory, Lucy Peck of St. Augustine and her friends sang "Cape
Anni," a unison work sung by J. I. Hutchinson, and the part-song "The
Grave of Bonaparte." The former was "a song about people who see the
same sight but identify it variously." The latter was a meditation on the fall
of a hero.

The concerts of the Hutchinson family were reported in Florida newspapers as early as 1848, but their crusades against whiskey and slavery were
not uniformly popular in the state. Parlor singers from Pensacola to St.
Augustine sang the partisan verses of the family repertory, even when their
sons and brothers were fighting Santa Anna in Texas and the Hutchinsons
were singing,

War and slavery perplex us
And ere long will surely vex us
Oh, we're paying dear for Texas
In the war with Mexico.

Such a demonstration
Is beneath our station

> When by arbitration
> We can settle every war.[92]

Another source for musicmaking in the home, at social occasions, or in solitude was the songster. These pocket-sized song collections usually contained the words only, though some had the tunes and a few had both the air and a bass. Illustrations were not uncommon. These were the popular songs of the day and reflected regional beliefs, taste, and biases. Some collections were put together for specific campaigns or purposes, and for them words were expressly written to be sung to familiar tunes. *The Republic Campaign Songster of 1856* was brought to St. Augustine. "Slavery is the great topic of interest from one end of the country to the other," it proclaimed. The small volume was dedicated to Col. J. C. Fremont, political leader of the Friends for Freedom, and espoused the antislavery movement and the temperance movement. It boldly called their leaders agitators and reformers and suited the verses to the causes. An earlier publication collected by an American officer was titled *The Rough and Ready Songster,* containing many verses written in commendation of Gen. Zachary Taylor. He was praised as a southern gentleman, as hero of the Florida Indian Wars and the Mexican campaigns by which Texas became "The Young Tree of Freedom." His Florida assignment was mentioned in the first song of the collection.

> I knew him first, the soldier said,
> Among the Everglades
> When we gave the savage red-skins
> Our bayonets and our blades.
> I think I hear his cheerful voice:
> "On column!" Steady! Steady
> So hardy and so prompt was he
> We called him *Rough and Ready.*[93]

Another verse, this one to the tune of "Dan Tucker," recalled:

> In eighteen twelve 'ganst twelve to one,
> He bravely saved Fort Harrison,
> And made Miami's red skins fly,
> From the lead of his guns, and the fire in his eye,
>   Hurrah, Hurrah. (repeat)

> At Florida in Thirty seven,
> With five hundred men—the foe eleven,
> He burnt "red alligators" Toby,
> And conquered Lake Okeechobee
>   Hurrah, Hurrah. (repeat)[94]

Then, to the tune of "Fine Old Englishman," was sung:

> When of vet'rans old the blood ran cold
>   at the savage Indian's yell,
> "Old Zachary" stood 'midst death and blood,
>   and earned his laurels well—
> Nor was the voice of charity e'er driven
>   from his heart,
> Which still hath been, 'mid every scene, fair
>   mercy's counterpart
> He's a fine old Southern gentleman—one of
>   the present time![95]

A battle scene illustration in this publication showed Zachary Taylor at Okeechobee and memorialized the general's service in the Seminole War. *The Rough and Ready Songster* was a laudatory document fit for use by the Whigs in their 1848 campaign to elect Taylor president of the United States.[96]

The musicians who moved to St. Augustine in the first half of the century brought with them a substantial collection of music for dancing. A Mrs. Smith had collections of Scottish music published in Edinburgh and London: airs, melodies, strathspeys, reels, and lancers. A collection by William Marshall contained sixty pages, each with three or four tunes and basses. Two volumes of thirty-eight pages each contained slow strathspeys and dances published by Niel Gow and Sons of London, John Gow of London, and Gow and Shepherd of Edinburgh. The latter also published Nathaniel Gow's "The Favorite Dances of 1812," which contained both court dances and country dances. In about 1808 the Gows had published one of the earliest dances in the collection, "The Earl of Moira's Welcome to Scotland." This piece was a favorite strathspey by Johann Georg Christoff Schetky, the German cellist, composer and friend of Robert Burns.

TAYLOR AT O-KE-CHOO-BEE.

ZACHARY TAYLOR AT OKECHOOBEE

Nineteenth-century small books called songsters were collections of popular songs of the day. This illustration from one of them appeared with a song praising Zachary Taylor for his military victories in Florida and Mexico. (Reprinted from The Rough and Ready Songster, *by an American Officer, p. 193)*

Lucy Peck's collection included a set of fashionable quadrilles from *Gustavus the Third (The Masked Ball)* by D. F. E. Auber, as danced by Niblos and Charrauds Assemblies. A set of quadrilles by Henry R. Bishop from his 1816 musical adaptation of the Walter Scott novel *Guy Mannering* was in her library. Also included was a waltz from Rossini's *The Barber of Seville* and a march from Bellini's *Norma*. From the ballet repertory was D. F. E. Auber's *La Bayadère Waltz,* C. Spahn's *The Taglioni Galopades,* celebrating Marie Taglioni, a star of the 1820s and 1830s. From the repertory of the greatest ballet star of the time, Fanny Elssler, were editions of "La gitana" and her lively Polish dance "La Cracovienne." A novelty among the dances was "The New York Capriccio," which its composer subtitled "a waltz in moto contrario" and designated "an Elssler dance." The composer was Anthony Philip Heinrich, a Bohemian who immigrated to America between 1815 and 1820 and became a militant patriot of his new countryland. This piece was published by the composer in 1840. Another piece dedicated to Elssler was the "Fanny Galopade" by A. Lewis Krugell. It, too, was danced by the young generation of St. Augustine.

The stately, slow Spanish dances, thought by several visitors to be gracefully performed by St. Augustine ladies, were also in Lucy Peck's library. These dances more closely resembled the minuet than the heel-clicking gypsy dances later associated with Spain, or "La cachucha," a castanet dance performed both by Fanny Elssler and the energetic St. Augustine dancers. Aside from the variety of Spanish dances, Lucy played waltzes named for girls, youths, nations, or lakes, and gallopades named for the Tyrol, Heidelburg, or Leipzig. One of the most popular was the "Bird Waltz," published by Firth and Hall in New York. At least fifteen issues of this title appeared in the early nineteenth century, the earliest in America being that of G. Graupner in Boston in 1819. The composer was Francis Panormo, an Italian flutist who lived for a period of time in Paris, London, and Dublin. A Charleston edition of this piece found in Lucy Peck's collection was arranged as a duet for two players and published in 1828 by J. Siegling. In another St. Augustine collection was William Dressler's four-hand settings ("The Twin Sisters") of waltzes, polkas, quicksteps, and galops, published in 1853.

Fifteen or more quicksteps and marches were in Lucy Peck's music collection. This music was used for dancing as well as for parlor piano performance. The quicksteps moved at about 108 steps per minute and were popular with young army men of the local post. Most of these works that

"LA CRACOVIENNE"

Pianists of early Florida were eager to play sheet-music releases of Fanny Elssler's new dances. (Courtesy Library of Congress, no. USZ62, 70518Q)

Lucy brought down from Connecticut date from 1829 to 1840. A few are undated and may be from earlier years. Many were dedicated to military officers or the men of their units. They were advertised as having been played by the Boston Brigade Band, the Boston Brass Band, and Dodsworth's Brass Band of New York. Allen Dodsworth, whose "Ocean Wave Quickstep" was included, directed the National Brass Band and was also the most fashionable dance instructor in New York. There was a quickstep, too, for Gen. William Henry Harrison, "The Tippecanoe or Log Cabin Quick Step," by Henry Schmidt, published by Henry Prentiss in 1840. In Louisville, W. C. Peters published "Queen Victoria's Coronation March" by Charles Czerny, and Ella Duncan played it in St. Augustine. An item of greater local interest was brought to St. Augustine at a later date but related to a Florida city and a Florida lady. It was the "Fernandina Polka" by H. C. Sherman, published in New York by S. T. Gordon in 1857. It was dedicated to Mrs. D. L. Yulee, wife of David Yulee, the U.S. senator from Florida who helped the territory achieve statehood and who was the first Jewish member of the U.S. Senate. It is in the collection of Mark Edward Fretwell.

Few keyboard instruments played in Florida as early as the 1840s are now on public display. The piano of Lucy Peck, however, still sits in the second-floor St. Augustine drawing room where she played it. It was brought from Connecticut and was bequeathed by her father to Lucy in 1841. It is an ornate square piano with heavy rosewood carved legs. It was built by Jonas Chickering, a New Hampshire cabinetmaker who went to Boston and in 1823 began manufacturing pianos. The same type of piano by the same manufacturer appeared in lithographs on sheet-music covers and was owned later by Jenny Lind and Abraham Lincoln.

An eclectic collection of sheet music in the St. Augustine Historical Society is composed of works for piano and for voice. Many are undated. Those bearing copyright dates are from 1852 to 1867. In text or title several relate to the Civil War, though the collection as a whole discloses no exclusive bias for the northern or southern cause. Included are marches for Gustave Beauregard, Robert E. Lee, and Stonewall Jackson. "The Drummer Boy of Shiloh" (Will S. Hays) carried the full message on a title-page lithograph and was one of the most popular songs of the war.

> On Shiloh's dark and bloody ground
> The dead and wounded lay;

WILLIAM MILLER SQUARE PIANO
*In the Tallahassee parlor of the Goodwood Plantation were this William Miller piano
and an older instrument by Mathushek of New Haven, Connecticut. In the Seminole
Wars and the Civil War, soldiers sang and danced at the plantation. (Courtesy
Florida State Archives)*

> Among them was a drummer boy,
> Who beat the drum that day.
>
> A wounded soldier held him up
> His drum was by his side
> He clasped his hands and raised his eyes,
> And prayed before he died.
>   (four other verses)

It was matched by the Union soldier's "Tell Mother I Die Happy" (Jabez
Burns). Soldiers from both sides remembered their girls at home. The
southern boy sang "Her Bright Smile Haunts Me Still" (William T.
Wrighton), while his northern brother sang "Beautiful Dreamer," a Stephen Collins Foster serenade. In the collection was a song and march

dedicated to "all true Union patriots" (Herman Fluegel) and also a very popular Confederate recruiting song transformed into a piano elaboration, "Tremolo on Harry McCarthy's 'Volunteer,'" by E. O. Eaton. The "Switzer's Song of Home," a German melody set by J. Moschelles, had both English and German texts. From the British repertory came a song from Michael W. Balfe's "Bohemian Girl," and from the American, one of the Hawthorne Ballads for piano on "Listen to the Mocking Bird," composed by Alice Hawthorne, pseudonym of the Philadelphia composer Septimus Winner. Most of the collection was composed of dance music: "The Contraband Schottische" (Charles Young), "Tit-Bit Polka" (E. O. Eaton), "Peri Waltzes" (Charles D'Albert), "The Electric Mazurkas" (H. V. Shannon), "The City of Cairo Schottish" (Charles Young), and others.

Numerous amateur musicians were among the Indian River residents in the 1840s. James Price, an English sailor from Liverpool, was a singer of sea songs. Lawyer Ossian B. Hart, future Republican governor of Florida, enjoyed playing the violin. Among the settlement's other professional men was Dr. Moses Holbrook, eccentric and talented recluse from a distinguished Charleston family who became a "veritable virtuoso" on the eight-keyed flute. From St. Augustine to Lake City to Jacksonville, Marcellini, a Negro, was the most respected violinist for dances.[97] While the fiddle was the most popular instrument of early days, the guitar was a close second. The *St. Augustine News* on June 7, 1845, published this poem:

Whilst others wish for pleasures gay
and seek for these in scenes afar,
I ask to feel no sweeter sway
Than softening strains from my Guitar.

When trouble presses on my mind
And cares the nervous system jar—
Oh! then what great relief I find
Touching the strings of my Guitar.

Oh, then let others pleasure find,
Contentment be my guiding star,
With this I'm blessed—thus speaks my mind,
When I awake—My mild Guitar.

Horatio

It was customary for Florida newspapers to publish poetry from time to time and to indicate a tune to which it might be sung. One example of the practice in East Florida was the appearance of the Goethe poem "Kennst du das Land?" which in the early part of the century had been set to music by numerous German composers, including Beethoven and Schubert. The editor, in this instance, chose no composer for his singers, but he did publish the entire poem in translation, which began,

> Knowest thou the land
> Where citrons scent the glade,
> Where grows the orange
> In the scented vale, where
> Softer breezes fan the azure skies.[98]

Goethe might have been thinking of an imaginary paradise, but Florida singers needed only to look about them to bring the text alive.

Because of Florida's long coastline and its many rivers and lakes, marine transportation has played an important role in its history. Sailing vessels from northern ports put in at Jacksonville, St. Augustine, Key West, then Havana, Apalachicola, Pensacola, Mobile, or New Orleans. Riverboats plied the St. Johns, Suwannee, Kissimmee, Calossahatchee, and Apalachicola. Water transportation served in the absence of roads and railways to join scattered settlements in the upper half of the peninsula. Many of the vessels brought in supplies and equipment essential to frontier living and left with cargoes of cotton, citrus fruit, turpentine, hides, and sugar.[99] Informal music began on many of them as they raised their flags. But it was the excursion boats that took entertainment, especially music, seriously.

On the St. Johns River were luxury liners *Cherokee, Iroquois, Algonquin, Seminole, Commanche,* and *Shawnee.* The smaller craft included the *Osceola, City of Jacksonville, Mary Draper, H. B. Plant,* and *H. J. Baya.*[100] The entertainment consisted of extemporaneous performances by fiddlers, banjoists, singers, small bands, and, by the 1840s, the full instrumentation of a military band. Winter visitors, English sportsmen, and local gentry came on these boats to Florida ports and resort hotels. There were steamers, shallow-draft vessels, ferries, and packets. The steamboats built in Charleston and Savannah in the 1820s brought visitors from New York, Baltimore, and Philadelphia. John James Audubon and William Cullen Bryant came in the 1830s. Jacob Brock, originally from Vermont and Con-

ON THE OLAWAHA FLORIDA.

ON THE OKLAWAHA

Early riverboats were rarely without informal music by fiddlers or banjoists. Later, luxury liners of the Atlantic and Gulf ports included bands and singers. (Reprinted from Edward King, The Great South *[Hartford, Conn.: American Publishing, 1879], frontispiece)*

necticut, opened Brock House, a resort hotel on the St. Johns at Enterprise, Florida, and by about midcentury it was visited by Ulysses S.
Grant, Grover Cleveland, Gen. William Sherman, Joseph Jefferson,
William Jennings Bryan, James G. Blaine, Gen. Benjamin Butler, Jay and
George Gould, and James Rockefeller. The steamboats had one or two
decks, side wheels, and comfortable accommodations for passengers.
Brock's *Darlington* had two decks, two saloons, and staterooms. It made
excursions from Jacksonville to Green Cove Springs and Palatka. The following account of a lively excursion appeared in the *Jacksonville News* in
1847:

> In the absence of theatres and concerts and circuses, a steamboat ex-
> cursion will always prove a safety valve for the superfluous activity of
> any young and enterprising town. Since last summer, Jacksonville has
> been abandoned to its own means of amusement, and balls, Spanish
> dances and serenades have taken up the spare time of all its young
> men in the absence of a greater variety of pleasures. Great, therefore,
> was our delight when it was rumored that an excursion was to be
> made by the *Gaston*. The town was in an uproar—ladies were in ec-
> stasies, and ladies' maids were exhausted in their efforts to effect
> sundry profound combinations of ribands and lace, and diverse in-
> scrutable harmonies between old dresses and new dresses. The *Gaston*
> arrived, and we are happy to state that all expectations were answered.
> It left here with the sound of music and dancing and returned with
> the sound of music and dancing. Its hospitable and generous owner
> Mr. Sorrel and her officers, seemed to have resolved to leave nothing
> unattempted which could contribute to the amusement of the party.
> After touching at Black Creek, Picolata and Palatka the boat returned,
> and a splendid dinner was served up to the hungry multitude on
> board, and well did they do justice to it. Champagne and generous
> Madeira flowed freely, and the inspiring strains of the Savannah Brass
> Band soon invited the joyous company to the waltz and cotillion
> upon the promenade deck. Amid the delights of the dance they ar-
> rived at Jacksonville, regretting the short life of pleasure, yet happy
> that no thorns had marred its existence during the previous twenty-
> four hours.[101]

In 1852 one New York visitor to St. Augustine reported, "There is no
desperate struggle [here] for wealth; and none of the pulling and tearing,

the jostling and struggling that are witnessed elsewhere. The quiet and contentment that are so generally perceptible are the greatest recommendations to the stranger, who is fagged and weary with the worldly struggle from which he has temporarily escaped."[102] He was impressed by the absence of pretense and by the general kindness of the people. He was introduced to a local recreation called marooning, a camping expedition to nearby Matanzas riverbanks. One historian reported that while camping out, "music was on hand to be sure, and the soft mellow notes of the guitar were certain to be heard out on the river as some youth sang the popular ballad of the day, Lightly row, etc."[103] He thought everyone dressed well, behaved well, and danced well. He observed the dancing and singing Negro servants and their "Christie imitations." He was a sophisticated observer of the social scene wherever he went and at home he attended performances at the Astor Opera House. After his long trip to Florida, New Orleans, St. Louis, then to Minnesota, he observed: "Political agitators, theatrical novelties, and strange exhibitions, will always attract crowds in this country. Calvin, Edson, Joice Heath, the wooly horse, Celeste the dancer, and Jenny Lind the singer were followed by crowds, until some fresher novelty succeeded them."[104]

One foreign author who observed the East Florida scene in the 1850s was Fredrika Bremer, a Swedish lady who wrote of her travels when she reached home. She found that Americans were interested in Jenny Lind, universal education, the slave bill, and "Spiritual Rappings or Knockings." She was fascinated with songs and celebrations of the Negroes. She visited Jacksonville, Palatka, and St. Augustine, which she called the most southern city of the United States. While on a cruise on the steamer *Magnolia* up the St. Johns River to Palatka, she recalled, "The moonlight nights were glorious, and we sat out till late on the little triangular piazza aft of the steamer, and two young sisters with sweet voices sang 'Dearest May,' and other delightful Negro melodies."[105]

Early Key West residents were not the usual pioneer homesteaders who settled the eastern or western American frontier. They were hardy and industrious, just as their western counterparts, but their frontier was the sea, not the land. They followed no plow to open the plains. Their occupations were fishing, diving, sponging, turtling, and, most of all, salvaging wrecked ships. They were Cockney Englishmen and Negroes who had migrated first to Nassau, then to the Florida Keys in the early years of the nineteenth century. They ran vessels up and down the coast looking for wrecks among the treacherous coral reefs. They were licensed to strike bargains with sea captains for salvaging their cargo, and many of them became wealthy businessmen. They were called Key West Conchs. Folk songs were devised that told of their occupations, notably "Down in the Diving Bell" and "The Wrecker's Song." They brought other songs from Nassau. Commentaries on these songs are made in chapter II below.

The first Key West lighthouse was erected in 1823, just two years after Florida was made a territory of the United States. A naval depot, a marine hospital, an army post, and Fort Taylor were built between the years 1831 and 1845. Enterprising families from New England and the Midwest came to the little settlement as business, professional, and social life prospered. Before midcentury the steamer *Isabel* called at Key West every two weeks delivering mail, foodstuff, and other cargo from New York, Charleston, and Havana. Smaller craft came on irregular schedules from St. Marks, Pensacola, Mobile, and New Orleans.[106]

Dancing was a popular recreation of Key Westers as early as 1826. One young man wrote of its beginning. "I was at a great ball two days since, and had the honor of paying my attentions to a fair one from Nassau. It was the first ball ever had on the Island. The fiddlers unfortunately got intoxicated, and thus interrupted the dance. They tried their best to play on, but for the soul of them, they could not manage their violins."[107] Several other balls were mentioned in the correspondence of this young man with his family.

Another young bachelor arrived on the island in 1828. He was a twenty-two-year-old lawyer. He led an active social life while young, though he preferred billiards, euchre, piquet, chess, and whist to dancing. He was William Randolph Hackley from Virginia. "There was a dance at the house tonight and I do not partake in such amusements in this place. . . . They kept the fiddle going until two this morning," he wrote.[108] He also wrote of other dances. Attorney Hackley led a life of sober rectitude after his marriage. He became attorney general, and his days were spent with law-enforcement problems involving drunken sailors, disorderly houses, assaults, and duels. In the evenings he read *Harper's, Putnam's, Godey's Lady Book, Knickerbocker Magazine, Weekly National Intelligencer,* and *Saturday Evening Post.* There were four o'clock dinners honoring officers of the *Princeton* or other ships, followed by numerous toasts, then dances that ended at 2:30 in the morning. Hackley subscribed to these citizen-supported events which were held in the district courthouse, but rarely did he attend. He never lost his penchant for musicmaking, and when a piano belonging to the captain of the *Bary Rainbow* was offered for sale, Hackley bought it at auction for $130. The day it was delivered, his friends the Pattersons came and played it. "I like the tone very much," the attorney remarked. Two months later a music teacher-technician named McChesney repaired it and began teaching two of Hackley's daughters. His fee was twenty-five dollars per quarter.[109]

While Yankee skippers were building their New England houses in Key West, commercial enterprises attracted other newcomers from many other ports, speaking many other languages. Cuban emigrants came to work in the first cigar factory in 1828. Others came to engage in commercial sponging and fishing. Negroes came to work in salt production beginning in the 1830s, in limited production of coconuts or other crops, and in support of the army and navy posts. Their presence was felt in churches, their workplaces, and in evening recreation.

Catholic St. Mary's, Star of the Sea, was incorporated under the jurisdiction of the bishop of Savannah, Georgia, in 1828. Priests from Havana, Cuba, occasionally sang High Mass on the second floor of the city hall in the 1840s before the first church building was dedicated in 1852. The first service at St. Paul's Episcopal Church was on Christmas Day 1832, and the first two organs were constructed by Henry Erben in 1847 and 1852. The Episcopal church had a congregation of five hundred people. The Methodist had seven hundred, and the Baptist three hundred. Each of the churches had Sabbath schools by midcentury. There were four private schools and one county school.[110] Fatherless children attended the county school free, but others paid one dollar a month. Few boys attended school after they became adults and could work for a living. Few of the Negroes received an education, but there was work and music for all, regardless of education. "I wish you could hear the niggers sing when they have to pull the ropes about the ship," a northern observer wrote. "They have got into such a notion that they can't do anything without singing as loud as they can hollow [holler]. It is so throughout the South."[111]

Dr. Benjamin Beard Strobel came to Key West as a young medical officer in the army. He also found time to edit the first newspaper on the island. His newspaper writing and later his memoirs recorded his literary preferences and vignettes of how life was lived in this multicultured enclave. Poems published in his newspaper, some of them set to music, were by Schiller, Robert Burns, Molière, and Lord Chancellor Brougham, as well as by local lyricists. Occasional articles appeared in Spanish or French, but most were in English. They had been borrowed from *Blackwood's Magazine, New England Review, New England Galaxy, Edinburg Review, Edinburg Literary Journal,* and other sources. Local events generated few stories. Short stories of romance in exotic settings were featured in early issues. Illustrative of the titles were "A Gypsy Encampment," "Mutiny in the Harem," and "The Reveries of a Bachelor."

In his recollections, Strobel told of attending a ball at Indian Key. Seafaring men in jackets, pantaloons, white shirts, silk stockings, and pumps brought along their wives, daughters, and young children, whom Strobel described as "clean, chubby-faced, hearty little dogs." When the fiddle struck up, they danced with all their might figures called "Fore and Afters," then the jig. Years later Strobel remembered the happiness of that evening when he "entered into the poor man's amusement and participated in his feelings."[112]

The ambience and social life of the Florida Keys at this early date were not as traditional as in St. Augustine or as proper as in Tallahassee. Society there was no less stratified but less sophisticated than in Pensacola, even after the temporary reforms of straight-laced Rachel Jackson. Two articles from the 1837 *Charleston Courier* are illustrative of the point. One is the story of a spellbinding French major who entertained his Key West friends with stories of his heroic deeds as aide to Gen. (le comte) René Charles Ligniville at the siege of Moscow. His skill in music and dance enhanced the major's social standing. Strobel wrote, "On one occasion the Baron and the Major opened a ball with a waltz *à la mode de Paris.* The vulgar citizens who had never seen anything of the kind, stood around idle spectators of the scene, mute in wonder and astonishment. After the dance came the song; at this the Major was adept, and favored us with Berenger's latest,[113] which was loudly encored."[114] Only after he had borrowed substantial amounts of money was the major pronounced "an imposter and a notorious swindler." He retired from the Key West social scene and went to Havana, where he purchased and exported cigars on credit.

The parents of Stephen Russell Mallory were among the earliest residents of Key West, and their son became an important figure in the political arena of Florida and the military staff of the Confederacy. His eminence as a U.S. senator and secretary of the Confederate navy is described further in chapter 11. His relationship to music began when he was a youth.

He was born in Trinidad in 1812 of a father who was a civil engineer from Reading, Connecticut. The family moved to Key West about 1820. Young Mallory was sent to the Moravian schools of Nazareth, Pennsylvania, where he heard and participated in the extraordinary musical life of the pietists. It was there he learned to play the flute and piano and learned French and Spanish well enough to read both. He later wrote that he allowed nothing to interfere with his reading and study. He was not a cultural provincial. He sometimes went over to Cuba for a brief visit or hunted on the islands adjoining Key West. He learned to ride, fence, box, row, shoot, and dance. In his early twenties, he wrote, he had formed an ideal of the woman he would marry. He met her in Pensacola. She was Catholic, spoke Spanish, French, and English, and was musical.[115] Her name was Angela Moreno. They were married in 1838 and moved to Key West, where they maintained residency for more than twenty years. Mallory was elected to the U.S. Senate and lived most of the 1850s in Washington, D.C. Jefferson Davis appointed him secretary of the Confederate Navy in 1861, and he and his wife moved to Richmond, where they participated in the active musical life of the city.

Key West remained a Union stronghold during the Civil War. There were about 2,500 local residents and 5,000 troops at Fort Jefferson and Fort Taylor. About three hundred blockade runners were seized by federal ships and brought to Key West. Union military men attended church services and wrote their families of music they heard. One of them, a trumpet player from Rochester, New York, who later was killed in action, wrote of the Negroes and their music. "They are as ignorant as a jackass and funny as a clown. . . . There are a lot of slaves on the island and every day you can hear them singing. . . . And when they are at work you might hear them sing. . . . They live by dancing all together."[116] The young writer's father did not respond to the report of the Negroes' singing, but he did warn his Catholic son against long-faced Protestant ministers who were distributing prayer books among the troops. Correspondence of the day had the war as its subject, whether from the North or the South. One wealthy man of Key West who had a large investment in slaves sent his children to expensive northern schools. In 1862 he wrote his son that his slaves had all run away. The boy could be supported no longer and returned to Key West. His father wrote of his bitterness over the change in circumstance: "The abolitionists are determined at any hazard to let the slaves free, without compensation for his [the owner's] loss; they are also determined to make the South a wilderness and give the nigger more privileges than the white man."[117]

Parades of military men through the Key West streets included the Fifteenth Regiment, Corps d'Afrique (510 men), later named the Ninety-ninth Colored Infantry. They also included the Forty-seventh Regiment of Pennsylvania Volunteers, who were stationed at Camp Brannan in 1862. On Washington's birthday they paraded through town to Fort Taylor, heard an address by the chaplain, and fired a thirty-four-cannon salute, one for each state in the Union. Later there were sack races, wheelbarrow races, foot races, and a greased pig to be caught. "The band struck up with their splendid music between each action," one volunteer wrote his family.[118] He also wrote that men of the Forty-seventh Pennsylvania Volunteers had heard a report that their band, and all others in Union service, were to be discharged on March first. He listened as they played the solemn hymn "Throne of Grace" and remembered how music had been with the regiment from its beginning.

They had sailed for Key West on the large transport steamer *Oriental* on January 27, 1862. The band had twenty-three members and played on board. At church services they played the hymn "From All That Dwell below the Skies," sung to the tune "Old Hundred," and "Lord Dismiss Us with Thy Blessing" and the Doxology. A string band played, and Danny Fritz danced a hoedown. Ferdinand Fisher and Joseph Fisher of Company G "enlivened the spirits of the men by playing the fiddle." As the ship approached Key West, the band played national songs.

After arrival, there were regular calls by beat of the drum at daybreak for reveille, and drill call was at 5:30 A.M. The band played for dress parade at 5:30 P.M. Taps was sounded at 8:30 P.M. These duty hours did not exhaust the energy of the Pennsylvania youths. The men acquired a violin and a banjo, and there was music for dancing and singing every evening.[119] The band played concerts and serenaded their officers. Musician Henry D. Wharton and the men of Company C attended the Episcopal church and listened to the Union rector. Pvt. Alfred C. Pretz played the melodeon for the service. Men of the regiment gave minstrel shows on two or more occasions.[120]

Key Westers celebrated the Latin-Catholic carnival season with parties and dances. One young Pennsylvanian compared the social occasions with those of his home town. "Their masquerades are similar to our old fashioned Bell snickles, only they have the fun to themselves—do not throw apples, cakes or nuts to the children for their regular scramble, but march through the streets, headed by a Negro and a Dago [Spaniard] with fiddle and guitar, and after satisfying their ambition in making themselves ridiculous, retire to some private house, where young ladies have already assembled, and end the evening with performances on the heel and toe."[121] Balls were the rage among the men of the Forty-seventh, with as many as sixty women attending. German poems were written to celebrate these and other occasions. Many of the volunteers were foreign born. Soldiers took parts in a play "Charles Brandon; or The Gambler's Fate," which local citizens attended. The band led by William H. Pomp was disbanded, but a new regimental band was formed in January 1863.

Music was brought to the island by other troops who were on Key West for temporary duty or short-term stays. The frigate *Niagara* with one thousand men aboard arrived with a musical cargo. One volunteer wrote, "There is a good band of music aboard and in the evening many volunteers from the different camps visit the wharf to listen to the sweet notes produced by their players."[122] In celebration of Union victories, the band of the Ninetieth New York Regiment once staged a full-dress parade, followed by a concert of vocal and instrumental music and dancing. Citizens of Key West were invited to a four o'clock reception. In the evening the company streets were festooned with colored lanterns. Illuminations and transparencies shone on the streets of the little town.

Even with these frequent celebrations, the men's spirits sagged. One musician reported that it took the men only two and a half months to tire of paradise.[123] A corporal at Fort Jefferson wrote that he was "sick and tired of this cursed rebellion and nigger freedom."[124] Another volunteer wrote his sister that the Conchs were going back to the blessed Bahamas, and the Yankees to the north. He observed that Key West would be dull socially. "The prospect seems that we are not going to have any terminus of the war at present. There seems to be a prospect of having lots of widows in the matrimonial market, so I may have a good showing yet," he cynically added.[125]

10

✳ ✳ ✳ ✳ ✳ ✳ ✳ ✳

Jump, Isabel,
Slide Water

Music of the Negroes

Sing on, poor hearts!
  Your Chants shall be
Our sign of blight or
  bloom,
The Vala-song of
  Liberty
Or death-rune of our
  doom!
—Anonymous

Panfilo de Narváez brought at least two Negroes with him on his ill-fated Florida expedition of 1528. His countryman Hernando de Soto brought a few Negro slaves when he made his 1539 expedition.[1] Tristán de Luna y Arellano brought many others in the large contingent of civilians that accompanied his 1559 settlement in Pensacola.[2] The first continuous settlement of Negroes in what is now the United States was made by those who came with Pedro Menéndez de Avilés in 1565.[3] That they built Spanish fortifications was confirmed both by a Spanish historian and a French captain.[4]

Negroes in early Florida were few in number and were not often the subjects of writers. The music they brought with them was described infrequently and casually. Dena J. Epstein has provided the best summation of music brought from Africa to the New World in an article that was based on sixteenth- and seventeenth-century accounts of English and French Caribbean observers.[5] Large numbers of Africans were not brought to Florida until English slavers brought them in the 1760s to 1780s. They had been brought to Jamaica, the Bahamas, Antigua, and Barbados many years ear-

240

lier, and observers wrote of their music and dancing soon after their arrival. William Beckford, who was in Jamaica in 1777, described the caramantee—flute and percussion instruments called the bender, the cotter, and a gamba, which were constructed of a variety of pebbles, wood, and stone. To them were added animal jawbones and other items, which produced a harsh and disagreeable sound to the author's ears.[6] This jawbone instrument was popular with Florida Negroes through the eighteenth and nineteenth centuries. An illustration of children playing on it in Tallahassee was drawn by Comte de Castelnau in 1842 and included with other lithographs of Middle Florida in his *Vues et souvenirs de l'Amérique du Nord*. He observed that the instrument produced a variety of sounds when scraped with a hollow reed.[7]

TALLAHASSEE, 1842

This lithograph of a Tallahassee street is from Vues et souvenirs de l'Amérique du Nord, *by Count Francis de Castelnau. On the lower left he depicted Negro boys dancing, accompanied by jawbones, tambourine, and drum. (Courtesy Library of Congress, no. USZ62, 3965Q)*

In 1784 the German naturalist Johann David Schoepf wrote of African music aboard a ship on which he sailed from St. Augustine to the Bahamas. Slaves on board were being sent to Providence for sale.

Another sort of amusement was furnished us by several among the Negroes on board, native Africans. One of them would often be entertaining his comrades with the music and songs of their country. The instrument which he used . . . he called *Gambee:* a notched bar of wood, one end of which he placed against his breast. In his right hand he held a small stick of wood, split lengthwise into several clappers . . . in his left hand also a small thin wooden stick, unsplit. Beating and rubbing both of these, vigorously and in time, over the notches of the first stick, he produced a hollow rattling noise, accompanied by a song in the Guinea tongue. . . . The Guinea Negroes are extremely fond of this rude, barbaric music, and sing or hear their folk-songs never without the greatest excitement; and they are at such times capable of any enterprise.[8]

African singing and dancing persisted, but acculturation began early. Slaves had few recreational hours, but they did observe British masters dance the stately minuet and cotillion. They were not long in attempting hip-swinging versions of their own, nor did they abandon their African dances that were judged to be curious, lascivious, and graceful. These were the terms used by Sir William Young to describe a St. Vincent ball at Christmastime 1791.[9]

Slaves who were brought to clear the land or build the forts sometimes left the Spanish settlements and went to live with the Indians. To their African music and folklore and the thin Spanish cultural patina, they added the green corn dance and the chants of the Indians. Among the Negro population were freemen, mulattoes, and slaves, but whatever their status, they were subject to both the protections and the hazards of life in the New World. To their importers, they were valuable property to be protected. It was their mobility that caused the Spanish and later the English and Americans to devise policies and pass laws governing their movement. The price of their freedom with the Indians was their vulnerability to raiders. From Georgia and South Carolina, hostile predators came across the Florida borders and stole slaves and freemen as well from Indian villages, plantations, and small-town streets. The niceties of legal proceedings were not observed.

But slave thievery was not a one-way street. As early as 1726 fugitive slaves came from the border states to the Spanish colony at St. Augustine. They were welcomed by the Spanish. They intermarried with the Creek Indians. An English missionary complained to the secretary of the Society for the Propagation of the Gospel that Negroes were leaving a South Carolina parish because they had been promised freedom in Florida. Florida governor Manuel de Montiano did indeed give some of them their liberty in 1738. They formed a black community two or three miles north of St. Augustine, and there thirty-eight families were instructed in the Catholic faith by Rev. Josef de Leon. There they chanted the litany of their dogma.

Negroes emigrated from the Bahamas to Key West from about 1783. Many Key West Conchs are descendants of these Bahamians, who, along with earlier English settlers, entered the marine salvage business or commercial fishing. On Saturday nights they gathered at waterfront cafés, bars, and coffee shops, and music poured out of every door. They competed with "shouting meetings" of the fundamentalist religious groups, black and white, after the turn of the century.[10]

The bias of almost any person on the subject of the treatment of slaves in Florida can be accommodated by first-hand observers, some native, some visitors. But whether slave owners were gentle or harsh, strict or liberal, they reported musicmaking among the blacks. One who encouraged singing and dancing was Zephaniah Kingsley.

Both a slaver and humanist, Kingsley was the embodiment of human contradictions. The son of a Quaker, he acquired a fortune as a large-scale slaver. In 1803 he settled on a 3,300-acre plantation at the confluence of the St. Johns River and the Atlantic Ocean. With him were about fifty African Negroes, many of whom he had brought over himself. He built a mansion on Fort George Island and slave quarters of coquina rock, a sedimentary rock formed of seashells and sand. He organized schools, or processing stations, along the St. Johns for the purpose of teaching English and orienting Africans to tasks that would be required of them in the New World. "I taught them nothing but what was useful, and what I thought would add to their physical and moral happiness. I encouraged as much as possible dancing, merriment and dress, for which Saturday afternoon and night were dedicated . . . they vied with each other in dress and dancing, and as to whose woman was the finest and prettiest. . . . My object was to excite their ambition and attachment by kindness; not to depress their spirits by fear and punishment," he wrote.[11] Kingsley invited neighbors to join in the weekend festivities at his plantation. Yet, a counterforce appeared in the form of a minister who preached that it was sinful to dance, work, or catch fish on Sunday. He justified stealing from Kingsley because Negroes were kept in bondage by him. He made the Negroes a sorrowful group by convincing them "that all pastime or pleasure in this iniquitous world was sinful; that this was only a place of sorrow and repentance, and the sooner they were out of it the better."[12] Kingsley, who was married to a Negro woman, called these religious precepts dangerous and hurtful superstition.

Gregor MacGregor, an English adventurer, and others filled their schooners or sloops with human cargo as well as with spoils of their piracy. Crowded, unsanitary conditions on the ships led to suffocation, tropical fevers, or other diseases and ultimately to the death of many slaves. Richard Drake, a notorious slaver, described conditions aboard his own ship as half bedlam and half brothel. Slaves were packed like herring below, while above the captain and his two mates stripped themselves and danced with black women to the accompaniment of a fiddle played by a crazy mulatto cook, according to exhibitionist Drake.[13]

Congress passed the Embargo Act, prohibiting the importation of African slaves after 1808. But on the east coast of Florida, "moccasin Boys" continued their blackbirding. Fernandina had become a strategic port for slavers to land their cargo, then transship to Florida or Georgia camps for resale. In 1817 Pres. James Monroe was still attempting to cope with the difficulties of enforcing the Embargo Act when he reported to Congress that Amelia Island was "a channel for the illicit introduction of slaves from Africa into the United States, and a port for smuggling of every kind."[14] Each state dealt with the problem in its own way. In Florida a legislative act in 1822 imposed a three-hundred-dollar fine for each Negro imported into the state from without the limits of the United States. It also gave freedom to a Negro if he or she was imported from another country. Those who came only across state or territorial lines did not acquire this status.[15] In 1840 Florida had 25,717 slaves and 817 free Negroes in a total population of 54,477. Five years later when the territory became a state, the total population had grown to approximately 70,000. Of these, 50.7 percent were white, 48.5 percent were slaves, and 0.8 percent were free Negroes.

The slavery issue appeared in songs sung by both blacks and whites well before midcentury. The celebrated Higginson family created a sensation in Philadelphia by insisting that colored ladies and gentlemen should sit on the front seats at their concerts. The editor of the *Quincy* [Florida] *Times* ridiculed the Higginsons by declaring that they were attached to the Negro race by ties of kindred and affinity. He suggested that whites would be summarily expelled if they insisted on an equal right to occupy the best seats in the concert house.[16] The antislavery sentiment of the Higginsons' songs had found its mark.

A song with words by John Greenleaf Whittier grew out of a Florida incident that illustrated the ambivalence, or perhaps the division, of views on slavery in territorial and early statehood days. Jonathan Walker, a Massachusetts man who became a Pensacola resident in 1837, was charged with helping slaves to escape. He had promised to take them to Nassau by boat, but his plan was discovered. His defense was that it was no crime peaceably to aid those robbed of their freedom. Some Pensacolans agreed, but Walker was convicted of the crime, fined, and sentenced to fifteen days in jail and an hour in the pillory. As additional punishment the letters *SS* (slave stealer) were branded on his right hand. Outrage at this act caused Whittier to write the poem "March! Here Comes the Branded Hand!" It was promptly set to music by George W. Clark and sung at antislavery rallies. Walker spoke and exhibited his mutilated hand at abolitionist meetings in New England. When he returned to Pensacola, he wrote of his reception. "Although what they term the laws in Florida could have been executed with greater severity, and I subjected to more cost and longer imprisonment, yet was a strong abhorrence on the part of the citizens of Pensacola, generally, to any further infliction of punishment; and many were opposed to its execution thus far. During my residence in Pensacola, I had formed an acquaintance with most of the people of that place, and was on social and friendly terms with all; never having any difficulty or misunderstanding with any." Walker stated that he was accepted because he acted on the principle that God made the people of the earth of one blood and that they were born free and equal.[17]

Long-term observers who came from northern states wrote their views of the labor force as candidly and as casually as they commented on the weather. One who spent thirteen years in the South wrote about both blacks and whites in St. Augustine. "The old population, in their old Spanish houses, of various tongues and nations, and all living in loving harmony and happiness, may never again be hoped for. Yes, they were indeed happy. Avarice and ambition seemed quite unknown among them; and good natured simplicity appeared to be the rule of social intercourse, with most rare exceptions. And of all that happy population, the Negro slaves seemed most happy . . . the loudest music was the laughing and whistling and singing of the Negroes proceeding to their easy tasks of the day."[18] He concluded that the southern slave was a joyous fellow and inevitably compared his lot with that of the northern laborer, black or white, to the Negro's advantage. His theme was humanitarian: "In the last century, the poor of New England were annually sold at auction to such men as could sustain them at the cheapest rate. And they were treated most unfeelingly. . . . In the last century, many masters may have treated their slaves as badly as people of the north their poor neighbors and relations; and in some cases even worse—if worse *can* be."[19] His final conclusion, along with John Greenleaf Whittier, was that folly and fanaticism were hard taskmasters.

A journalist, writing of his 1857 visit to Florida after an absence of forty-four years, did not join in the popular vituperation of the prewar years. He wrote:

> It is worthy to note here in justice to the old days of the Floridian society, a society now utterly extinct and a subject of history, that the kindliness to the slaves seemed universal on the St. Johns River. It was a kindly and indulgent community . . . the Negro quarters were as merry as the days were long and the Negro was a more important and better appreciated element of social life than in the north. I never heard of the punishment of a slave or saw a discontented Negro; the black children were the jolliest little creatures I ever saw and the adults seemed to do as much or as little as they pleased.[20]

After surviving forty or more years of Indian raids in which their houses were burned, now Floridians were faced with the abolition of slavery, secession from the Union, and the strong possibility that their way of life was to be lost altogether. It would seem that there was little to sing about, but nobody told the Negroes. Some of the words and tunes changed, but the singing continued—sometimes mournful, sometimes muted, or sometimes raised in praise and hope.

It was not unusual for a Negro to attempt to escape bondage by running away from his home. Owners usually offered a reward for the return of their property. Crossing a state line, however, could mean freedom. An advertisement for one runaway slave appeared in a Tallahassee paper when a Negro escaped in nearby Thomas County, Georgia: "$100 reward. Ran-Away from me Thomas County, Georgia: Monday, a yellow Negro, about 40 years of age, about six feet high as well as recollected, some teeth out in front, white eyes, a rough shoe-maker and plays the violin. Henry Marsh. Clinton, Jones County, GA."[21] Sandy, a Tallahassee slave, ran away in an attempt to reach his wife, and his owner placed an advertisement in the local paper describing him: "Runaway from my plantation a few weeks ago. He is strong and active, a good carriage driver, fiddler and dancer and pretends to be religious. Was seen a few days since near Governor Call's plantation where he has a wife."[22]

Blacks and whites both placed a high value on fiddlers. A few slaves were both carriage drivers and fiddlers, assuring music day and night for hosts of house parties. Guests would sometimes bring their own violinist to a party, as Prince Murat did at a Welaunee Plantation dance in May 1828.[23] The most celebrated fiddler in eastern Florida in the 1830s to 1860s was Marcellini (sometimes, Marsellino) who lived in St. Augustine. He played there and in Jacksonville, Live Oak, and points between. An army surgeon stationed in St. Augustine in 1836–38, during the Seminole Wars, wrote of him, "It was really delightful to see the beautiful Minorcan girls moving through their intricate waltz to the music of the violin and tambourine, which discoursed most sweet harmony under the scientific touch of Marcellini the black fiddler in one of his Spanish tunes, which are very beautiful and peculiar to this place alone."[24] Marcellini received equally encouraging appraisal from a winter visitor. "There was Marcellini, the Orpheus of the place, with his two sable attendants, with violin and tambourine. This music is highly respectable, and I have often listened to it at night, with great satisfaction."[25] This comment was made by a New York man of sophisticated taste in music. Marcellini's fame was immortalized by an anonymous lady who wrote:

> I see him yet, his rolling eyes,
> His scanty woolen hair,
> His swaying form, his conscious pride,
> His almost lordly air.
> Then all the white folks waiting stood
> Till he would draw his bow;
> And when he touched the familiar notes,

YOUNG NEGRO FIDDLER

On some plantations, young Negroes who aspired to be fiddle players improvised not only their music but their instruments as well. This woodcut is of a Florida youth. (Courtesy Florida State Archives)

The sober and the staid
Just felt the music in their heels,
When Marcellini played.[26]

   Playing for residents of the slave quarters for casual shuffling, barn dances, or frolics, the fiddler kept spirits high. In his absence, other instruments were improvised to accompany dancing and singing. In the diary of Helen Moore, daughter of Kidder Meade Moore, an early Jefferson County resident, is a description of such an event at Pinetucky Plantation, seven miles from Waukeenah. "The Negroes used to come to the house and dance in the yard under the big mulberry tree. No one made them do it . . . they loved to dance and seemed so happy, such laughing, singing and clapping of hands. One of the men had a tambourine, then one of them had a horse's jawbone with pieces of tin tacked on, which he could beat. It made a fuss and they kept time with their feet."[27]

   The dark side of the fiddling Negro's assignment was that he was sometimes required to lead a slave coffle while playing his instrument. Keeping slaves in good spirits was not a job for Saturday night only. Few of the tunes the Negro fiddlers played on these occasions are recorded. Titles of some of the spirituals are. Among those sung in Florida were "Great Camp Meetin' in de Promised Land" and "Heaven, Heaven, Everybody Talkin' 'bout Heaven Ain't Goin' There." These songs and others communally composed supplemented the Episcopal hymns and prayers taught to the slaves of Octavius N. Gadsden under the great oak trees of his estate near Waukeenah.[28] Gadsden was the brother of Gen. James Gadsden, an aide to Gen. Andrew Jackson who moved to Jefferson County in 1827.

   Acie Thomas, a slave, grew up in Jefferson County and remembered being given time off for "frolics." Singing or dancing were the chief diversions at cane grindings, hog killings, chicken killings, candy pullings, quiltings, and weddings. Douglas Dorsey, another slave, remembered dancing "Cut the Pigeon Wing" and a version of the Indian green corn dance. At the Folsom plantation where Acie Thomas worked, the youngest of the white masters furnished music by playing the fiddle. He liked to see the Negroes dance "Cutting the Pigeon Wing." This dance was popular with blacks and country people of Florida throughout the nineteenth century. The music was published in the 1830s in Baltimore and introduced to minstrel show audiences by Thomas Dartmouth Rice, a white performer in blackface. He danced it to the music of "Sich a Gitting Up Stairs" and these words:

> Trike de toe and heel, cut de pigeon wing,
> Scratch gravel, slap de foot, dat's just de ting.

On New Year's Day 1839 an army surgeon, writing of his experiences on the Florida frontier, told of visiting a Negro camp in the evening to witness their dancing. "The Negresses were decked out on the occasion with considerable taste, some having on white frocks which formed quite a contrast to the naked legs of the Negroes who cut up all imaginable capers before their dusky sweethearts to music play'd on a crack'd fiddle and a tin pan. Roasted pigs, softki, sweet potatoes and hominy constituted the bill of fare."[29]

Throughout the century, writers told of Negroes singing and dancing late at night.

> Negroes travel at night by these torches over their heads, sometimes 10 or 15 in company serenade a neighborhood with their rustic songs. The most gifted gives out one line, all then join in, and such music I never heard; "Jim Crow," "Long Tailed Blue," and other comics they sing and act to perfection. Since Mrs. Hammond [the writer's wife] has been ill I have been up sometimes all night; and the Negroes were seldom still before midnight—dancing, fiddling on one or two strings—a Negro is on the que vive the minute the fiddle squeaks. Such odd manuevers—comic sayings—you could but laugh to hear them. They have Negro preachers who often evince considerable talent; many of their comparisons are laughable.[30]

Because these late evening celebrations enervated the revelers and disturbed the peace during late evening hours, restrictions were placed on Negroes in several Florida towns. In 1845 the curfew hour was nine o'clock in St. Augustine. A similar ordinance at Key West was published as early as 1829. Negroes there were not permitted on the streets after 9:30 at night, when the town bell was rung. Neither were they permitted "to play the fiddle, beat a drum, or make any kind of noise after bell-ring without permission of the mayor or alderman, under penalty of being whipped or put to labor on public streets." One song grew out of the practice of jailing Negroes who broke curfew. The Market House was the jail, and James Filor was the town marshal in Key West in the late 1850s.

RUN NIGGER RUN
Oh! Filor's sly as a mouse
Locked the niggers in the market house;
Kept them there till half past nine,
Five dollars was their fine.
Run, nigger, run! Filor will get you!
Run, nigger, run! Filor will get you!
Wish I was in Filor's place
To give them niggers a longer race.[31]

Only a note signed by a slave's master could assure safe passage after the hour of curfew. Early constraints placed on late night Negro dancing gave way in Key West after large numbers of immigrants came from Nassau, Cuba, and the nearby islands.

The Bahama Islands became a British Crown Colony in 1717. Buccaneers, pirates, and Spaniards supplied the early antecedents of Bahamian folk songs and folk tales. Black slaves were brought to the island by Loyalists during the American Revolution, some of them from the American colonies. Others came in larger numbers directly from Africa. By 1789, three-fourths of the island's population was black. Slavery was abolished there in 1834, but the Negro influx continued until 1865. The songs brought to Key West, and much later to Riviera (Florida), grew out of this setting and were sung in the patois of this national and racial mixture.

British ballads, sung by both black and white residents, were found by Elsie Clews Parsons, an early researcher of Andros Island folk tales and songs. Among them were "Young Beichan" (Child Ballad no. 53), which remained close to the Child version. This ballad was also sung in Punta Gorda, according to folk-song collector Alton C. Morris.[32] Several ballads were transformed into folk tales told in spoken and sung narratives. "The Maid Freed from the Gallows" (Child, no. 95) and "The Cruel Brother" (Child, no. 11) are examples of this type of transformation. Names of central characters were sometimes changed, and the stories were told in local speech idioms. Story lines were kept for a few ballads, but more often, local characters or imaginary incidents rounded out the tale. Song-tales described the supernatural powers of devils, witches, or animals. A monkey chewed tobacco and spit lime juice. A cockero bird jumped from bank to bank, but one leg never touched water. The devil rode a three-legged donkey. Phrase repetition was common, as were onomatopoeic words to many tunes. Muttering songs, chants, or parlando passages occurred in many of these folk tales. The eel in one sang, "Voom marimpa teya voom."

Ring dances, believed to have come from Africa, were popular in the Bahamas before they were brought to Key West. Within the ring, solo dancers improvised movement and were accompanied by "knockers" or "clavers," utilitarian noise makers. Use of the goatskin drum and exclamation of the word *Gimbay* signaled the beginning of a celebration featuring the jumping dances. These dances are described by historian Charles L. Edwards.[33] The present-day fire dances and limbo are not of Bahamian origin. Secular subjects of the songs changed little through the years: ships, sailing, sponge fishing, and problems of love and living. The plots were simple, the words few. Clapping and body movement were observed as "vibrant enhancement to the dance," or accompaniment to the songs.[34]

Evenings were playtime for children, just as they were dance time for young men. The folk songs, dances, and folk tales were most popular with children and were handed down from generation to generation principally by them.[35] Among the children's songs that came from the Bahamas were "Ripe Tomato," "Green Peas," "Blue Hill Water Dry," and "Josie Put He Hand in He Pocket," according to one writer.[36] Many others filled in the narratives of folk tales or were fragmentary nonsense verses issued by characters in the tales. In the song "The Witch Spouse" a man married a wife who turned into a witch in the form of an egret. This was her incantation:

> Kitty Katty kee wang wah
> Kitty Katty kee wang wah
> Kee bottom, kee bottom, kee pyang
> Kitty Katty Katty kee wang wah, kee pyang.[37]

These were the songs and dances brought to the tip of Florida by Conchs from the Bahama Islands. Of the Caribbean and Gulf Negroes, George W. Cable wrote, "The surrounding scene belonged to his master. But love was his, and toil, and anger, and superstition and malady. Sleep was his balm, food his reinforcement, the dance his pleasure, rum his longed-for nepenthe, and death the road back to Africa."[38] To Bahama songs were added the improvised songs that told of life on the new island and the waters that surrounded it. Added also were songs of Negroes who had come from the deep American south. The new songs, secular and sacred, contained echoes from all of these sources.

The St. Johns and other rivers have been called commercial arteries for travel to the interior of Florida. Before highways and railroads, they were a major mode of travel and transport. The Apalachicola and St. Marks rivers were cleared for navigation in 1828. Steamboating on the St. Johns began a year later, and activity increased during the Second Seminole War with such vessels as the *Cherokee*. The *Minerva* and *Izard* plied the Suwannee in 1836, and by 1845 the *Orpheus* was in service from Cedar Key to Columbus. Regular service from Palatka to Savannah began in the 1830s. By the early 1850s the steamers ran on the St. Johns from Jacksonville to Enterprise and Mellonville on Lake Monroe. Negroes poled barges ladened with lumber, cotton, and other merchandise through the twisted Oklawaha from Silver Springs to the St. Johns. Direct service from Jacksonville to Charleston via Savannah began with the *Florida* in 1851 and the *Carolina* a year later.

The Suwannee River was immortalized by Stephen Collins Foster in 1851 in his song "Old Folks at Home." The composer spelled it Swanee, thus confusing generations of tourists who have visited his memorial on the banks of the river in White Springs. The song was adopted as the state song in 1935. Foster never saw the Suwannee but preferred its euphonious sound to that of the Pee Dee, which he had originally written. Etymologists do not agree on the origin of the name of the river. The two leading theories propose a derivation from the Cherokee word *sawani,* meaning "echo river," and an alteration of the Spanish *San Juan*.[39]

The steamboats that made their way up and down these rivers had the appearance of houseboats because of the tortuous course of the rivers. The early ones had recessed stern paddlewheels, turned by a pair of steam engines. A single boiler and furnace supplied steam from the piston engines. The second decks usually had rows of windows. Later vessels, when passenger service was greater, had one or two decks, side wheels, one stack amidship, and luxurious passenger accommodations. They traveled from one small town to another. Northern visitors were attracted by the spectacle of alligators, egrets, cormorants, and limpkins. After sunset, they observed eerie shadows on the inky streams. In the daylight, there were the pellucid waters of Silver Springs.

Early writers reported musicmaking by Indian oarsmen. Negro boatmen continued the tradition and added their own improvised words. When John Bulow brought the body of his Prussian planter father by waterways from his plantation to St. Augustine for burial in 1823, he prepared stroke lines to be sung by the Negro boatmen, rather than depending on them to improvise words with flattering sentiments appropriate to the occasion.

> Old Bulow's dead and gone to Hell,
> And here lib' young Massa, doing well.

Young Bulow was described by contemporaries as handsome, dissipated, quarrelsome, tyrannical, and the murderer of three Negroes.[40] One author wrote that John Bulow had graduated in all the devilment to be learned in Paris, France, where he received his education.[41]

The singing of Negro boatmen in Florida was also documented in an account of a trip up the St. Johns River during the Seminole Wars.

> A dozen stout Negro rowers . . . struck up a song to which they kept time with their oars; and our speed increased as they went on, and became warmed with their singing. The words were rude enough, the music better, and both were well-adapted to the scene. A line was sung by a leader, then all joined in a short chorus; then came another solo line, and another short chorus, followed by a longer chorus, during the singing of which the boat foamed through the water with redoubled velocity. There seemed to be a certain number of lines ready-manufactured, but after this stock was exhausted, lines relating to surrounding objects were extemporized. Some of these were full of rude wit, and a lucky hit always drew a thundering chorus from the rowers, and an encouraging laugh from the occupants of the stern-seats. Sometimes several minutes elapsed in silence; then one of the Negroes burst out with a line or two which he had been excogitating. Little regard was paid to rhyme, and hardly any to the number of syllables in a line: They condensed four or five into one foot, or stretched out one to occupy the space that should have been filled with four or five; yet they never spoiled the tune. The elasticity of form is peculiar to the Negro song.[42]

A later observer wrote similarly of the Negro worker. "He can plunk almost any string instrument and produce lively, toe-tickling harmonies from a battered mouth organ. Dancing comes as naturally to him as singing. He often makes up lyrics to fit current popular songs and no matter how many extra words are interpolated, usually finds room for them without impairing the melody."[43]

Count de Castelnau visited Middle Florida in 1837–38 and told of music aboard a boat in the Flint River near the Indian village of Hitchelan in Gadsden County. "The evening was warm, and the crew of the boat on which I was, composed entirely of black slaves, was occupied on deck in part, with those foolish and ridiculous dances peculiar to Negroes while others raised their voices and sang almost savage melodies."[44] He was only twenty-five years of age when he visited Florida, and his views on slavery were not yet mature. He believed that Negroes on southern plantations were certainly happier than those in the free states of the North; yet he mistrusted their gaiety. He wrote, "Nothing proves better the moral degradation of the Negro than the joy and content he shows in the state of slavery. Draw near to a plantation, and the noisy outbursts of laughter that you will hear there will make you forget the overseer who goes about provided with his huge whip; then come the rest days, and all the miseries of the week are forgotten in the wildest dances and the most ridiculous capers; the orchestra is provided with a sort of mandolin made of gourd, and a horse's jawbone, the teeth of which are scraped with a hollow stick."[45]

Charles H. Olstead visited the Kingsley Gibbs family at Fort George when he was a youth. He returned from nearby Jacksonville by way of the St. Johns River in a boat rowed by Negroes from the Gibbs plantation. The Negroes sang all the way down the river, a distance of over twenty-five miles. Olstead wrote that there was even more enjoyment in this way of traveling than in the larger craft.[46]

Anna Maria Dummett, daughter of a wealthy English family who moved to Florida in 1825, wrote that one of their greatest pleasures was their races in boats with their neighbors. The Negro men kept time with their six oars and voices. One of their songs was:

> O! O! Long tongue Sally!
> He head like a buckshot
> He neck like a whale-bone, honey!
> O! O! Sally my good gal,
> And wah you hab fer supper, honey!
> Possom fat and hominy
> An shove around de mutton, honey!

The rowers were rewarded with a little whiskey or a bottle of molasses.[47]

An anonymous northern gentleman left one of the best descriptions of the singing of Florida boatmen. He, a doctor, and a German-Spanish man of Picolata were rowed by black oarsmen from St. Augustine to the St. Johns River upstream to Drayton Island, in Lake George. The Negroes sang as they rowed during the day and as they sat around the campfire at night. His account follows:

> On the second day, having been rather disturbed through much of the night, by their songs and laughter around their blazing fire, our sympathies for their toil at the oars was not particularly painful. Indeed every night they seemed by no means so weary as we were; and during the whole excursion, they manifestly enjoyed it as though it had been entered upon and prosecuted for their special gratification. It gave us pleasure, to the full amount of our capacity for enjoyment, but, with all our supposed advantages, the much greater amount of real pleasure very plainly fell to their lot.
>
> What most surprised us in the Negroes,—strangers till then to their peculiarities—was their remarkable talent of improvisation. Their extemporaneous singing was not uncommon among them.
>
> The Negro boatman of the South seems inspired by the improvising muse whenever he seizes the oar; and especially if it be to row a company of agreeable people on a party of pleasure. If there be young ladies of the number, they may be quite sure to be introduced by the muse, and to receive not only compliments, but admonitions.
>
> Further to pursue this subject . . . there may be told a brief story of a case of improvisation, on a subsequent occasion, of a very striking and characteristic nature; and by no means a bad illustration of the scope and power of the poetic muse.
>
> At the time alluded to, there was an unmarried planter of large property in the country, whose character was not enviable, as either a Gentleman or a Master; although he had received an education which should have made him a model in both characters.
>
> A party of ladies and gentlemen were passing down the river on a retiring tide, and the oarsmen had little other labor but to keep time with their oars. After a low preparatory talk among themselves, they entered upon an extemporaneous song of considerable length, and not without artistic merit. The chorus had evidently been concerted among them; for the whole united in it at the first recurrence, so as to make the name of the victimized planter. He was described by the leader of the music, as a rich and handsome young man, with fine

house and gardens;—horses and carriages; and all desirable things for comfort and elegance. But all these advantages are represented as more than counterbalanced by bad qualities of heart and conduct, described and exemplified to excite abhorrence. And all the unmarried ladies, by name, one after another are warned not to be tempted by his wealth and splendor to marry him; because bad masters make bad husbands.—"Don't you marry———." The name in itself was replete with melody, and its structure and vowel sounds wonderfully adapted to musical effect. I know of no name in our language to compare with it in musical sound; and when it came back in echo to our ears from the distant shore of the broad St. Johns, the effect was wonderful.[48]

The Negroes of Esperanza Plantation on Amelia Island composed a song about the six-oar rowboat *Isabel* which carried them along the Amelia River and Nassau Sound. The elegant boat was ordered from Lord and Taylor of New York by Judge Henry O'Neill of Fernandina. It was named for his youngest daughter, Isabel, and her name was inscribed on the bow in blue and gold lettering. It was delivered in early 1860, a luxurious vessel that stirred the pride of the oarsmen as well as the owner. Mrs. Isabel O'Neill Barnwell was interviewed by a WPA musician and writer in 1939 and sang five verses of the Negro song that began:

> Jump, Isabel, slide water,
> Ho, my aunty, ho,
> Jump, Isabel, slide water,
> Ho, my aunty, ho.
> "Where's you gwine?" I says to her,
> Ho, my aunty, ho.[49]

Susan Bradford Eppes, daughter of a former governor who was an ardent secessionist, wrote of Negro cotton pickers singing their songs while working. One group sang, "One was John de Baptist, some say he was a Jew, But the holy bible says, he was a preacher too." Another continued, "Mary and Marthy, feed my lambs, feed my lambs, on de golden altar, oh, that bleeding lamb—that bleeding lamb—one found worthy." The narrator commented, "The music was just simply glorious."[50]

As Florida agriculture and industry developed, field hands and other laborers came with their calls, chants, and songs. Those who worked in the turpentine camps sang:

> When I left de State of ol' Virginia
> I left in de winter time,
> Where you gwine nigger?
> I'se gwine to Florida, I'se gwine to Florida
> Gwine to Florida to work in de turpentine.
> Day gimme a hack an' a stock
> An' put me in a crop
> An' say ol' nigger
> If you wanna see dat double line
> You shorley got to chop
> Gwine to Florida, Gwine to Florida, I's
> Gwine to Florida to work in de turpentine.[51]

If the men were not working and the overseer approached, a chant rang through the trees,

> Boss man's a-ridin' by
> Look out, boy, look out!

A Foley woodcutter sang this work song, accented by the stroke of the ax:

> I'm a gonna drink my licker ev'y place I go, uh huh,
> It make me feel good from my haid to my toe, uh huh,
> I'se so bad I don' never wanna be good, uh huh,
> I'se goin' to de debbil an' I wouldn' go to hebbm, uh, huh,
> No, I wouldn' go to hebbm ef I could.
> (each line is repeated)[52]

The loggers had another chant as their axes split the wood. The heavily accented first syllables of each line kept the crew cadence together. The final lines kept up their spirits as they toiled.

> Oh ho in the morning
> Oh ho in the morning
> Oh ho halleluiah
> Ain't gwine be here all my days.[53]

Some of the work songs told about work conditions among the lumber crews.

> The work ain't hard
> The man ain't mean
> The food's alright
> But the cook ain't clean.[54]

Others gave a reason for continuing in a difficult job.

> De boss man he is evil,
> De job is hard as hell,
> But I'm gonna stay wid it,
> On 'count o' my big brown gal.[55]

In other songs, loggers sang of a novel way of getting to heaven.

> Want to get to heaven?   (wham)
> Tell you what to do   (wham)
> Grease your feet   (wham)
> in possum stew   (wham)
> Slip on out   (wham)
> the devil's hand   (wham)
> Ooze right in   (wham)
> the promised land   (wham, wham, wham)
> Nice and easy now
> Go, greasy.[56]

The subject of many work songs was not the work itself but women and relations between the sexes. The following words were sung by cane cutters:

> Oh Mary Brown, where have you been so long?
> Say you been to town, my sweet high brown, oh huh,
> Ain't no blade in dis yere town
> Dat cuts like mine, baby, baby,
> Dat cuts like mine, uh huh,
> I ask mister police to turn me loose
> I said I ain't got no money but a good excuse, uh huh.[57]

Women were favored subjects of nineteenth-century Negro songs. The trouble between men and women continued to be a frequent theme, even when the original songs of the workers were replaced by commercial modifications in minstrel shows and sheet music. One example was a textual change of "Troubled in Mind" to relate to the tie choppers job.

Mama, I sure am blue
Seems like I gwine lose my min'
Sometimes I feel like laughin'
Other times I feel like dying.

I'm gwine lay my head
Out yonder on dat railroad line,
Jes' to feel dat Special
Runnin' cross my min'.

My yaller gal done quit me,
An' my min' is in a mess,
I try to sleep at night,
But my heart won't let me rest.[58]

A captain of a government coast-survey team described to Harriet Beecher Stowe the evening recreation of his Negro crew. She wrote, "He had known them, after a day of heavy exposure, travelling through mud and swamps, and cutting saw grass, which wounds like a knife, to sit down at evening, and sing songs and play on the banjo, laugh and tell stories, in the very best of spirits."[59] The plantation singers sang spirituals, ballads, minstrel songs, and work songs of their own devising. After the stevedores, railroad workers, truck farm laborers, sawmill gangs, and field hands had lightened their labors with song during the day, the evening songs were about how they happened to be in Florida, how the folks back home wanted them to return, and how their romances were either a sweet memory or a bitter disappointment. Balladlike songs were fashioned from their own experiences. Jailhouse inmates, for instance, had plenty of time to become songsmiths.

Religion, often of their own devising and derivative of both black and white, Catholic and Protestant heritages, played a large role in the lives of the slaves. In records of their memories of slavery days, they recalled the music and rituals of their churches. Many of them, when old, remembered attending church with white congregations. One said he remembered sitting in the wagon in the churchyard and hearing the sermon while he waited for the white family to return home. Most of them, however, recalled attending services inside the church. One said Negroes sat with whites, another that they sat in the front pews, another, the back rows, and still another, the gallery. One remembered that first they would hear the white minister preach, then they would have a sermon by a black minister.

Music figured conspicuously in all of their services. Among the songs Cindy Kinsey, a former slave, remembered were "Gimme Dem Golden Slippers" and "Ise Goin to Heben in de Charot ob Fiah." Louis Napoleon, a former slave, remembered congregational singing and shouting by the "happy ones."

The happy ones were described by a white lady novelist of the period who had observed them.

> "Gin me dat holy land," screamed an old woman.
>
> "Don't throw sand in my eyes, Satan," cried a younger one. Then there was a bass of groans, and a soprano of screams from the entire congregation. Then a sister . . . fell shouting and kicking, sprawling to the door.
>
> "See my bretherin and sisters, our sister is fairly smoking in her sins; bless be de Lord."
>
> Then what a volume of music poured forth, from the great healthy throats of the assemblage—so rich, pure, strong, clear, that I felt myself soaring on the strains, and for the time I was wafted into the presence of the spiritual.[60]

Before midcentury, few Negro ministers were ordained or licensed. Their sermons made frequent references to liberation by dying and going to heaven. Heaven was described as a place where one worked no more, and an orchestra of a thousand musicians played with brilliant effect.

> Dar music trow de spirit aron,
> An de gol' arches catch de banjo's sound;
> While bloomin' darkies fill'd wid lub appear,
> And Cupid shoot he arrows bery near.[61]

The mixing of biblical and secular elements only served to reinforce the concept of everlasting love.

Methodist and Baptist Negro workers in the turpentine industry attended church services outdoors or in schoolhouses on alternate Sundays. To exhort them was a visiting preacher or a fellow worker who changed his overalls for a frock coat. One observer described the sermon. "He preaches the gospel as he interprets it and does not mince words. There is no pussyfooting with absolute orthodoxy. The gory meat of Deuteronomy is hurled straight into the teeth of the congregation."[62]

A Boston journalist with Union troops in Fernandina at a late stage of the Civil War described Sunday Methodist church services. The congregation present was composed of about 30 white and 250 to 300 black communicants. A white Reverend Mr. De Forrest officiated. The correspondent set the scene and told the story. "The women come to church arrayed in turbans in which all colors of the rainbow are represented and commingled. Their singing is after the congregational manner; the hymn being read two lines at a time by the minister. I regret to say that it disappointed me. Yet when the colored people sing their own songs and an enthusiastic sister leads, as I have heard on a Sunday morning, with a chorus of two hundred male and female voices on the refrain, the effect is grand."[63] A week later, after the final doxology and benediction, "an enthusiastic colored sister" sang a response to General Sherman's orders regarding the treatment of Negroes.

> O, sisters, hear this good news!
> Good news! good news!
> O, brothers, hear dis good news!
> Good news! good news!
> O, Jesus is a coming!
> Good news! good news!
> We've 'listed for the battle!
> Good news! good news!
> We've 'listed for the battle!
> And he'll lead us *to the end*!

"The effect," the correspondent wrote, "was absolutely thrilling."[64]

At the Jerusalem Methodist Church on Spring Hill Road, northeast of Thomasville, Georgia, near the Florida border, music played its part in arousing and sustaining a high emotional pitch. The scene was described by William E. Curtis, a visiting journalist from the *Chicago Record*.

A deacon led the singing, lining out the verses from a ragged, coverless hymn book; it was "Amazing Grace" but to an unrecognizable tune. A bible lay upon the desk but was not read. . . . As the exhortation grew fervid the women on the mourner's bench and other parts of the congregation asked the spirit to move them, gathered in the area in front of the pulpit, singing, crying and screaming, and with the deacons and three or four others joined in a "walk around" or "shouting dance." Their eyes shone with unnatural light and seemed fixed upon something far away, like a hypnotized subject, and every now and then, with a fearful shriek, some overwrought girl would throw her arms into the air and fall under the feet of others in a hysterical frenzy.[65]

One hymnbook from which congregations sang was an edition of Isaac Watts's *Psalms and Hymns*. It was used by both white and black congregations in Florida and Georgia at this time.[66] Harriet Beecher Stowe confirmed that Negroes sang hymns by Watts.[67]

The "walk around" was not actually a dance but a shuffle. The distinction between the two was clear. In a shuffle, the feet were not lifted entirely from the floor; women placed hands on hips with arms akimbo; feet were kept close together but never crossed. The words of a spiritual warned, "Watch out, sister, how you walk on de cross. Your foot might slip an' your soul get lost." William E. Curtis added that the head and upper part of the body swayed in unison to the music. He concluded that the shuffle was inherited from African ancestors and adapted by Christianized Negroes "as a method of arousing fervor and exciting the emotions."[68] Another description of the "shout" was similar. Dancers walked around in a ring hardly moving the foot from the floor. A journalist wrote, "Sometimes they dance silently, sometimes as they shuffle they sing the chorus of the spiritual, and sometimes the song itself is also sung by the dancers. But more frequently a band, composed of some of the best singers and of tired shouters, stand at the side of the room to 'base' the others, singing the body of the song and clapping their hands together or on their knees." A handshake or love feast sometimes followed the sermon.[69]

One former slave remembered that generally the spiritual songs were sung at church or at camp meetings out of religious fervor by Christians praising God. She also remembered that others attended meetings because it gave them an opportunity to indulge in illicit lovemaking or to show off their fine clothes or buggy. Achille Murat had made a similar report of behavior at white camp meetings.

Singing spirituals was not confined to the all-day church services. Field hands sang spirituals as they worked. Duncan Gaines, a former slave from Madison, remembered that his mother sang them while returning from the fields, no matter how tired she was. Squires Jackson, a black minister, grew up on a Madison plantation where slaves were not allowed to sing as they worked, but he recalled that "nothing could stop those silent songs of labor and prayers for freedom."[70] Church rituals and celebrations were quite as likely to take place on the plantation as in township churches. A white observer remembered that a favorite congregational song of a Tallahassee plantation was:

> I'se a rollin' an' a rockin'
> An' I'se boun' ter go
> True bee-lee-bers fare-ye-well.[71]

Eli Boyd, a former slave of Miami, recalled that his grandfather was brought directly from Africa to Port Royal, South Carolina. His grandmother, he remembered, would hold up her hand, look at it, and "sing out of her hand." She sang in Geechee, a dialect, or in English, as she made up rhymes and songs while looking at her hand. If the diversity of their places of origin enriched the growing spiritual song literature, Christianization was a common bond that encouraged a core literature shared by all. The universals throughout most of the century were those unison songs, the shouts, and call and response songs. The early accounts report the Florida favorite was "Roll, Jordan, Roll." The version quoted in this early research was:

> My brudder sittin' on de tree of life
> An' he year-de when Jordan roll.
>
> Little Chil'en learn to fear the Lord
> and let your days be long.
>
> O let no false nor spiteful word
> Be found upon your tongue.[72]

Each verse ended with a repeat of the line "Roll, Jordan, Roll." Neither the words nor the tune of this early version have remained constant to the twentieth century.

William Francis Allen, an early researcher, stated, "Those [slave songs] from Florida and Tennessee are most like the music of the whites."[73] Corroboration is absent by black authors, but it is certain that white church holidays and rituals became important to black people of the state even as they and their churches achieved a degree of independence. One former slave remembered that at Christmastime on her northern Florida plantation a large fire was built, and the Negroes danced around it while the master and mistress distributed gifts of red woolen stockings and shoes. The old Negroes were served hot toddy. Singing in the slave quarters or under the trees surrounding the main house was a usual Christmas custom.

Each plantation had its own traditions for the observance of the Christmas holidays, but none were more persistent than the retelling of a Christmas legend by the Negro mammy to the white children in her care. She told the tale of marvelous happenings on Christmas Eve. "'At Midnight,' she said, 'all the cows kneeled and prayed out loud.' 'What for?' the children asked. 'Why chile alive! Dey was axin de Lord ter change dey hide to pritty white skin, an' change dey horns to curls, and change dey hoofs to pretty lil' feet, an' let 'em dance de Lancers Christmas nite; dat what dey was prayin.'"[74]

Other writers reported on the repertory of spirituals sung before the Civil War in Florida. Among songs heard in the state were "My Father, How Long?" "I'm in Trouble," "O Brother, Don't Get Weary," "I Want to Join the Band," "Jacob's Ladder," and "O Daniel."

> You call yourself a church member,
> You hold your head so high,
> You praise God with your glittering tongue
> But you leave all your heart behind
> O my Lord delivered Daniel
> O why not deliver me too?[75]

One of the most highly ritualized ceremonies of the church was baptism. Both the slaves and their children gave similar descriptions of the event. Edward Lycurgas, son of an English free Negro of the same name, described a St. Augustine ritual. Penitents dressed in long white robes, stockings, and towels wound around their heads. "Two by two they marched to the river from the spot where they had dressed. There was always some stirring song to accompany their slow march to the river. 'Take me to the water to be baptised' was the favorite spiritual for this occasion." Cindy King gave the most telling testimony to the efficacy of total immersion. "I'se a Baptist and proud of it," she said. "When de Preacher-mans baptize me he had duck me under de water twell I mos dron, de debbil got such a hott hold on me an jes won't let go, but de Preacher-mans he kep a dunkin me and he finally shuck de debbil loose an he ain't bother me much sence, dat is not very much, an dat am a long time ago."[76]

The religious ceremonies at one's death were important to plantation slaves. Uncle Davie, a Negro gardener trained in France, who died at age ninety-eight near Tallahassee, arranged his own. "The night he died, at his own request, a number of the best singers on the place collected in and around his house. For hours their weird, sad music rose and fell upon the summer air, with every now and again the solemn refrain:

> Roll on! Roll on! Sweet moments, roll on, and let this
> poor pilgrim go home, go home!"[77]

At Key West, Bahamian mourners were silent as their old people expired, but young and old acquaintances gathered outside their huts and sang songs of consolation. Old hymns were intoned until midnight, then refreshments were served, and folksongs were sung. Historians have termed the events "peculiarly touching," "weird and intensely sad." A favorite hymn for the gathering was "I Looked o'er Yander." The first line of the text is similar to the one in the well-known American spiritual "Swing Low, Sweet Chariot" ("I looked over Jordan, and what did I see?"), but there are no other similarities either in text or melody. Bahamian instrumentalists and singers formed a parade of mourners, and their music accompanied the deceased one to his or her grave. Mournful tunes of the escort ended as the body was lowered into its resting place. They were replaced by lively tunes, in celebration of the saint's ascent into heaven, when the procession made its journey homeward. The musical resources were small and the repertory limited, but spirits soared.

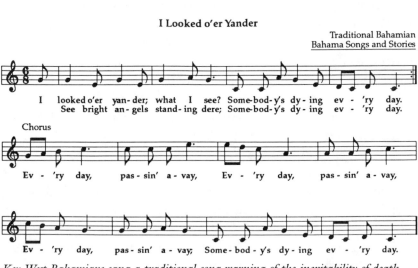

Key West Bahamians sang a traditional song warning of the inevitability of death. (Reprinted from Charles E. Edwards, Bahama Songs and Stories, *p. 23)*

Many spirituals of Bahamian Negroes, like those of the American South, grew out of biblical contexts. For example:

> Didn't it rain, Great Sestern,
> Didn't it rain in Key West, too,
> Didn't it rain forty days.[78]

Bahamian emigrants had accepted the religions of island missionaries and preachers. They knew well the hymns of the Wesleyans and the chants of the Anglicans. The Methodist hymns were those published in London, rather than those of the American North or South. Biblical stories were told in native narratives, and sinners were warned to mend their ways and pray.

> See dem people with a concubine
> Dey live in de worl' like swine
> Dey can't go ter heaven,
> Wid a villain mind.[79]

Regardless of the sources of their spirituals, Negroes retained songs about dying, about their views of heaven, and about how to get there. From the prewar years when congregations were racially mixed, they continued to sing with little or no change the funeral thought of Isaac Watts,

> Hark! from the tombs, a doleful sound
>   Mine ears attend the cry,
> Ye living men, come view the ground
>   Where you must shortly lie.
>
> Princes, this clay must be your bed
>   In spite of all your towers;
> The tall, the wise, the reverent [head]
>   Must lie as low as ours.[80]

Some of their own songs spoke of life's burdens, but many of them were optimistic views of heaven.

> Sometimes I'm up, sometimes I'm down
> Sometimes I'm almost level with the ground
> I feel like I'm on my journey home.[81]

Others had such lines as:

> Arise and shout glory, for de angels beckon me to come,
> . . . It look like King Jesus . . .
> See dat halo round His head, he's dressed in white.
> Hear dose wings a-fluttering, for de angels beckon me to come.[82]

Another song said:

> When I get to heaven, I want to sit right down,
> I won't turn back no more,
> Goin' to ask my savior for a starry crown,
> I won't turn back no more.[83]

The jubilation of reaching heaven was addressed as follows:

> There's a band of angels coming for me
> God's little angels coming for me,
> Oh, my soul's gwian' t' shine, shine!
> Oh, my soul's gwian' t' shine, shine![84]

Another lyric listed soul-shining lights on earth to a syncopated melody.

> This little light o' mine,
> I'm goin' a-let it shine,
> Let it shine, let it shine.[85]

Humane treatment was coupled with music instruction for children in the household of Unionist Richard Keith Call in Tallahassee. Describing the education of the daughter of a slave, Ellen Call Long wrote, "Delia was a young colored girl, my own age, belonging to my mother. She grew up from infancy in the house, and there was very little difference in the treatment she received from that extended to my sisters and brothers. We ate the same food, we performed the same task, we learned to sew together, and she learned to read and write by listening and observing the white children of the family; she even picked up a little Latin and French from my brothers, and went ahead of me in music, and of course had the same religious instruction as the rest of us."[86]

Children of white families recalled lullabies sung to them by black nurses. Mrs. Isabel Barnwell, at age eighty-five, remembered one sung to her at Esperanza Plantation.

> Sweet Summer is come,
>   Cold Winter is gone,
> The little birds sing on eb'ry green tree,
>   Kokay! Kokay!
> With a free good will,
>   Ah do declar'
> Ah luvs yuh still.
>
>   .   .   .
>
> When I hab money,
>   I gibs you mah pa'at,
> So when I hab none,
>   I gibs you mah heart.
>   Kokay! Kokay!
> With a free good will,
>   Ah do declar'
> Ah lubs you still.[87]

The sentiment of the last verse is not far removed from that of the Christina Rossetti poem "Mid-Winter," set as a Christmas carol by Gustav Holst.

> What can I give him,
> Poor as I am?
> If I were a shepherd
> I would bring a lamb
> If I were a wise man
> I would do my part;
> Yet what I can I give him—
> Give my heart.[88]

A black Aunt Dinah taught the children in the day nursery at Pine Hill Plantation "a goodly number of catchy little songs."[89] One segment of the Negro song legacy especially susceptible to improvisation was the singing games of the children. Because many of these games began with forming a circle, the Florida children invariably called them ring play. The name stuck, even for those that were not circle games. Choosing games made it possible, even mandatory, that when chosen for the center position, a child demonstrated his or her own interpretation of the words by singing a solo line or, more commonly, improvising a solo dance or gesture appropriate to the lyrics. In "Aunt Dinah Is Dead," players pantomimed their answers to "How did she die?" by indicating the afflicted body organ. In one version of the song, Aunt Dinah did not die at all; she only moved to town.[90]

> She's livin' in the country,
> She's goin' to town
> She's gonna shake that shimmy
> Till the sun goes down.

With no break in rhythm, each child moved to the center to become leader for succeeding verses. The words were chanted to an improvised tune. One ring play was an adaptation of the old white man's song, "Run, Nigger, Run."

> Some folks say that niggers don't steal,
> But I caught one in my corn field.

A children's version substituted "a preacher" for "niggers." It adapted to the local scene by the following verse:

> Some folks say, Gator can't run
> Stop and let me tell you what the gator done.
> He left Alabama half past one
> He got to Oklahoma, setting of the sun
> Now didn't that gator run, now didn't that gator run?[91]

From the reservoir of ancient English folk songs, Florida Negro children made one their own by singing the familiar first verse, then invariably adding another that enlivened the action potential.

> Little Sally Walker, sitting in a saucer,
> Rise, Sally rise, Wipe your weeping eyes
> Turn to the east and turn to the west
> Turn to the very one that you love best.

> Put your hand on your hip and let your backbone slip.
> Shake it to the east,
> Shake it to the west,
> Shake it to the very one you love the best.[92]

This song was sung throughout Florida by both blacks and whites. Grace Fox, a recreation researcher, recorded nine variants of it among the black singers; the collector Alton C. Morris recorded two among the whites.

Another Negro children's song-game grew out of an old English funeral dirge. Alton C. Morris documented the Delray version of a white singer. Grace Fox recorded a lively tune to the words sung by Negroes in Pensacola and the Bahamas. The Delray version remained close to the original English.

> Green Gravel, green gravel,
> The grass is so green,
> The fairest of maidens
> That ever was seen.
>
> Miss Mary, Miss Mary,
> Your sweetheart is dead;
> The King sends you a letter
> So turn back your head.[93]

The Bahamian version changed the final three lines to:

> Your lover is here
> He left you a letter
> To bring you a cheer.[94]

The Pensacola tune consisted of a repetitive quarter-note figure on the third, second, and first notes of the scale. The Bahamian tune retained the quarter-note rhythm but otherwise resembled the other version not at all.

Many of the Negro games were played to courting songs. One example was "Three Dukes." The tune with slight modifications to accommodate the words remained constant with singers throughout the state. Singers in Chipley, Milton, and Pensacola sang texts that varied little from the early versions reported by English researcher Alice B. Gomme.

> Dukes: Here come three dukes a riding,
>   a riding, a riding.
>   Here come three dukes a riding
>   To court your daughter, Miss (Mary)
> Mother: My daughter, Miss (Mary) is quite too young,
>   To be controlled by flattering tongue.
> Dukes: Your daughter, Miss (Mary) is not too young,
>   To be controlled by a flattering tongue.
> Mother: Go back, go back, you saucy man
>   Choose the fairest in the land.

> Dukes: Of all the fairest I can see
>   Come, Miss Mary, and walk with me.[95]

The Daytona Beach and Tallahassee versions vary widely from the thirty versions quoted by Alice B. Gomme in her collection of games from the British Isles.

Florida Negro children sang fourteen songs for the Grace Fox study that have counterparts in the Gomme collection. Forty-nine others did not. Games were also played to versions of "Paw Paw Patch," "Steal Liza Jane" ("Little Liza Jane"), "Shoo Fly, Don't Bother Me," and other songs familiar to the white community. Some of the others grew out of their experiences in Florida, such as:

> First time I played in the sand,
>   Sand got in my eye.
> Second time I played in the sand,
>   Sand made me cry.
> We all around, we all around
>   Mama say give that gal some cake.
> Sardine and ricey, don't taste so nicey, nicey,
> Mama rock the cradle
> Daddy shake the cradle down.[96]

Reminiscences of Florida residents were not only of early Negro singing but of the changing styles of slave music. Thomas Brown, second statehood governor of Florida (1849–53), recalled music and dancing at wheat harvestings and corn shuckings in his native Virginia. At the winter corn harvest-home, Negroes assembled in two parties, each with a leader. One began a song while marching back and forth along the line of corn while all responded to him; then the new leader mounted the bank of grain with a new song in wild rivalry. Brown wrote:

> On my uncultivated ear . . . it seemed to fill the whole vault of heaven and the stars to dance in harmony with them. There was never any jarring or wrangling with them. All was good humor and hilarity. . . . Now these old customs are forgotten even in the Old Dominion and their melodious corn songs are never heard except in Yankee imitations of "Negro Melodies," which I never heard without disgust, and if I could have my voice in the Southern Confederacy, there never should be an exhibition of the kind allowed amongst us;

and the old fashioned corn shuckings should be revived when we could hear the Negro songs in true character and have no more Yankee imitations, which I have always regarded as so far short of the good taste of the native Negro song as to become a burlesque on our Negroes.[97]

A St. Augustine visitor agreed with the governor, at least in part. "The Christie imitation of Negro dancing and singing is tolerable; but like all imitations, somewhat of a caricature."[98] A historian of Bahama culture agreed with Governor Brown and the visitor. He wrote that Bahamians of Nassau and Key West continued to improvise their own songs in the 1830s. To them they added such American folk songs and fiddle tunes as "Old Virginny Nebber Die," "Settin' on a Rail," "Old Dan Tucker," "Long Tailed Blue," "Zip Coon," and "Jim Crow." These were accepted into the Negro repertory without question. Reservations arose when minstrelsy was perceived to have replaced honest Negro feelings with specious emotions and straightforward songs with contrived melodies. The historian wrote, "Soon after 1841, a mass of spurious sentimental songs and miserable parodies flooded the country, and Negro minstrelsy fell into disrepute. The real minstrel, who loved the sunshine and the moonlight of the old plantation, was replaced by the corked imitation of the stage."[99]

Concerts by black performers were given in principal towns of Florida in the 1840s. One of them was advertised as follows: "The celebrated Negro Melodists and Serenaders expect to arrive in Tallahassee about the 5th of April instant, and will give a series of concerts of Negro melody and extravaganzas. The Melodists and Serenaders have met with great success wherever they have been, and they feel confident that their performance cannot be excelled if equalled."[100] Other concerts by Negro performers followed, as did minstrel shows by Negro troupes and by white men in blackface. Two concerts by a white man who sometimes appeared in blackface and played music of the minstrels were given by Joel Walker Sweeney in Tallahassee in December 1855. Sweeney was the most renowned banjo player of his time, advertised as the prince of performers on the instrument. He popularized the five-string banjo throughout the States and in England, Scotland, and Ireland before his Tallahassee appearances.[101] His off-beat rhythms accompanying the jig were picked up and popularized by other minstrel musicians.

Not all of the performances of minstrelsy music took place on the stage. Songsters, or inexpensive song collections, included favorite lyrics from

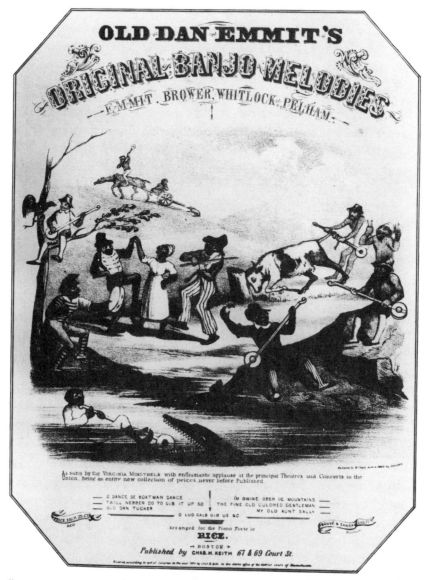

"OLD DAN EMMIT'S ORIGINAL BANJO MELODIES"

Thomas Brown, second statehood governor of Florida, declared the music of Negro minstrels, such as the work pictured here, to be lacking the good taste of native Negro songs. He disapproved on the grounds that they were imitations and a burlesque on Negroes. (Courtesy Florida State University Music Library)

the minstrels as well as the sentimental songs of Stephen Collins Foster during the years before the Civil War. Of the several publications by Ned E. P. Christy known in Florida, *Christy's Panorama Songster* was one of the most enduring. The frontispiece was a drawing of an animated black lady with castanets dancing a cachucha, with an insert of a smiling black man. The title-page drawing is of a seated black man in formal attire playing claves. The romance of Lucy Neal and Young Clem Brown was described in a song bearing the young man's name. "The Colored Fancy Ball" was a favorite of Christy's Minstrels through the remainder of the century. It appeared in five songsters from 1847 to 1851.[102] "The Rail Road Trabbler" told of a new invention: "Oh de telemagraph good for to transport the lightnen, / Or to git the news from Mexico, when the Yankees is a fitin'." The story of how ole Dan Tucker vanquished Ole Bull in a fiddling contest was told in a lyric bearing the contestants' names.

> Ole Bull and Tucker met one day
> Five hundred dollars for to play,
> De women ran an' de men too,
> To hear dem fiddle up something new.
>   Loud de banjo talked away
>   And beat Ole Bull from de Norway,
>   We'll take de shine from Paganini,
>   We're de boys from ole Virginny.[103]

One of the sentimental songs was "Car'lina."

> For dar's de ole log cabin
> Whar she sang so sweet to me
> And dar's de stringles banjo
> Dat she played so charmingly
> And her voice was soft and tuneful
> As de bluebirds in de tree
> Down in ole Car'lina.[104]

From other Christy collections, Floridians sang numerous Stephen Collins Foster songs, including "Ring de Banjo," "Come Where My Love Lies Dreaming," "Oh, Boys, Carry Me Long," "Uncle Ned," and "Dolly Day." Lyrics to the last song were:

> I've told you bout de banjo,
>   De fiddle and de bow

> Likewise about de cotton field
>   De shubble and de hoe;
> I've sung about de bulgine [railway engine]
>   Dat blew de folks away;
> And now I'll sing a little song
>   About my Dolly Day.
> *Chorus:* Oh! Dolly Day looks so gay
>   I run all round and round,
>   To hear her fairy footsteps play
>   As she comes o'er the ground.[105]

"De Ole Jaw Bone," sung in Florida as well as in other east coast states, was a comic favorite, even after minstrel shows were no longer popular. Its final verse was sung by Sam, a leading character in the folk opera *Susannah* by twentieth-century composer Carlisle Floyd. The final verse of the original was:

> Jay bird pon a swinging limb
> Winked at me, I winked at him
> Cotched up a stone, hit him on de shin
> And dats de way we sucked him in.[106]

The social issues of slavery appeared in numerous guises in popular songs sung by the blacks.

> Hurrah, hurrah for freedom!
> It makes de head spin' roun'
> De nigga' in de saddle
> An' de white man on de groun'.[107]

Yet at war's end some Negroes could sing,

> Ob all the old plantashun
> I'se de onliest one what's lef'
> But I'll sing erbout de good times
> 'Twell de Lord cuts off ma
>   bref'.[108]

If after the Civil War some of the Negroes sang of their loss, they were not alone. A New York minister who recalled his 1832 visit to Florida wrote a lengthy account that raised valid issues about Negroes and music of his time. He crossed the Suwannee river and commented that it seemed to be hiding from sight beneath the trees along its banks; yet he found himself humming the familiar Foster tune.

It is the echo of the old plantation melodies, though the words and the music were by a northern composer. Yet he must have made a study of the native songs, till he caught their peculiar rhythm and was infused with their spirit. What a pity that these old melodies, that charmed a past generation, are dying out! It may be said that they are "slave songs," which were born of a state of servitude, and now that the Negroes are free, we cannot expect them any longer to sing the songs of the captivity. This may be one reason, and yet I cannot help thinking that there is another still more potent, viz: that they are ashamed of them, as if they were reminders of their old state of bondage.

The evening before I left St. Augustine, there was a gathering of the colored people in the Opera House, which was chosen as the only building in the town large enough to hold them. As I sat on the platform, between the principal speaker and Dr. Paxton of New York, and looked over the assembled multitude, it was a stirring scene. The choir, composed wholly of colored singers, sang a number of pieces, and sang well, as such singers always do, for they have an instinct of melody; and yet I felt a disappointment, and said to the leader, "Why did you not sing some of the old plantation melodies?" "Because," he answered, "I thought I would educate my people to something higher!" That tells the whole story. It is in the effort to rise to "something higher," that they have lost what gave their songs such a wonderful pathos and power. The feeling may be a natural one, but the result is to be lamented, for so perishes what we would not willingly let die. These songs have still a place in a world that is full of breaking hearts. Slavery is dead, but sorrow is not dead, and the time has not yet come, and perhaps never will come, when mourning hearts will not need to sing:

> Nobody knows the sorrows I've seen,
> Nobody knows but Jesus,

and

> Keep me from sinking down.[109]

A counterpart to the sorrows of Negro life was the white poet's deeply sentimental remembrances of Negro fireside music. In the 1845–53 scrapbook of a Tallahassee man was the tribute of Claudie Vincent Courtney to "Uncle Thomas."

He never seemed tired when he came from work
But would take his fiddle down
And play all the good, old fashioned tunes
That are never heard in town.
We loved them then, and I love them still
For the memory of the past,
And the dear, brown hands that then held the bow
For the last time—oh! the last.

Then he'd sing for us, and that voice so deep
Had an almost magic spell
Oh! Those winter nights by the old fireside
Oh! Sweet voice we loved so well!
Where are you now? Gone forever more
And we knew not half your worth
'Till you slipped by on the wings of time
To return no more to earth.

I remember well all his favorite songs
And the three he loved the best
Were "The Dark Eyed Sailor," "Lily Dale"
And "The Lily of the West."
And when we sing them now at our household work
Mother's eyes oft fill with tears
And we know her heart is reviewing all
Those joys of vanished years.[110]

* * * * * * * *

Fire, Maringo,
Fire Away

Folk Music

When night comes on
we dance and sing,
Whilst de current some
vessel is floating in
When daylight comes a
ship's on shore,
Among de rocks where
de breakers roar.
—*"The Wrecker's Song"*

I guess all songs is folk
songs, cause I never
heard no horse sing 'em.
—*Big Bill Broonsy*

The usual people of frontier Florida were farmers, woodsmen, housewives, teachers, ministers, and others who were willing to take a chance on survival in primitive housing while threatened by animals, insects, the weather, disease, flooding, fire, and Indians. Their compensations were independence, freedom, and clean air. Urban conveniences, urban arts, or urban distractions were known by few. Most of the music was the homemade kind. One could learn to read church music by attending singing school, and a few settlers had been taught to play the flute, piano, or violin before deciding to be a pioneer. A few others sent their children to schools where music was taught, but many were self-taught. It was their way of bringing variety, refreshment, and beauty into their lives, a small but reliable triumph over loneliness and boredom.

The songs they preferred were deceptively simple. Some of them were ancient, so old that the meaning of the original ballad stories had been lost and was no longer understood, even by the singer. Some of them were improvised for the occasion, retelling a local tragedy or recalling a love affair. They were seldom artless. The lyrics had local fla-

vor in word order, dialect, and vocabulary. The singing style eschewed
extravagance, but emotional shading of a word or breaking a phrase for
emphasis was common practice. There appear to have been no apologists
for colloquialism or untutored delivery. The singer's message was sung
unself-consciously and with painstaking care. Among these people, sophisticated or art music came off badly when compared with their own folk
music. Italian music, specifically opera, always lost out to Scotch song.
Editors of small-town newspapers disdained roulades as much as top hats
and white gloves. The simple songs had their subjective magic. They defined the people, their place, and their time. The spirit and the events of
their lives were recorded in their songs and the morals drawn from them.
Every song had its rhetoric. Whatever its use or meaning in years gone by,
it served Floridians and gave meaning to their lives from generation to
generation. At times the boundaries between the people in the songs and
the people who sang them were hard to find.

The active social life of the plantation set had its parallel in the gatherings of country folk where music was fiddled or sung. Instead of weekend
house parties at plantation homes, the settings were crude houses or the
outdoors, and the occasions were hog killings or cane grindings. Florida
was a frontier territory of small population, scattered Scotch, English,
and Irish settlers of peasant stock who were semiliterate. Attitudes toward
music, as toward life itself, were practical, unself-conscious, and assured.
They were shaped by the values of settlers, transients, and even military
men who came to Florida ports and forts. In 1821 a soldier stationed at St.
Augustine asked his comrade one evening to accompany him to a dram
shop to hear a fiddler. His friend replied, "None of your fusty music for
me; give me the roaring of a 24 pounder, a clap of thunder, and now and
then an earthquake."[1] Ladies were convinced that skill in practical arts
preceded that of the aesthetic. Upon entering a lady's apartment, one
young man exclaimed, "I thought I heard music. On which instrument
were you playing, Miss?" She replied, "On the grid iron, Sir, with the
accompaniment of the frying pan! My mother says I must learn to finger
these instruments sooner or later, and I have this day commenced taking a
course of lessons."[2] The editor who reported this episode commented that
a duet of these two instruments was a melodious combination; he admired
the lady's taste.

Very little music in territorial and statehood days was made by professional musicians. It was made by farmers, loggers, fishermen, cowboys,
and their families. These people, like many others who lived in sparsely

populated settlements or in small towns, had chosen this style of life and were convinced of its superiority over city dwelling. Preference for the plain and unelaborated extended to their music, even by those who had lived in or visited urban settings and heard art music. A St. Joseph newspaper editor challenged the preference of the *Savannah Republican* editor for opera over the simple ballad. According to the former:

There is a vast difference between the old ballads that thrill upon the heart strings and the artificial demi-semi-quavers of the opera. The one is the memory of youth—fresh, artless, unstained and embodied in the image of our first love. The other is of Miss Bebee of Broadway, studied, artificial, and unnatural. It may be, however, that the city exquisites prefer the intricate medley of sweet sounds to the simple and harmonious strains which nature teaches us. Not so, however, with the uninitiated, for we remember years ago when on a visit to New York, as was our nightly custom, we *brought up* the theatre. It was an opera night, the music shook and quavered the tintinabulum of the ear, without a single echo from the heart. The fashionable were frantic, Bravo! Bravissimo! echoed from all parts of the house. The rattaned and whiskered dandies threw an arm here and a leg there, as if seized with Saint Vitus' dance, when by way of interlude, or in pity to the uncultivated boobies like ourselves, the band struck up, accompanied by sweet and silvery voices, the old song of *Robin Adair,* and straightway there welled up from the heart, the gushing tenderness of boyhood years, the sweet and plaintive tones of the blue-eyed and sunny-haired girl who taught us that song of our youth. We went home satisfied that we had been paid for our dollar with *Robin Adair,* and from that time till now, we have eschewed operas.[3]

Sons and daughters of wealthy families, descendants of Thomas Jefferson and other aristocrats who populated Middle Florida, had heard concerts in New York, Philadelphia, Baltimore, and Washington, D.C., either before coming to their adopted state or on annual visits to these urban centers. The absence of Puritan influence in these early Florida years allowed music to diffuse throughout the area without the constraints imposed by New England divines.

Given their sources of origin, it is not surprising that little discrete folk music may be identified as Floridian. Early settlers sang the songs of the homes they had left in the British Isles, Africa, and the American North and West. Dominating the repertory were the songs of England, Scotland, and Ireland. Few African elements survived the transplantation and acculturation into the statehood days. Black music that evolved, or that was brought from other states, was absorbed so completely into the repertory that it bore little or no geographical distinction. A few exceptions, because they referred to local people, jobs, or locations, are identified in chapter 9.

The region adopted the songs of the dominant cultural strains. Old lyrics were sustained by the stories they told and by the Elizabethan language, the Scottish dialect, or the Irish humor. Some of the tunes were little changed over the years. Others were adapted to new words, and only their skeletons remained. In the acculturation process some songs retained a verse or two of an old ballad, then hybridized into a regional story or moral. Florida folksingers neither knew nor cared about the age of a song or its origin. They sang some of the most ancient British ballads without knowing the historical references to kings, lords, or ladies who were their subjects. They knew little of the upheavals in the north of England and in Scotland which generated the tales of "Lord Derwentwater" or "John of Hazelgreen."

Oral tradition, broadsides, and songsters, domestic and foreign, brought these songs to Florida. The new setting and the new dialect gave them their new verses and a new identity. Archaic language and modal melodies were retained as long as they could be remembered, but modifications were made of either if the singer had a tale to tell. Local subjects or happenings began to be subjects of ballads, here as elsewhere. Poverty, danger, hard labor, and natural disasters are traditional subjects of folk songs, and Floridians had their share of all. Their ballads told the stories, and the abandonment of tradition did not hurt their conscience. The historical songs with ancient tunes held their places in the folksinger's repertory as did fiddle tunes and children's game-songs, and to them were added the stories of events that had brought excitement, passion, or contentment in Florida. This genre of song was popular among a large segment of settlers and was distributed across the state as transportation improved. Class distinctions were muted, and the songs were sung by local aristocrats as well as by hardscrabble farmers. Small children of all social classes sang many of the same play-party songs. Youths sang courting songs at outdoor social occasions. Love songs were no respecters of social class. They addressed a sweet temper and beauty and seldom raised the question of ancestry.

Francis J. Child, an American, produced his seminal study of English and Scottish folk ballads in the late nineteenth century.[4] Of the 305 ballad texts he studied, more than 100 of them have been found in oral tradition in the United States of America, and at least 34 were known by Floridians.[5] Tunes for about 80 of the ballads have been identified across the nation.[6] Those sung in Florida were transcribed by Leonard Deutsch for the Alton Morris collection. From the eastern seaboard, the English and Scottish ballads and folk songs moved with the impoverished sons and young brothers of gentry, the poor farmers, and workmen to the South. A large-scale study of these was made by Cecil Sharp, an English collector, and Maud Karpeles, his assistant, in 1916, 1917, and 1918.[7] Of the Child ballads collected for the Sharp study, 30 were also collected by Morris in Florida. Among them were "The Elfin Knight," "The Two Sisters," "Lord Randal," "The Cruel Mother," "The Cherry Tree Carol," "Lord Lovel," "Barbara Allen," and other popular narratives. Less well known were the four Child ballads collected by Morris in Florida which were not collected by Cecil Sharp in Appalachia: "The Lass of Roch Royal" (Child, no. 76), "Lord Derwentwater" (Child, no. 208), "Get Up and Bar the Door" (Child, no. 275), and "Lady Alice" (or "George Collins"; Child, no. 85).

The Florida version of "The Lass of Roch Royal" is similar to the *D* version in Child. The lovers vow to be faithful as Gregory leaves for a foreign land. He returns to find her in her "cold cloudy coffin" and grieves. Gregory, the narrator, is not named in the Florida variant, and no love tokens are exchanged. The text was a well-known eighteenth-century ballad set to a succession of tunes. Morris saw two borrowings, the first from Robert Burns's "O, My Luv's like a Red, Red Rose."

> She's like one pink, one pink or rose,
>   That blooms in the month of June;
> She's like one bright new instrument
>   That's never out of tune.[8]

The lines "Who will shoe your pretty little foot, / And who will glove your hand" occur not only in numerous variants of this text but in other ballads as well. The last stanza borrows from Child, no. 85 ("Lady Alice"), the poignant lines:

> O don't you hear that lonesome turtledove,
>   That flies from pine to pine;

It's mourning the loss of its own true love,
And why not me for mine?

"Lord Derwentwater" made its first documented appearances on this
side of the Atlantic Ocean in Georgia and Florida. It was one of few ballads based on British historical events to survive that trip. Morris identified it as variant *D* in Child, no. 208, though the lord's name was changed
from Derwentwater to Ballanter. The lord from the north of England was
convicted of treason in 1716 and executed. The Florida singer of this ballad
was Mrs. G. A. Griffin, who was born in 1863 and learned the story from
her father, who was a singing-school teacher in Georgia. The Florida version omits the reason for the lord's death.

"Get Up and Bar the Door" is a Scotch narrative which continued the
dialect in variants reaching America. The Florida version tells the story of
a couple who had prepared pudding for a feast on Martinmas (November
11), when they argued about which of them should bar the door from the
cold winter wind. They made a pact that the first to speak should bolt the
door. At midnight two travelers wandered in and ate the puddings, but
neither man nor wife spoke a word.

Then said one unto the ither,
"Here man, take ye my knife, O;
Ye cut off the old man's beard,
An' I'll kiss the guid wife, O."

Then up starts our guid man,
An' an angry man is he, O,
Woud ye kiss my wife before my face
An' scad me wi puddin bree, O?

Then up jumps our guid wife
Gae three skips roond the floor, O,
"Guid man ye've spoken the foremost ward;
Gae up an bar the door, O."[9]

A fourth Child ballad, no. 85, titled "Lady Alice" (or "George Collins"),
was heard in Florida in two versions by Morris. Lucy Holt Harrison,
singer of version *A*, learned it from her grandfather, who was born in 1792,
and he learned it from his English grandmother. The traditional ballad
told of the death of a man and the grief of his widow. One of two final

verses closed most of the variants. Version *A* in Florida contained neither of these but closed with a stanza in which the widow also died. A lily grew on her husband's grave and touched the lady's breast.

In 1950 Morris declared "Bonny Barbara Allen" (Child, no. 84) to be the favorite popular ballad in Florida from an English or Scottish source. Of the numerous variants, four are included in the Morris collection. Sweet William on his deathbed sent for Barbara to comfort him, or by her love to save his life; but hard-hearted Barbara only said, "Young man, I think you're dying." Sweet William died that day, and Barbara the next. From his grave a red rose sprang, from hers a briar. They grew to the top of the church and there "twined in a true-lovers' knot; the big red rose and the briar."[10] The essential story line is followed in each Florida version, but in each the choice of words or the dialect is regional: in version *A,* "Young Massa's sick"; in *B,* "she turned all 'round and stared off a-laughing"; in *C,* "I co'ted her for seven long years"; and in *D,* "Fore I heard death bells a-ringing."

From the New World, one of the oldest ballads based on a historic event was "Revolutionary Tea; or, The Old Lady over the Sea." The Stamp Act and Boston Tea Party spawned this song, which later appeared in singing-school manuals such as L. O. Emerson's *The Golden Wreath* (1857).[11] Like many other ballads, it was composed of four-line stanzas. The lines alternated between iambic tetrameter and iambic trimeter, with rhymes occurring on lines two and four. The story is told in a dialogue between the mother (England) and daughter (the colonies).

Almost every hamlet in colonial America had a rhymester who wrote about a special event and set his words to the tune of "Yankee Doodle." The version sung in Florida was brought from Connecticut and sung by Mrs. Charles T. Bodifield of Cocoa. It, too, told of the Boston Tea Party, then the American Revolution, and ended with three verses praising the tune itself.

> A long war they had in which
> John was, at last, defeated,
> And "Yankee Doodle" was the march
> To which the troops retreated.
> Cute Jonathan to see them fly
> Could not restrain his laughter
> "That tune," said he, "suits to a 'T';
> I'll sing it ever after."

With "Hail Columbia" it is sung
In Chorus full and hearty;
On land and main we hear the strain
John made for his tea party:
"Yankee doodle ho! ha! he!
Yankee doodle dandy,
We kept the tune but not the tea,
Yankee doodle dandy."

No matter how you rhyme the words,
The music speaks them handy,
And where's the fair can't sing the air
Of "Yankee Doodle Dandy"?
Yankee doodle firm and true,
Yankee doodle dandy,
Yankee doodle doodle doo,
Yankee doodle dandy.[12]

English and American ships sailed along the eastern seascoast from Boston, New York, Baltimore, Charleston, and Savannah to Florida ports in territorial and statehood days. The English also sailed directly from Liverpool to Pensacola, St. Marks, and other Gulf ports. The Napoleonic Wars and the War of 1812 ended in 1815, and by 1818 the first American packet ships engaged in the shipping trade crossed the Atlantic from New York to Liverpool. The design of the American clipper made it the fastest transatlantic transportation at a time when maritime activity was increasing at a rapid rate. These ships and others put in along Florida's long coastline, and their trade flourished until the Civil War. At work aboard or sporting ashore, their crews rived the air with song.

Floridians may have heard sea songs during the English hegemony. It is likely that English seamen sang work songs while in St. Augustine and Pensacola. A few sea songs were distributed in broadsheets in England in the eighteenth century. If, while they were in England, the officers or their crews had attended musical theater performances, they may have heard the popular sea songs of Charles Dibdin, composer of *The Recruiting Sergeant, The Padlock,* and *The Benevolent Tar.*

BALLAD

A sailor's life's the life for me,
He takes his duty merrily,

If winds can whistle, he can sing!
Still faithful to his friend and king,
He gets belov'd by all the ship,
And toasts his girl, and drinks his flip.

Dibdin also wrote:

TRUE ENGLISH SAILOR

Jack dances and sings, and is always content,
In his vows to his lass he'll ne'er fail her;
His anchor's a-trip when his money's all spent—
And this is the life of a sailor.

Alert in his duty he readily flies,
Where the winds the tried vessels are flinging
Though sunk to the sea gods, or toss'd to the skies,
Still Jack is found working and singing.[13]

These, however, were songs by landsmen about the sea. The songs of the working seamen had a different ancestry and a different sound. They had developed from the sing-song chant or howl of the sailor who bawled out orders to the crew, regulating their work. By the early nineteenth century the usual form was a solo line or a stanza to which a chorus responded. The variety of work tasks generated a variety of musical structures to accompany them. There were songs for short haul, or halyard songs for topsails, bowline shanties for boarding sheets, and others for working the braces. There were songs for heaving the anchor, hoisting sails, and pumping, and each served as a rhythmic punctuation to the physical function. These songs were called chanteys. Songs sung by sailors when off watch were called forebitters or main-hatch songs.[14]

Crews that plied the Florida waters were either local short-haul men aboard ships from Charleston or Savannah to Jacksonville or deep-water men who were linked to foreign ports. Seamen on these vessels signed on for reasons of their own or were shanghaied from tough seaport neighborhoods. They were Irish, Scotch, Welsh, English, Scandinavians, Germans, French, and Negroes. They were tough, hard-living men escaping from life at home or looking for adventures abroad. Fragments of their lyrics and tunes came from ballads or folk songs of their countries of origin. They sailed to ports around the world, heard the stevedores chant their tunes, and stored away their misanthropic views of human beings and life in songs. It was these songs that originated in, or were brought to, Florida ports or were later sung about experiences of sailors who remembered Florida. The exchange of songs was as brisk as the exchange of cargoes.

The invention of the cotton gin and the improvement of deep-water shipping encouraged a lively cotton trade between Florida and England. English droghers filled the ports and bays of Pensacola, Apalachicola, and St. Marks. Cotton production for 1860 was 65,153 bales, and much of it, since the 1830s, was stowed in the holds of these ships bound for Liverpool or London. By men heaving on powerful jackscrews, the cargo was packed in. These stevedores were southern blacks and white sailors from the North Atlantic packets, English, Irish, and Bostonians. When mates of the Black Ball Line faced the prospect of cold winter service in Newfoundland, some of them jumped ship and made their way to Pensacola, Mobile, and other warm Gulf ports. These men worked there through the winter and shipped out to England or elsewhere in the spring. Their music making in Mobile in the late 1840s was described by Charles Nordhoff in his 1857 account of sailor life.

> The gang . . . take hold of the handles of the screws, the foreman begins the song, and at the end of every two lines the worm of the screw is forced to make one revolution. . . . Singing, or chanting as it is called, is an invariable accompaniment of songs . . . answering well the purposes of making all pull together, and enlivening the heavy toil. The foreman is the chantey-man, who sings the song, the gang only joining in the chorus, which comes in at the end of every line, and at the end of which comes the pull at the screw handles. The chants . . . have more of rhyme than reason in them. The tunes are generally plaintive . . . as are most of the capstan tunes of the sailors, but resounding over still waters . . . they had a fine effect.[15]

One collector of shanties has called these Gulf ports shanty marts, or exchange bureaus of the work song. New Englanders, most of them Irish, brought their songs from the seven seas, while the Negroes chanted similar songs that they had learned as boatmen on the great rivers—the Mississippi, the Ohio, and the Missouri.[16]

Four titles are cited as typical capstan or cotton songs or chants. The tunes of "Fire, Maringo, Fire Away" and "Oh, We Work for the Yankee Dollar" are lost, but variants of the lyrics of the latter have emerged in the Caribbean set to a tune with a Latin beat. Tunes and several folk variants have survived for the other two: "Stormalong" and "Highland Laddie."

The text to "Fire, Maringo, Fire Away" tells of the jackscrew process, while giving rhythmic encouragement to the workers. A vivid account of the jackscrew workers and their song was written in 1859 by a British passenger aboard one of the cotton ships: "The men keep the most perfect time by means of their songs. These ditties, though nearly meaningless, have much music in them, and as all join in the perpetually recurring chorus, a rough harmony is produced, by no means unpleasing. I think the leader improvises the words of which the following is a specimen; he singing one line alone, and the whole then giving the chorus, which is repeated without change at every line, till the general chorus concludes the stanza:

> I think I hear the black cock say,
>   Fire the ringo, fire away!
> They shot so hard, I could not stay;
>   Fire the ringo! fire away!
>
> So I spread my wings and flew away
>   All the way to Canaday."

A political verse had as its subject the victory over the British at New Orleans.

> Gin'ral Jackson gain'd the day;
>   Fire the ringo, blaze away
> At New Orleans he won the day;
>   Fire the ringo, fire away![17]

"Oh, We Work for the Yankee Dollar" was a simple solo and response, with the solo voice praising the Yankee dollar, and the chorus responding with "Hurrah, see-man-do" and a final request to the captain to pay the men. "Stormalong" told the story of the death and burial of a respected bosun. This shanty with its music and many mutants has remained in the repertory of the genre. "Highland Laddie" was sung both by sailors and stevedores in Florida Gulf ports in the 1840s.

> Were you ever in Quebec,
> Bonnie laddie, Highland laddie,
> Stowing timber on the deck?
> My bonny Highland laddie, oh.

These same songs were sung by men who loaded the logs into droghers that put in to Pensacola and Apalachicola. The budding Florida timber industry brought the Quebec fleet as well as those from New England and England. Men of these ships sang variants of "Highland Laddie" as "Donkey Riding" or "A Young Thing Left Her Mammy O." They also heard chants and songs of Negroes who worked with them and whose songs they took back to the shantymen of Quebec. Hugill described the setting and named their songs: "One of the world's toughest sailortowns grew up around Lower Palifox Street, Pensacola, a sailortown inhabited and frequented by a knifing, eye-gouging, kicking and rum-swilling bunch of French-Canadian and Irish timbermen. A shanty, probably of Negro origin, popular with these pitch-pine gangs was 'Way Down in Florida.'"[18] Not only did these men exchange shanties. They combined fragments of Irish and Negro rhymes and sang them to new or traditional tunes. "Clear the Track and Let the Bulgine Run" had Negro words and was set to the Irish tune "Shule Agra." "Johnny Come Down to Hilo" is a similar combination that was popular among Gulf crews. "Lowlands" got new verses from Negro cotton screwers, such as the following:

> Lowlands, lowlands away my John
> Five dollars a day is a stevedore's pay,
> Five dollars and a half a day.

> A dollar a day is a nigger's pay
> Lowlands, lowlands, away my John
> I thought I heard our old man say
> Five dollars and a half a day

> That he would give us grog today,
> Lowlands, my lowlands, away my John,
> When are we leaving Mobile Bay,
> My dollar and a half a day.[19]

The tune to which these words were sung was not that with the subtitle "The Golden Vanity" but similar to that with the alternate title "Lowlands Away." William Doerflinger quoted it in the citation above. Stan Hugill gave a different version.[20] Both versions follow the familiar solo-and-chorus format. Although all collectors agree that the song went through the coastal shanty mart and was a Negro version, there is little agreement as to its origin. It is thought to be a British song brought to Gulf ports by Irish or English seamen.

Alton C. Morris, whose collection of folk songs of Florida was published in 1950, contains ten titles that are specified sea songs, plus several others that appear in other classifications that are chanteys or songs about the sea.[21] Some versions of "Captain Kidd" catalog "Rabelaisian adventures with fancy-women," but the Florida version stays closer to the 1701 broadside telling that the captain murdered William Moore and was tried and executed. "High Barbary," as brought to the state, tells of a sea battle, the sinking of a pirate's ship, and the crew's futile attempt to swim ashore. A second version names the pirate ship the *Prince of Luther* and the victorious English ship the *Prince of Wales*. Opening words to the topsail halyard shanty "Blow, Bullies, Blow" were:

> One night off Cape Horn I remember quite well,
> It was dark and a-raining and blowing like hell.

This Florida version departs from other versions which place the storm aboard Yankee China clippers, other ships, or Guinea slavers that carried for cargo "black sheep that have run the Embarger," that is, slaves who have run the embargo of about 1800.

The usual story of Ruben Ranzo was that of a shanghaied tailor who was an incompetent sailor but married the captain's daughter and rose to the rank of captain. The "Ranzo's Son" brought to the Florida Gulf coast was a triple-meter tune, a sequel to "Ruben Ranzo," though bearing no relation to the earlier ditty. The soloist speculated on what he would do if he were Ranzo's son: build a ship of ten thousand tons and give his sailors plenty of rum.

Among the many alphabet songs, "The Seaman's Alphabet" emerged among the commercial fishermen of Punta Gorda. Singing it, the novice seaman learned nomenclature of the ship's fittings. "Nancy Lee" was a paean to an incomparable girl who was to be a sailor's wife. "Down in the Diving Bells" was the Florida version of the old story of the diver who was welcomed by a colony of mermaids. The fish-women shook hands with their tails and made a clothesline of the Atlantic telegraph before discovering it was a very bad place to dry. One became the sailor's bride.

We married in a fancy church made of oyster shells;
The parson wore his bathing gown; the goldfish rang the bells;
And now since we are married, you girls are in a shade,
For there's none so fair as to compare with my pretty little
    mermaid.[22]

THE WRECKER

Hardy black and white singing men, descended from English, Bahamian, and German stock, salvaged cargoes of ships wrecked off the shores of Key West. (Courtesy Florida State Archives; reprinted from Harper's New Monthly Magazine 18 [1858–59]: 577)

Unique among the songs of Florida was one called "The Wrecker's Song." The first documented performance took place aboard the schooner *Jane,* where Dr. Benjamin Strobel, a Key West physician, was a supper guest on September 12, 1829. His account follows:

> As soon as we arrived on board the vessel, a German sailor, who performed remarkably well on the violin was summoned to the quarter deck, where all hands, with a "good will and cheerily," danced to the lively airs which he played, until supper was ready. The table was laid in the cabin, and was literally loaded with venison, curlews, pigeons and fish. Supper being ended, toasting and singing followed. Among other curious matters produced, I succeeded in preserving the following song which was chanted by the fiddler who accompanied his voice with his instrument. The fiddler is the reputed author of the song. I shall make no apology for the poetry; it is certainly quite characteristic. . . . The singer, who had a broad German accent, laid great emphasis on his words. Between each verse he played a symphony, remarking—"I makes dat myself." The chorus was trolled by twenty or thirty hoarse voices, which in the stillness of the night, and at a little distance, produced no unpleasant effect.[23]

The words were sung to a London tune, "The Garden Gate."

THE WRECKER'S SONG
Come ye goot people von and all,
Come listen to my song,
A few remarks I have to make,
Which von't be very long.
Chorus: Along de reef, etc.

'Tis of a vessel stout and goot
As ever yet was built of woot,
Along de reef where de breakers roar,
De wreckers on de Florida shore.

The tavernier's our rendezvous
At anchor dere we lie
And see de vessels in de Gulf
Carelessly passing by.

When night comes on we dance and sing,
Whilst de current some vessel is floating in;

When daylight comes a ship's on shore,
Among de rocks where de breakers roar.

When daylight dawns den we're under veigh,
And every sail we set,
And if de wind it should prove light,
Why den our sails we'll vet.

To gain her first, each eager strives,
To save de cargo and de people's lives,
Amongst de rocks where de breakers roar,
De wreckers on de Florida shore.

When we get longside we find she's pilged,
We all know what to do;
Save all de cargo dat we can,
De sails and de rigging too.

Den down to Key West we soon will go,
Where quickly our salvage we shall know,
When every ting is fairly sold,
Our money down to us it is told.

Den von week's cruise we'll have on shore,
Before we do sail agen
And drink success to de sailor lads
Dat are ploughing of de main.

And when you're passing by dis way
On de Florida-reef should you chance to stray,
Why we will velcome you on shore,
Amongst de rocks where de breakers roar.[24]

During the Seminole Wars, Charles Walker, a graduate of Philips Exeter, Harvard, and a citizen of Concord, New Hampshire, wrote his observations of Key West to relatives. He reported in 1838 that three or four hundred inhabitants lived on the end of a little coral island. He suspected that all were wreckers, excepting only the Episcopal priest, the judge, and the tax collector. He was surprised to find on the island a large number of good books, reviews, and late publications. One seaman described the Key West Conchs as a "hardy, dare-devil sort of people, who seem as much at home in the water as a muskrat or alligator."[25] Their business was described as fishing and wrecking. They were descendants of Cockney and Tory English and Bahamian blacks and whites.[26]

Stephen R. Mallory, who was inspector of customs in 1828 and later a U.S. senator from Florida and then Confederate secretary of the navy, also wrote of Key West. The village was made up of Bahama wreckers, fishermen from Mystic, Connecticut, shipwrecked sailors, and gentlemen refugees, according to Mallory. Among these men he found a companion or two. They and Roberto, a Negro fiddler, often joined Mallory, who with his flute and companions wandered about the neighborhood serenading ladies on moonlit nights. These were seagoing men, and it is not unlikely that they sang their forebitters. "The Key West Hornpipe" was their favorite fiddle tune.

In territorial and early statehood days, fiddlers and callers were equally essential for formal dances or hoedowns. The favorite dance was the

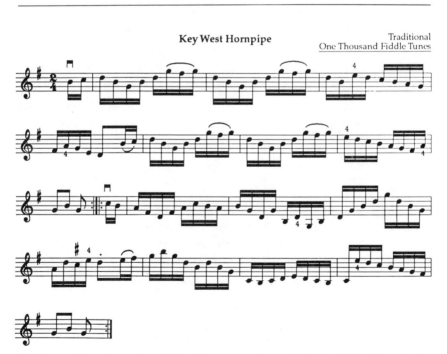

Key West Hornpipe

Traditional
One Thousand Fiddle Tunes

To this traditional tune, hardy Key West seamen danced with local girls. (Reprinted from One Thousand Fiddle Tunes, *p. 97)*

cotillion, which required eight dancers and a caller who choreographed the dance and reminded them of the next steps. They were accompanied by a fiddler and, sitting at right angles to him, a "beater," who with straws beat time across the strings, making a light percussive sound. Favored tunes included "Cindy," "The Girl I Left behind Me," "Hell after the Yearling," "Sugar, Babe," "Weevly Wheat," "Arkansas Traveler," "Mississippi Sawyer." "Honey I Hate to Leave You," and "Drunkard in the Sawgrass."[27] The person calling the figures began, "Honor your partner, lady on the left, balance all." Then followed, "Swing your partners, your corners too," and the dancers were off to intricate patterns of sashaying, "ladies floating," and promenades. Services of the fiddlers that accompanied the dance cost less than ten dollars each, and few backwoods settlements were without one. The man who could play a fiddle was a man of special value. Every Protestant denomination opposed dancing, and church members were regularly "turned out," or excommunicated, for engaging in this frivolous pastime. Yet when the fiddle began to play, it was Saturday night. Sunday morning could take care of itself.

Children played singing games such as "Mr. Coffee Likes Sugar and Tea," "We're Marching 'round the Level," "Steal Partners," and "Fishing for Love."[28] At Fort White they sang "The Paw Paw Patch," "Jemmy Crack Corn," and "The Jolly Miller." Popular in northern Florida were "Coffee Grows on White Oak Trees" and "Sweet Pinks and Roses." These games were played not only by children but by teenagers whose parents objected on religious grounds to dancing. One of them was a courting, kissing game that used the following lines:

> Coffee grows on white oak trees,
> River flows with brandy,
> Go to the east; go to the west
> Choose the one that you love best.
> Now on this carpet you must kneel,
> Sure as the grass grows in the field.
> Salute your bride and kiss her sweet
> As she rises to her feet.
>
> Go in and out the window
> Go in and out the window
> Go in and out the window,
> For he has gained the day.[29]

A homey nostalgia song was popular among emigrants from Georgia. It was set to a familiar fiddle tune, "I Want to Go Back to Georgia."

> The coon he takes a ringy tail,
> The possum takes a slick 'un;
> Oh, the coon he eats my new-ground corn,
> And the possum catches chicken.
>
> I wouldn't have you to save your life
> Because you are my cousin,
> And I can get a-plenty more
> For eighteen cents a dozen.
>
> The higher you climb the cherry tree,
> The riper is the berry;
> The more you court that pretty l'il gal,
> The sooner she will marry.
>
> *Chorus:* I want to go back to Georgy,
> And I want to go back to Georgy.[30]

The final stanza of this song picks up a universal symbol that recurs in many others. The cherry tree verse was used in another song popular in early Florida, "Yonder Comes a Young Man." A final verse gives advice to a penniless young bachelor.

> Don't court one with two blue eyes;
> She's sure to cost too much money.
> Go court one with two black eyes;
> She'll kiss you and call you honey.[31]

The Florida tune lacks the melodic appeal of the pentatonic tune recorded by Cecil Sharp in North Carolina under the title "The Higher Up the Cherry Tree."

"The Foggy, Foggy Dew" was known in a number of variants in the United States. The most familiar was that which later was popularized by Carl Sandburg and Burl Ives.

> When I was a bachelor I lived alone
> I worked at the weaver's trade
> And the only, only thing that I did that was wrong
> Was to woo a fair maid.

> I wooed her in the wintertime
> Part of the summer too;
> And the only, only thing that I did that was wrong
> Was to keep her from the foggy, foggy dew.[32]

In Florida this tune was titled "The Bugaboo." It retained the essential story line, but both the verse and tune have been modified.[33]

In the early days of Florida, even before the legend of Capt. John Smith and Pocahontas, there was a local story of a white man's being saved by an Indian princess. But fear and hatred of Indians during the wars with them in Florida generated few local ballads about them. Secular songs on Indian subjects were brought to the state, but even those passed down in the oral tradition used the language of the cultivated tradition. "Young Albin" was an example. It was the story of Amanda, captured by the Indians and about to be burned to death, who was saved by Young Albin, the chieftain. The couple then rowed to safety through the wild willows.

> A moment of parting was passed on the shore
> And young Albin, the chieftain, was heard of no more.[34]

At about the time this folk song was brought to Micanopy, Frank Hatheway, a young New Hampshire bookkeeper, brought to Tallahassee a manuscript copy of "The Indian Maid." Though a simple love song, it was clearly in an art-song setting, a style not unlike that of Franz Joseph Haydn.

Love songs brought to Florida were on those themes dear to every folk-song singer: songs in praise of the single state ("I'll Not Marry at All" and "The Jolly Bachelor"), anxiety about not having a lover ("I Wonder When I Shall Be Married?"), mother's advice to her daughter to marry a wealthy man ("Billy Grimes"), the girl who chose a lowly shepherd over a haughty wealthy man ("Young Henry Green"), sorrow at the death of a young bride ("Kitty Wells"), the carefree man who married a shrew ("Devilish Mary"), and a constant lover ("Betsy, My Darling Girl").

"The voice of the cowboy was no better than his actions when he was full of liquor," one observer wrote.[35] While singing "Rye Whisky," cowboys added a refrain that sounded like "a combination of an Indian war whoop, a panther scream, and a drunk just going into the d.t.'s.," another wrote.[36] Cowboy songs were never intended to be high art. They bragged about horsemanship, gambling, drinking, and love affairs. But above all, they were plaintive ballads that speculated on loneliness and death.

Not until the Indians had been removed from central and southern

CRACKER COWBOYS OF FLORIDA

Cowboys sang their way from Florida to Texas and back in the 1840s. Frederic Remington immortalized them in his drawings of 1895. (Courtesy Florida State Archives; reprinted from Harper's New Monthly Magazine *91 [August 1895])*

Florida did cattle raising become a large-scale industry in the state. Little time elapsed, however, until cattlemen brought their herds and the cowhands to manage them to the prairies along the St. Johns, to Lake Okeechobee, to the Peace and Caloosahatchee rivers, and to Fort Myers. Also in the 1840s a cow belt ran from mid-Florida to the Guadalupe River in Texas between San Antonio and Fredericksburg. The cowboys from Florida were sons of ranchers and Negroes. Songs of both the Southeast and Southwest were sung on the trails, and over a period of years they became common property.

"Rye Whisky" was a favorite of the trail. It was composed of two-line stanzas with a two-line refrain, easily remembered. The earliest verses formed a defense of drinking and independence. Others carried the subplot courting story to a cynical conclusion.

> I'll eat when I'm hungry, I'll drink when I'm dry;
> If the hard times don't kill me, I'll live till I die

Refrain: Rye whisky, rye whisky, rye whisky, I cry,
   If you don't give me rye whisky, I surely will die.

I'll tune up my fiddle, and I'll resin my bow,
And make myself welcome wherever I go. (Refrain)

They say I drink whisky; my money's my own,
All them that don't like me can leave me alone. (Refrain)

My foot's in the stirrup, my bridle's in my hand;
A-courting fair Mollie, to marry if I can. (Refrain)

Her parents don't like me, they say I'm too poor;
They say I'm unworthy to enter her door. (Refrain)

I've no wife to quarrel, no babies to bawl;
The best way of living is no wife at all. (Refrain)

You may boast of your knowledge, and brag of your sense,
 Twill all be forgotten a hundred years hence. (Refrain)[37]

Most versions of "Whoopee Ti Yi Yo, Git Along Little Dogies" were only recitals of the hardships to be endured by a cowboy. The Florida version ended with the cowboy carousing, getting shot in the heart, and dying. Among other cowboy songs sung in Florida were "The Old Chisholm Trail," "Strawberry Roan," "The Cowboy's Lament," "The Texas Ranger," and "The Texas Gambler," all collected by Alton C. Morris. "The Texas Gambler" was a ballad love story with one reference to the "country sing," a folk custom that continued in Florida long after the early singing schools in the South and Southwest.

    'Twas on one Sunday morning
    In the merry month of May;
    'Twas to a country singing
    I happened to stray.
    'Twas there I met a damsel,
    The finest I ever saw;
    My feeling at the moment, boys,
    Revives within me now.[38]

Both this song and "The Dying Ranger" were sung in Florida but narrated tales of Texans who left their native state. The gambler went to Mexico and the ranger to a forest far away from his Texas home, where he expired "beneath the shade of a palmetto and the sunset silvery sky." The ranger's companions promised to shield his orphan sister from harm, then, "laid him down to rest, with his saddle for a pillow, and his gun across his breast." While the dates of these two songs are not documented, it is speculated that they grew out of experiences in the war with Mexico. After the Seminole Wars, Florida youths followed their commanding officers to Texas to engage in the war with Santa Anna. The name *ranger* may refer to a man of the Texas Rangers rather than a cattleman.

One of the most poignant death scenes in American balladry is that of the victim in "The Dying Cowboy." Unlike the nearly identical Florida and Texas versions of "The Dying Ranger," this Florida title accommodates neither verse nor tune that may be called a variant. They share only a pentatonic scale and triple meter. John and Alan Lomax amalgamated thirty-six separate sources for their version, a slow melancholy tune which supports the pathetic request, "Oh, bury me not on the lone prairie, where the wild coyotes will howl o'er me."[39] The Florida version of the same title, subtitled "Tom Sherman's Barroom," is a touching narrative of a cowboy's last request.

> As I rode by Tom Sherman's barroom,
> Tom Sherman's barroom quite early one morn,
> I spied a young cowboy all dressed in white linen,
> All dressed in white linen and fit for the grave.
>
> Go beat the drums slowly and beat the fife lowly,
> Beat up the death march that will carry me through,
> And on my coffin put a bottle of brandy
> That the cowboys may drink as they carry me along.
>
> Then bury beside me my knife and six-shooter,
> My spurs on my heels, my rifle by my side,
> And when I am gone don't weep for this cowboy
> Although this poor cowboy has made his last ride.[40]

Drovers sang the trail songs and campfire songs of their companions, but not until the Civil War were books written of their exploits that included songs that they themselves wrote, songs about real Florida cowboys in local settings.

12

To Live Unchained or Bravely Die

Music of the Civil War

The Armed Occupation Act of 1842 brought many new homesteaders to Florida. The Seminole Indian Wars were winding down with the removal of Indians to the West and a truce that promised greater safety to new settlers. The interior of the state was mapped, and new roads led to a network of forts that spawned new villages and towns. The territory became a state and a full-fledged member of the Union in 1845. But that status had been legitimized only a few years before the secession controversy arose. At midcentury, the Southern Rights Association adopted the motto, "Equality in the Union or Independence out of it."[1] Floridians were divided on this issue, just as they had been on their loyalty to England at the outset of the revolution for independence in the late eighteenth century. Speeches at a Fourth of July celebration in 1851 at the Madison courthouse illustrated the dilemma. The day had begun with spirited music by fife and drum, firing of the cannon, and a procession through the town led by a band of music. Between speeches the band played "Hail Columbia" and "Yankee Doodle." Regular toasts were proposed to heroes of the Revolution, but volunteer toasts were commentaries on abolitionists, the Union, southern rights, and compromise. The Unionists spoke with firm voices. One citizen, Miles A. Warren, declared,

> A union of lakes, a union of lands,
> A union that none can sever,
> A union of hearts, a union of hands,
> The American union, forever.

Capt. C. C. Coffee elicited loudest applause with his ringing speech as a Union man. Compromise measures were both supported and opposed by other speakers. A few zealots spoke of withdrawing southern trade, of sectional ambition, and of wicked fanaticism. J. G. Putnam, Esq., spoke to the abolitionists of the North and the ultras of the South: "The first should be deported to their brethren in Africa and the latter kept in strait jackets, until returning sanity becomes manifest."[2]

The sentiment continued to burn in Tallahassee when the Fourth of July was celebrated by the Florida Riflemen in 1855. After the usual toasts to the memory of Washington, the Constitution, the Union, and the ladies, P. J. Pierce rose and proposed, "May all abolitionists be embarked in a craft without a rudder or compass and be wafted to the coast of Africa, where it is likely they will be received by real know-nothings."[3]

Union sympathizers in St. Augustine bought sheet music and sang sentimental songs on issues of the day. One example was the John G. Whittier poem, "Little Eva, Uncle Tom's Guardian Angel," set to music by Manuel Emilio and dedicated to Mrs. Harriet Beecher Stowe, author of *Uncle Tom's Cabin*. Among prominent Union nationalists were Columbus Drew, Jacksonville newspaper editor; Gov. Thomas Brown; Whig candidate for governor George T. Ward; and Richard Keith Call, military leader, plantation owner, and a territorial governor of the state. Call described the act of secession as treason, but ardent secessionists prevailed, and Florida left the Union in 1861. Given its geographical position and the base of its economy, the move was not unexpected.

The Whigs were destroyed in the South by the issue of slavery in the territories. The Republican party had lost public support as a result of the debates between Abraham Lincoln and Stephen A. Douglas, John Brown's raid of 1859, and the election of Lincoln to the presidency in 1860. Democrats were in the ascendancy. An eleventh-hour campaign to save the Union was launched nationally and in the South by the Union party.

Those who opposed secession distributed handbills in an attempt to win the governor's race and keep Florida in the nation. One of the notices read, "Voters of Florida! Are you national men or disunionists? Will you vote for Genl. Edward Hopkins, a conservative Union loving man, or will you vote for Genl. John Milton, who was in 1838 . . . a nullifer and is now an avowed secessionist and disunionist?"[4]

The Union party's cause was lost, and the Democrat John Milton was elected governor. Even so, Florida gave the Unionist a strong minority vote in the gubernatorial campaign of 1860. They voted against secession at the secession convention. Once the ordinance was signed on January 10, 1861, however, their sense of duty transferred to the state of Florida and the welfare of the South. Many of them agreed with a Virginia patriot who also had opposed secession. "Any scruples which I may have entertained as to the right of secession were soon dispelled by the mad, wicked and un-constitutional measures of the authorities in Washington and the frenzied clamor of the people of the North for war upon their former brethren of the South."[5]

On the night before the secession ordinance was signed at the state capitol, there was a torchlight parade through the Tallahassee streets headed by a band of local musicians. After the governor spoke, the enthu-siastic crowd danced in the streets. The secession ordinance document was bound by Elizabeth Eppes, descendant of Thomas Jefferson, and on the following morning Princess Catherine Murat lit the fuse of the first of a fifteen-cannon salute to the Confederacy. State volunteer units were or-dered to occupy federal military installations. This order included Forts Clinch, Marion, Jefferson, Taylor, Pickens, and Barrancas. Men volun-teered for twelve months of military service and were paid eleven dollars per month. Their units usually bore the names of their counties. There were the Taylor Eagles, the Calhoun Rangers, and the Jackson Black Hawk Cavalry. Units of the Third, Fourth, and Tenth Florida infantries occupied Fort Clinch in January, before it was completely built. The sentiment of the Confederate recruits was described by a private of the Perote Guards stationed at Barrancas Barracks when he wrote of a theatrical performance at nearby Warrenton.

> A gentleman soloist, and a fine singer he was, advanced to the front of the stage bearing a large blue silk flag with a golden star in the center. Slowly unfurling the banner he began to sing the song of the "Bonnie Blue Flag." As he named each state in the order of its secession, the

soldiers from these respective states cheered with the greatest enthusiasm. But as he completed the last stanza,

> For the lone star of the Bonnie Blue Flag
> Has grown to eleven,

he at the same time reversed the banner, displaying on the opposite side a galaxy of eleven stars, representing the eleven states of our new born Confederacy. The sentiment, the occasion, the highly dramatic rendition of the whole recitation electrified the great assembly. Every man at once seemed to lose his reason. They sprang to their feet, rushed forward frantically waving their caps and wildly gesticulating, some out of joy beating comrades with fists, others embracing and kissing, still others shouting and yelling like mad men. The reign of Bedlam lasted ten minutes.[6]

The navy yard at Pensacola, the only one south of Norfolk, had become the first military camp organized in Florida for the Confederacy. About nine thousand troops from Florida, Alabama, and Louisiana, the best of the volunteer organizations, replaced Union forces for part of the year.[7] During their brief residency young volunteers sang new songs supporting the southern cause, played cards, and drank whiskey punch. "Though the nation was going down to battle, its banners were flaunting gaily and its bands were playing anything but dirges," one observer wrote.[8]

In March 1861 Abraham Lincoln was inaugurated as the sixteenth president of the United States. The Confederate army was organized that same month in Florida, with cheering, singing, martial music, and tears.[9] The Fourth of July was no longer a cause for celebration. Ellen Call Long wrote, "[George] Washington, all the heroes of the Revolution, together with the signers of that Declaration heretofore held in such reverence, are now as nothing, and I often hear the wish expressed that England had held us in subjection; and most certainly would it be treason to award this day any of its former prestige."[10] As if in agreement, schoolmasters of East Florida State Seminary arranged closing exercises for the year but omitted the usual patriotic music, though fourteen musical selections were included on the program. At its conclusion Susannah Bruton sang, to the tune of "Dixie," a song specially written for the occasion by the seminary's principal, Robert P. Price.[11]

The young men of Florida had happy prospects in the 1850s, but the turn of events in the early 1860s sent many to their deaths and others to unending poverty. The changes in their lives were illustrated in the diary and letters of Washington M. Ives, Jr. Ives, a youth in Lake City, began keeping his diary in 1860, six months before his seventeenth birthday, and closed it three months after his nineteenth in 1862. The diary documents his encounters with music and events in northeast Florida that led to his enlistment in the Florida Fourth Regiment.

Life had not been without its pleasures when Washington Ives was sixteen. He spent a good bit of his time fishing, bathing, boating, and hunting. He played whist, euchre, checkers, backgammon, and billiards. At the right seasons he gathered hickory nuts and haws. Neighbors came for afternoon tea and for dancing in the evening. On Sundays he visited Methodist, Presbyterian, or Episcopal church services and Sunday schools and heard their music. The arrival of a piano in the community was news that was welcomed by relatives and visitors. Washington's sister played the piano, as did several neighbors. Hannah Carter, a neighbor, played "The Child's Wish." Others played "The Grave of Bonaparte," "Do They Miss Me at Home?" and "Clystat and Rainbow Schottische." A. A. Ochus, one of Jacksonville's finest pianists, played at a nearby Micanopy school. Washington's uncle played the accordion, and Washington himself became proficient on that instrument. He also learned to play the violin and the flutina. He mentioned the name of no teacher, so it must be assumed that he was self-taught. He does mention the title of one piece he played on the accordion—"Old Dog Tray." His violin and flutina accompanied singers or dancers. He attended school in Jacksonville, where he studied drawing, arithmetic, history, Latin, literature, and penmanship. He traveled by the recently completed railway to hear music in the nearby city.

"I first saw a harp today," he wrote. "It was played by an Italian accompanied by the violin and flute; there was a grand jubilee to some of the Negroes of Jacksonville who got up a band amongst themselves, came up on the railroad cars and played about wherever and whenever they pleased. They followed the speakers and played several tunes while the speaking was going on. From there they came up town and played before the doors of the two hotels; their instruments consisted of a bass and three tenor drums, two brass pieces and a violin."[12] He attended a Catholic church for the first time in Jacksonville on April 7, 1861, and there heard an organ. Back in Live Oak he heard Sam Mattair play the violin and P. O. Rogerson the banjo. Other local musicians were the banjoist Tully and the accordionist Hernandez. Two unnamed Negroes who worked for Dr. Bexley played the violins for neighborhood evening entertainments. The best-known violinist of the region was the Negro Marcellini, who played at the Trezevant house on March 20, 1862. Ives called him a splendid performer. Marcellini was from the St. Augustine household of William Travers.

Washington attended two musical events by Negro performers in Palatka, which he referred to as concerts and ministrels, the former being more accurate for the proceedings. At Live Oak he attended dramatic productions by the Estelle Troupe, which featured songs and "fancy dances." Their drama repertory included *Margery; or, The Rough Diamond, Black Eyed Susan, Cox, King and Dutchess,* and *Cousin Joe.*[13]

Among the books he owned was *The Home Melodist,* a ninety-six-page collection of songs and ballads published by Oliver Ditson Company in 1859. From it and other similar collections he and his friends played and sang at the frequent musical evenings held in their homes. The Micanopy Brass Band practiced regularly, and Washington thought they played very well, though he was not a member.

The clouds of war had begun to gather, and on September 21, 1860, the Lake City citizens formed a vigilance committee. The Regulators began holding meetings. On December 26 the news came that South Carolina had seceded from the Union. A regimental muster began the following morning. Washington was attending school in Jacksonville that winter and commented on the trains of volunteers from Levy and Clay counties passing through, but he never reduced his schedule of music making or concert attendance as a concession to war.

The military bands fascinated him. On May 8, 1861, he heard Capt. J. J. Daniels's company beating their drums at drill and heard A. A. Ochus rehearse the brass band. A few days later news came of the Charleston blockade. Dixie Stars, Columbia Rifles, and other regiments prepared to go to Virginia. Among the regiments passing through Live Oak en route to Jacksonville was one from Mississippi, and in February 1862, Washington heard their band play a concert. As the Thirty-fourth Mississippi Regiment under Colonel Dawd came through on their way to Tennessee, their band played several tunes. The war soon came closer to home. Fernandina and Jacksonville were occupied by Union troops in March. A month later Washington Ives joined Captain Dial's company (Company C), third regiment, Florida Fourth Infantry. The New Hampshire and Ninety-seventh Pennsylvania regiments had leveled most of the city. Except for the Union troops, the city was deserted. The music had stopped.

The only sounds were made by guards calling the watch, bells ringing occasionally, and sentinels calling "boat ahoy" when a boat came alongside. The Fourth Florida left Lake City on May 29, 1862, and Washington began his long assignment with them. In letters to his parents and sisters, he wrote of music he heard the bands play and of the battles he and his companions fought for the Confederacy.

From the early days of statehood, Florida had maintained state militia units. Well equipped and colorfully uniformed, they paraded through small-town streets, usually headed by a local musical aggregation of small scale. Their public appearances were on national holidays, inaugural ceremonies for governors, or local celebrations. Soon after Florida withdrew from the Union in January 1861, the militia was discontinued. By April 5, a sufficient number of men had joined the Confederate army to form the First Florida Infantry. A week later they left for Pensacola and active duty. They were composed of two companies each from Leon and Alachua counties and one each from Franklin, Jackson, Madison, Gadsden, Jefferson, and Escambia.[14]

Florida had the smallest population of any Confederate state, but the percentage of its manpower placed in the service of the new alliance was remarkable. Florida retained eight or ten companies of home guards, and at first enlistment sent 10,527 men. A total of about 15,000 men were actively engaged in the war. The voting population of the state was 13,000, and the total population about 140,000. Among the highest-ranking Confederate officers were Floridians, such as major generals Edmund Kirby Smith, William Wing Lorin, and James Patton Anderson, and brigadier generals Joseph Finegan, Edward A. Perry, George Davis, William Miller, and Jesse J. Finley. Some of them had been mustered into service early enough to engage in the protection of Florida seaports, and others in battles fought on Florida soil at Marianna, Olustee, or Natural Bridge. A much larger number were sent out of state to join such Confederate units as the Army of Northern Virginia or to fight in the Tennessee campaign, the Western Army, the Maryland campaign, and others. Florida men, supported and sometimes called to battle by their musicians, fought in such engagements as Corinth, Manassas, Chickamauga, Chattanooga, Missionary Ridge, Cold Harbor, Williamsburg, Chancellorsville, and Gettysburg. From these widespread military engagements they told their stories of the war. In interim respites they sang their songs, danced with the local girls, and heard bands play their newly written patriotic tunes.

Even when some of them were imprisoned at Fort Delaware, they wrote letters about the music they heard. The presence of music, particularly of the men singing songs, became recurring symbols of patriotism, sentimentality, and occasional humor among the troops.

Early recruitment drives in Florida consisted of parades with fifes, drums, flags, volunteers, and children tagging along with broomsticks, mops, or rakes over their shoulders simulating rifles. Bands played in the towns that were large enough to sustain them. They had had a role at civic and patriotic functions since the early 1850s, when they had been attached to rifle companies of the state guard.

Florida bands played on a variety of occasions in the war. Their presence was noted as early as June 1861. At that time the Florida Fourth Infantry and other Confederate units were preparing the defense of Apalachicola from the Federal blockade. The Methodist chaplain wrote that they had fine bands that frequently serenaded the officers. He described one event: "About nine o'clock the band and singers came. They opened up my room

FERNANDINA JUVENILE BAND

Fernandina Negro children improvised musical instruments for their own bands.
Their models were early Confederate recruitment bands and Union bands of the black
regiments stationed in Fernandina. (Courtesy Florida State Archives)

at full blast with that grand hymn, 'Before Jehovah's Awful Throne Ye Nations Bow with Sacred Awe.' The moon was bright, our headquarters were on the Bay. The sound of the many instruments and fine voices swept over the Bay, and all the air seemed alive with music."[15] The minister and his general agreed that there were no songs like the songs of Zion. On this occasion the musicians may not have agreed. Their usual reward for a serenade was a round of drinks led by field officers, who set the example. But Methodist ministers in Florida approved of neither drinking nor dancing, and the reward this night was a round of Apalachicola oysters on the half shell.

Twenty-eight-year-old John Hosford enlisted at Apalachicola on March 10, 1862, and was serving with the Army of Northern Virginia near Fredericksburg, Georgia, when he wrote:

> We repair to some place designated for preaching at eleven o'clock in the forenoon. We have no chaplain for our Reg't, but some of the men preach and it is sublime to visit one of our humble churches. We have no music save that of vocal and that consists of our men's voices who have been exposed to all the dews of heaven and cold till it is somewhat hoarse and harsh. Still the music is good and grand when collected in some grove with leaves for our seats and no one present but the masculine sex. The preacher reads his text and gives out the hymns something like they do in churches built of finer material than ours, as well as I can recollect. The choir takes up the time which consists of nearly all present and makes the woods ring with its melody, and I think if you were here you would be obliged to say it was good music.[16]

Many hymns were so well known that they were sung from memory,[17] but pocket-sized music collections were distributed to Confederate troops. Among them were *The Soldier's Hymn Book,* published by the South Carolina Tract Society, and *The Army Hymn Book,* published by the Richmond Presbyterian Committee on Publications.

A Florida youth whose father was a minister and Unionist joined the home guard at Baldwin on his seventeenth birthday. He was assigned guard duty and described the recreation of his comrades. "Of night large fires were built just out of camp; and around them the boys of the entire battalion would gather and group themselves according to their taste and inclination. Around one fire would be wrestling, boxing, and all manner of athletic exercises; around another would be gathered the more sober minded who indulged in story telling, song and reading and sometimes dancing; around another would be card playing, throwing dice, fox and geese, and tricks with cards."[18] Another observer wrote, "Round many a smoky campfire were sung clever songs, whose humor died with their gallant singers, for want of recording memories in those busy days." He remembered that there were songs about battles and skits written and produced by members of the regiment. Parodies of old songs were popular, as were satires set to Union tunes. "Everything," he wrote, "tended to pathos."[19] Robert Watson was a native of Ragged Island, Bahamas, who settled in Key West at age twenty-five in 1860. He mustered into Confederate service with Company K, Seventh Florida Infantry Regiment, a year later. His company was composed of "Yankees, Crackers, Conchs, Englishmen, Spaniards, Frenchmen, Italians, Poles, Irishmen, Swedes, Chinese, Portuguese, Brazilians . . . all [were] good southern men."[20] He played his flutina with a fiddler as his multinational company sang, danced, and went serenading.

G. H. Dorman, a Floridian who lived at Jaskes and later at Live Oak, was on active duty with the Tenth Florida Regiment. After the bloody crusade of Ocean Pond (Olustee) and the slaughter of Confederates at the Wilderness Battle, there was a lull in the fighting. Union and Confederate units were camped on opposite banks of the Rappahannock River. Dorman described an event that has been retold by many Civil War historians.

One night, one of the brass bands on our left struck up to playing "Dixie," the next one joined in, and then the next, and so on along down the line. The drum rattled on the other line to drop in; so they struck up with "Yankee Doodle." As far down both lines as we could hear a band, our band was playing "Dixie" and the others "Yankee Doodle." This was calculated to make the boys feel better. They would sometimes bunch up in little groups at night and sing some of our favorite songs such as "Dixie," "The Bonnie Blue Flag," "The Girl I Left behind Me," etc., then wind up with a few good old spiritual songs, bid each other good night, and go to our places on the line where we would be more handy to our muskets.[21]

Thomas C. DeLeon wrote an assessment of bands of the Confederacy.

The bands of the southern army—so long as they remained existent as separate organizations—were indisputably mediocre, when not atrociously bad. But it must be recalled that there was little time to practice, even in the beginning; literally no chance to obtain new music, or instruments; and that the better class of men—who usually make the best musicians—always preferred the musket to the bugle. Nor was there either incentive to good music, or appreciation for it, among the masses of the fighters. The drum and fife were the best they had known at musters; and they were good enough still, to fight by. So, recalling the prowess achieved constantly, in following them, it may be wondered what possible results might have come from inspiration of a marine band, a Grafulla, or a Gilmore![22]

Sophisticated critics agreed that Confederate bands heard by Florida soldiers did not match those of the Federal units. An English professional soldier observed, "Many of the regiments had little bands of three or four musicians who played rather discordantly. The Southerners are said to be extremely fond of music, though they seldom take the trouble to learn to play themselves, and seem not very particular as to whether the instruments they hear are in tune or not. The bandsmen are almost all Germans."[23] In agreement was another English military observer who described a droll procession of another band. He wrote, "First came eight or ten instruments braying discordantly, then an enormous Confederate flag, followed by about four hundred men moving by fours—dressed in every variety of costume, and armed with every variety of weapon . . . all had six-shooters and bowie knives."[24] The circumstances under which the bands sometimes performed were reasons enough not to be fastidious about intonation. Lt. Col. Arthur Fremantle cited one instance at the battle of Gettysburg. "When the cannonade was at its height, a Confederate band of music, between the cemetery and ourselves, began to play polkas and waltzes, which sounded very curious, accompanied by the hissing and bursting of shells."[25] The assessments of Florida regimental historians and bandsmen did not always agree with cosmopolitan critics. They told their own stories.

The most lengthy and specific account of a Florida band and of other bands heard by Florida military units in the war was written by Washington M. Ives, Jr., in letters to members of his family in Live Oak. As a member of the Fourth Florida Regiment, Ives was sent through northwest Florida to Montgomery and Mobile, Alabama, in June and July 1862. He drilled, stood guard, lay in the mud in wet clothes, and had neither tent nor fire. When his unit was assigned to Camp Ward, near Warrington,

West Florida, he was appointed company clerk. His morning report of August 4 listed the following personnel: 6 captains, 18 lieutenants, 18 sergeants, 27 corporals, 14 musicians, and 461 privates.[26]

In August, Ives's unit was joined by others from Florida. Among them were the Third, Seventh, and Eighth regiments, Martin's Artillery, and the First Battalion. He observed that the brass band of the Third Regiment played very well. That of the Fourth Regiment was rehearsing under H. Crane from Tampa. They had received their instruments only a week earlier.[27] Members of the band, two lieutenants, and a colonel attempted to persuade Ives to join the band. He refused on the grounds that his berth as clerk was better than one blowing a horn; yet the appeal of the assignment was growing.[28] In October he wrote his sisters that the band had played very well at guard mounting. Among their current repertory were "The Troubadour," "Rosalie," "Grand Norma March," "The Mobile Quickstep," and "Cheer, Boys, Cheer." He reported that in the fight at Lavergne, the band of the Thirty-second Alabama lost all of its instruments but that the Fourth Florida allowed its members to play on theirs. He thought they performed splendidly. Their interpretation of "Down in Alabama," he wrote, made "anyone's blood rise to the point necessary of charge bayonets."[29]

Ives survived the fierce fighting of the early months of 1863 while at Tullahoma, Tennessee, though Union sharpshooters did cut the hair off his right temple and leave a hole in his pants. By July he wrote that he was marching with remnants of the Fourth's band. Many men were either "worn out" or sick and had been sent to the rear. Many of Ives's old friends had not survived, and his new ones were members of the band. With them he formed a mess at Camp Hurricane, Mississippi, in August. Their names were L. C. Canora, William G. Broe, M. C. Pemberton, Socrates Prosperos Bowin, Jimmie Rawls, J. H. Young, Elias Bingham, Charles Young, James McCradie, J. A. Pollard, William Pennington, and Sherman Daniels. He commented, "Most of these are good men and well disposed and we get along splendidly."[30] Their current repertory included "Military Band Polka," "Viva Polka," and "Rival Polka." Less than a month later he wrote his mother, "Our brass band is the best in this army. It has been playing a piece which Katie [his sister] plays, viz., 'Kissing through the Bars' or 'The Switzer's Farewell.'"[31] The sentimental songs and light-hearted dance tunes soon were to be replaced by the reports of rifles and cannons and the moans of dying men.

Overpowering Union forces and bad management forced a Confederate retreat at the battle of Chickamauga. It was a major Union victory. While Ives wrote that the several Florida units fought nobly, he wrote his sister that the battle was "dearly bought." Sitting on his knapsack and writing on the head of Moses Pemberton's drum, he reported seeing 500 or 600 dead men, 100 horses dead, and about 2,500 men badly wounded. He wrote of the ghastly faces of the dead and the blood-soaked battlefield. He also wrote that a diphtheria epidemic had begun. Ives himself was soon a victim, though he survived.[32] Other Florida men survived both the battle and the disease, though their numbers were reduced. Among them were the First Cavalry and the First, Third, Fourth, Sixth, and Seventh regiments. None of Ives's Fourth came from east of Madison, and he was not convinced of support from East Floridians. "The boys don't talk much about peace now," he wrote. "It does not seem one able bodied man will be spared to tell the tale," he concluded.[33] He had once thought a hard blow struck by the Confederacy would end the war but now speculated that there was little likelihood that it would end in his lifetime.[34]

On Christmas Eve 1863, Ives heard the brigade band play "My Old Kentucky Home," "Dixie," "The Marseillaise," and a piece known to the band as "Lovely Waltz." The boys of the Fourth Regiment band had been out serenading that evening and had been rewarded by ample refreshments, which Ives called "evil spirits." They played "Dixie" and "Let Me Kiss Him for His Mother" but were too boozy to compete with the better performance by the brigade band. Ives remarked, too, upon the lack of sobriety among the officers who attempted to speak before the crowd.

By mid-January 1864, the Fourth Florida Regiment was in winter quarters at Dalton, Georgia. Ives then wrote of their repertory and that of the Fourth Kentucky. He wrote that the excellent Kentucky band had not played since the battle of Missionary Ridge, as three of its principal musicians had deserted to the enemy. He remembered that they played an excellent variety of pieces, including "The Washington Artillery Quickstep" and "Diamond Schottische." These two were in the repertory of the Florida Fourth Regimental band, as were "Sultan Polka," "Share My Cottage Quickstep," "Captain Shepphard Quickstep," "Verona Waltz," "Let Me Kiss Him for His Mother," "Lorena," "F. L. Village Quickstep," and several other marches and quicksteps. He added, "The brigade band plays some beautiful pieces and Bates band plays a great many old familiar pieces, viz., 'Annie Laurie,' 'Ever of Thee,' etc."[35]

Washington Ives's letters to his family continued until February 13, 1865, but none others told of music made or heard by the boys from Florida. His only other 1864 reference to the band was to reassure his father of his son's comparative well-being. "Musicians," he wrote, "get the best of supplies as they are always at the rear and pass off as good soldiers."[36] He had marched nearly six hundred miles from the time he left Florence, Alabama, until the Tennessee campaign. At rates of twelve to twenty-two miles per day through cold and snowstorms, he had earned the epithet of good soldier.

Young bandsman Washington Ives had stayed the course. "I don't think there can be enough ill feelings left to stir up another war during my lifetime," he wrote. His commentary on his future was equally candid. "There is really a great deal of romance and affectation yet in the south which I wish would give way to something like the realities of life."[37] The men who survived the war came home to pick up the pieces of their lives or to begin new ones. The prosperity and order of the 1850s were gone. The wounds of failure and bitterness of defeat were deep and slow in healing. For many, music made the pain bearable. The inveterate Confederates (Richard B. Harwell's term) were strong enough to write their own song. They wanted no northern pity. Their hate for the Yankees would sustain them.

O, I'm a good old rebel, that's just what I am;
For this "Fair Land of Freedom" I don't care a damn!
I'm glad I fit against it, I only wish we'd won,
And I don't want no pardon for anything I've done.

I hates the Constitution, this great Republic too,
I hates the Freedman's Buro in uniforms of blue;
I hates the nasty eagle with all his brag and fuss,
The lyin', thievin' Yankees, I hates them wuss and wuss!

I hates the Yankee nation and everything they do,
I hates the Declaration of Independence, too;
I hates the glorious Union—'tis dripping with our blood,
I hates the striped banner, I fit it all I could.

Three hundred thousand Yankees lie stiff in southern dust;
We got three hundred thousand before they conquered us!
They died of Southern fever and Southern steel and shot,
I wish they was three million instead of what we got!

Oh, I'm a Good Old Rebel

Arr. by Philip Egner
"Sound Off!"

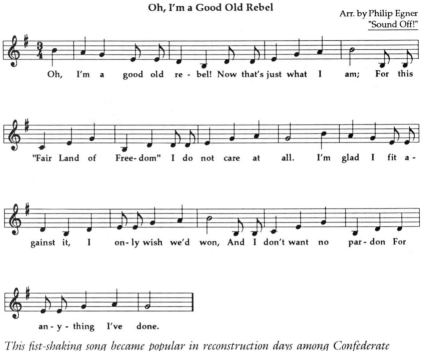

Oh, I'm a good old re-bel! Now that's just what I am; For this "Fair Land of Free-dom" I do not care at all. I'm glad I fit a-gainst it, I on-ly wish we'd won, And I don't want no par-don For an-y-thing I've done.

This fist-shaking song became popular in reconstruction days among Confederate veterans. Other versions cropped up in collections in the South, Southwest, and Midwest. (Reprinted, by permission, from Edward Arthur Dolph, Sound Off!, *p. 361)*

> I can't take up my musket and fight 'em now no more,
> But I ain't a-going to love 'em, now that is sartain sure;
> And I don't want no pardon for what I was and am,
> I won't be reconstructed, and I don't care a damn![38]

For those who accepted defeat, there was to be little rest and few comforts on earth. They sang their songs of longing for eventual rest in heaven. The words of one were by Isaac Watts and set to the music of William Mather.

> When I can read my title clear
> To mansions in the skies,

Several collections of hymns that early settlers brought to Florida included a setting of
"When I Can Read My Title Clear." This one was arranged by Thomas Hastings.
(Reprinted from Thomas Hastings, Sacred Songs for Family and Social Worship
[New York: American Tract Society, 1842])

I bid farewell to every fear
And wipe my weeping eyes.

There shall I bathe my weary soul
In seas of heavenly rest,
And not a wave of trouble roll
Across my peaceful breast.[39]

Young recruits for the Union army also had their eyes on heaven. For one of them there was not a heavy line between religiousness and patriotism. William B. Smith was fifteen years of age in 1863 when he attended a meeting at his church in a small Illinois town, but years later he remembered it well. He recalled, "Now, instead of the sweet, peaceful songs of Zion, lined by the venerable minister in clerical black and white cravat, and sung fervently by the devout worshipers, the rostrum was occupied by the stalwart Union officer in blue with shoulder straps of gold. Patriotic war songs were heartily sung, and stirring speeches were made. Martial music of fife and drum filled the air and all was enthusiasm and excitement." William joined in as the crowd sang,

Yes, we'll rally round the flag, boys,
We'll rally once again.[40]

When the singing stopped, he stepped forward and signed up to go to war. It was like being saved at a religious service. William served in the Seventeenth Army Corps and the Fourteenth Illinois Volunteer Infantry. Before his army career was over, he came with his unit to Jacksonville, Florida. He always remembered that rallying song. It was written by William B. Bradbury, the gospel-hymn writer who wrote "Just As I Am, without One Plea" and "He Leadeth Me." This recruiting song led him to enlistment and capture and a term as prisoner of war at Andersonville before he returned to Illinois.

William Smith was only one of many young men who were to leave their homes for the first time in the service of their country. From the East Coast and the Midwest, they received orders to travel to the southern sector and there to engage in battle with the Confederate rebels. Some of them reached their destination and completed their mission in Florida.

In 1861 the U.S. army table of organization for large units included positions for bandsmen. War Department General Orders no. 15, issued

May 4, 1861, authorized a band of twenty-four musicians for each regiment. In addition, two others were authorized for martial music purposes for each company and two principal musicians for the regiment as a whole. It was estimated that by June 30, 1862, a total of 27,248 enlisted men were serving as musicians. Of this number approximately 14,832 served as bandsmen in 618 or more bands. Many of these were professional musicians of superior ability. Music was at its best among the Union bands from the spring of 1861 to midsummer 1862. On July 17, 1862, Congress passed a bill mustering out the regimental bands because of the excessive cost of maintaining them. Within thirty days, these professional musicians returned to their homes. The bill did allow the organization of volunteer brigade bands of sixteen members. These men, however, essentially were ambulance corpsmen who carried rifles in action or on march. They played their instruments in camp or on parade. The bands were formed principally of personnel from the martial music corps of regiments. The music of the octave flutes, fifes, and drums served the functional purposes required for marching or battle but were judged monotonous for concert or recreational purposes. The bill disbanding professional bands was not a popular one.

An officer of the First Regiment, Massachusetts Cavalry Volunteers, wrote, "In a land where amusements were scarce, the band's performances were always welcome, and the order which came from the War Department to discharge all regimental bands was heard with dismay."[41] The colonel of the Twenty-fourth Regiment, Massachusetts Volunteers, wrote, "I think it a great mistake (to discharge the band) and that the service will lose more than the treasury will gain."[42]

Officers and men of other Union military units agreed with the colonel, but rarely have military men been unable to find ways around unacceptable regulations. The order to muster bandsmen out of service hardly reached regimental headquarters before new bands were raised within the units and supported by volunteer company funds. It was these groups that were heard in Florida, except for those who arrived on the scene early in the war. One early arrival was the Sixth Regiment New York Volunteers Infantry, known as Wilson Zouaves, who came to Santa Rosa Island in 1861, before the order was published. They had not only a fine band but a talented, well-equipped theatrical troupe. Many of these soldiers were firemen recruited from "the dregs of the city [New York], pug uglies and criminals . . . fearful and dazzling to behold." Their colorful uniforms only romanticized their appearance to their East Side sweethearts. One girl sang,

> My love he is a Zou-Zu, so gallant and bold,
> He's rough and he's handsome, scarce nineteen years old;
> To show off in Washington he has left his only dear,
> And my heart is abreaking because he's not here.

Septimus Winner, Philadelphia composer of many lighthearted popular songs of the period, wrote about one of these men in the chorus of "Abraham's Daughter; or, Raw Recruits."

> And I belong to the Fire Zou-Zous,
> And don't you think I oughter?
> We're goin' down to Washington
> To fight for Abraham's daughter.[43]

They were stationed on Santa Rosa Island, near Fort Pickens and over-looking Pensacola Bay, and participated in that battle on October 9, 1861. since they were serving essentially a blockade function and had ample free time, they amused themselves by producing a form of entertainment they called "private and public theatricals." They were, in fact, variety programs which usually included a dramatic sketch. An undated program included in their regimental history lists an opening chorus by the troupe, an overture by the band, and numerous songs, readings, and dances. The performance closed with a dramatic farce, *Uncle Dad's Cabin,* a parody on Harriet Beecher Stowe's popular work. Some of the New Yorkers could sing well, others could dance a breakdown or jig well enough to please a Bowery audience. "The Zouave Theatre was an immense success, with an audience composed of old and stiff backed regular officers, young and enthusiastic ditto, the 6th own contribution of shoulder straps, and an outlying fringe of peering Ethiopians," according to the regimental historian.[44]

Of all the Federal troops that served in Florida during the war, the Wilson Zouaves were one of the most colorful. An anonymous Scotsman who served with the unit described their off-duty antics.[45] The Scotsman had immigrated to New York in 1850 and, while under the influence of liquor in June 1861, volunteered to become a member of the New York Sixth Regiment. To sum up the character of the men, he wrote, "The regiment had got such a name in the North, and had been represented in

SIXTH REGIMENT
ZOUAVE THEATRE.
PENSACOLA, FLA.

PROGRAMME.
Part First.

OPENING CHORUS, ...	Troupe.
GET ALONG HOME YALLER GALS . .	Mr. J. Durning.
MY LOVE HE IS A ZOUAVE, . .	" J. Garvey.
SEEING NELLY HOME, . . .	" G. Clark.
POMPEY'S LAMENT, . . .	" J. Powers.
ELLA REE, ...	" J. Durning.
ANNIE LISLE, ...	" C. Trigler.
THE BOY WITH THE AUBURN HAIR, .	" J. Garvey.
HAZEL DELL, ...	" C. Trigler.
OVERTURE, ...	Band.

PART SECOND.

DANCE, (jig), ...	Mr. J. Comfort.
SONG, (comic), ...	" E. Rice.
DANCE, (challenge plantation), . .	" Garvey & Foley.
SONG, ...	" E. Havey.
JULIESS'S IDEAS ABOUT THE WAR, .	" J. Garvey.
SONG—THE UNLUCKY MAN, . .	" J. Comfort.
DANCE, ...	" W. Tiffany.
SONG, ...	Union Children.

The Performance will conclude with the laughable farce of

UNCLE DAD'S CABIN.

OLD DAD BROWN, . . .	Mr. J. Durning.
PEDLER, ...	" W. R. Haynes.
ARABELLA, ...	Miss E. Smith.
LUCY, ...	" E. Havey.

Doors open at 3½ o'clock, P. M.   Performance to commence at 4.
☞ You are respectfully invited to attend by

LIEUT. V. VANGIESON,
SIXTH N. Y. VOLS.

SIXTH REGIMENT ZOUAVE THEATRE

Brilliantly costumed in imitation of French army Moorish soldiers, men of the New York Sixth Regiment Volunteers occasionally traded their usual fezzes, vests, baggy pants, and leggings for less colorful stage costumes when they gave programs of songs, dances, and drama in Pensacola. (Reprinted from Gouverneur Morris, The History of a Volunteer Regiment, *p. 79)*

the Southern newspapers as such cutthroat blackguards, that even the sharks in the bay of Pensacola had forsaken their haunts on our account."[46] The general commanding the unit himself was not admirable. He had an obsession for pianos and ordered his men to gather all of them they could find to be brought to his quarters. About eight or ten of them were on display there after he raided and destroyed civilian residences to no military purpose.

In St. Augustine, performances of minstrel shows were reported by Company K, Seventh Connecticut Volunteer Infantry; the Ninety-seventh Regiment, Pennsylvania Infantry; and the Third Rhode Island Heavy Artillery Regiment. Other units produced a variety of plays acted by men of the company. Female parts were taken either by the men or by drummer boys, just as they had been when Florida was a British colony a hundred years before. The New York Forty-eighth had been sent to the Ancient City in August 1863 and were replaced in October by the Twenty-fourth Massachusetts. The forty-eighth had brought down from Fort Pulaski, Georgia, stage fixtures for their theatrical productions. From New York, their costumes cost five hundred dollars. Music was furnished by bands from the Twenty-fourth Massachusetts and the Tenth Connecticut. The regimental glee club and actors came from the same units. The Olympic Theatre proscenium drop curtain, measuring thirteen by twenty-six feet, was painted with the seal of the New England Guards, and the chocolate and gold well panels depicted scenes from St. Augustine. The repertory included *To Paris and Back for Five Pounds, The Bachelor's Bedroom, My Wife's Second Floor, Bombastes Furioso, An Object of Interest, A Blighted Being, Aunt Charlotte's Maid, Number One around the Corner, An Ugly Customer,* and *Two Buzzards.*

Union soldiers and sailors who occupied Florida coastal towns were reputed to have several well-trained musicians within their units.

The New England troops excel in the music faculty, and in every regiment from Massachusetts, Connecticut, or New Hampshire, music teachers or good singers abound, and many an otherwise tedious evening has thus been beguiled by the elevating influence of music. In this respect, perhaps, no regiment is more favored than the Massachusetts Twenty-third, composed chiefly of Salem, Marblehead, Danvers, and Boston men. Many of the officers were members of the best musical societies and leaders or pillars in their church choirs at home. Could their friends have looked in upon us on board the *High-lander*, during many of the boisterous nights we have been anchored in this Sound [Hatteras Inlet, N.C.], while the storm howled without, they might have heard:

> Perhaps Dundee's wild, warbling measures rise,
> Or plaintive martyrs, worthy of the name,
> Or noble Elgin beat the heavenward flame.

On board the *Huzzar*, which carries the left wing of the Twenty-third, they have their full share of sweet singers, and a very excellent band of music, under the lead of Henry C. Brown of Boston. In the centre of the fleet, which covers an area of some two miles of the bay, is anchored the *S. R. Spaudling*, the present flagship of Gen. A. E. Burnside. From her high deck he can survey the entire fleet, and observe all that is going on. On the deck of one or two vessels near us are gathered quiet groups of soldiers, and the sublime strains of "Old Hundred" which float across the waters, human voices mingling with the bands, testify that they are engaged in religious worship. To many of these brave men it will be, perhaps, their last Sabbath on earth.[47]

The Massachusetts Twenty-fourth Regiment entered fully into the social and religious life of St. Augustine. They offered colorful dress parades with bands playing, feasts and balls at Florida House, and evening performances at the Olympic Theatre. At St. George Episcopal Church the regimental glee club sang, and a member of the band played the organ. So content were they that their favorite hymn became:

> My willing soul would stay
> In such a frame as this,
> And sit and sing itself away,
> To everlasting bliss.[48]

Most of the regiments reported informal singing and dancing as the principal recreations. That of the First Light Battery, Connecticut Volunteers, was illustrative. "The time not required by the care of horses was passed in singing, playing on the violin, banjo, bones and other instruments. In the evening there was dancing—full sets were formed for cotillion, Virginia Reel, and the comrades proved that they could waltz as well as any."[49]

Social life was no less lively among Union naval personnel. Eugene

SPANISH CATHEDRAL, ST. AUGUSTINE
Federal bandsmen are photographed at the entrance to the Spanish Catholic cathedral in St. Augustine during the Civil War. (Courtesy Florida State Archives)

Chapin, a navy paymaster who during the blockade was stationed at Key West, Tampa, St. Joseph, and Cape St. Blas, wrote of his recreation. "While at Key West I made some pleasurable acquaintances, and was invited to several small parties, consisting of music and private fandangoes. I also received an invitation to a grand ball which was given by the officers of the U.S. Steamer *San Jacinto,* which I accepted, and which was a most brilliant affair." It was attended by the Spanish consul, his retinue, Spanish ladies and gentlemen, and Cubans. "The officers, all dressed in their showy uniforms, and the ladies, in their rich, gay colors and expensive ornaments of diamonds and jewels, all gracefully dancing, made, indeed, a very interesting and dazzling scene to look upon, and one which seldom occurs in a person's lifetime. I took part in the dancing and enjoyed myself very much, until the early hours of the morning, when I retired to my quarters on board the ship."[50]

Religious services gave one Union soldier the privilege of attending a singing school. Stationed in Jacksonville, he commented that he had attended church and heard a sermon by Rev. John Swaim. "It was one of the pleasantest Sabbath mornings I have spent in a long time," he commented. "The singers collected together and sang very finely. Hereafter there is to be a singing school meeting at Mr. Swaim's every Saturday evening, and as I have been specially invited, I think I will attend occasionally to revive old times a little."[51]

The chaplain of the Seventh New Hampshire Volunteers, stationed in Fernandina, inspired little religious zeal among his flock. The tall somber chaplain, wearing a long frock coat, would rise on his toes and sink in the sand "looking like the avenging angel out seeking young devils whom he might devour."[52] In another unit, it was the music that was remembered by the historian. "The Religious Association held prayer meetings, and comrade Hotchkiss would stand, tuning fork in hand, leading the singing."[53]

Holidays and reunions were celebrated by Union army and navy men with music, speeches, parades, banquets, and dancing. While stationed on Amelia Island in 1863, officers of the Ninety-seventh Pennsylvania joined their naval counterparts on the gunboat *Flambeau* for a reunion. If the purpose of the social occasion was to encourage rapport between branches of the services, the event was a success. According to the official historian, "The merry sailors, with song and viol, alternated music with jest, and with witty repartee in genuine cordiality filling the hours with pleasure."[54] At Fernandina on Thanksgiving 1863, the string band of the Pennsylvania Ninety-seventh Regiment played "America," "Star Spangled Banner," "Red, White, and Blue," "Hail Columbia," and "Old Hundredth." They played at Col. Henry R. Guss's headquarters in the afternoon and several serenades that evening. On Christmas Day that year there was target shooting, a hurdle race, a blindfold wheelbarrow feat, a boat race, and a jig dance competition. A minstrel show with vocal and instrumental music was produced as the evening entertainment.[55]

Union bands were heard in the coastal towns Fernandina, St. Augustine, Key West, and Pensacola. New York newspapers reported that Union bands animated parades and that in the Jacksonville celebration of

FEDERAL TROOPS MARCHING

Five drummers set the cadence for these Federal troops as they marched down Second Street, Fernandina, during the Civil War. (Courtesy Florida State Archives)

the anniversary of the Emancipation Proclamation, Negro children sang "Thrice Happy Days" and John Greenleaf Whittier's "Negro Boatman Song."[56] Bands of the Twenty-fourth Massachusetts and Tenth Connecticut regiments played in St. Augustine on New Year's Day 1864 in their celebration of the first anniversary of the Emancipation Proclamation. A platform had been built in the plaza, and several hundred black citizens marched up to the stage while the bands played. Union officers and men were present for the reading of the proclamation and speeches by Chaplains H. Clay Trumbull and Willson and unnamed black ministers. Negro children sang songs, including "John Brown's Body" and "The Year of Jubilo." The two bands played "Hail Columbia." A collation was prepared in the courthouse hall for officers and bandsmen. A regimental historian wrote:

> The Negroes formed on the plaza, while the officers and musicians devoured the food within the hall. The soldiers standing around had infinite amusement hearing the colored folks sing their own peculiar melodies. After the bands had filled up with food, they came out and again tuned their instruments, giving many national airs, ending with Yankee Doodle. Later came amusements of their own in the several quarters of the companies. Gander or stag-dances were the order of

UNION BAND IN ST. AUGUSTINE, 1862

The Civil War blockade brought several Union bands to Florida coastal towns, such as this one marching in review in St. Augustine. (Courtesy Florida State Archives; reprinted from Frank Leslie's Illustrated Newspaper *15 [1862]: 177)*

the evening, and if the music was primitive, the light fantastic was energetic and the fun ran merrily on till a late hour, and well it was that it should, for as yet these men realized nothing of the exactions of the approaching Battle Summer. . . . Many a brave boy in blue who on this New Year's night is so blithe and gay, will sleep beneath the soil of Old Virginy, an offering for his country's need.[57]

Gen. William Burney, Union commander of the District of Florida, with headquarters in Jacksonville, ordered a bandstand built near his headquarters in 1864. There the band of the Seventeenth Regiment Connecticut Volunteer Infantry played on Mondays, Wednesdays, and Fridays from 7:30 to 8:30 in the evening. One volunteer wrote his cousin that the music was beautiful and inspiring. Of his commanding officer, he wrote that the general had quite a taste for wine, music, and the fine arts.[58] The general sometimes took excursions on the St. Johns River accompanied by the band. The Seventeenth Regiment string band and the 107th brass band were in demand for social occasions. On November 8, 1864, they played for a farewell dance honoring Gen. John P. Hatch, which continued until four o'clock in the morning. On January 5, 1865, the string band played for a masquerade ball, a grand affair exceeding anything of its kind ever before undertaken in Jacksonville. Guests from Hilton Head and St. Augustine attended.[59]

The Negro Boatman's Song

J. G. Whittier, Esq.

L. O. Emerson
Trumpet of Freedom

At the 1864 anniversary program celebrating the Emancipation Proclamation, Jacksonville Negro children sang "The Negro Boatman's Song," and Union bands led parades through the streets. (Reprinted from Trumpet of Freedom)

Each of the Union musical units that came to Florida during the Confederate struggle for independence had its military mission. Units dispatched early in the war reclaimed federal forts and defended the seacoast. Later, others continued to cut Confederate supply lines and open their own outlets for cotton, lumber, salt, meat, and other provisions in the warehouses of Florida. They also obtained Negro recruits and attempted "to inaugurate measures for the speedy restoration of the State of Florida to her allegiance to the United States."[60] Many military units engaged in

Florida had musical aspects or music performers that they brought to the state. A sampling of their official histories illustrates events of musical life during the war period.

The Chatham Artillery fought in the battle of Olustee. In florid language, its historian remembered the "sweet bugle" of a member of the company called Old Hetterick. "How often at tattoo its silvery notes, mingling in soft cadence with the gentle ripple of the swelling tide in perfect unison with the whisper of the evening winds as they lingered among the beautiful trees silvered all over by the rays of a full-orbed moon, filled the air with thoughts of alternate joy and sadness, love and pleasure, peace and war. Now an aria, now a ballad, now a lively waltz, now a soul stirring march, and now strains so soft and pensive, that they seemed the voice of a young mother in her first sorrow."[61]

The Seventh Regiment, New Hampshire Volunteers, saw service at Fort Jefferson (situated on Dry Tortugas Island, one of the Florida Keys) and later in St. Augustine. Six of the companies had been brought to the Keys aboard the full-rigged clipper ship *S. R. Mallory.* A lieutenant of the regiment described their arrival. "The sun came out in all its glory followed by a beautiful, bright moonlight, and the boys enjoyed it immensely by sitting on deck until near morning, singing and story-telling. We anchored in the bay at night, and in the early hours of morning the jolly singing of the sailors at the capstans, plainly told us they were weighing anchor and were about to get under way once more."[62]

The Forty-fifth Regiment, Massachusetts Volunteer Militia, was mustered into service on September 15, 1862. Their band was organized by searching among the companies for men who had "more or less knowledge of musical instruments." The search produced a leader, Sgt. John A. Spofford, and seventeen bandsmen. Cpl. Augustus S. Lovett recalled, "Soon discordant sounds from the retreat of the musicians, indicated that they were getting together and exerting themselves to produce harmony of action, which in due time, bore fruit in making our band a great credit to our regiment as whole, and the admiration of each individual."[63] Instruments had been donated by the men and friends of the regiment. They were declared delicate tools of war, and it was difficult to protect them in inclement weather on the march. Bandsmen were led on dress parades by an elderly drum major from Gilmore's Band, named Mariani. A member of the band described him as very tall, commanding in appearance, proud, and jolly. He wore a colorful uniform, including a bearskin hat topped with a pompom, and carried a gold-headed baton. By the time they reached the southern sector, the band had a repertory sufficient to play for both military and social occasions. The favorite tune of the band was at first called "that squawking tune," then the "cut, cut, cut-a-cut, cut" tune. It was properly titled "Cadet Waltz," written by R. A. Burditt, and it was remembered as a solo cornet piece for John A. Spofford, the band leader. The Forty-fifth Regiment fought in the battle of Olustee.[64] The 115th Regiment, New York Volunteers, and their Cayadutta Brass Band arrived at the mouth of the St. Johns River on February 7. As they sailed up to the dock, the bands "discoursed national airs." They occupied Jacksonville and moved through Baldwin and also fought in the battle of Olustee. After their defeat and a raid on Palatka, they returned to Jacksonville. As they sailed away on April 16, the band played, "To the Mississippi I Am Going." The regiment had impressive music resources. There were fifteen members of the band. In addition, there were twenty-five other musicians of the corps.[65]

Union men, like soldiers in every war, welcomed correspondence from home. While in Florida, one man received assurance of his girl's undying love. At the same time she urged him to prove himself true both to her and to the flag of the Union. She enclosed a copy of one of the most popular songs of the time.

> Dearest love, do you remember
> When we last did meet
> How you told me that you loved me,
> Kneeling at my feet?
> Oh! how proud you stood before me,
> In your suit of blue
> When you vowed to me and country
> Ever to be true.
> *Chorus:* Weeping sad and lonely
>   Hopes and fears, how vain;
>   Yet praying
>   When this cruel war is over
>   Praying that we meet again.[66]

Maj. Seth Rogers, surgeon of the Thirty-third U.S. Colored Infantry, the first freedmen's regiment to be organized, was ordered to service along the coastal towns of Georgia and Florida in 1862–63. His were among the most extended accounts of Negro singing in such places as Beaufort, South Carolina, Fernandina, and Jacksonville. In one letter he wrote, "When I sit down at evening it always seems as if there could be but one subject to write upon, the music of these religious soldiers, who sing and pray steadily from supper time till taps at 8:30, interrupted only by roll call at eight. . . . At this moment the camp resounds with the John Brown hymn, sung as no white regiment can sing it, so full of pathos and harmony." He had sympathy for Negroes but did not find them perfect, any more than he had the whites in Worcester.[67]

Major Rogers wrote of the troops' marching to the music of their own voices and of a flag ceremony when Negro men and women inspired the company by singing "My Country 'Tis of Thee." But he was impressed most with the sadness of their spirituals and the spirit with which they sang in adversity. He gave two illustrations of boatmen singing. "Our black soldiers sang as they rowed—not songs of common soldiers—but the hymns of praise mingled with those pathetic longings for a better world, so constant with these people. There are times when I could quite enjoy more earthly songs for them, even a touch of the wicked, but this generation must live and die in sadness. The sun can never shine for them as for a nation of freemen whose fathers were not slaves." They left Fernandina on March 8, 1863, to reoccupy Jacksonville. Uncle York, an old Negro, rowed one boat quietly past the Confederate steamers by covering the oars with sheepskin.[68] He told the story himself. "An' de moon was berry shine, an' when at las' we done got by de danger, I whoop, an' de master ob de gun boat *Paul Jones* say 'come on' and din I make rowers raise a sing."[69]

Many of the northern troops who came to Florida during the war were black soldiers with white officers. One of the young officers wrote his father from Jacksonville of the music in his black regiment. "While I am seated here I can hear singing along the line—'tis good—some of the officers have some of the men in their tent with violins and banjos—they make good music and there are many good singers."[70]

Several Union officers recorded the texts of Negro songs they heard during their assignments to the southern sector. Few gave precise dates and places of their first hearing. That they were heard or sung by units which served in Florida is documented in official regimental histories or memoirs of those present. That there were textual variants was verified by the officer who wrote one of the fullest accounts of the spirituals during the war years—Col. Thomas Wentworth Higginson.

> It is not strange that they differed, for the range seemed almost endless, and South Carolina, Georgia and Florida seemed to have nothing but the generic character in common, until all were mingled in the united stock of camp melodies. Often in the starlit evening I have returned from some lonely ride by a swift river, or on the plover-

Federal picket boats and rowboats patrolled rivers near Fernandina in 1863. Negro oarsmen sang as they rowed. (Courtesy Florida State Archives; reprinted from Joseph T. Wilson, The Black Phalanx, *p. 276)*

haunted barrens, and, entering the camp, have silently approached some glimmering fire, round which the dusky figures moved in rhythmical barbaric dance the Negroes call a "shout," chanting, often harshly, but always in the most perfect time, some monotonous refrain. . . . These songs, are but the vocal expression of the simplicity of their faith and the sublimity of their long resignation.[71]

This summary was apt for the song Higginson reported as their favorite. To the question, "What makes ole Satan for follow me so?" the answer was "Hold your light, Brudder Robert, Hold your light." The advice was given to each member of the assembly by name, a personal reassurance that being a shining example on earth would lead to a heavenly reward. The Negro troops sang spiritual songs of the church militant, boat songs, narrative songs, answering songs, special occasion songs, marching songs, and improvised wartime or freedom songs.

As to Higginson's reference to "shouts" or praise meetings of the Negroes, they are described by officers of several Union military units.

Some members of the Eleventh Maine Regiment, en route to Fernandina, were present at such a meeting near Beaufort, South Carolina. The description was written by Col. William W. Davis of the 104th Pennsylvania Regiment.

> They [church members] formed themselves in a circle around the room, all standing. Three men, seated on a bench at one side, now commenced to chant, which increased in volume as they proceeded, when the worshipers began to move around the room, keeping hold of hands. They kept time to the music with their bodies and limbs and repeated the words of the refrain. Sometimes they moved backward—sometimes sideways, all the while wriggling and twisting their bodies forward into many attitudes, shuffling their feet to time, and beating the cadence with their hands. The music of the chant was wild, melancholy, and monotonous, but not entirely devoid of harmony. Sometimes the voices would swell into a loud and full chorus, then sink again almost to a whisper; but at no time did they reach the shouting pitch. The leader of the three singers changed the words and the tune at pleasure, apparently impromptu and without method. His hands were kept in lively motion and his action reminded one of a darkie beating Juba. At one time the refrain had some application to boating, when the Negroes as they swept round the room in measured cadence worked the arms as though pulling at the oar. The dances of some of our western Indian tribes is not unlike what I witnessed. It was evidently a heathen ceremony handed down from their African ancestors, somewhat modified by their Christian training.[72]

Negro church revival meetings were a novelty to the New England troops who came to the southern section. Regimental historians wrote that such gatherings occasioned considerable amusement for the troops and that some troops attended for the sake of getting a little cheap entertainment. One especially patronizing historian repeatedly described the service as "ludicrous in the extreme" in such passages as "a sister fat and forty but as black as the ace of spades, threw out her arms right and left and grabbed the wool of a young brother who was near her, pulled it, calling 'I've got him, bress de Lawd!'"

It was not surprising that a fistfight between troops and congregation ensued when soldiers failed to contribute a dime to the collection plate at one service. But before the men were restricted for their behavior, they heard a favorite revival hymn:

> Little children sitting on the tree of life,
> To hear when Jordan roll;
> O' roll, Jordan, roll; roll Jordan roll!
> We march the angel march;
> O, march the angel march;
> Oh, my soul is marching heavenward,
> To hear when Jordan roll.
> O my brother sitting on the tree of life,
> To hear when Jordan roll.
> Sister Mary sitting on the tree of life,
> To hear when Jordan roll.[73]

Singing of the First Union Regiment under Thomas Wentworth Higginson was described in colorful detail by their commanding officer. When the men were advised that they were en route to Florida, they marched as they sang "John Brown," "Marching Along," and "Gwine in de Wilderness."[74]

Negro troops continued their singing even after some of them were captured and in prison. One account, written almost thirty years after the event, told of Union Negroes who after capture at Wagner were imprisoned at Charleston. "Often after nine o'clock at night, when by the rules we were confined to our quarters, I have been aroused from a doze by the singing of the colored prisoners. At such a time the voices coming down from the upper floors of the jail sounded very sweet, and there was a certain weird, indescribable sadness in the minor key melodies, that told of camp-meeting days and the religious hope that seemed to be confined exclusively to these poor fellows."[75] A similar account was written by another observer.

> At the close of the day the Negro prisoners made a practice of getting together in the jail, and singing their plaintive melodies till late in the evenings. The character of their songs was universally mournful, and it was often affecting to listen to them,—always embodying as they did those simple childlike emotions and sentiments for which the Negro is so justly celebrated. The harmony and the rich melody of

their voices are rarely surpassed. . . . One song which appeared to be a special favorite with them, was written by Sergeant Johnson. . . . He intended it as a parody on "When the Cruel War Is Over."

> When I enlisted in the army,
> Then I thought 'twas grand,
> Marching through the streets of Boston
> Behind a regimental band.
> When at Wagner, I was captured
> Then my courage failed;
> Now I'm dirty, hungry, naked,
> Here in Charleston jail.
> *Chorus:* Weeping, sad and lonely,
> Oh! how bad I feel!
> Down in Charleston, South Carolina,
> Praying for a good, square meal.
> (two more verses)[76]

Civilians of the Florida Confederacy welcomed the symbol of the new nation and soon were singing the song about it, "The Bonnie Blue Flag." The Confederate congress adopted the first national flag, the Stars and Bars, on March 4, 1861. It was this flag that was raised at Fort Marion, St. Augustine, on March 23, 1861, less than a month after the design was officially adopted.[77] The burden of the song about it was that southern natives had acquired their property by honest toil and their rights to it had been threatened. Union men had been friends and brothers but now were treacherous. Men of the eleven states of the Confederacy were cheered for their strength and bravery. They rallied round "The Bonnie Blue Flag" to save their heritage and made it their most popular song. Each of the states was named. The third verse was:

> First gallant South Carolina noble made the stand;
> Then came Alabama who took her by the hand;
> Next, quickly, Mississippi, Georgia, and Florida,
> All raised on high, the Bonnie Blue Flag that bears a single star.

This device of naming the states also appeared in several other songs. In "Flight of Doodles" the Florida reference was in the final verse.

SEMINOLES AND CAPTAIN HENDRY
Seminole Indians are photographed here with Capt. Francis A. Hendry, who was a Confederate cattleman in the Fort Myers area during the Civil War. (Courtesy Florida State Archives)

> Old Florida came in with a terrible shout,
> She frightened all the Yankees till their eyes stuck out—
> Oh! It don't make a niff-a-stifference to neither you nor I,
> Florida's death on Yankees, root, hog, or die.[78]

These songs were sung in the homes and around campfires of the South. Northern sympathizers bought broadsides of the lyrics published by New York booksellers.[79]

Secession was the subject of the early war songs. Only seven states had seceded when the northern "Wait for the Wagon" (music by R. B. Buckley) was answered by "The Southern Wagon." The third verse was:

> There was Tennessee and Texas also in the ring;
> They wouldn't have a government where cotton wasn't king,
> Alabama and Florida have long ago replied;
> Mississippi and Louisiana were anxious for the ride.

Chorus: Wait for the wagon,
   The Dissolution wagon;
   The South is our wagon
   And we'll all take a ride.[80]

Songs sung by Florida soldiers, sailors, or their families at home did not belong to them exclusively. Only a few were written in the state and usually only the poetry was published in local newspapers. Songsters and a few out-of-state periodicals occasionally printed music scores, and they filled in part the void created by the obstruction of sheet music from northern presses. Floridians, however, continued to buy sheet music from publishers in Augusta, New Orleans, Mobile, Macon, and other southern suppliers. Local dealers continued to advertise sheet music and music instruments. Myers and Garman of Tallahassee advertised violins, guitars, banjos, flutes, accordions, flagolets, fifes, drums, violin strings, and bows.[81] McDougald's Book Store in Jacksonville offered pianofortes, organs, and melodeons, even though insolvency notices were appearing about town.[82] Fannie Raney of Apalachicola went to New Orleans early in the war and bought a piano. Shipment was delayed because of the blockade, but eventually the instrument was delivered to nearby St. Joseph, then to her home. Mrs. Raney's sheet-music collection contained a wide selection of titles from Paris, Boston, New York, and Philadelphia publishers and a few from Cleveland and Louisville, all from the 1840s and 1850s. The flow was interrupted precipitously in the 1860s.

Compounding the problem was the scarcity of songs having a strong regional identity with the South and a near absence of any from or about Florida. The declaration of secession had hardly been made before rhymesters began writing patriotic verses ascribing to their sons heroic deeds yet to be done. As the struggle wore on, events of the war and conditions at home became the subjects, as did the battle generals, the weary soldiers, and their mothers, sweethearts, wives, and children at home. The musicians who composed these words included anonymous amateurs and such professional composers as John Hill Hewitt. At home, many songs of the 1850s were sung. They had pushed the limits of sentimentality when they were new, and time had not dulled their appeal. Separation from loved ones had idealized their relationship.

But sentiment for absent soldiers or praise of earthly heroes was not enough. Ultimately, those who engaged in war had to convince their constituency that God was on their side. William Billings had written a hit song of the Revolutionary War, "Chester," for that purpose.

> Let tyrants shake their iron rod
> and slavery clank her galling chains.
> We fear them not; we trust in God
> New England's God forever reigns.

Now, a similar sentiment shone through a hymnlike paraphrase of "God Save the Queen" with the title "God Save the South." A prayer addressing the Deity ended with the plea:

> God made the right
> Stronger than might;
> Millions would trample us
> Down in their pride.
> Lay down legions low
> Roll back the ruthless foe.
> Let the proud spoiler know
> God's on our side.

The words were by Earnest Halphin, pseudonym for George H. Miles, the music by Charles W. A. Ellerbrock. The song was published by Blackman and Brothers.[83] It was sung in Florida.

A new version of "Dixie" appeared in the *St. Augustine Examiner* in 1861. "Dixie" had first been notated and distributed in 1859 by Daniel Decatur Emmett as a walk-around for the Bryant Minstrels and was an instant success. It became a staple finale of minstrel shows, north and south. In some instances it became the epicenter of a bitter controversy on the culture and character of southerners. A writer for the *New York Herald* declared, "Good martial, national music is one of the great advantages we have over the rebels. They have only bands of guerrillas and bridge burners, and are as destitute of musical notes as they are rich in shinplasters. They have not even one good national theme, if we except the "Rogue's March," for "Dixie" belongs exclusively to our own Dan Bryant. . . . Having thus no music in their souls, they are, as Shakespeare says, only fit for treason, rebellion, strategems, masked batteries, spoils and knaveries."[84] The writer confused the composer's name with that of Dan Bryant, who was a banjoist, comedian, and dancer of the minstrel company. "The Rogue's March" is a traditional British tune dating from the late 1700s, having nothing to do with the South.

If the evidence of publisher John Tellery Lewis and composer-poet John Hill Hewitt is reliable, Emmett's "Dixie" was a mutation of an old Negro stevedore song played by bands and sung by steamboat roustabouts before 1859.[85] In his autobiography Hewitt commented:

> The crude, yet stirring air of "Dixie" which seemed so full of inspiration to the Southern soldier, answered very well to remind him of his home and the many wrongs that were heaped upon him by a more powerful foe, but the melody was contraband, having originated among northern counterfeit Ethiopians known as "cork opera." In our opinion it was more properly *brought out* by these dark minstrels; for we have a vivid recollection of having heard it on the levee of Savannah long before it was given to the public by the press of itinerant singers. It was sung by a gang of stevedores while loading vessels with cotton. We were at that time struck with its peculiarity, and the strange power it had over the stalwart Negro—the power of inspiration—if we may be allowed to use the term under such circumstances. If the "Dixie" of the present day be the same we heard fifty years ago, it is certainly of indigenous origin and claims a southern nativity.[86]

Music retailers from Virginia to New Orleans continued to announce new publications in Florida newspapers. Copies of their sheet music have appeared in inventories of collections now in Florida libraries, donated by residents of the period or their relatives. The advertisement of George Dunn of Richmond, Virginia, and Julian C. Selby of Columbia, South Carolina, in the *Florida Sentinel* issues of October 22 and November 10, 1863, may be cited as samplings of sheet music available to residents of the state on those dates. Three songs were by the most eminent southern bard, John Hill Hewitt. Hewitt was a son of the English violinist-composer James Hewitt, who immigrated to America and was active in the music life of the new republic. His ballad "Rock Me to Sleep, Mother," was first published in Baltimore and Philadelphia in 1861. The version advertised in Tallahassee was published a year or two later in Columbia, South Carolina, by Julian A. Selby and lithographed in Richmond by George W. Dunn. This title and "All Quiet on the Potomac Tonight" were the two most popular published by Selby. Words to the former were by Florence Percy, pseudonym for Mrs. Elizabeth Ann (Chase) Akers Allen. Those to the latter were attributed to Maj. Lamar Fontaine, C.S.A., but were actually by Mrs. Ethel Lynn Beers. They were first published in *Harper's Magazine*, November 20, 1861. The song was sung in both the North and the South. Picket duty, thought to be more boring than dangerous, was an unlikely song subject. The lyrics told of the fatal wound of a sentry by a sniper's bullet and of the victim's concern for his family as his blood flowed. The singer commented on the lack of notice taken that a mere enlisted man had become a casualty of the war.

A third Hewitt song, with text by Charlie Wildwood (pseudonym for Samuel Leroy Hammon), was the song of a patriot and was written in response to such northern lyrics as those of Finley Johnson, set to *Maryland, My Maryland,* where southerners were depicted as rebel scum coming from hell. Wildwood had no flattering language to describe northerners. He called them base tyrants and foul demons. Hewitt was equally bitter in a lyric he wrote for a song by Arnand Preot, also with the title "The South."

> Men of the South! Your homes
>> Where peace and plenty smiled
> Have been assailed by thieving bands
>> And by their tread defiled.
> The canting traitors of the North
>> With lying tongues declaim
> And spit at you their slime and froth,
>> Their venom and their flame.

Recruitment songs included "Harp of the South" (music by C. L. Peticolas, words by J. M. Kilgour).

> Harp of the South, Awake!
>> and strike the strain once more
> Which nerved the hero's hearts
>> in glorious days of yore.

These lyrics recalled the heroic deeds of Sir Walter Scott's novels and fantasies of southern manhood. No less stirring were the "Virginian Marseillaise," available in Florida both in French and English editions, and the other mutations of Roget de L'Isle's French national anthem such as "The Southern Marseillaise," published in Augusta, "La Louisianaise," in New Orleans, and "Succession March," in Mobile. Sentimental songs pub-

"GOD SAVE THE SOUTHERN LAND"

A Confederate chaplain adapted this song text to an English ballad tune. It was published by the Richmond, Virginia, firm George Dunn and Company in 1864 and sold for the benefit of needy soldiers and their families. (Courtesy Florida State University Music Library)

lished in earlier years continued their appeal through the war. Two of them were "Kathleen Mavourneen" (music by F. N. Crouch, words by Julia Crawford) and "Annie of the Vale" (music by J. R. Thomas, words by George P. Morris). No less sentimental was "My Wife and Child" (music by F. W. Rosier, words by Gen. Henry Rootes Jackson of Georgia, written during the Mexican War). Popular songs were sometimes answered. One answer-song heard in Florida was to John Hill Hewitt's "Rock Me to Sleep, Mother." It was "Keep Me Awake, Mother!" (music by Henry Schoeller, words by M. W. Stratton), published in Augusta by Blackmar and Brothers. One of the saddest "mother songs" bore as its title the question asked by a southern child, "Mother, Is the Battle Over?" by Benedict Roefs.

> Mother is the battle over?
> Thousands have been killed they say.
> Is my father coming? Tell me,
> Have the Southrons gained the day?

Popular, both north and south, was "Weeping Sad and Lonely," also known as, "When This Cruel War Is Over," the preferred title in the South. The music was by Henry Tucker, who also wrote "Sweet Genevieve"; the words were Charles Carroll Sawyer, who also wrote "Who Will Care for Mother Now?" Critics found little musical or literary merit in the song, but it evoked "answer ballads" and was published in many editions.

One concert artist who appeared on the Florida circuit toward the end of the war was Thomas Greene Wiggins, better known as Blind Tom. His contribution to the Civil War repertory was "The Battle of Manassas." He played it on a concert in Tallahassee in February 1864. The performance was described by a girl who attended. "The Battle of Manassas begins with the booming of cannon, the rattle of musketry and above all the clear notes of the bugle. Faintly in the distance the strains of Dixie float upon the air; these strains grow louder and louder and mingle with the clashing of guns, the trampling of horses and the sharp commands of officers. He [Wiggins] interspersed the music with the names of generals who took the most prominent parts in the day's work."[87] Wiggins was only fifteen years of age when he gave this concert, but with this piece and others, he created such a sensation that he continued to return to Tallahassee for twenty-seven years. His reception in Florida from the beginning was suitable for the worldwide celebrity which he was to become.

While new music repertory items were not always available, singers in Florida continued to sing songs of the 1850s, such as "Twinkling Stars Are Laughing, Love" (John P. Ordway), "Listen to the Mocking Bird" (Alice Hawthorne), "Darling Nellie Gray" (B. R. Hanby), and "Jingle Bells"

"WHEN THIS CRUEL WAR IS OVER"

Families and friends of soldiers in both the North and the South sang this sad but popular ballad in the Civil War. (Courtesy Florida State University Music Library)

(J. Pierpont). From the early sixties they played from their collections "Gideon's Band" (arr. Charles R. Dodworth), "Folks That Put on Airs" (W. H. Coulston), and "Billie Rhee; or, Carry Me Back to Tennessee" (Septimus Winner). These pieces were in their collections before the blockade. They were supplemented by sheet music of Confederate publishers.[88]

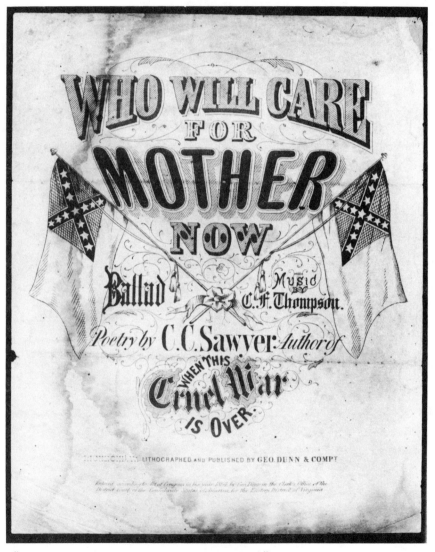

"WHO WILL CARE FOR MOTHER NOW?"

A youth dying on the battlefield sang of his concern for his mother in this song. The sentiment knew no sectional bias. (Courtesy Florida State University Music Library)

"THE MOCKING BIRD QUICKSTEP"

Septimus Winner's "Listen to the Mocking Bird" was not only a popular song. This quickstep version, published in Richmond in 1864, became a favorite parlor piece for piano. (Courtesy Florida State University Music Library)

A few Floridians acquired hymn collections and patriotic songbooks that were written or compiled by northern composers, published in the North and with decidedly northern sentiments. Among them were Leonard Marshall's *The Sacred Star; or, Union Collection of Church Music,* published by Oliver Ditson and Company, 1861. A cheap paper music edition with timely patriotic songs could be carried by soldiers or civilians. Titled *The Patriotic Song Book,* it contained "We'll Camp Awhile in the Wilderness," "Home, Sweet Home," "Oft in the Stilly Night," and "Freeman's Gathering," set to the "Marseillaise" tune. It also included Stephen Collins Foster's "Sorrow Shall Come Again No More."[89] In a Florida collection, too, was George F. Root's *The Bugle Call,* designed to arouse love for the Union. A song "The Union League" cursed the hand that attempted to sever the Union. Included was "The Ship of Union" with words by Longfellow. Two songs were by Henry C. Work, "Brave Boys Are They" and "Kingdom Coming."[90] Another collection was *Silver Bell* by Charles Butler, a teacher of music in the Boston schools. It also contained songs of the times: "Poor Old Slave," "The Contraband of Port Royal," "When This War Is Over," "Break It Gently to My Mother," "We Are Coming Father Abraham," "Do They Think of Me at Home?" "We're Tenting Tonight," "Kathleen Mavourneen," "Cheer, Boys, Cheer," and "Annie Laurie."

Not all the battles of these years were fought on the military front. Churches at home had their disputes and verbal skirmishes. Some Florida Episcopalians felt that their Bishop Polk should not leave to accept appointment to the army, but Tallahassean J. H. Randolph wrote, "I think ours being a holy cause, we need holy men to carry it on."[91] The Reverend L. R. Studemayer, rector of Trinity Church, St. Augustine, was ordered by Union troops and his church vestry to leave St. Augustine because he was a southern sympathizer. Specifically, he refused to continue the ritual prayer for the president of the United States and substituted "the Confederate States" instead. Divisions within the church continued at such a pitch that Elvira, the organist, quit in disgust, as did others of the congregation.[92]

Economic pressures on Floridians were felt early. J. H. Randolph, medical officer of the Confederate department in Tallahassee, complained, "We are getting in a very deplorable way here, for the want of money! . . . Many persons of large property cannot collect or borrow money to buy meat for their Negroes. What must we do? . . . We get bad news from Key

West. Lincoln has put his iron heel upon the necks of the inhabitants."[93] In Jacksonville a city guard found the city very dull because of the blockade of the St. Johns River. The few activities were military operations and the excitement of an occasional schooner slipping through the blockade.[94] In Lake City things were no better. A citizen there wrote, "Things look blue indeed, in Florida; but [there is] little doing and prices going up, up, up every day. The acts of the Lincoln congress have cast a gloom over all. It would seem that the war must go on indefinitely."[95] In the absence of owners, theft and confiscation of private property was a major problem. Union soldiers, vandals, and informers carried off books, furniture, clothing, food, and other property. Private residences were occupied by contrabands.[96]

Social changes were no less difficult to accept. The men of St. Augustine were at war or in the home guard. Women were forced to fend for themselves. They could not get enough to eat, servants would not work, and livestock was starving. To protest publicly risked confinement for treason. To their diaries, they could write their states of mind: "A dreadful and unheard state of things, . . . an awful life to lead. . . . Everybody feels bad, a miserable, unpleasant day."[97] One complained that Union troops drank too much liquor and were boisterous. She especially disapproved of Union officers who walked arm in arm with yellow girls on the St. Augustine sea wall. At a grand dance one week she observed that the officers "danced till morning with the nigger caddies."[98] A few more-charitable women began receiving soldiers into their parlors, and some of them summoned enough courage to appear in public with men who seemed no longer to be the enemy.

Citizens in St. Augustine were arrested because their husbands or sons were in the Confederate army, according to one of them. She wrote that the mother of Gen. Edmund Kirby Smith was exempted only because she was seventy-seven years of age and in ill health.[99] Merchants in St. Augustine were compelled to sign an oath of allegiance to the United States if they were to continue their business. They were not allowed to sell to customers unless they too had signed an oath. Union lines extended ten miles into the mainland. Gen. David Hunter commanded that all relatives of Confederate soldiers be sent over rebel lines.[100] When Noah Brooks, a newspaper correspondent, visited Florida in June 1863, he found only about a thousand people in Fernandina and seven hundred in St. Augustine. "It is a puzzle to know how they live," he wrote.[101]

As if to solve the puzzle, women across northern Florida sang a song which had many variants and was popular with folk singers for generations. The tune was an adaptation of "The Irish Jaunting Car." It had been popularized as "The Bonnie Blue Flag" by the actor Harry McCarthy. It now served a new text, "The Homespun Dress." The origin of the lyrics is obscured, but it has been attributed to Carrie Bell Sinclair of Augusta, Georgia, and to a Lieutenant Harrington of Alabama. The latter is cited in folklore to have written the song after attending a dance in honor of Gen. John Hunt (Jack) Morgan, where the women wore homespun dresses.[102] The Florida girls sang not only of the dresses but of their hats made of palmetto.

Yes, I know I am a Southern Girl; I glory in the name,
And what a prize far greater than glittering wealth of fame;
I envy not the Northern girl her robes of beauty rare,
Though pearls bedeck her snowy neck, and diamonds in her hair.
Chorus: Hurrah! Hurrah! For the sunny south so dear,
        Three cheers for the homespun dress the Southern ladies wear.

My homespun dress is plain, I know; My hat is palmetto, too;
But now you see what Southern girls for Southern rights can do.
We sent the bravest of our land to battle with the foe,
And we would lend a helping hand; we love the South, you know.
    (two more verses)[103]

A version of this song appeared in *The Jack Morgan Songster,* compiled by a captain in Gen. Robert E. Lee's army and published in 1864 in Raleigh, North Carolina, by Branson and Farrar. This songster appeared in Florida, but it is not known whether it came to the region during or after the war.[104]

A few songs sung by civilians referred to specific battles during the war. One of them grew out of the encounter between the Fifty-fourth Massachusetts Regiment (colored) and Fortieth Massachusetts Mounted Infantry and the Confederate forces at Baldwin, a village twenty miles west of Jacksonville. In February 1864 these battle-proven Union units attempted to capture supplies of food and equipment and cut off Florida from other southern states. Confederate soldiers prevailed and left this song legacy of the event. They called it "I Can Whip the Scoundrel."

> The Yankees came to Baldwin
> They came up from the rear [pronounced "rare"]
> They thought they'd find old Abner
> But old Abner was not there.
> *Chorus:* So lay ten dollars down
>   Or twenty if you choose,
>   For I can whip the scoundrel
>   That stole old Abner's shoes.

> Jeff Davis was a gentleman;
> Abe Lincoln was a fool.
> Jeff Davis rode a dapple gray
> Abe Lincoln rode a mule.[105]

The origins of both the text and music are so obscure that few researchers will speculate on them. The words with variants have been sung by folksingers throughout the South. This version is that of Mrs. J. E. Maynard of Micanopy, Florida, who herself heard it after the war.

A few Florida residents and northern missionaries did not allow the war to interrupt their children's education. Two Florida fathers wrote letters about music instruction for their daughters during the war. Rabun Scarborough from Cedar Grove Plantation, Apalachicola, wrote that he had selected two teachers for their school but added, "I do not yet know who our music teacher will be."[106] The reality of war had not yet dampened the ardor for music in this prosperous little port city when he wrote his daughter on April 19, 1861. Earlier in that year Mrs. A. A. Miller, who had been entrusted with the care of George R. Fairbanks's children during the war, wrote that she had rented a piano for five dollars per month, and that his daughter Flora was studying music with a competent teacher from whom she had received encouragement.[107]

The American Missionary Association sent their first teachers to St. Augustine in 1863. Their mission was to teach black children. They were not welcomed in every community, but by 1865 they had established schools in Key West, Jacksonville, St. Augustine, Strawberry Mills, Tallahassee, Ocala, Monticello, Gainesville, and Magnolia. Music was taught in these schools and became the cause of a disturbance in 1866 when local white citizens objected to black students singing "Rally 'round the Flag, Boys," a song that stirred bitter memories among Confederate veterans.[108]

In 1863 three hundred Negro children were taught in the Fernandina Schools. A report of their singing was made in the July 21 *Wisconsin State Journal* and an extract reprinted in the *Rebellion Record,* 1864.

> Among the songs by the school, interspersed throughout the exercises—and every child sings in these schools—was the following, which, aside from its intrinsic merit and affecting pathos, was particularly interesting from the fact that just before the rebellion, a congregation of slaves attending a public baptism on Sunday, at Savannah, were arrested, imprisoned, and punished with thirty-nine lashes each for singing the song of spiritual freedom—now a crime since slavery had become a "divine institution."

> SLAVE SONG
> My mother, how long! Mothers, how long?
> Mothers, how long! Will sinners suffer here?
> *Chorus:* It won't be long! (Three times)
>   That sinners 'ill suffer here!"

Other verses sang of the pleasure of walking the golden streets, singing the praises of the Lord, and freeedom when the Lord called them home.

A newspaper correspondent reported that the "expressive and pathetic" verses were added to by other singers on other occasions. He did not speculate on the origin of this or other spirituals sung by Florida Negroes, but he did identify the source of the inspiration. "In patient faith and enduring hope, these 'Songs of Zion' have been sung by generations of these bondmen, as the only relief for bleeding hearts and lacerated bodies, and now God comes in judgement to requite the nation for the wrongs inflicted upon his oppressed and suffering poor."[109]

The daughter of Gov. Thomas Brown expressed her attitude to the social changes after the war. The formerly prosperous governor was sick and in financial ruin. His daughter wrote of the poverty of other families. She and her daughter taught music, reading, and writing to their young relatives. "If we charged," she wrote, "we could get a good school, but, as yet, I don't care about placing myself upon the level of these Yankee School Marms who teach darkies. . . . This is truly the dark age, for the darkies have everything, do as they please, and can get what they please."[110]

Yet, neither poverty nor discomfort could still the sound of music. Music events were both the most popular public entertainment and the most useful among the arts of raising money for war-related causes. Bands played for charity groups, and concert-suppers were given. Tableaux and minstrel shows were staged frequently. Singers and pianists, soloists and ensemble concerts raised money for poor families, for clothing of soldiers, and for a variety of equally worthy causes. Performances of plays included the burlesque *Bombastics Furioso* and an original melodrama based on historical events of early Tampa.[111] These events, aside from their artistic and humanitarian purposes, sustained morale of those who remained on the home front. Dances were not frequent, but when they did occur, for a few hours, the fiddle and the banjo set the tempi and the tunes for the pigeon-wing, the chicken-in-the-bread-tray, the double shuffle, and the Virginia reel. It no longer mattered whether the escape from the war was a barn dance or a squire's ballroom (if it ever did).

On April 9, 1865, a Tallahassee hospital benefit concert was arranged. The performers included Susan Eppes's cousin Jewel, who played a nocturne. Her sister Mart and cousin Jennie sang a German duet, cousin Bettie played "Une pluie du perle," and her cousin Fannie Nash played "Sleeping I Dreamed Love." "Dixie" opened the program, this time and again, "sweet old-time airs were sung, operatic music enchanted the educated ears; touching Confederate songs brought tears to the eyes of many."[112] Then,

> A magnificent quartette began singing "The Southern Marseillaise" when a gentleman entered the door and advanced rapidly up the aisle, bearing aloft in his hand a telegram. All hearts stood still, and waiting was agony, for no one knew where the blow would fall. Ascending the steps he stood at last upon the platform. Twice he tried to speak and twice his voice failed him. Then he made a mighty effort and in a loud and unnatural voice, he read: "General Lee surrendered the army of Northern Virginia today, at Appomattox. . . ." Few slept that night and the sun arose upon a miserable, broken-hearted people—far too miserable to even talk it over with each other.[113]

The war was over, and Florida's men returned to their families. One northern man wrote an essay entitled "Sentiment of the People" and sent it to G. R. Fairbanks of St. Augustine, who was to become a Florida historian.

> In my conversation with the few white citizens I met, I was persuaded to the belief that the majority of the inhabitants of Florida are tired of

the war and heartily desire a return to the Union. There can be no question that the rebel government has dealt severely with them, and pushed not only the young and vigorous but the old and decrepit into the ranks of the army. Our coming to occupy the state has been looked for with much anxiety for months past. As we passed a dwelling on our way to Baldwin, an old lady came to the door and cried, "God bless the old flag!" I believe it will not be two months before we shall see but one popular sentiment in Florida, and that sentiment—the Union.[114]

U.S. Col. George F. Thompson made a lengthy tour of Florida in the spring of 1866 and reported that he found no disloyalty to the United States. He even concluded, "So far as the hostility of the people is concerned, I would as soon live in any part of southern Florida as in the city of Washington or Boston."[115] Only a few years passed before Abby Hutchinson Patton and her brothers came to Florida and there sang camp-meeting songs of the Florida freedmen. One of them was a new song which echoed the sentiment of the old hymn by Isaac Watts and William Mather.

> The King's high road to happiness,
>   We will sing the new song.
> O blest are all the paths of peace,
>   Then we'll sing a new song.
> *Chorus:* Wait a little while
>   Then we'll sing the new song. (repeat)

> When I can read my title clear,
>   Then we'll sing the new song.
> All darkness then will disappear,
>   When we sing the new song.
>   (two more verses)[116]

*   *   *   *   *   *   *   *

Epilogue

The Indians of early Florida had religions and myths that had grown out of their relationship with the planets, the animals, the vegetation, and their ancestors. Their songs and dances celebrated their environment and the events that took place in it. Their spirits and cultural patterns rose from encounters in their small world. The white man came and observed them with little understanding.

The Spanish and French came in search of gold and political advantage. Their cultural models were renaissance European. While they endured hardships and disasters of the new land, their music and dance was of the Old World. The history of Western music in what is now the United States did not begin with black-coated, psalm-singing New England Puritans. It began with elegantly costumed Spanish and French noblemen, Catholics and Huguenots, who came to the Gulf of Mexico and Atlantic coasts of Florida. They brought with them small chamber orchestras and well-trained singers. Here they chanted the Catholic rites, sang the Huguenot psalms, and played the instrumental music of sixteenth-century Europe on strings, keyboard, and wind instruments. They taught music to the Indians but ultimately left only small traces of their music traditions, since both they and the Indians were removed or killed by superior military or political forces. Some residents of St. Augustine, however, have kept alive the heritage of their solemn church music, the dramas of Lorca, and the graceful Spanish dances.

The British left their heritage of pleasure-garden ditties, sea songs, and sentimental love songs. Their small military bands played marches and music from Handel's operas. While this music is occasionally heard today, the British brought other racial and national strains to Florida whose music has also had strong impact. The large number of Negroes created a vast repertory, some of which is still heard throughout the state. Of small scale but no less vigorous are the Minorcan and Greek songs and dance festivals now held on the east coast. The Fromajadas tradition continues during the carnival season in St. Augustine.

In territorial and early statehood days there were settlements of Scots and English, but Florida's immigrants came from all points, including down from New England and New York and from the closer-to-home Carolinas and Virginia. The core repertory of music came from European sources and was absorbed when the environment could accommodate it, that is, when instruments and performers were present. The small-town aristocrat reserved a small reservoir of time for music. Music dipped into his religion and defined special species of repertory. It accompanied the events of his social life, at home with his family or at political rallies, at national holiday celebrations, or at dances where he courted the young lady who was to become his wife. Musicians were not alienated from society as long as they did not take their singing or playing too seriously. Amateur musicians enriched the social scene. Becoming a professional musician was a different matter. That was for Negro fiddlers, beautiful women of questionable reputation, freaks, or eccentrics who had little value beyond that as exhibitionists.

As the flow of population increased, so did the richness of the repertory. The raffish rural culture, black or white, was as lively as the decorous small-town life. Its music was not as well mannered, but it was sometimes more spontaneous. Its roots were sometimes just as ancient. It was ad hoc rather than rehearsed, free-flowing rather than self-conscious. It lacked eloquence occasionally, but it had the merit of simplicity. Its song delivered its message directly. It was utilitarian if it was a fiddle tune, because it determined the measure, the speed, and the order of the dance.

Florida has not been indifferent to music. It built few, if any, musical fences or seawalls at its borders. Even in the early years, there was nothing hermetic about the music field in Florida. There was a curiosity about music, and a staggering diversity was brought to the peninsula after it became a state. There were few peaks of music activity or extraordinary achievement. No towering composer grew out of this agar. No iconoclastic musician came to declare independence from European traditions, or even those of New England. Generation after generation made music a function of their lives in the parlor, in the choir, at the dance, or river excursions, on the stage, at war, or in love. Emotional attachment has kept it alive and caused it to take root in Florida soil. This book is a narrative of music choices, music events. The socialization of diverse groups produced a musical landscape as lush and varied as the flora that surrounded it.

Settlers and visitors wrote of the cluster of tastes. As they traveled out of state in war or peace, they wrote of music in their letters, diaries, and memoirs. When they returned, they resumed their singing and playing and dancing.

Appendix A

William Cullen Bryant— Mahones "Fromajadas"

In 1843 William Cullen Bryant heard the Mahones "Fromajadas" serenade in St. Augustine and asked a native of the city for a written copy of the hymn. He presumed that this version was the first to be printed. The song was first published in Bryant's *Letters of a Traveller,* in New York by George P. Putnam, 1850, pp. 114–20.

Disciarem lu dol,
Cantarem anb' alagria,
Y n'arem a dá
Las pasquas a Maria.
  O Maria!

Sant Gabriel,
Qui portaba la anbasciada;
Des nostro rey del cel
Estarau vos prenada.
Ya omiliada,
Tu o vais azui serventa,
Fia del Deu contenta,
Para fe ló que el vol.
  Disciarem lu dol, etc.

Y a milla nit,
Pariguero vos regina;
A un Deu infinit,
Dintra una establina.
Y a millo dia,
Que los Angles van cantant
Pau y abondant
De la gloria de Deu sol.
  Disciarem lu dol, etc.

Y a Libalam,
Alla la terra santa,
Nus nat Jesus,
Anb' alagria tanta.

Infant petit
Que tot lu mon salvaria;
Y ningu bastaria,
Nu mes un Deu to sol.
   Disciarem lu dol, etc.

Cuant d'Orien lus
Tres reys la stralla veran,
Deu omnipotent,
Adora lo vingaran.
Un present inferan,
De mil encens y or,
A lu beneit Señó,
Que conesce cual se vol.
   Disciarem lu dol, etc.

Tot fu gayant
Para cumplí lu prumas;
Y lu Esperit sant
De un angel fau gramas.
Gran foc ences,
Que crama lu curagia;
Deu nos da lenguagia,
Para fe lo que Deu vol.
   Disciarem lu dol, etc.

Cuant trespasá
De quest mon nostra Señora,
Al cel s'empugiá
Sun fil la matescia ora.
O emperadora,
Que del cel sou eligida!
Lu rosa florida,
Me resplenden que un sol.
   Disciarem lu dol, etc.

Y el tercer giorn
Que Jesus resuntá
Deu y Aborama,
Que la mort triumfa.
De alli se ballá
Para perldra Lucife,

An tot a seu peudá,
   Que de nostro ser el sol.
    Disciarem lu dol, etc.

After this hymn, the following stanzas, soliciting the customary gift of cakes or eggs, are sung.

Ce set sois que vam cantant,
   Regina celastial!
Dunus pau y alagria,
   Y bonus festas tingau
Yo vos dou sus bonas festas,
   Danaus dinés de sus nous;
Sempre tarem lus mans llestas
   Para recibí un grapat de ous.

Y el giorn de pasqua florida
   Alagramos y giuntament;
as qui es mort par darnos vida
   Ya viú gloriosament.

Aquesta casa está empedrada,
   Bien halla que la empedró;
Sun amo de aquesta casa
   Baldria duna un do.
Furmagiada, o empanada,
   Ducatta o flaó;
Cual se vol cosa me grada,
   Sol que no me digas que no.

The shutters are then opened by the people within, and a supply of cheesecakes or other pastry or eggs is dropped into a bag carried by one of the party, who acknowledge the gift in the following lines, then depart:

Aquesta casa está empedrada,
   Empedrada de cuatro vens;
Sun amo de aquesta casa,
   Es omo de compliment.

If nothing is given, the last line reads, "No es omo de compliment." In Spanish, this final stanza is as follows:

Aquesta casa está empedrada,
   Empedrada de cuatro vientos;
El amo de aquesta casa
   Es hombre de cortesía.

※　※　※　※　※　※　※　※

Appendix B

Prince Achille Murat's Farewell

On September 9, 1830, a Tallahassee newspaper reported the farewell of Prince Murat as follows:

> The late events in France have rendered it necessary for our esteemed fellow citizen, Col. Achille Murat, to leave this society to which he has endeared himself by his hospitality and republican manners. Desirous of expressing their esteem for him and his accomplished lady, as well as the deep interest they feel in the triumph which the French people have won for liberty and the rights of man over usurped and arbitrary power, our citizens have made arrangements for a ball, which will be given this evening at the Planters' Hotel. The decorations and transparencies will be suitable to the occasion, and will have reference to the two events most auspicious to liberty, the American and late French Revolution.

A note of invitation to the colonel is addressed to Lipona, his place of residence, and is signed by a committee of ten distinguished citizens including R. K. Call. It is followed by an elegant acceptance by the colonel.

> This, gentlemen, is the land of my adoption. I have seen many improvements raised up, as by magic, in the bosom of the wilderness. I have seen the members, composing a delightful society, arrive one by one from their distant homes—and it would be impossible for me, in whatever situation I may be placed, to forget the strong feelings which all this has excited.
>
> When I first came to the United States, my object was to live under a government whose laws were in accordance with my political principles—this I very soon found to be the case, beyond my most sanguine expectations. But what I was not prepared for: I found among you, a most pleasant and enlightened state of society—I very soon found friends as dearly beloved, as any I ever had—and lastly contracted those ties, in which, our fair country men are so apt to enslave us.

He declared that he had no intention of leaving until a few days before he was to sail, and he hoped to return in a year's time unless political events rendered it necessary to remain abroad.[1]

Later newspaper accounts describe the farewell ball honoring Prince Murat.

According to arrangements, a ball was given at the Planters' Hotel, on the evening of the ninth inst. Our citizens availed themselves of the departure of Colonel Murat to give this public expression of respect for him, as well as the deep interest they feel in the late events of France, his native land with the glory of which his family is so intimately connected.

There was an unusual display of beauty and fashion to the occasion. Great credit is due to Captain Brown, for the elegance and taste with which the decorations were got up. The tri-colored flag of France and our own Star-Spangled Banner, with intertwining folds, waved over a bust of LaFayette, which occupied one extremity of the hall; at the other was a splendid transparency of Washington, with the emblems of Liberty and Fame in the act of placing on his brow a wreath of laurels. On the right was a transparency of Jackson and at a distance were seen the American arms and colours floating over the memorable defenses of cotton bags. On the left was also a transparency of LaFayette. While in the background the banner of France surmounted the castled embattlements of a Gothic Fortress. The whole was brilliantly illuminated and surrounded with appropriate devices, wrought with evergreens and flowers. Rich and brilliant shrubbery, which none but a Southern forest can supply, was arranged upon the walls while ornamental vines, with their massy foliage hung in graceful festoons, and the deep verdure of the laurel and myrtle was relieved by wreaths and bouquets of rose and jessamine—the effect of the whole was picturesque and beautiful to the highest degree. One, who many years ago was a resident in this place, could hardly believe in the reality of what he saw or reconcile the presence of so many sylph-like forms, floating through the mazy dance to the wild and thrilling airs of Castaly.

At eleven o'clock the supper room was thrown open and ample justice was done to the refreshments prepared. The room was ornamented in keeping with the ball. The table was set with great elegance and decorated in a tasteful and fanciful manner with miniature flags, the work of some fair hand. Nothing occurred to mar the festivities of the evening, save the sentiment that one who endeared himself to all by his unaffected hospitality and republican simplicity of manner, and another, who had been so long the life and attraction of this society were participating, perhaps for the last time in innocent and social amusement.[2]

✳ ✳ ✳ ✳ ✳ ✳ ✳ ✳

Appendix C

The Florida State Songs

Written by Stephen Collins Foster and popularized by E. P. Christy in his Negro minstrels, "The Swanee River" was adopted as the Florida state song in 1935. The Suwannee River rises in the Okefenokee Swamp and empties into the Gulf of Mexico. Foster never saw the river that his song immortalized. The following is the house of representatives resolution by which the song was adopted:

Be It Resolved by the House of Representatives of the State of Florida, the Senate Concurring:

That, from and after the adoption of this amendment the official song of the State of Florida, to be sung in the schools and at all other public or official gatherings, shall be "The Swanee River (Old Folks at Home)," written by Stephen Foster and entered according to an act of Congress by Firth, Pond and Co., in 1851, in the Clerk's office of the District Court of the Southern District of New York. The following is the song:

> Way down upon de Swannee ribber,
> Far, far away,
> Dere's wha my heart is turning ebber,
> Dere's wha de old folks stay.
> All up and down de whole creation,
> Sadly I roam,
> Still longing for de old plantation,
> And for de old folks at home.

> *Chorus:* All de world am sad and dreary,
> Eb-ry where I roam,
> Oh! darkeys how my heart grows weary,
> Far from de old folks at home.

> All round de little farm I wandered
> When I was young,
> Den many happy days I squandered,
> Many de songs I sung.
> When I was playing wid my brudder

Happy was I.
Oh! take me to my kind old mudder,
Dere let me live and die.

One little hut among de bushes,
One dat I love,
Still sadly to my mem'ry rushes,
No matter where I rove.
When will I see de bees a humming
All round de comb?
When will I hear de banjo tumming
Down in my good old home?

B E   I T   R E S O L V E D That House Concurrent Resolution No. 24, the Laws of Florida, Acts of 1913, be and the same is hereby repealed.
Approved May 28, 1935.
Filed in Office Secretary of State, May 29, 1935.[3]

Before the Stephen Collins Foster song could be adopted, it was necessary to repeal a 1913 law which had designated "Florida, My Florida" as the state song. Below is the resolution:

HOUSE CONCURRENT RESOLUTION NO. 24

Be it resolved by the House of Representatives of the State of Florida, the Senate Concurring:

That Whereas, In view of the fact that many of the Public Schools of the State are now singing, as part of their daily exercise, the song "Florida, my Florida," a song written in 1894 by Rev. Dr. C. V. Waugh, for many years an honored Professor of Languages in the old Florida Agricultural College at Lake City, and whereas,

The said song has both metrical and patriotic merit of the kind calculated to inspire love for home and native State, there, be it

Resolved, that this song, "Florida, my Florida," be and the same is hereby declared by the Legislature to be sung to the tune of "Maryland, my Maryland," and that it is recommended for use in the daily exercises of the public schools of the State of Florida, as well as at all public gatherings where singing forms a part of the program.

The following is the song:

FLORIDA, MY FLORIDA
(State Patriotic Song for Schools, C. V. Waugh.)

Land of my birth, bright sunkissed land,
Florida, my Florida,

Laved by the Gulf and Ocean grand,
   Florida, my Florida,
Of all the States in East or West,
Unto my heart thou art the best;
Here may I live, here may I rest,
   Florida, my Florida,

In country, town, or hills and dells,
   Florida, my Florida,
The rhythmic chimes of thy school bells
   Florida, my Florida,
Will call thy children day by day
To learn to walk the patriot's way,
Firmly to stand for thee for aye,
   Florida, my Florida,

Thy golden fruit the world outshines
   Florida, my Florida,
Thy gardens and thy phosphate mines,
   Florida, my Florida,
Yield their rich store of good supply,
To still the voice of hunger's cry,—
For thee we'll live, for thee we'll die,
   Florida, my Florida,

Th' oppressors' rod can't rest on thee,
   Florida, my Florida,
Thy sons and daughters free must be,
   Florida, my Florida,
From North and South, from East and West,
From freezing blasts they come for rest,
And find in thee their earnest quest,
   Florida, my Florida,

When ills betide and woes o'ertake.
   Florida, my Florida,
Thy sons and daughters quick will make,—
   Florida, my Florida,
The sacrifice of loves and life
To save from woe, from ills and strife,
To fell thy foes in danger rife,
   Florida, my Florida.[4]

✳ ✳ ✳ ✳ ✳ ✳ ✳ ✳

Notes

PREFACE

1. One exception is the brief reference in Robert Stevenson's *Protestant Church Music in America*, pp. 3–4.
2. Charlton W. Tebeau, *A History of Florida*, p. xiii.

CHAPTER 1: *A Solemn Elevated State of Mind*

1. Álvar Núñez Cabeza de Vaca, *The Journey of Álvar Núñez Cabeza de Vaca*, trans. Fanny Bandelier, p. 5.
2. Álvar Núñez Cabeza de Vaca, "The Narrative of Álvar Núñez Cabeza de Vaca," in *Spanish Explorers in the Southern United States, 1528–43*, ed. F. N. Hodge, p. 26.
3. Ibid., p. 29.
4. Garcilaso de la Vega, *el Inca, La Florida of the Inca*, trans. Benita B. Lewis and W. H. Wilkinson, pp. 24–25.
5. Garcilaso de la Vega, *The Florida of the Inca*, trans. and ed. John Grier Varner and Jeannette J. Varner, p. 576.
6. Gonzalo Solís de Meras, *Pedro Menéndez de Avilés*, trans. Jeannette Thurber Connor, p. 147. These events are also told in Barcia's *Chronological History of the Continent of Florida*, trans. Anthony Kerrigan, pp. 104–6.
7. Jonathan Dickinson, *Jonathan Dickinson's Journal*, ed. E. W. Andrews and C. M. Andrews, p. 47.
8. James Adair, "The History of the North American Indians," in Kingsborough's *Antiquities of Mexico*, 8:349–52.
9. Ibid., pp. 327–28.
10. Frances Densmore, *Seminole Music*, p. 39.
11. Núñez Cabeza de Vaca, *Journey*, p. 21.
12. Jacques Le Moyne, "Brevis narratio," in *The New World*, ed. Stefan Lorant, p. 38.
13. Adair, "History," p. 356.
14. William Bartram, *Travels through North and South Carolina, Georgia, East and West Florida*, p. 369.

15. *Pensacola Gazette and West Coast Advertiser,* May 29, 1824.

16. William Bartram, *Bartram's Travels,* ed. Francis Harper, p. 502.

17. Ibid., p. 243.

18. Ibid., pp. 505–6.

19. Ibid., pp. 502–3.

20. Ibid., pp. 234–35.

21. A. P. Canova, *Life and Adventures in South Florida,* p. 90.

22. James Franklin, *The Philosophical and Political History of the Thirteen United States of America . . . and of East and West Florida,* pp. 25–26.

23. Jacob Rhett Motte, *Journey into Wilderness,* p. 209.

24. Theodore Baker, *Über die Musik der nordamerikanischen Wilden,* p. 10.

25. Motte, *Journey into Wilderness,* p. 209.

26. John T. Sprague, "Macomb's Mission to the Seminoles," ed. Frank F. White, Jr., *Florida Historical Quarterly* 35, no. 2 (October 1956): 144, 159, 164.

27. Ibid., pp. 183, 132.

CHAPTER 2: *Te Deum Laudamus*

1. Núñez Cabeza de Vaca, *Jouney,* p. 5.

2. W. H. Prescott, *History of the Conquest of Mexico,* p. 238; and Bartolomé Barrientos, *Pedro Menéndez de Avilés,* p. 148.

3. Lota M. Spell, *Music in Texas,* p. 6.

4. George N. Heller, "Juan de Padilla," in *The New Grove Dictionary of American Music,* ed. H. Wiley Hitchcock and Stanley Sadie, 3:459.

5. Lota Spell, "The First Teacher of European Music in America," *Catholic Historical Quarterly,* n.s., 2 (1923): 372–78.

6. Victor Francis O'Daniel, *Dominicans in Early Florida,* p. 129. See also Francisco Javier Allegre, *Historia de la Provincia de la Compañía de Jesús de Nueva España,* vol. 1 (Rome: Institutum Historicum, S.J., 1956).

7. The event is described in a prose translation by A. F. Falcones: "Songs of welcome were sung in accompaniment with the organ which wise Father Chozas had presented to them. He had held classes in organ playing twice a day for the Indians. On the occasions that the Indians prayed or sang in the church, the sonorous and grave tones of the organ presented a suitable musical background for them" (James Covington, ed., *Pirates, Indians, and Spaniards,* p. 25). Geiger's translation reads, "Great happiness prevailed as a result of Father Chozas' return [from Tama]. The Indians sang their songs to the accompaniment of the organ; for Father Chozas, musically talented, had given them two lessons each day" (Luís Gerónimo de Oré, *The Martyrs of Florida, 1513–1616,* trans. and ed. Maynard Geiger, p. 80).

8. Alonso Gregorio de Escobedo, "La Florida," in Luís Gerónimo de Oré, *Relación histórica de la Florida,* ed. P. Atanasio López, 1:32–33.

9. "Cantando a punto de órgano canciones" would seem to translate, "singing

songs to the accompaniment of an organ," but musicologist Robert Stevenson has presented strong evidence that *canto de órgano* is an idiom meaning "polyphonic music." In his *Music in Mexico* (p. 177), Stevenson quotes Tomás de Iriarte (1750–91), author of the "didactic poem" *La música*, in *Discurso sobre la música* (published in the October 24, 1807, issue of the *Diario de México*), as the authority for defining *canto de órgano* as polyphonic music. Gerard Behague, Latin American music historian, consistently translates *canto de órgano* to mean polyphony: "In Quito, the Franciscans organized the Colegio de San Andrés (1550–81) for songs of Indian chiefs; its music instruction consisted mainly of familiarizing the natives first with Gregorian chant and later with *canto de órgano,* or polyphony" (*Music in Latin America,* p. 3).

10. Michael V. Gannon, *The Cross in the Sand,* p. 53.

11. Ibid., p. 52.

12. Jerald T. Milanich and William C. Sturtevant, *Francisco Pareja's 1613 Confesionario,* p. 34.

13. Ibid., p. 31.

14. J. T. Lanning, *The Spanish Missions of Georgia,* p. 72.

15. Luís Gerónimo de Oré, "Simbolo católico indiano," 1598, cited in Robert Stevenson, *The Music of Peru,* p. 44.

16. Oré, *Martyrs of Florida,* p. 130.

17. Ibid., p. 104.

18. List of the ornaments and furnishings for divine services in thirty-four doctrina (missions) of the Florida conversions, St. Augustine, June 16, 1681 (Archivo General de Indias [AGI] 54-5-20, W.L.—9 U.F.). See Robert Allen Matter, "The Spanish Missions of Florida," pp. 127–28.

19. The "Vexilla Regis Prodeunt" (The banner of the king advances) is a hymn usually sung at vespers on the first Sunday of the Passion. It was the plainsong setting sung in Pensacola, but the text was also set by Juan Navarro, Diego Ortiz, Giovanni Pierluigi da Palestrina, and Tomás Luís de Victoria.

The "Litany of Loreto" is a thirteenth-century litany sung at Loreto, Italy, every evening in honor of the Virgin Mary. A litany is a supplication usually sung responsively between the priest and the congregation. This one has often been used as processional music sung by the congregation. Settings have been made by numerous composers.

20. Antonio Ponce de Leon, February 26, 1687, SD 864/6 JTC6; idem, January 29, 1702, SD 863/43 JCT6; Charles Arnade, *The Siege of St. Augustine in 1702,* p. 61; Juan de Pueyo and Juan Bendit Horroytiner, November 10, 1707, SD 847/10 JTC6.

21. Amy Bushnell, *The King's Coffer,* p. 40.

22. Lota M. Spell, "Music Teaching in New Mexico in the Seventeenth Century," *New Mexico Historical Review* 2, no. 1 (January 1927): 27–36.

23. Michael Gannon, *The Cross in the Sand,* p. 117.

24. Amy Bushnell, "Privilege and Obligation," p. 56.

25. They bore such names as Our Lady of the Conception, Our Lady of the Solitude, and Our Lady of the Milk.

26. Alonso de Leturiondo to the Crown, June 14, 1690.

27. Gov. Lucas Fernando de Palacio y Valenzuela to the Crown, August 5, 1760, AGI 86-7-22/3-5.

28. Gustave Reese, *Music in the Renaissance,* p. 600.

29. Eugenio Ruidiaz y Caravia, *La Florida,* 1:155; and Solís de Meras, *Pedro Menéndez de Avilés,* pp. 145–46. The vihuela de arco is a Spanish version of the lute, played with a bow. A clarine is a small-bore trumpet.

30. *The New Grove Dictionary of Music and Musicians,* 8:197.

31. Reese, *Music in the Renaissance,* p. 620.

32. This instrument was among the property of soldier Juan Ponpeyo. The property was divided or sold at St. Augustine on July 1, 1576, but this item was not sold at auction. *Archivo General de Indias,* EC 154-A, folio 783v.

33. Ibid., fol. 784v.

34. Andrés González de Barcia Carballido y Zúñiga, *Chronological History of the Continent of Florida, 1512–1722,* p. 74. For more information on Spanish music of the period, see *Monumentos de la música española,* 41 vols. (Barcelona: Consejo Superior de Investigaciones Científicas, Instituto Español de Musicológica, 1941–). Music for tecla, harp, and vihuela of 1557 and 1578 by Luys Venegas de Henestrosa and Antonio de Cabezón is examined, as is other music for later periods.

35. Milicia, Equilicia, *Discurso y regla militar, 1595,* fols. 12, 20–21, 63. Standard military calls of the second Spanish period in Florida, specifically the years 1779–80, have been recorded by Ricardo Fernández de la Torre, *Antología de la música militar* (Madrid: Graf. Eoco, 1972).

36. Francisco Barado, *Museo militar—historia del ejército español,* 3:546–47.

37. Ibid., pp. 551–54.

38. Bushnell, *King's Coffer,* p. 65.

39. R. P. N. Otaño, ed., *Toques de guerra,* p. 5.

40. "Testimonio sobre las reales fiestas que se hicieron en la ciudad de la Florida," March 4, 1702, AGI, Santo Domingo, file 840.

41. John Jay TePaske, *The Governorship of Spanish Florida, 1700–1763,* pp. 177–78.

42. Charles W. Arnade, "The Failure of Spanish Florida, *Americas* 16, no. 3 (January 1960): 271.

CHAPTER 3: *Distant and Strange Lands*

1. Gabriel Gravier, ed., *Deuxième voyage du dieppois Jean Ribaut à la Florida en 1565,* p. ii.

2. Edward Dickinson, *Music in the History of the Western Church,* p. 361.

3. Gravier, *Deuxième voyage,* p. ii.

4. René Laudonnière, *Three Voyages,* trans. and ed. Charles E. Bennett, pp. 11–13.

5. Nicolas Le Challeux, "Brief discours et histoire d'un voyage de quelques

Francois en la Florida," in Girolamo Benzoni, *Histoire nouvelle du Nouveau Monde*, p. 96.

6. Laudonnière, *Three Voyages*, pp. 41–42.

7. Charles E. Bennett, "Fort Caroline, Cradle of American Freedom," *Florida Historical Quarterly* 35, no. 1 (July 1956): 3–16.

8. Charles E. Bennett, *Laudonnière and Fort Caroline.* p. 55.

9. Le Moyne, *"Brevis narratio,"* p. 38.

10. Ibid.

11. Stefan Lorant, ed., *The New World*, pp. 38, 109.

12. Bennett, *Laudonnière and Fort Caroline*, p. 89.

13. Challeux, "Brief discours," p. 96.

14. An example of the practice is Claude Goudimel's setting of Psalm 65 in an edition prepared by Carleton Sprague Smith, published by the New York Public Library in 1938.

15. From "Deposition of Jean Menin," in Paul Gaffarel, *Histoire de la Floride française*, pp. 145 and 445; and René Laudonnière, *L'histoire notable de la Floride*, p. 196.

16. Quoted in Percy A. Scholes, *The Oxford Companion to Music*, p. 156.

17. Jean Ribault, *The Whole and True Discoverye of Terra Florida*, part 2, chap. 10, p. 132.

18. Jacques Le Moyne de Morgues wrote his "Brevis narratio" in London about twenty years after he left Florida. The Latin narrative was published first, then the German translation and engravings were published by Theodore de Bry in Frankfort in 1591. An English translation of the original Latin text and the de Bry engravings were published in Boston in 1875 by James R. Osgood. A modern publication of the narrative and the engravings is in Stefan Lorant's *New World*, pp. 33–119. The most extensive recent studies are those of Charles E. Bennett: *The Settlement of Florida*, *Laudonnière and Fort Caroline*, and *Fort Caroline and Its Leader*. Accounts here are based on those of Le Moyne and these other sources.

19. C. W. Baird, *History of the Huguenot Emigration to America*, p. 68.

20. Dominique de Gorgues, "Histoire mémorable de la reprinse de l'isle de la Floride [1568]" in *Les Français en Amérique*, ed. Suzanne Lussagnet, p. 243.

21. Bennett, *Laudonnière and Fort Caroline*, p. 49.

22. Marot and other poets who wrote metrical psalms sometimes departed from the biblical texts. The psalm numbering here is that of Pierre Pidoux in his *Psautier Huguenot du seizième siècle*.

CHAPTER 4: *I Long to Hear the Grenadiers March*

1. William Roberts, *An Account of the First Discovery and Natural History of Florida*, p. 86.

2. Barcia Carballido y Zúñiga, *Chronological History*, p. 174.

3. 1564–65, vol. 1, p. 263, Alex Lacy. "Have over the water to Floryda," ms Ashmoleon 48, no. 76, in the Bodleian Library, Oxford.

4. Gov. George Johnstone to James Johnston, *Georgia Gazette,* January 10, 1765.

5. Henry George Farmer, *Memoirs of the Royal Artillery Band,* pp. 36–38.

6. Capt. Robert Hinde, comp., *A Third Collection of Twenty-four Quick Marches, with Basses as performed by the Guards Light Horse and other regiments,* p. 9.

7. Charles Thompson and Samuel Thompson, *A Second Collection of Twenty-four Marches in seven parts as they are perform'd by his Majesty's Foot and Horse Guards,* set for two clarinets, violins, German flutes or hautboys, and two French horns and bass.

8. Lewis Butler, *The Annals of the King's Royal Rifle Corps,* 1:335.

9. Robert R. Rea, "Pensacola under the British (1763–1781)," in *Colonial Pensacola,* ed. James R. McGovern, p. 74.

10. R. L. Campbell, *Historical Sketches of Colonial Florida,* pp. 83–84.

11. Campbell to Germain, Pro, Co 5:597. Quoted in Max von Eelking, "German Mercenaries in Pensacola during the American Revolution, 1779–81," *Pensacola Historical Society Quarterly* 9, no. 1 (November 1977): 9.

12. Albert W. Haarmann, "The Third Waldeck Regiment in British Service, 1776–1783," *Army Historical Research* 48, no. 195 (Autumn 1970): 182.

13. Lewis Winstock, *Songs and Music of the Redcoats,* pp. 28–36.

14. Col. Henri Bouquet to Lewis Ourry, June 17, 1763, quoted in Butler, *Annals,* 1:335.

15. Raoul F. Camus, *Military Music of the American Revolution,* p. 111.

16. R. I. [John Reid], *A Set of Marches for two clarinets, hautboys, or German flutes, two horns, and a bassoon,* inscribed to the Rt. Honable Lady Amherst, pp. 20–21 and 24–25.

17. Butler, *Annals,* 1:335–36.

18. Charlton W. Tebeau, *A History of Florida,* pp. 78–79; Robert L. Gold, *Borderland Empires in Transition,* p. 147.

19. Cecil Johnson, *British West Florida, 1763–1783,* p. 167.

20. T. Sternhold and J. Hopkins, *The Whole Book of Psalms Collected in English Metre,* printed 1562.

21. Nahum Tate and Nicholas Brady, *A New Version of the Psalms of David,* first printed in 1696.

22. Isaac Watts, *The Psalms of David Imitated in the Language of the New Testament,* from 1719.

23. Nicholas Temperley, *The Music of the English Parish Church,* 1:122.

24. General Grant, to General Gage, February 18, 1771, Gage papers, William M. Clements Library, University of Michigan. Quoted by C. L. Mowat, "St. Augustine under the British Flag, 1763–1775," *Florida Historical Quarterly* 20, no. 2 (October 1941): 139.

25. Advertisement of the publisher in Mathias Vento, *A Third Book of Six Sonatas for the Harpsichord, with accompaniment for a violin or German flute,* dedicated to His Most Serene Highness Charles, hereditary Prince of Brunswick Lunebourg, etc. (London: Welcker, n.d.).

26. *Rutherford's Compleat Collection of 112 of the most celebrated minuets, with their basses both old and new, which are now in vogue perform'd at court and at all publick assemblies; the tunes are proper for the German flute, violin, or Harpsichord.* Volume 1 was published by D. Rutherford, volume 2 by John Rutherford, 1775–80.

27. *Thompson's Compleat Collection of Two hundred Favourite Country Dances, performed at Court, Bath, Tunbridge, and all Public Assemblies with proper figures or Directions to each tune Set for the Violin, German flute and Hautboy,* vol. 1. This volume is a reprint of an earlier, 1760 edition.

28. *Warlike Musick, Books I, II, III, IV in one volume, Being a choice collection of marches and Trumpet Tunes for a German flute, violin, or harpsichord. By Mr. Handel, St. Martini, and the most eminent masters.*

29. Butler, *Annals,* 1:337.

30. Alfred E. Zealley and J. Ord Hume, *Famous Bands of the British Empire,* p. 25.

31. John Farmer, *Scarlet and Blue,* p. 14.

32. Ibid., p. 177.

33. Ibid., pp. 200, 196, 194.

34. James Oswald, *A Collection of the Best Old Scotch and English Songs,* pp. 16–17.

35. Jane Quinn, *Minorcans in Florida,* p. 12

36. William Stark, *An Account of East Florida,* pp. 12–13.

37. Wilbur H. Siebert, "Slavery and White Servitude in East Florida, 1726–1776," *Florida Historical Quarterly* 10, no. 1 (July 1931): 3–23.

38. Edwin L. Williams, Jr., "Negro Slavery in Florida," *Florida Historical Quarterly* 28, no. 2 (October 1949): 93.

39. Clinton N. Howard, *The British Development of West Florida, 1763–1769,* p. 45.

40. *Florida Acts,* 1822, pp. 21–23, cited in Dorothy Dodd, "The Schooner Emperor," *Florida Historical Quarterly* 13, no. 3 (January 1935): 117.

41. *East Florida Gazette,* March 3, 1784.

42. H. W. Pedicord and F. L. Bergmann, eds., *The Plays of David Garrick,* 1:69–104.

43. David Garrick, *Miss in Her Teens,* p. 23.

44. Josiah Smith, Jr., "Diary, 1780–1781," *South Carolina Historical and Genealogical Magazine* 33, no. 1 (January 1932): 20–25.

45. Joseph Johnson, *Traditions and Reminiscences* (Charleston, 1851), p. 30, quoted by Charles L. Mowat, *East Florida as a British Province,* p. 124.

46. J. Leitch Wright, "British East Florida: Loyalist Bastion," in *Eighteenth Century Florida: The Impact of the American Revolution,* ed. Samuel Proctor, pp. 1–13.

CHAPTER 5: *Before the Ending of the Day*

1. Joseph B. Lockley, *East Florida, 1783–1785,* p. 448.
2. Michael J. Curley, *Church and State in the Spanish Floridas, 1783–1822,* p. 116.
3. Ibid., p. 109.

4. Helen Hornbeck Tanner, "The 1789 Saint Augustine Celebration" *Florida Historical Quarterly* 38, no. 4 (October 1959): 280–93.

5. Ibid., p. 292.

6. George R. Fairbanks, *The History and Antiquities of St. Augustine, Florida*, p. 17.

7. Ibid., p. 177.

CHAPTER 6: *The Roll of a Drum, the Sound of an Old Song*

1. *A Subaltern in America* (1833), quoted in Lewis Winstock, *Songs and Music of the Redcoats*, p. 86.

2. Rachel Jackson to Eliza Kingsbury, July 23, 1821, quoted in James Parton, *Life of Andrew Jackson*, 2:602.

3. Mark F. Boyd, *Florida Aflame*, p. 108.

4. Among the military figures were Winfield Scott, Edmund P. Gaines, Thomas S. Jesup, William J. Worth, Duncan L. Clinch, Francis L. Dade, Ethan Allen Hitchcock, Alexander McComb, George A. McCall, William Tecumseh Sherman, and Richard Keith Call.

5. John Bemrose, *Reminiscences of the Second Seminole War*, ed. John K. Mahon, pp. 80–81.

6. Ibid., p. 78.

7. Erasmus D. Keys, *Fifty Years' Observation of Men and Events, Civil and Military*, pp. 48, 52–53. The words of this song are by Col. A. T. Lee, who served with the Eighth Army Infantry in the Florida war.

8. Edward Arthur Dolph, *Sound Off!* p. 455.

9. Bartholomew M. Lynch, "Journal, 1837–1839," pp. 129, 138, 192.

10. Ibid., pp. 131, 158, 161, 166.

11. Keys, *Fifty Years, Observation*, p. 165.

12. Ibid., p. 17.

13. Arthur E. Franke, Jr., *Fort Mellon, 1837–42*, p. 79.

14. Felix P. McGaughy, Jr., "The Squaw Kissing War," p. 16.

15. Lynch, "Journal," p. 129.

16. George Ballentine, *Autobiography of an English Soldier in the United States Army*, p. 247.

17. Ibid., pp. 282–83. This account was written after the author's unit had left Florida and gone to fight in Mexico in 1847. For another description of bucking and gagging, see Dolph, *Sound Off!* p. 394.

18. George A. McCall, *Letters from the Frontier*, p. 315.

19. John T. Sprague, *The Origin, Progress, and Conclusion of the Florida War*, pp. 526–49.

20. Bemrose, *Reminiscences*, p. 11.

21. Ethan Allen Hitchcock, *Fifty Years in Camp and Field*, p. 189. This music is now in the Florida State University Music Library, Tallahassee.

22. Rumsay, ed., *Letters*, pp. 81, 93, 100.

23. Bemrose, *Reminiscences,* pp. 10–11.

24. R. L. Goulding, "William Hackley's Diary, 1830–1857: Key West and the Apalachee Area," *Apalachee* 6 (1963–67): 35.

25. "Come o'er the Sea" was first published in America in Philadelphia, 1815–16, in the John Andrew Stevenson collection, *A Selection of Irish Melodies,* pp. 36–37. It was reissued in New York by Geib and Walker, 1829–43. It is set to the tune "Cuishlih ma chree."

26. Ballentine, *Autobiography,* pp. 61–62.

27. Ibid., pp. 92–93.

28. Ibid., p. 96.

29. Ibid., pp. 23–24.

30. John K. Mahon, *History of the Second Seminole War, 1835–1842,* p. 303.

31. Charles Millard, Jr., to his brother, July 29, 1818, Fernandina, Amelia Island, *Florida Historical Quarterly* 40, no. 1 (July 1961): 96–97.

32. Susan L'Engle, *Notes of My Family and Recollections of My Early Life,* pp. 29, 47, 61.

33. *Pensacola Gazette and West Florida Advertiser,* November 5, 1852.

34. Dolph, *Sound Off!* p. 456.

35. John T. Sprague, "Macomb's Mission to the Seminoles," ed. Frank F. White, Jr., *Florida Historical Quarterly* 35, no. 2 (October 1956): 154, 156. This article is based on Sprague's journal kept during April and May 1839. Lieutenant Sprague is identified as aide-de-camp to General McComb, Eighth Army Infantry, in the Seminole War of 1839.

36. Sprague, "Macomb's Mission to the Seminoles," p. 144.

37. Mahon, *History,* pp. 256–57.

38. John Hammond Moore, "A South Carolina Lawyer Visits St. Augustine, 1837," *Florida Historical Quarterly* 43, no. 4 (April 1965): 361–78.

39. John Pickell, "Brief Notes of the Campaign against the Seminole Indians in Florida in 1837," ed. Frank White, Jr., p. 115.

40. Moore, "South Carolina Lawyer," p. 373.

41. W. Stanley Hoole, ed., *Florida Territory in 1844: The Diary of Master Edward C. Anderson, U.S. Navy,* pp. 23, 30.

42. Ballentine, *Autobiography,* p. 64.

43. Hoole, *Florida Territory in 1844,* pp. 25–26.

44. Ibid., p. 61.

45. Randolph B. Marcy, *Border Reminiscences,* pp. 149–50.

CHAPTER 7: *Safety at Home and Respectability Abroad*

1. *The American Naval and Patriotic Songster, as sung at various places of Amusement,* pp. 29–30.

2. *Floridian* (Pensacola), October 8, 1821.

3. *Florida Journal,* (Apalachicola), March 17, 1841.

4. *Pensacola Gazette,* September 30, 1848.

5. *Floridian,* (Pensacola), July 19, 1823. Following toasts, the music included "Adams and Liberty," "Union and Force," "Eighth of January," "Decatur and Victory," "Pike's March," "Cortez and Constitution," and "The Marseillaise Hymn."

6. *Pensacola Gazette and West Florida Advertiser,* August 7, 1824. Among the music was "Monroe's March," a slow march, and a song "Is There a Heart That Never Lov'd?"

7. Ibid., July 13, 1827. The music included "Tars of Columbia," "Here's Columbia Forever," "The American Star," "Walk In and Tak a Gud Pint Stoup," "It Was Dunois the Young and Brave," "The Irident Neptune," "To Ladies Eyes a Round Boys" "Hail Columbia," and "Auld Lang Syne."

8. *Pensacola Gazette and West Florida Advertiser,* July 15, 1828. To the all-time favorites were added "Away with Your Pouting and Sadness," "The Wounded Hussar," "Let Merit Have Her Reward," "Home, Love, and Liberty," "The Free and Accepted Mason," and "Haste to the Wedding."

9. *St. Joseph Times,* July 9, 1839. The music repertory expanded to include "March to the Battle Field," "Constitution and Gurriere," "Jefferson's March," "Liberty Tree," "Yankee Doodle," "Does Your Mother Know You Are Out?" "Jersey Blue," "Marseillaise Hymn," "Kosciousko's March," "Dead March" from *Saul,* "Handcock's March," "Up Rouse Ye Then My Merry Men," "Sich a Gitten Down Stairs," "Sons of Vulcan," "All by the Merry Green-wood Trees," "Sons of Freedom," "Exile of Erin," "They Fought for Freedom," "Landlord Fill the Flowing Bowl," and "Columbia, the Land of the Free."

10. Ibid., August 4, 1840.

11. *Apalachicola Commercial Advertiser,* July 6, 1844.

12. *Florida Intelligencer* (Tallahassee), August 11, 1831.

13. *The News* (St. Augustine), May 24, 1845.

14. *The Republican Campaign Songster* (New York and Auburn: Miller, Oeton and Mulligan, 1856). Other lyrics were devised to be sung to such familiar tunes as "The Old Oaken Bucket," "Alley Croaker," "Scots Wha Hae," "Camptown Races," "Ben Bolt," "The Soldier's Tear," "Once Upon a Midnight Dreary," "Rory O'More," "Oh, Hard Times Come Again No More," "Lucy Long," "Kathleen Mavoureen," "I Dreamed That I Dwelt in Marble Halls," "Some Love to Roam," "The Minstrel Boy," "The Last Rose of Summer," "Yankee Doodle," "Old Dan Tucker," "Uncle Ned," "Widow Machree," Old Dog Tray," "Hail Columbia," "My Boy Tommy," and "Nelly Bly."

15. George J. F. Clarke to Capt. J. R. Bell, September 3, 1821, published in the *East Florida Herald,* March 8, 1823.

16. John Lee Williams, *A View of West Florida,* p. 77.

17. Clarence E. Carter, ed., *The Territorial Papers of the United States,* 22:877.

18. *Key West Register,* June 4, 1829.

19. *St. Joseph Times,* June 22, 1839.

20. Ibid.

21. *East Florida Herald,* May 10, 1823.

22. *Florida Herald,* July 22, 1829.

23. *Pensacola Floridan,* February 9, 1829.

24. *Florida Democrat* (Pensacola), January 16, 1846.

25. Ibid., July 15, 1846.

26. ibid., April 8, 1846.

27. John D. G. Shea, *History of the Catholic Church in the United States,* 3:699.

28. Joseph D. Cushman, Jr., *A Goodly Heritage,* pp. 33–34.

29. William G. Dodd, "Early Education in Tallahassee and the West Florida Seminary, now Florida State University," *Florida Historical Quarterly* 27, no. 1 (July 1948): 1–27.

30. *Florida and Advocate,* December 8, 1829.

31. *Floridian,* November 7, 1835.

32. *Florida Sentinel,* August 3, 1847.

33. *Floridian* (Tallahassee), October 21, 1837.

34. *Florida Sentinel,* November 18, 1843.

35. *Floridan and Journal,* April 5, 1856.

36. Ibid., September 20, 1856.

37. B. H. Groene, "Lizzie Brown's Tallahassee," *Florida Historical Quarterly* 28, no. 2 (October 1969): 155–75.

38. Nita Pyburn, *Documentary History of Education in Florida, 1822–1860,* p. 70.

39. *Apalachicola Gazette,* January 25, 1840.

40. *Florida Sentinel,* (Tallahassee), November 4, 1842.

41. Ibid., January 6, 1846; December 23, 1851.

42. *The American Musical Directory, 1861,* p. 29.

43. John L. McKinnon, "History of Walton County (Florida)."

44. *Florida Senate Journal,* appendix, pp. 15–19.

45. James O. Knauss, "Education in Florida, 1821–1829," *Florida Historical Quarterly* 3, no. 4 (April 1925): 22–35.

CHAPTER 8: *Of Thy Indulgence, Love, and Power*

1. George A. McCall, *Letters from the Frontier,* pp. 16–17.

2. *Pensacola Gazette and West Florida Advertiser,* March 27, 1824.

3. Ibid., April 24, 1824.

4. *East Florida Herald,* January 22, 1825.

5. John Cole Ley, *Fifty-Two Years in Florida,* p. 45.

6. J. Moore, "South Carolina Lawyer," p. 373.

7. Arthur W. Thompson, "A Massachusetts Traveller on the Florida Frontier," *Florida Historical Quarterly,* 38, no. 1 (October 1959): 140–41.

8. Edgar L. Pennington, "The Church in Florida, 1763–1892," *Historical Magazine of the Protestant Episcopal Church* 7 (March 1938): 24.

9. *Pensacola Gazette,* January 13, 1829.

10. Thomas Douglas, *Autobiography of Thomas Douglas, Late Judge of the Supreme Court of Florida*, p. 94.

11. *Pensacola Gazette and West Florida Advertiser,* May 31, 1832.

12. Julia J. Yonge, *Christ Church Parish, Pensacola, 1827–1927,* p. 11.

13. *Pensacola Gazette,* July 11, 1835.

14. Yonge, *Christ Church Parish,* p. 17.

15. W. H. Carter, "History of St. Johns Church Tallahassee," p. 18.

16. I am indebted to John Ogasapian for supplying these dates and other information about Henry Erben. The builder's inventory lists correct dates but is not reliable as to church names. They have been corrected here.

17. Dorothy Dodd, "Apalachicola: Antebellum Cotton Port," manuscript, p. 9, Florida State Library.

18. *Commercial Advertiser* (Apalachicola), April 27, 1844.

19. Lowell Mason, *The Boston Handel and Haydn Society Collection of Church Music,* p. v.

20. Peter Haskew, "A St. Joseph Diary of 1838," ed. F. W. Hoskins, *Florida Historical Quarterly* 17, no. 2 (October 1938): 134.

21. Ibid., p. 140.

22. *Florida Journal of Apalachicola,* May 21, 1842.

23. James C. Bryant, "Indian Springs: The Story of a Pioneer Church in Leon County, Florida," p. 64.

24. Joshua Knowles, "Methodism in Tallahassee in the Year 1836," p. 2.

25. "Souvenir Centennial Celebration Program, 1838–1938," Bethel Baptist Church, Golden Jubilee, Jacksonville, Florida, July 18–24, 1938, Florida State Library.

26. Pisgah Methodist Church, "Bulletin," n.d., Florida State University Library, Tallahassee.

27. J. Bryant, "Indian Springs," p. 64.

28. Jefferson B. Browne, *Key West, the Old and the New,* p. 31.

29. Henry P. Cook, "Pensacola Mission," *Methodist Magazine* 8 (1825): 111–12.

30. Noah Laney, "St. Augustine Mission," *Methodist Magazine* 8 (1825): 112–13.

31. John S. Tappan, "Tallahassee and St. Marks 1841," *Florida Historical Quarterly* 24, no. 2 (October 1945): 108–12.

32. Etta Bell Willis, "History of the Methodist Church of Quincy, Florida." "Lining out" was the practice of speaking, chanting, or singing a line or two of a hymn before it was sung by the congregation.

33. Ibid.

34. *Tallahassee Democrat,* October 7, 1976.

35. Ibid., April 24, 1966.

36. Norman E. Booth, *A History of Old Pisgah, 1830–1876,* p. 11.

37. Ibid.

38. "History of Monticello Baptist Church," *Florida Baptist Witness,* February 3, 1916, p. 2.

39. Dr. Charles A. Hentz, "Diary," Marianna and Quincy, Florida, May 3–31, 1863, p. 4, Florida State University.

40. *Gentleman's Magazine* 51 (1781): 369.

41. A. Mervyn Davies, *Presbyterian Heritage*, p. 119.

42. Cooper Clifford Kirk, "A History of the Southern Presbyterian Church of Florida, 1821–1891," pp. 164–65.

43. Ibid., p. 112.

44. Ibid., p. 119.

45. Jean P. McCord, "History of the First Hundred Years of the First Presbyterian Church in Tallahassee, Florida," typescript, p. 42.

46. Kirk, "History," pp. 158–59.

47. Prince Achille Murat, *America and the Americans*, pp. 100–101.

48. Ibid., p. 172. Reverend Sparrow was formerly president of Hampden-Sydney College in Virginia.

49. Isaac Watts, *Hymns and Spiritual Songs*, hymn 66.

50. *Pensacola Gazette*, September 13, 1823.

51. John L. Rosser, *A History of Florida Baptists*, p. 8.

52. *Florida Intelligencer*, January 20, 1831.

53. J. Bryant, "Indian Springs," p. iii.

54. W. T. Cash, "Taylor County History," *Florida Historical Quarterly* 27, no. 1 (July 1948): 43.

55. Aenon Baptist Church, "Records, 1842–1864," January 15, 1843.

56. Cash, "Taylor County History," p. 43.

57. Murat, *America and the Americans*, p. 99.

58. *Plymouth Collection of Hymns and Tunes*, p. iv.

59. Ibid., p. vii.

60. Samuel Worcester, *An Address on Sacred Musick*, delivered before the Middlesex Musical Society and the Handel Society of Dartmouth College at a joint meeting held at Concord, New Hampshire, September 19, 1810, (Boston-Manning and Loring, 1811), pp. 19–20.

61. Andrew Law (1749–1821) was a singing-school master and notation innovator.

62. Richard A. Crawford, *Andrew Law, American Psalmodist*.

63. George C. Osborn, "A Religious Revival in Tallahassee in 1843 by the Rev. Dr. Nathan Hoyt," *Florida Historical Quarterly* 32, no. 4 (April 1954); 293–94.

64. Murat, *America and the Americans*, pp. 96–97.

65. Ibid., p. 103.

66. *The Middlesex Collection of Church Music; or, Ancient Psalmody Revived*.

67. *The Suffolk Selection of Church Music*, p. 3.

68. *The New England Harmony; or, New England Repository of Sacred Music*, preface, 17th ed.

69. Ibid.

70. Edward Hamilton, *Songs of Sacred Praise*.

71. Lowell Mason and George James Webb, *Cantica Laudis,* preface.

72. C. J. Latrobe, *The Rambler in North America,* 1:51.

73. *St. Joseph Times,* July 2, 1838.

74. *Tallahassee Florida Sentinel,* July 22, 1842.

75. Simon Peter Richardson, *The Lights and Shadows of Itinerant Life,* p. 69.

CHAPTER 9: *Where Gen'rous Hearts and Beauty Dwell*

1. McCall, *Letters from the Frontiers,* pp. 14–15.

2. Ibid., pp. 70–71.

3. Ibid., pp. 76–77.

4. Ibid., pp. 51–52.

5. Joseph Strutt, *Sports and Pastimes of the People of England,* p. 45.

6. McCall, *Letters from the Frontiers,* p. 20.

7. Ibid., pp. 108–19.

8. *West Florida Advertiser,* May 26, 1829.

9. William G. Dodd, "Theatrical Entertainment in Early Florida," *Florida Historical Quarterly* 25, no. 2 (October 1946): 121–74.

10. *Pensacola Floridian,* October 22, 1821.

11. *Floridan,* August 18, September 8, October 8, 1821.

12. *Floridian,* October 22, 1821.

13. Ibid., May 4, 1822.

14. McCall, *Letters from the Frontiers,* pp. 81–83.

15. *Pensacola Gazette,* June 22, 1822.

16. Ibid., April 18, 1828.

17. Ibid., February 17, 1829.

18. Ibid., March 10, 1829.

19. Hans Nathan, *Dan Emmett and the Rise of Early Negro Minstrelsy,* p. 52.

20. W. Dodd, "Theatrical Entertainment," pp. 121–74.

21. *Pensacola Gazette,* March 11, April 28, 1837.

22. Gilbert Chase, *America's Music,* p. 114.

23. "Air National: God Save the Queen, variations; À la occasion due couronnement de sa majesté Victoire, reine d'Angleterre," by F. V. Beutel de Lattenberg, op. 15 (Prague: F. Hoffman), and "Grand duo du couronnement composé pour deux pianos et dedie a sa majesté la reine d'Angleterre," by H. Herz, op. 104 (Paris: Mayence et Anvers).

24. *Floridian* (Pensacola), May 31, 1823.

25. *Pensacola Gazette,* December 1, 1826.

26. Ibid., July 20, 1827.

27. Ibid., July 1, 1826.

28. Thomas C. DeLeon, *Four Years in Rebel Capitals,* pp. 298–99.

29. Malcolm B. Johnson, *Red, White, and Bluebloods in Frontier Florida,* pp. 18–20, 49–56, 75–78, 43–44, 58–66.

30. George G. Smith, *History of Methodism in Georgia and Florida from 1785 to 1865*, pp. 387–88.

31. William G. Dodd, "Ring Tournaments in Tallahassee," *Apalachee* 3 (1948–50): 55–70.

32. A. J. Hanna, *A Prince in Their Midst*, p. 47.

33. Achille Murat, "Florida," *American Quarterly Review* 1, no. 3 (September 1827): 232.

34. MSS, n.d., Tallahassee Centennial file, Florida State University Library.

35. Murat, *America and the Americans*, pp. 61–62.

36. *Florida Intelligencer* (Tallahassee), February 24, 1826.

37. Jerrell H. Shofner, *History of Jefferson County*, p. 36.

38. *Floridan and Advocate* (Tallahassee), September 9, November 16, 1830. See appendix B for the full account of this ball.

39. *Tallahassee Floridian and Journal*, October 19, 1850.

40. *Florida Sentinel*, September 24, December 3, 1850.

41. Murat, *America and the Americans*, pp. 258–59.

42. Groene, "Lizzie Brown's Tallahassee," p. 167.

43. Long, *Florida Breezes*, pp. 177–219.

44. The *Star of Florida*, January 1840.

45. Long, *Florida Breezes*, pp. 107–8.

46. Ibid., p. 133.

47. *Floridian* (Tallahassee), May 6, 1848; and Evelyn Whitfield Henry, "The May Party," *Apalachee* 2 (1946): 35–45.

48. Long, *Florida Breezes*, pp. 246–47.

49. *Newport Gazette*, August 31, October 26, 1847.

50. O. J. Hammond to Harvey Hubbard, Tallahassee, November 10, 1838, Florida State University Library.

51. Elizabeth F. Smith, *Tom Brown's Tallahassee Days*, 1825–1850, n.p.

52. John P. Kennedy, *Memoirs of the Life of William Wirt*, 2:389, 392, 390.

53. *Apalachicola Commercial Advertiser*, September 30, 1843.

54. Ibid., April 5–12, 1843.

55. *Floridian and Advocate*, January 27, 1831, *Floridian*, December 14, 1833, January 17, 1835, January 29, 1852, December 6, 1856, December 31, 1859.

56. Charles A. Hentz, "My Autobiography," 1:162.

57. Ibid., p. 335.

58. Ibid., p. 19.

59. Susan Bradford Eppes, *Through Some Eventful Years*, pp. 80–81.

60. Ibid., p. 86.

61. Ibid., p. 73.

62. Ibid., p. 233.

63. Ibid., p. 126.

64. Susan Bradford Eppes Collection, n.p., Florida State University Archives.

65. Eppes, *Through Some Eventful Years*, p. 236.

66. Ibid., pp. 237–38.

67. Long, *Florida Breezes*, p. 117.

68. Ibid., p. 124.

69. Ibid., p. 129

70. Alton C. Morris, *Folksongs of Florida*, p. 222.

71. Long, *Florida Breezes*, p. 307.

72. J. Miller, *Narrative of a Voyage to the Spanish Main in the Ship "Two Friends,"* p. 119.

73. Ibid., p. 122.

74. *East Florida Gazette*, August 4, 1821.

75. *St. Augustine Gazette*, November 1, June 14, 1823.

76. Motte, *Journey into Wilderness*, p. 112.

77. W. W. Marsh to Henry C. Pitney, February 7, 1853, chronological file, St. Augustine Historical Society.

78. J. T. Van Campen, *St. Augustine, Capital of la Florida*, p. 62.

79. Orson [pseud.], "Familiar Sketches of Life in Florida; number two, St. Augustine and Its Environs," *Knickerbocker* 8 (November 1836): 555.

80. George R. Fairbanks, *The History and Antiquities of St. Augustine, Florida*, p. 177.

81. Matilda D. Taylor, "Old Customs of the Early Days," *El Escribano*, no. 41 (October 1961): 7–8.

82. Lester B. Shippe, ed., *Bishop Whipple's Southern Diary, 1843–1844*, pp. 57–58.

83. Ibid., pp. 56–63.

84. Ibid., p. 57.

85. Thomas Graham, *The Awakening of St. Augustine*, p. 16.

86. William Cullen Bryant, *Letters of a Traveler*, pp. 104ff.

87. Rev. Fernando Marti, Archivist of the Arxin Diocesá de Cintadella, Minorca, to Philip D. Rasico, 1983.

88. D. Francisco Camps y Mercadal, *Folk-Lore menorquín de la Pagesia*, pp. 55–57.

89. Quinn, *Minorcans in Florida*, pp. 246–47. From the Rofger collection, other Minorcan songs still occasionally sung in St. Augustine include "Cants infantile" (pp. 238–39), "Cant de l'Advent" (pp. 243–46), "Enveure murtre Florida" (p. 73), and "Ferreries" (pp. 54–55).

90. It was acquired by Marguerite Porter of Daytona Beach, who was supervisor of music in the public schools of the city from the 1920s to the 1950s. Miss Porter left no ownership documentation for the volume but speculated that it was brought to the area either by a British military man or by an early English settler.

91. Scholes, *Oxford Companion to Music*, p. 502.

92. J. W. Hutchinson, *Story of the Hutchinsons*, 1:225.

93. *The Rough and Ready Songster*, p. 6.

94. Ibid., pp. 29–30.

95. Ibid., pp. 93–94.

96. Ibid., p. 193.

97. *Titusville Florida Star*, May 5, 1887.

98. *East Florida Herald* (St. Augustine), January 11, 1823.

99. Edward A. Mueller, "East Coast Florida Steamboating, 1831–1861," *Florida Historical Quarterly* 40, no. 3 (January 1962): 241–60.

100. James C. Craig, "Steamboat Days on the St. Johns River," *Jacksonville Historical Society Journal* 3 (1954): 138–45.

101. *Jacksonville News,* June 18, 1847.

102. Charles Clinton, *A Winter from Home,* pp. 20–21.

103. Thomas Frederick Davis, *History of Jacksonville, Florida, and Vicinity, 1513–1824,* p. 113.

104. Ibid., p. 44.

105. Fredrika Bremer, *The Homes of the New World: Impressions of America,* 2:473.

106. See chapter 10 for a folksong written about another vessel named the *Isabel.*

107. Hy M. Jenners to his mother, Mrs. D. Jenners, Waterford, Virginia, March 31, 1826, Florida State Library.

108. R. L. Goulding, ed., "William Hackley's Diary," p. 7, typescript, 1968, Florida State University Library, Tallahassee.

109. Ibid., p. 16.

110. Eugene L. Schwaab, ed., *Travels in the Old South,* 2:456; "Key West, Florida," *Merchant's Magazine,* January 1852, pp. 52–60, reprinted in *Florida Historical Quarterly* 8, no. 1 (July 1929): 48–63.

111. John R. Lytte to J. B. Stevenson, November 6, 1841, Monroe County Public Library.

112. Benjamin Beard Strobel, *Charleston Courier,* May 4, 1837.

113. Pierre Jean de Berlanger (1780–1857) was a popular French poet and songwriter.

114. Recollections of Benjamin Beard Strobel in the *Charleston Courier,* May 17, 1837, quoted in E. A. Hammond, ed., "Sketches of the Florida Keys, 1829–1833," *Tequesta* 29 (1969): 90–94.

115. "The Courtship of Mallory," unidentified newspaper clipping, University of North Carolina Library.

116. George Cromer to his family, January 26, March 2, 1862, Monroe County Public Library.

117. Christian Boyd to his son, from Key West, Florida, September 23, 1862, Monroe County Public Library.

118. David-Jacob E. Apple (?) to parents, brother, and sister, from Camp Brannon, Key West, Florida, February 23, 1862, Monroe County Public Library.

119. Lewis G. Schmidt, *A Civil War History of the Forty-seventh Regiment of Pennsylvania Veteran Volunteers,* p. 112.

120. Ibid., pp. 112, 115.

121. Ibid., p. 410.

122. Ibid., p. 120.

123. Henry D. Wharton, *Diary,* p. 129.

124. Schmidt, *Civil War History,* p. 340.

125. George D. Allen to his sister, Frances A. T. Allen, June 7, 1863, from Key West, Florida; Monroe County Library.

CHAPTER 10: *Jump, Isabel, Slide Water*

1. Buckingham Smith, trans., *Narratives of De Soto in the Conquest of Florida*, p. 269.

2. H. I. Priestly, *The Luna Papers*, p. xxxiv.

3. Charles A. Stakley, "Introduction of the Negro into the United States," *Magazine of American History* 26 (1891): 358–63.

4. See Barcia Carballido y Zúñiga, *Chronological History*, and Laudonnière, *L'histoire notable de la Florida*.

5. Dena J. Epstein, "African Music in British and French America," *Musical Quarterly* 59 (January 1973): 61–69. See also Epstein's *Sinful Tunes and Spirituals*.

6. William Beckford, *A Descriptive Account of the Island of Jamaica*, 1:215–17; 2:387.

7. Comte Francis de Castelnau, *Vues et souvenirs de l'Amérique du Nord*, p. 316.

8. Johann David Schoepf, *Travels in the Confederation (1783–1784)*, 2:260–61.

9. William Young, "A Tour through Several Islands of Barbados, St. Vincent, Antigua, Tobaga, and Grenada, in the Years 1791 and 1792," in Bryan Edwards, *The History, Civil and Commercial, of the British Colonies in the West Indies*, 4:258.

10. *A Guide to Key West*, WPA Writers' Program, p. 24.

11. Zephaniah Kingsley, *A Treatise on the Patriarchal, or cooperative system of society*, 2d ed., p. 14.

12. Ibid., 1st ed., n.p.

13. Alfred Jackson Hanna and Katherine Abbey Hanna, *Florida's Golden Sands*, p. 97.

14. Quoted in Hanna and Hanna, *Florida's Golden Sands*, p. 100.

15. *Florida Acts*, 1822, pp. 21–23.

16. *Quincy Times*, May 13, 1848.

17. Jonathan Walker, *The Trial and Imprisonment of Jonathan Walker*, p. 101.

18. David Brown, *The Planter; or, Thirteen Years in the South, by a northern man*, p. 64.

19. Ibid., p. 135.

20. W. J. Stillman, *The Autobiography of a Journalist*, vol. 1, n.p., quoted in Margaret Seton Fleming Biddle, *Hibernia, the Unreturning Tide*, p. 41.

21. *Florida Intelligencer* (Tallahassee), December 8, 1826.

22. *Tallahassee Floridian and Journal*, January 15, 1859.

23. Laura Randall to family, May 25, 1828, Florida State University Archives.

24. Motte, *Journey into Wilderness*, pp. 112–13.

25. Clinton, *Winter from Home*, p. 29.

26. T. Davis, *History of Jacksonville*, p. 51.

27. "Towns and Plantations," WPA, Corse Files no. 784, pp. 20–21.

28. Julia Floyd Smith, *Slavery and Plantation Growth in Antebellum Florida, 1821–1860*, p. 94.

29. Capt. N. S. Jarvis, "An Army Surgeon's Notes of Frontier Services, 1833–62," reprint from *Journal of the Military Service Institution,* State Library of Florida.

30. O. T. Hammond to Harvey Hubbard, Esq., Norwich, Chenango Co., New York, from Tallahassee, Fla., November 10, 1838, Florida State University Library.

31. Carita Doggett Corse Papers, WPA Writers Program, p. 22.

32. Alton C. Morris, *Folksongs of Florida,* pp. 259–62.

33. Charles L. Edwards, *Bahama Songs and Stories,* p. 17.

34. Basil D. Hedrick and Jeanette E. Stephens, *In the Days of Yesterday and in the Days of Today: An Overview of Bahamian Folkmusic,* p. 28.

35. C. Edwards, *Bahama Songs,* p. 18.

36. Gladys Brown, ed., *Third World Group,* Bahamas Independence Issue, p. 103.

37. Elsie Clews Parsons, *Folk Tales of Andros Islands, Bahamas,* p. 39.

38. George Cable, quoted in C. Edwards, *Bahama Songs,* p. 108.

39. Allen Covington Morris, *Florida Place Names,* p. 139. See also appendix C.

40. Bemrose, *Reminiscences,* p. 13.

41. Alice Strickland, "Prince of the Wilderness," *Florida Speaks* 5, no. 2 (April 1953): 28–29.

42. J. Kinnard, Jr., "Who Are Our National Poets?" *Knickerbocker Magazine,* October 26, 1845, pp. 331–41.

43. "The Story of Naval Stores," WPA, Florida Writers' Program, *Florida Highways,* May 1943, p. 36.

44. Comte de Castelnau, "Essai sur la Floride du milieu," trans. Arthur R. Seymour, *Florida Historical Quarterly* 26, no. 4 (April 1948): 316.

45. Ibid., 26, no. 3 (January 1948): 243.

46. Lilla Mills Hawes, ed., "The Memoirs of Charles H. Olstead," *Georgia Historical Society* 43 (June 1959): 170–86.

47. Anna Maria Dummett, "Remembrances of the Old Plantation . . . The Old Dummett Grove," *Literary Florida,* February 1949, p. 10.

48. D. Brown, *The Planter,* pp. 84–86.

49. Alton C. Morris, *Folksongs of Florida,* pp. 62–63.

50. Susan Eppes, *The Negro of the Old South,* pp. 17–18.

51. Corse Papers, p. 70.

52. Ibid., pp. 68–69.

53. Ibid., p. 72.

54. Ibid.

55. Ibid., p. 74.

56. Panhandle Pete, "Singin' Men and Singin' Rails, *Florida's Panhandle Life,* May 1982, p. 28.

57. Ibid., p. 69.

58. Ibid., p. 65.

59. Harriet Beecher Stowe, *Palmetto Leaves,* p. 284.

60. Long, *Florida Breezes*, pp. 181–82.

61. *Quincy Times*, May 20, 1848.

62. "Story of Naval Stores," pp. 14–15.

63. Correspondent *N*, "Letter from Fernandina, Fla., dated February 6, 1865, in *Boston Semi-Weekly Advertiser*, March 1, 1865. Quoted in Deane L. Root, *Music of Florida Historical Sites*, p. 80.

64. Ibid., pp. 80–81.

65. Quoted in William Warren Rogers, *Ante-bellum Thomas County, 1825–1861*, p. 196.

66. *Quincy Times*, May 20, 1848.

67. Stowe, *Palmetto Leaves*, pp. 46–47.

68. Quoted in W. Rogers, *Thomas County*, p. 196.

69. W. F. Allen, "Negro Dialect," *Nation* 1 (December 1865): 744–45.

70. WPA Florida Writers' Project, Papers, n.p., n.d., Jacksonville University Library.

71. Eppes, *Negro of the Old South*, p. 61.

72. William Francis Allen, Charles Pickard Ware, and Lucy McKim Garrison, *Slave Songs of the United States*, pp. xi, 19–20.

73. Ibid., p. xx.

74. Eppes, *Negro of the Old South*, p. 9.

75. Allen, Ware, and Garrison, *Slave Songs*, pp. xi, 112–17.

76. Remembrances of these slaves are taken from the typescript "Slave Narratives," WPA Writers' Project Florida, Jacksonville University Library.

77. Eppes, *Negro of the Old South*, p. 39.

78. Charles L. Edwards, *Bahama Songs and Stories*, p. 25.

79. Elsie Clews Parsons, *Folk Tales of Andros Islands, Bahamas*, p. 460.

80. Watts, *Hymns and Spiritual Songs*, vol. 2, no. 63. This hymn was sung by Maria Threet, a former slave in Coconut Grove, for Cara Mae Taylor, April 27, 1936, WPA Folk Lore Project, Florida Historical Society Papers, University of South Florida.

81. Jennie Jenkins, Miami, for Cora Mae Taylor, April 27, 1936, WPA Folk Lore Project.

82. Ibid., February 10, 1936.

83. Annie M. Coleman, Miami, for Cora Mae Taylor, March 10, 1936, WPA Folk Lore Project.

84. Hannah Wheeler, Miami, for Cora Mae Taylor, March 10, 1936, WPA Folk Lore Project.

85. Marie Collins, Miami, for Cora Mae Taylor, April 6, 1936, WPA Folk Lore Project.

86. Long, *Florida Breezes*, p. 181.

87. Corse Papers.

88. Percy Dearmer, R. Vaughan Williams, and Martin Shaw, *Oxford Book of Carols*, pp. 187–88.

89. Eppes, *Negro of the Old South*, p. 65.

90. Grace Fox, "Ring Plays and Other Games of the Florida Negro," pp. 45–48.

91. Ibid., pp. 49–53.

92. Ibid., pp. 91–98.

93. Ibid., pp. 74–76.

94. Alice B. Gomme, *The Traditional Games of England, Scotland, and Ireland,* 2:234.

95. Fox, "Ring Plays," p. 184.

96. Ibid., p. 60.

97. Thomas Brown, "Memoirs," p. 28, Florida State University Archives.

98. Clinton, *Winter from Home,* p. 29.

99. C. Edwards, *Bahama Songs,* p. 107.

100. *Floridian,* April 8, 1848.

101. *Floridian and Journal,* December 22, 1855.

102. Cecil Lloyd Patterson, "A Different Drum: The Image of the Negro in the Nineteenth Century Popular Song Books," p. 45.

103. Ned Christy, *Christy's Panorama Songster,* pp. 80–81.

104. Ibid., pp. 86–88.

105. *Uncle Ned Songster.*

106. This song is attributed to Joel Walker Sweeney and was published by Henry Prentiss in Boston, in 1840. It was reprinted in Nathan, *Dan Emmett,* pp. 464–66.

107. Popular song of the day quoted in Eppes, *Negro of the Old South,* p. 143.

108. Ibid., p. 129.

109. Henry M. Field, *Bright Skies and Dark Shadows,* pp. 92–93.

110. Frank Hatheway "Scrapbook, 1845–1853," clipping from unidentified source, Florida State University Library.

CHAPTER 11: *Fire, Maringo, Fire Away*

1. *St. Augustine Gazette,* November 24, 1821.

2. *Florida Advocate* (Tallahassee), November 25, 1829.

3. *St. Joseph Times,* January 29, 1840.

4. Francis James Child, *The English and Scottish Popular Ballads.* The five volumes were published between 1882 and 1898.

5. Bertrand Harris Bronson, *The Traditional Tunes of the Child Ballads.*

6. Alton C. Morris, *Folksongs of Florida,* p. 14.

7. Cecil J. Sharp and Maud Karpeles, *English Folk Songs from the Southern Appalachian Mountains.*

8. Alton C. Morris, *Folksongs of Florida,* p. 278.

9. Ibid., p. 321.

10. Ibid., p. 285.

11. Ibid., p. 19.

12. Ibid., pp. 20–22.

13. Elizabeth A. Sharp, "Charles Dibdin," in *Songs and Poems of the Sea,* pp. 76–79.

14. Stan Hugill, comp., *Shanties from the Seven Seas*, pp. 26–27.

15. Charles Nordhoff, *Nine Years a Sailor*, p. 32.

16. Stan Hugill, comp., *Shanties and Sailors' Songs*, p. 51.

17. Philip Henry Gosse, *Letters from Alabama*, pp. 305–6.

18. Hugill, *Shanties and Sailors' Songs*, pp. 52–53.

19. William M. Doerflinger, *Songs of the Sailor and Lumbermen*, pp. 80–81.

20. Hugill, *Seven Seas*, pp. 68–69.

21. Alton C. Morris, *Folksongs of Florida*, pp. 51–66.

22. Amelia Cabot Collection, Monroe County Public Library, Key West.

23. E. A. Hammond, ed., "Wreckers and Wrecking on the Florida Reef, 1829–1832," *Florida Historical Quarterly* 41, no. 3 (January 1963): 239–73.

24. A slightly different version of this song is given in "William Adee Whitehead's Reminiscences of Key West," ed. Thelma Peters, *Tequesta* 25 (1965): 41–42. Still another version is in Love Dean, "The Wreckers: Fiction, Fact, and Legend," *Florida Keys* 4, no. 4 (Fourth Quarter 1981): 32–39. A manuscript version is in the Monroe County Public Library, Key West.

25. Kenneth Scott, "The City of Wreckers," *Florida Historical Quarterly* 25, no. 2 (October 1946): 193–96.

26. J. A. Wilson, *Adventures of Alf. Wilson*, p. 210.

27. W. T. Cash, "Taylor County History," *Florida Historical Quarterly* 27, no. 1 (July 1948): 41.

28. W. T. Cash, ed., *Florida Becomes a State*, p. 15.

29. According to Francis Arlie Rhodes, a Tallahassee historian, this song was sung at Woodville cane grindings well into the twentieth century. A variant was recorded in MacClenny in 1934 by Alton C. Morris.

30. Stetson Kennedy, *Palmetto Country*, pp. 62–63.

31. Alton C. Morris, *Folksongs of Florida*, p. 142.

32. Burl Ives, *The Burl Ives Song Book*, pp. 60–61.

33. Alton C. Morris, *Folksongs of Florida*, pp. 160–61; and Sharp and Karpeles, 2:174.

34. Alton C. Morris, *Folksongs of Florida*, pp. 128–30.

35. Jim Bob Tinsley, *He Was Singin' This Song*, p. 156.

36. John A. Lomax and Alan Lomax, *Folk Song: U.S.A.*, p. 199.

37. John A. Lomax and Alan Lomax, *Cowboy Songs and Other Frontier Ballads*, pp. 164–65. (A few verses are omitted.)

38. Alton C. Morris, *Folksongs of Florida*, p. 46.

39. Lomax and Lomax, *Cowboy Songs*, pp. 48–49.

40. Alton C. Morris, *Folksongs of Florida*, p. 41. (Two verses are omitted.)

CHAPTER 12: *To Live Unchained or Bravely Die*

1. Constitution, Southern Rights Association, Centerville District, Leon County, in *Tallahassee Floridian*, July 19, 1851.

2. Program, "Celebration of the Fourth of July, 1851," at Madison courthouse, *Florida Sentinel,* 1851, Florida State Library.

3. *Tallahassee Floridian and Journal,* July 7, 1855.

4. Political Handbill, Edward Hopkins vs. John Milton, October 1860, State Library of Florida.

5. Jubal A. Early, *A Memoir of the Last Year of the War for Independence in the Confederate States of America,* pp. iii–iv.

6. Edward Young McMorries, *History of the First Regiment, Alabama Volunteer Infantry, C.S.A.,* pp. 21–22.

7. DeLeon, *Four Years in Rebel Capitals,* p. 69.

8. Ibid., pp. 2, 69–70, 82.

9. William Watson Davis, "The Civil War and Reconstruction in Florida," p. 93.

10. Long, *Florida Breezes,* pp. 324–25.

11. Samuel Proctor, ed., *Florida a Hundred Years Ago,* n.p.

12. W. M. Ives, Jr., "Journal," March 18, 1860.

13. Ibid., April 20, May 9–10, 1860.

14. Fred L. Robertson, comp., *Soldiers of Florida in the Seminole Indian, Civil, and Spanish-American Wars,* p. 38.

15. *The War of the Rebellion: A Compilation of the Official Records of the Union and Confederate Armies in the War of the Rebellion* (Washington, D.C., 1880–1901), 1; 6:286–87, quoted in W. Davis, "Civil War and Reconstruction," pp. 161–62.

16. Knox Mellon, Jr., ed., "A Florida Soldier in the Army of Northern Virginia: The Hosford Letters," *Florida Historical Quarterly* 46, no. 3 (January 1968): 249–50.

17. W. M. Ives, Jr., to his mother, September 6, 1863, Florida State Library Archives.

18. Joshua Hoyet Frier II, "Reminiscences of the War between the States," manuscript of a boy in the Florida Home Guard, p. 105, Florida State Archives.

19. DeLeon, *Four Years in Rebel Capitals,* p. 303.

20. Robert Watson, "His Confederate War Diary, 1861–65," p. 27.

21. George H. Dorman, *Fifty Years Ago,* p. 12.

22. DeLeon, *Four Years in Rebel Capitals,* p. 299.

23. Fitzgerald Ross, *Cities and Camps of the Confederate States,* ed. Richard B. Hartnell, p. 40.

24. Arthur Fremantle, *Three Months in the Southern States: April–June 1863,* pp. 74–75.

25. Ibid., p. 266. It has not been determined whether this was a Florida band, though Florida units were present at this battle.

26. W. M. Ives, Jr., to his father, August 10, 1862, from Chattanooga, Tennessee.

27. Ibid.

28. Ives to his father, August 16, 24, 1862, from Chattanooga, Tennessee.

29. Ives to his sisters, October 20, 1862, from Murfreesboro, Tennessee.

30. Ives to his sisters, August 11, 1863, from Camp Hurricane, Mississippi.

31. Ives to his mother, September 6, 1863, from a camp near Chattanooga, Tennessee.

32. Ives to his sister Katie, September 29, 1863, from Chattanooga, Tennessee, and to his mother on October 11, 1863.

33. Ives to his mother, October 31, 1863, from near Chickamauga.

34. Ives to his father, December 31, 1863, from Dalton, Georgia.

35. Ives to his sister Fannie, January 16, 1864, from Dalton, Georgia.

36. Ives to his father, July 17, 1864, from near Atlanta.

37. Ives to his mother, November 12, 1863, from Chickamauga, and to his sister Kate, November 8, 1864, from Chickamauga.

38. "Oh, I'm a Good Old Rebel" (words by Innes Randolph, music to the tune of "Joe Bowers," by R. Bishop Buckley), in Irwin Silber, *Songs of the Civil War,* pp. 356–57.

39. *The Amateur's Song Book,* pp. 102–3.

40. William B. Smith, *On Wheels and How I Came There,* p. 18.

41. D. H. L. Gleason, *A History of the First Regiment of Massachusetts Cavalry Volunteers,* p. 461.

42. Alfred S. Roe, *The Twenty-fourth Regiment, Massachusetts Volunteers, 1861–1866,* p. 146.

43. Willard A. Heaps and Porter W. Heaps, *The Singing Sixties,* pp. 80–81.

44. Gouverneur Morris, *The History of a Volunteer Regiment (Sixth New York Infantry),* p. 78.

45. *Recollections of a Checkered Life.*

46. Ibid., p. 62.

47. *Rebellion Record,* 4 (1860–62): 49.

48. Roe, *Twenty-fourth Regiment,* pp. 240, 248–249.

49. Herbert W. Beecher, *History of the First Light Battery, Connecticut Volunteers, 1861–1865,* p. 323.

50. Eugene Chapin, *By-Gone Days,* pp. 83–84.

51. Justus M. Silliman, *A New Canaan Private in the Civil War,* p. 85.

52. Henry F. Little, *The Seventh New Hampshire Volunteers,* p. 98, cited in Terence H. Nolan, *History of Fort Clinch,* p. 42.

53. Beecher, *History of First Light Battery,* p. 323.

54. Isaiah Price, *History of the Ninety-seventh Regiment, Pennsylvania Volunteer Infantry,* p. 216.

55. Nolan, *History of Fort Clinch,* p. 40.

56. *New York Times,* January 23, 1864; *New York Tribune,* January 23, 1864.

57. Roe, *Twenty-fourth Regiment,* pp. 251–52.

58. Silliman, *New Canaan Private,* p. 79.

59. Ibid., pp. 84, 90.

60. Charles Colcock Jones, *Historical Sketch of the Chatham Artillery,* p. 175.

61. Ibid., pp. 45–46.

62. Little, *Seventh New Hampshire Volunteers,* p. 28.

63. John R. Morse, "The Cadet Band," in Albert W. Mann, *History of the Forty-fifth Regiment, Massachusetts Volunteer Militia,* p. 188.

64. Ibid., p. 187.

65. James H. Clark, *The Iron Hearted Regiment*, p. 123.

66. Stanton P. Allen, *Down in Dixie*, p. 71.

67. Thomas Wentworth Higginson, ed., "Letters of Major Seth Rogers, M.D.," *Massachusetts Historical Society* 43 (February 1910): 342, 345.

68. Ibid., p. 342.

69. Ibid., p. 394.

70. Charles M. Duren, "Letters from Charles M. Duren," *Florida Historical Quarterly* 32, no. 4 (April 1954): 262–87.

71. Thomas Wentworth Higginson, *Army Life in a Black Regiment*, pp. 197–98, 222.

72. William W. H. Davis, *History of the 104th Pennsylvania Regiment*, p. 211.

73. Beecher, *History of First Light Battery*, p. 187.

74. Higginson, *Army Life*, p. 236.

75. *New York Times*, May 10, 1891.

76. W. Davis, *History of the 104th*, p. 417.

77. Alfred A. Miller to George A. Fairbanks, March 23, 1861, from St. Augustine.

78. "Songs of the Rebels," *Rebellion Record* 4 (1860–62): 51.

79. See H. DeMarsan, publisher, "Bonnie Blue Flag," in Library Company of Philadelphia Collection.

80. Paul Glass and Louis C. Singer, *Singing Soldiers*, p. 69.

81. *Florida Sentinel*, June 17, 1862.

82. *Florida Union*, July 4, 1863.

83. *St. Augustine Examiner*, May 18, 1861, p. 1.

84. *New York Herald*, January 11, 1862.

85. Richard B. Harwell, *Confederate Music*, pp. 48–49.

86. John Hill Hewitt, "Five Years under the Confederate Flag," John Hill Hewitt Collection, Emory University, quoted in Harwell, *Confederate Music*, p. 46, and in part in Coy E. Huggins, "John Hill Hewitt: Bard of the Confederacy," p. 77.

87. Eppes. *Through Some Eventful Years'*, p. 233.

88. These publishers were located in Georgia (Augusta, Macon, and Savannah), South Carolina (Charleston and Columbia), Virginia (Danville and Richmond), Tennessee (Nashville and Memphis), Alabama (Mobile), Louisiana (New Orleans), and North Carolina (Wilmington). See Frank W. Hoogerwerf, *Confederate Sheet Music Imprints*, p. xvii.

89. Horace Waters, comp., *Patriotic Song Book, 1862*.

90. George F. Root, ed., *The Bugle Call*.

91. J. H. Randolph to G. R. Fairbanks, July 4, 1861, Fairbanks Collection, Florida State University Archives.

92. L. R. Studenmayer to G. R. Fairbanks, August 16, 1862, from Camden, New Jersey.

93. J. H. Randolph to G. R. Fairbanks, October 17, 1861, from Tallahassee.

94. Andrew Fairbanks to G. R. Fairbanks, February 4, 1862, from Jacksonville.

95. J. M. Doty to G. R. Fairbanks, March 8, 1863, from Lake City.

96. L. R. Studenmayer to G. F. Fairbanks, n.d., Fairbanks Collection, Item 37.

97. Mrs. Joseph Lee Smith, "Journal," May 11, 1863, pp. 6–8.

98. Ibid., May 16, 1863, pp. 8–9.

99. Ibid.

100. P. J. Staudenraus, ed., "A War Correspondent's View of St. Augustine and Fernandina, 1863," *Florida Historical Quarterly* 41, no. 1, (July 1962): 60–62.

101. *Sacramento Daily Union*, July 21, 1863.

102. Irvin Silber, *Songs of the Civil War*, p. 54.

103. Alton C. Morris, *Folksongs of Florida*, pp. 31–32.

104. "The Homespun Dress" was here titled "The Southern Girl's Song." The collection also included "The Brightest Eyes," "Annie Laurie," "Bonnie Eloise," "Ever of Thee I'm Fondly Dreaming," "Bonnie Jean," "There's a Good Time Coming," "The Mocking Bird," "The Last Rose of Summer," "Root Hog or Die," "Oft in the Stilly Night," "Happy Land of Canaan," "A Life on the Ocean Wave," "Then You'll Remember Me," "O Boys, Carry Me Long," "When This Cruel War Is Over," "All Quiet on the Potomac," "The Southern Cross" (tune: "Star Spangled Banner"), "Annie of the Vale," "Pop Goes the Weasel," "Old Dog Tray," and "My Old Kentucky Home."

105. Alton C. Morris, *Folksongs of Florida*, pp. 28–29.

106. Rabun Scarborough, *The Civil War Letters of Rabun Scarborough, Apalachicola, Florida, 1861–1862*, ed. E. F. Smith, p. 2.

107. Mrs. A. A. Miller to George R. Fairbanks, February 4, 1861.

108. Joe M. Richardson, "We Are Truly Doing Missionary Work: Letters from American Missionary Association Teachers in Florida, 1864–1874," *Florida Historical Quarterly* 54, no. 2 (October 1975): 179.

109. "Songs of Zion," *Rebellion Record* 11 (1863): 61–62.

110. B. H. Groene, "A Letter from Occupied Tallahassee," *Florida Historical Quarterly* 28, no. 1 (July 1969): 72.

111. Eppes, *Through Some Eventful Years*, p. 240; *Florida Sentinel*, January 21, 1862, May 26, 1863; *Gainesville Cotton States*, May 7, 1864; *Quincy Semi-Weekly Dispatch*, March 15, 1865.

112. Eppes, *Through Some Eventful Years*, pp. 237–38.

113. Ibid., pp. 262, 266.

114. "Sentiment of the People," G. R. Fairbanks papers, manuscript with unidentified author, p. 41.

115. George R. Bentley, *A History of the Freedmen's Bureau*, p. 112.

116. Abby Hutchinson Patton, *Camp Meeting Songs of the Florida Freedman*.

APPENDIXES

1. *Floridan and Advocate* (Tallahassee), September 9, 1830.

2. Ibid., November 16, 1830.

3. *Florida Laws, 1935: General Acts and Resolutions Adopted by the Legislature of Florida at Its Twenty-fifth Regular Session, April 2 to and Including May 31, 1935.* Under the Constitution of A.D. 1885, published by Authority of Law (Tallahassee: Rose Printing, 1935), vol. 1, house concurrent resolution no. 22, p. 1540.

4. *General Laws Passed by the Legislature of Florida at Its Fortieth Session under the Constitution of A.D. 1885* (Tallahassee: T. J. Appleyard, State Printer, 1913), pp. 517–18.

✳ ✳ ✳ ✳ ✳ ✳ ✳ ✳

Bibliography

Note: The State Library of Florida, the Florida State Archives, and the Florida State University (including its Archives, Library, and Music Library) are all located in Tallahassee.

Adkins, Hector Ernest. *A Treatise on the Miltary Band*. London: Boosey, Hawkes and Belwin, 1945.

Aenon Baptist Church. "Records, 1842–1864." Florida State University Archives.

Alden, W. L. "Sailor's Songs." *Harper's New Monthly Magazine*, July 1882, pp. 281–86.

Allen, W. F. "Negro Dialect." *Nation* 1 (December 1865): 744–45.

Allen, William Francis, Charles Pickard Ware, and Lucy McKim Garrison, eds. *Slave Songs of the United States*. New York: A. Simpson, 1867. Reprint. New York: Oak Publications, 1965; Freeport, N.Y.: Books for Libraries Press, 1971.

An Amateur. See *The Amateur's Song Book*.

The Amateur's Song Book. By an Amateur. Boston: Elias Howe, Jr., 1843.

The American Musical Directory, 1861. New York: T. Hutchinson, 1861. Reprint, Introduction by Barbara Owen. New York: Da Capo Press, 1980.

The American Naval and Patriotic Songster. Baltimore, 1836.

An American Officer. See *The Rough and Ready Songster*.

American Sheet Music to 1830. Midland Park, N.J.: Archival Micrographics for Brookhaven Press, Washington, D.C., n.d. [c. 1975].

The American Songster, containing a choice selection of about 150 modern popular songs. New York: Nafis and Cornish, n.d. Stereotype ed. [c. mid-1840s].

Angles, Higini. *La música en la corte de Carlos V; con la transcripción del "Libro de cifra nueva para tecla, harpa, y vihuela," de Luys Venegas de Henestrosa*. Barcelona: Institute Español de Musicología, 1965.

———. *La música en la corte de los reyes católicos*. Madrid: Institute Dieg Belazquez, 1941.

Appleyard, John. *The First Presbyterian Church, Pensacola, Florida: Its Story . . . 1845–1976*. Pensacola: Mayes Printing, 1977.

Appleyard, Lula D. "Plantation Life in Middle Florida, 1821–1845." M.A. thesis, Florida State College for Women, 1940.

Arana, Luís Rafael. "The Exploration of Florida and Sources on the Founding of St. Augustine." *Florida Historical Quarterly* 44, no. 1 (August 1965): 1–16.

———. "The Sixtieth Foot in British North America." Typescript. St. Augustine Historical Society Library.

Armstrong, Henry Clay. *History of Escambia County, Florida.* St. Augustine: Record, 1930.

Arnade, Charles W. "The Failure of Spanish Florida." *Americas* 16, no. 3 (January 1960): 271.

———. *Florida on Trial, 1593–1602.* Coral Gables: University of Miami Press, 1959.

———. *The Siege of St. Augustine in 1702.* Gainesville: University of Florida Press, 1959.

Arnold, Sanford. "Music in Florida Schools." Typescript, 1962. State Library of Florida.

Attaingnant, Pierre. *Danseries a quatre parties.* Edited by Raymond Meylan. Paris: Heugel, 1969.

———. *Quart et cinquième livre de danceries, 1550.* Edited by Helmut Monkmeyer. Celle: Hermann Moeck, 1966.

———. *Second livre de danceries, 1547.* Edited by Helmut Monkmeyer. Celle: Hermann Moeck, 1966.

Baird, C. W. *History of the Huguenot Emigration to America.* Vol. 1. New York: Dodd, Mead, 1885.

Baker, George E. "St. Augustine and the Union Blockade." *El Escribano,* no. 23 (1986): 1–18.

Baker, Theodore. *Über die Musik der nordamerikanischen Wilden.* Leipzig: Breitkopf and Hartel, 1882.

Ballentine, George. *Autobiography of an English Soldier in the United States Army.* New York: Stringer and Townsend, 1853.

Banks, John. *A Short Biographical Sketch of the Undersigned, by Himself.* Austell, Ga.: Privately printed, 1936.

Baradoy Font, Francisco. *Museo militar—Historia del ejército español.* 3 vols. Barcelona: M. Soler, 1833–87.

Barbier, Pierre, and France Vernillat. *Histoire de France par les chansons.* Paris: Gallimard, 1958.

Barbour, George M. *Florida for Tourists, Invalids, and Settlers.* New York: D. Appleton. 1881. Reprint. Gainesville: University of Florida Press, 1964.

Barcia Carballido y Zúñiga, Andrés González de. *Chronological History of the Continent of Florida, 1512–1722.* Translated by Anthony Kerrigan. Gainesville: University of Florida Press, 1951.

Barco, Joseph. "Civil War Letters." Manuscript. Florida State University Archives, Tallahassee.

Barrientos, Bartolomé. *Pedro Menéndez de Avilés, Founder of Florida.* Translated by Anthony Kerrigan. Gainesville, University of Florida Press, 1965.

Completed in 1567, as *Vida y hechos de Pedro Menéndez de Avilés.* First published in 1902 in G. Garcías, *Dos antiguas relaciones de la Florida.*

Barrs, Burton. *East Florida in the American Revolution.* Jacksonville: Guild Press, 1932.

Bartram, John. *Diary of a Journey through the Carolinas, Georgia, and Florida from July 1, 1765, to April 10, 1766.* Annotated by Francis Harper. Philadelphia: American Philosophical Society, 1942.

———. *John and William Bartram's America: Selections from the Writings of the Philadelphia Naturalists.* Edited by Helen Gere Cruickshank. New York: Devin-Adair, 1957.

Bartram, William. *Bartram's Travels.* Edited by Francis Harper. New Haven: Yale University Press, 1958.

———. *Travels through North and South Carolina, Georgia, East and West Florida.* Philadelphia: James and Johnson, 1791; London, 1792. Reprint. Savannah: Beehive Press, 1973.

Bayne-Powell, Rosamond. *Eighteenth Century London Life.* New York: E. P. Dutton, 1938.

Beckford, William. *A Descriptive Account of the Island of Jamaica.* 2 vols. London: T. and J. Egerton, 1790.

Beckley, Alfred. "Memoir of a West Pointer in St. Augustine, 1824–1826." Edited by Cecil D. Eby. *Florida Historical Quarterly* 42, no. 3 (April 1964): 307–20.

Beecher, Herbert W. *History of the First Light Battery, Connecticut Volunteers, 1861–1865.* New York: A. T. De La Mare Printing and Publishing, n.d.

Behague, Gerard. *Music in Latin America.* Englewood Cliffs, N.J.: Prentice-Hall, 1979.

Bemrose, John. *Reminiscences of the Second Seminole War.* Edited by John K. Mahon. Gainesville: University of Florida Press, 1966.

Bennett, Charles E. *Fort Caroline and Its Leader.* Gainesville: University of Florida Press, 1964.

———. "Fort Caroline, Cradle of American Freedom." *Florida Historical Quarterly* 35, no. 1 (July 1956): 3–16.

———. *Laudonnière and Fort Caroline.* Gainesville: University of Florida Press, 1964.

———. *The Settlement of Florida.* Gainesville: University of Florida Press, 1968.

Benson, Louis F. *The English Hymn: Its Development and Use in Worship.* New York: Hodder and Stoughton, George H. Doran, 1915.

Bentley, George R. *A History of the Freedman's Bureau.* Philadelphia: University of Pennsylvania Press, 1955.

Benzoni, Girolamo. *Histoire nouvelle du Nouveau Monde. . . .* Geneva: Apud Eustace Vignon, 1579. Appended with half title "Brief discours et histoire d'un voyage de quelques François en la Florida [by Nicolas Le Challeux, from the account first published in Dieppe, 1566].

Berquin-Duvallon. *Travels in Louisiana and the Floridas, in the Year 1802, Giving a Correct Picture of those Countries*. Translated from the French, with notes, etc. by John Davis. New York: I. Riley, 1806.

Biddle, Margaret Seton Fleming. *Hibernia, the Unreturning Tide*. New York: Vantage Press, 1974.

Bilbo, Jack L., Jr. "Economy and Culture: The Boom-and-Bust Theatres of Pensacola, Florida, 1821–1917." Ph.D. Texas Tech University, 1982.

Bishop, Morris. *The Odyssey of Cabeza de Vaca*. New York: Century, 1933.

Black, Capt. Hugh. "Civil War Letters." Manuscript. Florida State University Archives.

Blassingame, Wyatt. *Seminoles of Florida*. Tallahassee: Peninsular, 1963.

Boalch, D. *Makers of the Harpsichord and Clavichord, 1440–1840*. 2d ed. Oxford: Clarendon Press, 1974.

Boggess, Francis Calvin Morgan. *A Veteran of Four Wars*. Arcadia, Fla.: Champion Job Rooms, 1900.

Boggs, William R. *Military Reminiscences of General W. R. Boggs, C.S.A.* Durham, N.C.: Seeman Printery, 1913.

Booth, Norman E. *A History of Old Pisgah, 1830–1976*. Tallahassee: Pisgah United Methodist Church, 1976.

———. "Tallahassee Trinity's Ante-Bellum Times, 1824–1861." M.A. thesis, Florida State University, 1971.

Boyd, Mark F. "Enumeration of Florida Spanish Missions in 1675." *Florida Historical Quarterly* 27, no. 2 (October 1948): 181–88.

———. *Florida Aflame*. Tallahassee: Florida Board of Parks and Historical Memorials, 1951.

———. "From a Remote Frontier, San Marcos de Apalache, 1763–1769." *Florida Historical Quarterly* 19, no. 3 (January 1941): 179–245; 20, no. 1 (July 1941): 82–92; no. 2 (October 1941): 203–9; no. 3 (January 1942): 293–310; no. 4 (April 1942): 382–97.

———, trans. "Diego Pena's Expedition to Apalachee and Apalachicola in 1716." *Florida Historical Quarterly* 28, no. 1 (July 1949): 1–27.

Boyd, Mark F., Hale Smith, and John W. Griffin. *Here They Once Stood: The Tragic End of the Apalachee Missions*. Gainesville: University of Florida Press, 1951.

Branch, Susan. [Two bound collections of music.] Florida State University Archives.

Bremer, Fredrika. *The Homes of the New World*. Vol. 2. New York: Harper and Brothers, 1853.

Brewster, C. Ray. *The Cluster of Jessie Mercer*. Macon, Ga.: Renaissance Press, 1983.

Brewster, Lawrence F. "The Later History of British West Florida, 1771–1781." M.A. thesis, Columbia University, 1932.

Brinton, Daniel G. *Notes on the Floridan Peninsula: Its Literary History, Indian Tribes, and Antiquities*. Philadelphia: Joseph Sabin, 1859. Reprint. Boulder, Colo.: Paladin Press, 1969.

Bronson, Bertrand Harris. *The Traditional Tunes of the Child Ballads*. Vols. 1–2. Princeton: Princeton University Press, 1962.

Brooks, Abbie M. [Silvia Sunshine]. *Petals Plucked from Sunny Climes*. Nashville: Southern Methodist Publishing House, 1880.

Brown, David. *The Planter; or, Thirteen Years in the South, by a northern man*. Philadelphia: H. Hooker, 1853.

Brown, Elizabeth. "Memoirs." Centennial File. Florida State University Archives.

Brown, Gladys, ed. *Third World Group*. Bahamas Independence Issue. Nassau: Nassau Printing and Litho, 1973.

Brown, Thomas. "Memoirs." Typescript. Florida State University Archives.

Browne, Jefferson B. *Key West, the Old and the New*. St. Augustine: Record, 1912.

Browne, Patrick W. "Salamanca and the Beginnings of the Church in Florida." *Ecclesiastical Review* 84 (1931).

Bryant, James C. "Indian Springs: The Story of a Pioneer Church in Leon County, Florida." 1971. Florida State University Archives.

Bryant, William Cullen. *Letters of a Traveller*. New York: George P. Putnam, 1850.

———. *Prose Writings of William Cullen Bryant*. 1884. Reprint, edited by Parke Godwin. New York: Russell and Russell, 1964.

Buchanan, James. *Sketches of the History, Manners, and Customs of the North American Indians, with a plan for their Melioration*. New York: Wm. Borradaile, 1824.

Bullen, Adelaide K. *Florida Indians of Past and Present*. Gainesville: Kendall Books, 1974.

Burke, Edmund. *An Account of the European Settlements in America*. 2 vols. London: R. and J. Dodsley, 1757.

Burney, Charles. *A General History of Music*. 2 vols. New York: Dover Publications, 1957.

Burns, Robert. *The Songs of Robert Burns (now printed with the melodies for which they were written)*. Notes by James C. Dick. London: Henry Frowde, 1903.

Burns, Thomas J. "The Catholic Church in West Florida, 1783–1850." M.A. thesis, Florida State University, 1962.

Bushnell, Amy. *The King's Coffer: Proprietors of the Spanish Florida Treasury, 1565–1702*. Gainesville: University Presses of Florida, 1981.

———. "Privilege and Obligation: The Officials of the Florida 'Caja Real,' 1565 to 1702." Ph.D. diss., University of Florida, 1979.

Bushnell, David Ives. *Drawings by Jacques Lemoyne de Morques of Saturioria, a Timorcan Chief in Florida, 1564*. (Smithsonian Misc. Coll. 81:4. Washington, D.C.: Smithsonian Institution, 1928.

Buswell, James O. III. "Florida Seminole Religious Ritual: Resistance and Change." Ph.D. diss., St. Louis University, 1972.

Butler, Lewis William. *The Annals of the King's Royal Rifle Corps*. 5 vols. London: Smith, Elder, 1913–32.

Cabeza de Vaca. *See* Núñez.

Calderón, Gabriel Diaz Vara. *A Seventeenth-Century Letter of Gabriel Diaz Vara Calderón, Bishop of Cuba, Describing the Indians and Indian Missions of Florida*. Transcribed and translated by Lucy L. Wenhold; introduction by John R. Swanton. Washington, D.C.: Smithsonian Institution, 1936.

Cameron, Evelyn. "Sheet Music Collection, 1837–1868." Florida State University Music Library.

Camin, Alfonso. *El Adelantado de la Florida, Pedro Menéndez de Avilés*. Mexico: Reviste Norte, 1944.

Campbell, James T. "The Charles Hutchinson Letters from Territorial Tallahassee." *Apalachee* 4 (1956): 13.

Campbell, Richard L. *Historical Sketches of Colonial Florida*. 1892. Reprint. Gainesville: University Presses of Florida, 1975.

Camps y Mercadal, D. Francisco. *Folk-Lore menorquín de la Pagesía*. Mahón: M. Sintes Rofger, 1918.

Camus, Raoul F. *Military Music of the American Revolution*. Chapel Hill: University of North Carolina Press, 1976.

Cannon, Richard. *Historical Record of the Ninth, or the East Norfolk Regiment of Foot*. London: Furnivall and Parker, 1848.

Canova, Andrew P. *Life and Adventures in South Florida*. Palatka, Fla.: Southern Sun, 1885.

Capron, Louis. *The Medicine Bundles of the Florida Seminole and the Green Corn Dance*. Washington, D.C.: Government Printing Office, 1953.

———. *Seminole History*. Fort Lauderdale: Fort Lauderdale Historical Society, n.d.

———. "The Spanish Dance." *Florida Historical Quarterly* 38, no. 2 (October 1959): 91–95.

Carlevoix, Pierre François Xavier de. *Journal of a voyage to North America*. London: R. and J. Dodsley, 1761. Translated from *Histoire et description général de la Nouvelle France*. Paris: Chez la veuve Ganeau, 1744.

Carter, Clarence E., ed. *The Territorial Papers of the United States*. 25 vols. Washington, D.C.: Government Printing Office, 1934–60.

Carter, W. H. "History of St. John's Church, Tallahassee." Typescript. State Library of Florida.

Caruso, John Anthony. *The Spanish Frontier*. Indianapolis: Bobbs-Merrill, 1963.

Casas, Bartholomé de las. *The Spanish Colonies; or, Brief Chronicle of the acts and gestes of the Spaniardes in the West Indies, called the New World, for the space of eleven yeeres*. Translated by M. M. G. London: William Brome, 1583.

Cash, W. T. "History of Trinity Methodist Church." *Apalachee* 2 (1946): 46–58.

———, ed. *Florida Becomes a State*. Tallahassee: Florida Centennial Commission, 1943.

Cash, William Thomas. *The Story of Florida*. 4 vols. New York: American Historical Society, 1938.

————. "Taylor County History." *Florida Historical Quarterly* 27, no. 1 (July 1948): 28–58.

Castelnau, Comte Francis de. "Essai sur la Floride du milieu." Translated by Arthur R. Seymour. *Florida Historical Quarterly* 26, no. 4 (April 1948): 300–324.

————. "Mémoire sur la Floride du milieu." *Comptes-Rendus* 14 (April 1842): 518.

————. "Note sur deux itinéraires de Charleston à Tallahassee (Floride), par le comte Francis de Castelnau." *Bulletin, Société de Geographie de Paris* 18, no. 2 (October 1842): 241–59.

————. *Vues et souvenirs de l'Amérique du Nord.* Paris: A. Bertrand, 1842.

Catlin, George. *Letters and Notes on the Manners, Customs, and Conditions of the North American Indians.* New York: Wiley and Putnam, 1841.

Chamberlin, Donald L. "Fort Brookes, a History." M.A. thesis, Florida State University, 1968.

Chapin, Eugene. *By-Gone Days.* Boston: By the author, 1898.

Chase, Gilbert. *America's Music.* Urbana: University of Illinois Press, 1987.

Child, Francis James. *The English and Scottish Popular Ballads.* 5 vols. Boston and New York: Houghton, Mifflin, 1882–98.

Child, Lydia Maria. *Letters from New York.* New York: C. S. Francis, 1852.

Christenson, R. P. *The Old Time Fiddler's Repertory.* Columbia: University of Missouri Press, 1973.

Christ-Janer, Albert, Charles W. Hughes, and Carlton Sprague Smith, eds. *American Hymns Old and New.* 2 vols. New York: Columbia University Press, 1980.

Christy, Ned. *Christy's Panorama Songster.* New York: William H. Murphy [c. 1850].

Clark, James H. *The Iron Hearted Regiment.* Albany; N.Y.: J. Munsell, 1865.

Clay Minstrel; or, National Songster. New York: Greely and McElrath and Thomas Copperwaite, 1844.

Clinton, Charles A. *A Winter from Home.* New York: John F. Trow, 1852.

Clio and Euterpe; or, British Harmony, a collection of celebrated songs and cantatas by the most approved masters. 3 vols. London: Henry Roberts, 1762.

Clubbs, Occie. "Pensacola in Retrospect, 1870–1890." *Florida Historical Quarterly* 37, nos. 3–4 (January–April 1959): 377–96.

Cobb, Buell E., Jr. *The Sacred Harp.* Athens: University of Georgia Press, 1978.

Coe, Charles H. *Red Patriots.* Cincinnati: Editor Publishing, 1898. Reprint. Gainesville: University Presses of Florida, 1974.

Coffin, T. P. *The British Traditional Ballad in North America.* Philadelphia: American Folklore Society, 1950.

Cohen, Myer M. *Notices of Florida and the Campaigns.* Charleston; S.C.: Burges and Honour, 1836. Reprint. Gainesville: University of Florida Press, 1964.

Colcord, Joanna C. *Songs of American Sailormen.* New York: W. W. Norton, 1938.

A Collection of above 150 Choice Songs and Ballads. London: T. Boreman, 1735.

Comic and Minstrel Songs. Boston: Oliver Ditson, 1890.

Confederacy and the South in Music and Song. Lester S. Levy Collection. Philadelphia: Musical Americana, 1956. Microform.

Connor, Jeannette M. Thurber, ed. and trans. *Colonial Records of Spanish Florida.* 2 vols. De Land: Florida State Historical Society, 1925–30.

Cook, Henry P. "Pensacola Mission." *Methodist Magazine* (New York) 8 (1825): 111–12.

Cooper, W. M., et al. *The B. F. White Sacred Harp.* Troy, Ala: Sacred Harp Book, 1960.

Cornish, Dudley Taylor. *The Sable Arm.* New York: W. W. Norton, 1966.

Corse, Carita Doggett. Papers. WPA Writer's Program. Jacksonville University Library.

Covington, James W. *The British Meet the Seminoles.* Gainesville: University of Florida Press, 1961.

———, ed. *Pirates, Indians, and Spaniards.* St. Petersburg: Great Outdoors Publishing, 1963.

Cox, John Harrington. *Folk Songs of the South.* Cambridge: Harvard University Press, 1925.

Coxe, Daniel. *A Description of the English Province of Carolana, by the Spanish call'd Florida and by the French La Louisiana and also of the great and famous river Meschacebe of Missisipi.* London: B. Cowse, 1741.

Craig, James C. "Steamboat Days on the St. Johns River." *Jacksonville Historical Society Journal* 3 (1954): 138–45.

Crane, Verner W. *The Southern Frontier, 1670–1732.* Durham, N.C.: Duke University Press, 1929. Reprint, Ann Arbor: University of Michigan Press, 1956. New ed., Preface by Peter B. Wood. New York: W. W. Norton, 1981.

Crawford, Richard, *Andrew Law, American Psalmodist.* Evanston, Ill.: Northwestern University Press, 1968.

Cromer, George. "Letters: Civil War, 1862." University of Rochester Library.

Crowinshield, Benjamin W. *A History of the First Regiment of Massachusetts Cavalry Volunteers.* Boston: Houghton, Mifflin, 1891.

Cuervo, Justo [O.P.]. *Historiadores del Convento de San Esteban de Salamanca.* 3 vols. Salamanca: Imprementa Católica, 1914.

Curley, Michael J. *Church and State in the Spanish Floridas, 1783–1822.* Washington, D.C.: Catholic University of America Press, 1940.

Cushman, Joseph D., Jr. "The Episcopal Church in Florida, 1821–1865." M.A. thesis, Florida State University, 1958.

———. *A Goodly Heritage: The Episcopal Church in Florida, 1821–1892.* Gainesville: University of Florida Press, 1965.

———. "The Indian River Settlement, 1842–1849." *Florida Historical Quarterly* 43, no. 1 (July 1964): 21–35.

———. *The Sound of Bells: The Episcopal Church in South Florida, 1892–1969.* Gainesville: University Presses of Florida, 1976.

Damon, S. Foster. "The History of Square Dancing." *Proceedings of the American Antiquarian Society* 62, no. 1 (April–October 1952): 63–98.

Darby, William. *Memoir on the Geography and Natural and Civil History of Florida.* Philadelphia: T. H. Palmer, 1821.

Davies, A. Mervyn, *Presbyterian Heritage.* Richmond, Va.: John Knox Press, 1965.

Davis, Jess G. *History of Alachua County.* Alachua; Fla.: Alachua Historical Commission, 1960.

Davis, Mary Lamar. "Tallahassee through Territorial Days." *Apalachee* 1 (1944): 47–61.

Davis, Thomas Frederick. *History of Jacksonville, Florida, and Vicinity, 1513–1824.* Jacksonville: Florida Historical Society, 1925. Reprint. Gainesville: University of Florida Press, 1964.

———. "Pioneer Florida: The Wild Tallahassee of 1827." *Florida Historical Quarterly* 24, no. 4 (April 1946): 292–94.

Davis, William W. H. *History of the 104th Pennsylvania Regiment.* Philadelphia: Jas. B. Rodgers, 1866.

Davis, William Watson. "The Civil War and Reconstruction in Florida." Ph.D. diss., Columbia University, 1913.

Dawson, Francis W. *Reminiscences of Confederate Service, 1861–1865.* Charleston, S.C., 1882. Reprint. Baton Rouge: Louisiana State University Press, 1980.

Dean, Love. "The Wreckers: Fiction, Fact, and Legend." *Florida Keys* 4, no. 4 (Fourth Quarter 1981): 32–39.

Dearmer, Percy, R. Vaughan Williams, and Martin Shaw. *Oxford Book of Carols.* London: Oxford University Press, 1964.

De Biedma, Luis, ed., and Richard Hakluyt, trans. *The Discovery and Conquest of Terra Florida by Don Fernando de Soto and six hundred Spaniards, his followers, written by a gentleman of Elvas.* New York: B. Franklin, 1966.

de Bry, Theodore. *Discovering the New World.* New York: Harper and Row, 1976. Original ed., *Grands Voyages—Historia Americae,* 1590.

DeLeon, Thomas C. *Four Years in Rebel Capitals.* Mobile: Gossip Printing, 1892.

Densmore, Frances. *Seminole Music.* Smithsonian Institution, U.S. Bureau of American Ethnology, Bulletin 161. Washington, D.C.: Government Printing Office, 1956.

Dewhurst, W. W. *History of St. Augustine, Florida.* New York: G. P. Putnam's Sons, 1881.

Díaz del Castillo, Bernal. *The Bernal Díaz Chronicles.* Translated and edited by Albert Idell. Garden City, N.Y.: Doubleday, 1956.

———. *The True History of the Conquest of Mexico.* Guatemala City, 1572. Reprint, trans. Maurice Keating. London: J. Wright and J. Dean, 1800.

Dibble, Ernest F. *Ante-bellum Pensacola and the Military Presence.* Pensacola: Pensacola News Journal, 1974.

Dibdin, Charles. *A Complete History of the English Stage.* 5 vols. London: By the author, 1800.

Dichter, Harry, and Elliott Shapiro. *Early American Sheet Music: Its Lure and Its Lore*. New York: R. R. Bowker, 1941.

Dickinson, Edward. *Music in the History of the Western Church*. London: Smith, Elder, 1902.

Dickinson, John J. *Military History of Florida*. Atlanta: Confederate Publishing, 1899.

Dickinson, Jonathan. *Jonathan Dickinson's Journal; or, God's Protecting Providence*. Edited by E. W. Andrews and C. M. Andrews. New Haven: Yale University Press, 1945.

Dodd, Dorothy. "Florida in 1845." *Florida Historical Quarterly* 24, no. 1 (July 1945): 3–29.

———. *Florida in the War, 1861–1865*. Tallahassee: Peninsular Publishers, 1959.

———. "Old Tallahassee." *Apalachee* 5 (1957–62): 60–71.

———. "The Schooner Emperor." *Florida Historical Quarterly* 13, no. 3 (January 1935): 117–28.

———. "The Wrecking Business on the Florida Reef, 1822–1860." *Florida Historical Quarterly* 22, no. 4 (April 1944): 173–99.

———, ed., *Florida Becomes a State*. Foreword by W. T. Cash. Tallahassee: Florida Centennial Commission, 1945.

Dodd, William G. "Early Education in Tallahassee and the West Florida Seminary, Now Florida State University." *Florida Historical Quarterly* 27, no. 1 (July 1948): 1–27.

———. "Ring Tournaments in Tallahassee." *Apalachee* 3 (1948–50): 55–70.

———. "Theatrical Entertainment in Early Florida." *Florida Historical Quarterly* 25, no. 2 (October 1946): 121–74.

Doerflinger, William Main, comp. *Shantymen and Shantyboys*. New York: Macmillan, 1951.

———, comp. *Songs of the Sailor and Lumbermen*. New York: Macmillan, 1951.

Doherty, Herbert J., Jr. "Florida in 1856." *Florida Historical Quarterly* 35, no. 1 (July 1956): 60–70.

———. "The Governorship of Andrew Jackson." *Florida Historical Quarterly* 33, no. 1 (July 1954): 3–31.

———. *Richard Keith Call: Southern Unionist*. Gainesville: University of Florida Press, 1961.

Dolph, Edward Arthur. *Sound Off!* New York: Cosmopolitan Book, 1929.

"Domestic Miscellany." *Army and Navy Chronicle* 7 (October 11, 1838): 236.

"Domestic Miscellany" (performance of "The Tragedy of Douglas" aboard the sloop of war *Concord*). *Army and Navy Chronicle* 5 (October 5, 1837): 221.

Donnelly, Ralph W. *History of the Confederate States Marine Corps*. Washington, D.C.: Donnelly, 1976.

Dorman, George H. *Fifty Years Ago, Reminiscences of 1861–1865*. Tallahassee: T. J. Appleyard, 1912.

Douglas, Marjory Stoneman. *Florida, the Long Frontier*. New York: Harper and Row, 1967.

Douglas, Thomas. *Autobiography of Thomas Douglas, Late Judge of the Supreme Court of Florida*. New York: Calkins and Stiles, 1856.

Douglass, Frances Elizabeth Brown. "Memoirs." Autograph photocopy, 1956. Florida State University Archives. Original written 1894–1904.

Dozier, Annie Randolph. "Early Settlers in Tallahassee, 1824–1850." *Tallahassee Historical Society Annual*, 1934, pp. 33–38.

Dummett, Anna Maria. "Remembrances of the Old Plantation . . . The Old Dummett Grove." *Literary Florida* 5 (February 1949): 9–15.

Duncan, Edmondstoune. *The Minstrelsy of England*. Vol. 2. London: Augener, 1909.

Duncan, Ella. *Collection of Sheet Music*. 3 vols. St. Augustine: St. Augustine Society Library.

Duncan, Francis. *History of the Royal Regiment of Artillery*. 2 vols. London: J. Murray, 1872.

Duren, Charles M. "Letters from Charles M. Duren." *Florida Historical Quarterly* 32, no. 4 (April 1954): 262–87.

Early, Jubal A. *A Memoir of the Last Year of the War for Independence in the Confederate States of America*. Toronto: Lovell and Gibson, 1866.

Eby, Cecil D., ed. "Memoir of a West Pointer in St. Augustine, 1824–1826." *Florida Historical Quarterly* 42, no. 4 (April 1964): 307–20.

Edwards, Bryan. *The History, Civil and Commercial, of the British Colonies in the West Indies*. 4 vols. London: J. Stockdale, 1793.

Edwards, Charles L. *Bahama Songs and Stories*. Boston: Houghton, Mifflin, 1895.

Eelking, Max von. *The German Allied Troops in the North American War of Independence, 1776–1783*. Translated by J. G. Rosengarten. Albany: J. Munsell's Sons, 1893.

———. "German Mercenaries in Pensacola during the American Revolution, 1779–81." *Pensacola Historical Society Quarterly* 9, no. 1 (November 1977): 1–36.

Egan, Clifford L. "The United States, France, and West Florida, 1803–1807." *Florida Historical Quarterly* 47, no. 3 (January 1969): 227–52.

Emmerson, George S. *A Social History of Scottish Dances*. Montreal and London: McGill-Queens University Press, 1972.

Eppes, Susan Bradford. "Collection." Florida State University Archives.

———. *The Negro of the Old South*. Chicago: Joseph G. Branch Publishing, 1925.

———. *Through Some Eventful Years*. 1845–46. Reprint. Macon, Ga.: J. W. Burke, 1926.

Epstein, Dena J. "African Music in British and French America." *Musical Quarterly* 59 (January 1973): 61–91.

———. *Sinful Tunes and Spirituals*. Urbana: University of Illinois Press, 1977.

Equilicia, Milicia. *Discurso y regla militar, 1595*. Fols. 12, 20–21, 63.

Escobedo, Alonso Gregorio de. "La Florida." In *Pirates, Indians, and Spaniards*, ed. James W. Covington. St. Petersburg: Great Outdoors Publishing, 1963.

Fairbanks, George R. "The Fairbanks Collection, 1861–1865." Manuscripts. Florida State University Archives.

———. *Florida, Its History and Its Romance, the Oldest Settlement in the United States . . . 1497–1898*. Jacksonville: H. and W. B. Drew, 1898.

———. *The History and Antiquities of St. Augustine, Florida*. New York: Norton, 1858; Jacksonville: H. Drew, 1881. Reprint. Gainesville: University Presses of Florida, 1975.

———. *History of Florida from its discovery by Ponce de Leon in 1512 to the close of the Florida war in 1842*. Philadelphia: Lippincott; Jacksonville: C. Drew, 1871.

———. *The Spaniards in Florida*. Jacksonville: C. Drew, 1868.

Farmer, Henry George. *Handel's Kettledrums and Other Papers on Military Music*. London: Hinrichsen, 1950.

———. *A History of Music in Scotland*. London: Hinrichsen Edition, 1947.

———. *Memoirs of the Royal Artillery Band*. London: Boosey, 1904.

———. *Military Music*. World of Music series. New York: Chanticleer Press, 1950.

———. *The Rise and Development of Military Music*. London: William Reeves, 1912.

Farmer, John. *Scarlet and Blue; or, Songs for Soldiers and Sailors*. London: Cassell, 1896.

Farmer, John S., ed. *Merry Songs and Ballads prior to the Year A.D. 1800*. Vol. 2. London: By the author, 1897.

Farmer, John Stephens. *The Regimental Records of the British Army*. London: G. Richards, 1903.

Field, Henry M. *Bright Skies and Dark Shadows*. New York: C. Scribner's Sons, 1890.

Fiske, Roger. *English Theatre Music in the Eighteenth Century*. London: Oxford University Press, 1973.

Fleming, Francis P. *Memoir of Capt. Seton Fleming of the Second Florida Infantry, C.S.A.* Jacksonville: Times-Union Publishing House, 1884.

The Forget Me Not Songster. New York: Nafis and Cornish, n.d. [c. 1850].

Fox, Grace. "Ring Plays and Other Games of the Florida Negro." D.P.E. diss., Indiana University, 1949.

Francke, Arthur E., Jr. *Fort Mellon, 1837–42, a Microcosm of the Second Seminole War*. Miami: Banyan Books, 1977.

Franco, Alonso. *Historia de la provincia de Santiago de México, orden de predicadores en la Nueva España*. Vol. 2. Mexico City: Museo Nacional, 1900.

Franklin, James. *The Philosophical and Political History of the Thirteen United States of America . . . and of East and West Florida*. London: J. Hinton and W. Adams, 1784.

The Free Masons Songs. Edinburgh: R. Bremner, 1760.

Fremantle, Arthur James Lyon. *Three Months in the Southern States: April–June 1863*. New York: John Bradburn, 1864.

Fretwell, Jacqueline K., ed. "Civil War Times in St. Augustine." *El Escribano,* no. 23 (1986): 1–117.

Frier, Joshua Hoyet, II. "Reminiscences of the War between the States." Manuscript of a boy in the Florida Home Guard. Florida State Archives.

Fuente, Julien, and Francisco Antonio Gussman. *Historia de Guatemala o recordación Florida.* Madrid, 1883.

Fuller, Bernard. *La France qui chante.* London: Wm. Heinemann, 1959.

Fuller, J. F. C. *British Light Infantry in the Eighteenth Century.* London: Hutchinson, 1925.

Gache, Louis-Hippolyte. *A Frenchman, a Chaplain, a Rebel.* Chicago: Loyola University Press, 1981.

Gaffarel, Paul Louis Jacques. *Histoire de la Florida française.* Paris: Firmin-Didot, 1875.

Galvao, Antonio, ed. *The Discoveries of the World from their first original unto the yeere of our Lord 1555.* London: Richard Hakluyt, 1601. Reprint. Cleveland: World Publishing, 1966; New York: Da Capo Press, 1969.

Gálvez, Bernardo de. *Yo Solo.* New Orleans: Polyanthos, 1978.

Gannon, Michael V. *The Cross in the Sand: The Early Catholic Church in Florida, 1513–1870.* Gainesville: University Presses of Florida, 1965.

García, Genaro. *Dos antiguas relaciones de la Florida.* Mexico: J. Aguilar Vera, 1902.

Garcilaso de la Vega, el Inca. *La Florida of the Inca.* 2d ed. Translated by Benita Brunson Lewis and Warren H. Wilkinson. Madrid, 1723. 1st ed., 1605.

———. *The Florida of the Inca.* Translated and edited by John Grier Varner and Jeanette J. Varner. Austin: University of Texas Press, 1951.

Garofalo, Robert, and Mark Elrod. *A Pictorial History of Civil War Era Musical Instruments and Military Bands.* Charleston, W.Va.: Pictorial Histories Publishing, 1985.

Garrick, David. *Miss in Her Teens.* London: J. Tonson and S. Draper, 1748.

Gastoue, A. *Le cantique populaire en France.* Lyon: Janin Freres, 1924.

Geiger, Maynard J. *Biographical Dictionary of the Franciscans in Spanish Florida and Cuba (1528–1841).* Paterson, N.J.: St. Anthony Guild Press, 1940.

———. *The Early Franciscans in Florida and Their Relation to Spain's Colonial Effort.* Paterson, N.J.: St. Anthony Guild Press, 1936.

———. *The Franciscan Conquest of Florida (1573–1618).* Washington, D.C.: Catholic University of America, 1937.

A Gentleman of Elvas. See *Virginia Richly Valued.*

Giddings, Joshua R. *The Exiles of Florida.* Columbus, Ohio: Follett, Foster, 1858. Reprint. Gainesville: University of Florida Press, 1964.

Glass, Paul, and Louis C. Singer. *Singing Soldiers.* New York: Grosset and Dunlop, 1964, 1968. Reprint: New York: Da Capo Press, 1975.

Gleason, D. H. L. *A History of the First Regiment of Massachusetts Calvary Volunteers.* Boston: Houghton, Mifflin, 1891.

Gleig, G. R. *The Subaltern.* Edinburgh: Blackwood, 1828.

Glen, John. *Early Scottish Melodies.* Edinburgh: J. and R. Glen, 1900.

"Glimpses of Life in Florida during the Seminole War." *Knickerbocker* 38 (September 1951): 214.

Gold, Robert L. *Borderland Empires in Transition: The Triple-Nation Transfer of Florida.* Carbondale: Southern Illinois University Press, 1969.

Gomme, Alice Bertha. *The Traditional Games of England, Scotland, and Ireland.* 2 vols. London: David Nutt, 1898.

A Good Templar. See *Recollections of a Checkered Life.*

Gore, Eldon H. *History of Volusia County, Florida.* De Land, Fla.: E. O. Painter Printing, 1927.

Gosse, Philip Henry, F.R.S. *Letters from Alabama.* London: Morgan and Chase, 1859.

Goulding, R. L. "William Hackley's Diary, 1830–1857: Key West and the Apalachee Area." *Apalachee* 6 (1963–67): 33–44.

Gourges, Dominique de. "Histoire mémorable de la reprinse de l'isle de la Floride." In *Les Français en Amérique pendant la deuxième moitié du seizième siècle,* ed. Suzanne Lussagnet. Paris: Presses Universitaires de France, 1958.

Graham, Thomas. *The Awakening of St. Augustine.* St. Augustine: St. Augustine Historical Society, 1978.

Gramling, Wilbur. "The Gramling Diary, 1864–1865." Manuscript. Florida State University Library.

Gravier, Gabriel, ed. *Deuxième voyage du dieppois Jean Ribaut à la Florida en 1565.* Rouen: Imprimerie de Henry Boissel, 1872.

Green, Stanley. *The World of Music Comedy.* London: Tantivy Presses, 1980.

Griffith, John. *A Collection of the Newest and Most Fashionable Country Dances and Cotillions.* London, 1788.

Groene, Bertram H. *Ante-bellum Tallahassee: It Was a Gay Time Then.* Tallahassee: Florida Heritage Foundation, 1981.

———. "A Letter from Occupied Tallahassee." *Florida Historical Quarterly* 28, no. 1 (July 1969): 70–75.

———. "Lizzie Brown's Tallahassee." *Florida Historical Quarterly* 28, no. 2 (October 1969): 155–75.

A Guide to Key West. WPA Writers' Program. New York: Hastings House, 1941.

Haarmann, Albert W. "The Third Waldeck Regiment in British Service, 1776–1783." *Army Historical Research* 48, no. 195 (Autumn 1970): 182–85.

Hall, Capt. Basil. *Travels in North America.* 3 vols. Edinburgh: Cadell, 1829.

Hall, Robert L. "The Social Cosmos of Black Churches in Tallahassee, Florida, 1865–1885." M.A. thesis, Florida State University, 1972.

Hamilton, Edward. *Songs of Sacred Praise.* Boston: Phillips and Sampson, 1845.

Hamilton, Peter J. *British West Florida.* Jackson: Mississippi Historical Society, 1903.

Hamm, Charles. *Music in the New World.* New York: W. W. Norton, 1982.

———. *Yesterdays: Popular Song in America.* New York: W. W. Norton, 1979.

Hammond, E. A., ed. "Sketches of the Florida Keys, 1829–1833." *Tequesta* 29 (1969): 73–94.

————, ed. "Wreckers and Wrecking on the Florida Reef, 1829–1832." *Florida Historical Quarterly* 41, no. 3 (January 1963): 239–73.

Hanna, A. J. *A Prince in Their Midst.* Norman: University of Oklahoma Press, 1946.

Hanna, Alfred Jackson, and Katherine Abbey Hanna. *Florida's Golden Sands.* Indianapolis: Bobbs-Merrill, 1950.

Hanna, Kathryn Abbey. *Florida, Land of Change.* Chapel Hill: University of North Carolina Press, 1941.

Harrison, Frank, and Joan Rimmer. *European Musical Instruments.* New York: W. W. Norton, 1964.

Harwell, Richard B. *Confederate Music.* Chapel Hill: University of North Carolina Press, 1950.

————. *Songs of the Confederacy.* New York: Broadcast Music, 1951.

Haskew, Peter. "Diary, 1836–1842." Manuscript. Florida State University.

————. "A St. Joseph Diary of 1838." Edited by F. W. Hoskins. *Florida Historical Quarterly* 17, no. 2 (October 1938): 132–51.

Hatheway, Frank. "Diary, 1845–53." Manuscript. Florida State University Archives.

————. "Scrapbook, 1845–1853." Florida State University Library.

Hawes, Lilla Mills, ed. "The Memoirs of Charles H. Olstead." Part 3. *Georgia Historical Society* 43 (June 1959): 170–86.

Hawkins, Benjamin. *Letters, Journals, and Writings of Benjamin Hawkins.* Vol. 1, *1796–1801.* Savannah: Beehive Press, 1980.

Haynes, Mary H. "Sheet Music Collection, 1831–1843." Florida State University Music Library.

Heaps, Willard A., and Porter W. Heaps. *The Singing Sixties.* Norman: University of Oklahoma Press, 1960.

Heart Songs Dear to the American People and by Them Contributed in the Search for Treasured Songs Initiated by the National Magazine. Boston: Chapple Publishing, 1909. Reprint. New York: Da Capo Press, 1982.

Hedrick, Basil D., and Jeanette E. Stephens. *In the Days of Yesterday and in the Days of Today: An Overview of Bahamian Folk Music.* Carbondale: Southern Illinois University, University Museum, 1976.

Heller, George N. "The Enigmatic Story of Fray Juan de Padilla." Typescript, 1986.

Henderson, T. R. *Freemasonry in the Royal Scots.* Wellington Works, Aldershot, England: Gale and Polden, 1934.

Henry, Evelyn Whitfield. "The May Party." *Apalachee* 2 (1946): 35–45.

Hentz, Charles A. "My Autobiography." 2 vols. Typescript, n.d. [c. 1893]. Southern Historical Collection, University of North Carolina.

Herd, David, ed. *The Ancient and Modern Scots Songs, Heroic Ballads, etc.* Edinburgh: Martin and Wetherspoon, 1769.

Hewitt, David Gerald. "Slavery in the Old South: The British Travelers' Image, 1825–1860." Ph.D. diss., Florida State University, 1968.

Higginson, Thomas Wentworth. *Army Life in a Black Regiment*. Boston: Fields, Osgood, 1870.

———. "Negro Spirituals." *Atlantic Monthly* 19, no. 66 (June 1867): 685–96.

Hind, Harold C. "Military Music." In *Grove's Dictionary of Music and Musicians*, 5th ed., 5:766–73. New York: St. Martin's Press, 1960.

Hinde, Robert, comp. *A Collection of Quick Marches*. British Library, 1770.

———, comp. *A Third Collection of Twenty-four Quick Marches, with Basses as performed by the Guards Light Horse and other regiments*. London: Longman, Lukey, 1775.

Hitchcock, Ethan Allen. *Fifty Years in Camp and Field*. New York: G. P. Putnam's Sons, 1909.

———. *A Traveler in Indian Territory*. Edited by Grant Foreman. Cedar Rapids, Iowa: Torch Press, 1930.

Hitchcock, H. Wiley, and Stanley Sadie. *The New Grove Dictionary of American Music*. 4 vols. London: Macmillan, 1986.

Hodge, Frederick W., ed. *Spanish Explorers in the Southern United States, 1528–43*. New York: Charles Scribner's Sons, 1907.

Holbrook, Lizzie. "Sheet Music Collection, 1850–1880." Florida State University Music Library.

Holbrook, William C. *A Narrative of the Services of the officers and enlisted men of the Seventh Regiment of Vermont Volunteers from 1862 to 1866*. New York: American Bank Note, 1882.

The Home Melodist. Boston: Oliver Ditson, 1859.

Hoogerwerf, Frank W. *Confederate Sheet Music Imprints*. Brooklyn: Brooklyn College of the City of New York, 1984.

Hoole, W. Stanley, ed. *Florida Territory in 1844: The Diary of Master Edward C. Anderson, U.S. Navy*. University: University of Alabama Press, 1977.

Hoskins, Frank W. *History of Methodism in Pensacola, Florida*. Nashville: Publishing House of Methodist-Episcopal Church, South, 1928.

Howard, Clinton N. *The British Development of West Florida, 1763–1769*. Berkeley: University of California Press, 1947.

Howe, Elias. *Howe's Complete Ball-Room Hand-Book*. Boston: Elias Howe, 1858.

Hubbard, Frank. *Three Centuries of Harpsichord Making*. Cambridge: Harvard University Press, 1965.

Huggins, Coy. "John Hill Hewitt: Bard of the Confederacy." Ph.D. diss., Florida State University, 1964.

Hughes, John. "The Tientos, Fugas, and Diferencias in Antonia de Cabezón's *Obras de musica para tecla, harpa, y vihuela*." Ph.D. diss., Florida State University, 1961.

Hugill, Stan, comp. *Shanties and Sailors' Songs*. New York: F. A. Praeger, 1969.

———, comp. *Shanties from the Seven Seas*. London: Routledge & Kegan Paul, 1961.

Hutchinson, J. W. *Story of the Hutchinsons*. New York: Da Capo Press, 1977.

Hutchinson, Thomas. *The American Musical Directory, 1861*. Reprint. New York: Da Capo Press, 1980.

International Musicological Society. *Report of Twelfth Congress, Berkley, 1977.* Kassel: Barenreiter, 1981.

Irving, Washington. *Wolfert's Roost and other papers first collected.* New York: G. P. Putnam, 1855.

Ives, Burl. *The Burl Ives Song Book.* New York: Ballantine Books, 1963.

Ives, W. M., Jr. "Civil War Letters." Florida State Archives.

———. "Journal, 1860–1862." Florida State Archives.

The Jack Morgan Songster. Raleigh, N.C.: Brandon and Farrar, 1864.

Jackson, Jesse J. "Negro and the Law in Florida, 1821–1921." M.A. thesis, Florida State University, 1960.

Jackson, William. *Observations on the Present State of Music, in London.* Dublin: A. Grueber, J. Moore, J. Rice, W. Jones, R. McAllister and R. White, 1791.

Jackson, William Richard, Jr. "Florida in Early Spanish Colonial Literature." Ph.D. diss., University of Illinois at Urbana, 1952.

Jarvis, Capt. N. S. "An Army Surgeon's Notes of Frontier Services, 1833–62." *Journal of the Military Service Institution.* State Library of Florida.

Jerome, Father [Jerome Joseph Wisniewski]. *Church and State in Florida in 1822.* St. Leo, Fla.: Abbey Press, 1963.

———. *They Came and They Remained.* St. Leo, Fla.: Abbey Press, 1964.

Jesup, Thomas S. *Seminole Saga, the Jesup Report.* Fort Myers Beach, Fla.: Island Press, 1973.

Johns, John E. *Florida during the Civil War.* Gainesville: University of Florida Press, 1963.

———. *Florida in the Confederacy.* Chapel Hill: University of North Carolina Press, 1958.

Johnson, Cecil. *British West Florida, 1763–1783.* New Haven: Yale University Press, 1943. Reprint. Hamden, Conn.: Archon Books, 1971.

Johnson, David. *Scottish Fiddle Music in the Eighteenth Century.* Edinburgh: J. Donald, 1984.

Johnson, Malcolm B. *Red, White, and Bluebloods in Frontier Florida.* Tallahassee: Rotary Clubs of Tallahassee, 1976.

Jones, Charles Colcock. *Historical Sketch of the Chatham Artillery during the Confederate Struggle for Independence.* Albany, N.Y.: Joel Munsell, 1867.

Jones, W. L. "Civil War Papers." Manuscript, 1862. Florida State University Archives.

Kadel, Richard W. "Evaluation of Hymnody in the Presbyterian Church in the U.S., 1850–1900." M.M. thesis, Florida State University, 1968.

Kastner, Georges. *Manuel général de musique militaire.* Paris: Typ. de Firmin Didst frères, 1848.

Keegan, P. Gregory Joseph, and Leandro Tormo Sanz. *Experiencia misionera en la Florida.* Madrid: Consejo Superior de Investigaciones Científicas, 1957.

Keiley, Anthony M. *In Vinculis; or, The Prisoner of War.* New York: Blelock, 1866.

Kell, John McIntosh. *Recollections of a Naval Life.* Washington, D.C.: Neale, 1900.

Kennedy, John P. *Memoirs of the Life of William Wirt.* 2 vols. Philadelphia: Lea and Blanchard, 1850.

Kennedy, Stetson, *Palmetto Country.* New York: Duell, Sloan and Pierce, 1942.

Keuchel, Edward F. A. *History of Columbia County.* Tallahassee: Sentry Press, 1981.

Keys, Erasmus D. *Fifty Years' Observation of Men and Events, Civil and Military.* New York: C. Scribner's Sons, 1884.

Kingsborough, Edward King. *Antiquities of Mexico.* 9 vols. London: R. Havell and Colnaghi, 1831–48.

Kingsley, Zephaniah. *A Treatise on the Patriarchal, or cooperative system of society as it exists in some governments.* . . . Tallahassee, 1829. 2d ed., Freeport, N.Y.: Books for Libraries Press, 1970.

Kinnard, J., Jr. "Who Are Our National Poets?" *Knickerbocker,* October 26, 1845, pp. 331–41.

Kirk, Cooper Clifford. "A History of the Southern Presbyterian Church of Florida, 1821–1891." Ph.D. diss., Florida State University, 1966.

Knauss, James O. "Education in Florida, 1821–1829." *Florida Historical Quarterly* 3, no. 4 (April 1925): 22–35.

———. "William Pope DuVal, Pioneer and State Builder." *Florida Historical Quarterly* 11, no. 3 (January 1933): 93–139.

Knowles, Joshua. "Methodism in Tallahassee in the Year 1836." Typescript. State Library of Florida.

Lacy, Alex. "Have over the Water to Florida." In Bodleian Library, Oxford, 1564–65, vol. 1, p. 263, ms 48, no. 76.

Laney, Noah. "St. Augustine Mission." *Methodist Magazine* 8 (1825): 112–13.

Lanning, John Tate. *The Spanish Missions of Georgia.* Chapel Hill: University of North Carolina Press, 1935.

Latrobe, Benjamin Henry. *Latrobe's View of America, 1795–1820.* New Haven: Yale University Press, 1985.

Latrobe, Charles Joseph. *The Rambler in North America.* 2 vols. London: R. B. Seeley and W. Burnside, 1835.

Laudonnière, René Goulaine de. *L'histoire notable de la Floride.* 1586. Reprint, edited by Martin Basanier. Paris: P. Jannet, 1853.

———. *Three Voyages.* Translated and edited by Charles E. Bennett. Gainesville: University Presses of Florida, 1975.

Lavin, Jack. "The Temperance Movement in Ante-bellum Florida." M.A. thesis, Florida State University, 1967.

Law, Andrew. *Harmonic Companion and Guide to Social Worship.* Philadelphia: Thomas H. Palmer, 1819.

Learned, Marion D., ed. *Philip Waldeck's Diary of the American Revolution.* Philadelphia: Americana Germanica Press, 1907.

Le Moyne, Jacques. "Brevis narratio eorum quae in Florida Americae." In Theodore de Bry, *Collection of Voyages,* 1591.

Le Moyne de Morgues, Jacques. *The Work of Jacques Le Moyne de Morgues.* 2 vols. Edited by Paul Hulton. London: British Museum Publications, 1977.

L'Engle, Susan. *Notes of My Family and Recollections of My Early Life.* New York: Knickerbocker Press, 1888.

Lescarbot, Marc. *Histoire de la Nouvelle France.* Paris: Jean Milot, 1609.

"Letter from Fernandina, Fla." [Signed by N.] *Boston Semi-Weekly Advertiser,* March 1, 1865.

Levy, Lester S. *Confederacy and the South in Music and Song.* Philadelphia: Musical Americana, 1956. Microfilm.

———. *Grace Notes in American History: Popular Sheet Music from 1820 to 1900.* Norman: University of Oklahoma Press, 1967.

———. *Picture the Songs.* Baltimore: Johns Hopkins University Press, 1976.

Ley, John Cole. *Fifty-Two Years in Florida.* Nashville: Publishing House of Methodist-Episcopal Church, South, 1899.

Liber Usualis. Edited by Benedictines of Solesmes. New York: Desclee, 1963.

Lisenby, Julie Ann. "The Free Negro in Ante-bellum Florida, 1821–1861." M.A. thesis, Florida State University, 1967.

Little, Henry F. W. *The Seventh Regiment New Hampshire Volunteers in the War of the Rebellion.* Concord, N.H.: J. C. Evans, 1896.

Lockley, Joseph B. *East Florida, 1783–1785.* Berkeley: University of California Press, 1949.

———. "Public Education in Spanish St. Augustine." *Florida Historical Quarterly* 15, no. 3 (January 1937): 147–68.

Lomax, John A., and Alan Lomax. *Cowboy Songs and Other Frontier Ballads.* New York: Macmillan, 1957.

———. *Folk Song: U.S.A.* New York: Duell, Sloan and Pierce [c. 1947].

Long, Ellen Call. *Florida Breezes.* 1882. Reprint. Gainesville: University of Florida Press, 1962.

Lorant, Stefan, ed. *The New World.* New York: Duell, Sloan and Pearce, 1946.

Lord, Francis A., and Arthur Wise. *Bands and Drummer Boys of the Civil War.* New York: Thomas Yoseloff, 1966. Reprint. New York: Da Capo Press, 1979.

Lowery, Woodbury. *The Spanish Settlements within the Present limits of the United States, 1513–1561.* 2 vols. New York: G. P. Putnam's Sons, 1901–5.

Ludlow, Noah M. *Dramatic Life As I Found It.* St. Louis: By the author, 1880. Reprint. New York: B. Blom, 1966.

Lussagnet, Suzanne, ed. *Les Français en Amérique pendant la deuxième moitié du seizième siècle.* Writings of Jean Ribault, René de Laudonnière, Nicholas Le Challeus, and Dominique de Gourges. Paris: Presses Universitaires de France, 1958.

Lynch, Bartholemew M. "Journal, 1837–1839." Microfilm. Florida State University Library.

Lyon, Eugene. "Captives of Florida." *Florida Historical Quarterly* 50, no. 1 (July 1971): 1–24.

————. *The Enterprise of Florida: Pedro Menéndez de Avilés and the Spanish Conquest of 1565–1568.* Gainesville: University Presses of Florida, 1976.

McCall, George A. *Letters from the Frontiers.* 1868. Reprint. Gainesville: University Presses of Florida, 1974.

MacCauley, Clay. "The Seminole Indians of Florida." In *U.S. Bureau of American Ethnology, Fifth Annual Report, 1883–84,* pp. 469–531. Washington, D.C.: Government Printing Office, 1887.

McCord, Jean P. "History of the First Hundred Years of the First Presbyterian Church, Tallahassee." Typescript, n.d. Private collection of Mrs. Guyte McCord.

McCoy, Martha C. "Sheet Music Collection, 1833–1852." Florida State University Library.

McGaughy, Felix P., Jr. "The Squaw Kissing War: Bartholomew M. Lynch's Journal of the Second Seminole War, 1836–1839." M.S. thesis, Florida State University, 1965.

McGovern, James, ed. *Colonial Pensacola.* Vol. 1. Pensacola: Pensacola News-Journal, 1974.

McGovern, James R. "Sporting Life on the Line." *Florida Historical Quarterly* 54, no. 2 (October 1975): 131–44.

McIlwain, William E. *The Early Planting of Presbyterianism in West Florida.* Pensacola: Mayes Printing, 1926.

Mackerness, E. D. *A Social History of English Music.* London: Routledge and Kegan Paul, 1964.

McKinnon, John L. "History of Walton County (Florida)." Typescript [c. 1909]. Florida State University Library.

Mackle, Elliot James, Jr. "The Eden of the South: Florida's Image in American Travel Literature and Painting, 1865–1900." Ph.D. diss., Emory University, 1977.

McMorries, Edward Young. *History of the First Regiment, Alabama Volunteer Infantry, C.S.A.* Montgomery: Brown Printing, 1904.

McPheeters, D. W. "A Comparative Study of Some Spanish Songs and Ballads Collected in Tampa, Florida." M.A. thesis, University of Florida, 1941.

McQueen, John. *The Letters of Don Juan McQueen to His Family, Written from Spanish East Florida, 1791–1807.* Columbia, S.C.: Bostick and Thornley, 1943.

Macy, Julia A. "Sheet Music Collection, 1844–1855." Florida State University Music Library.

Mahon, John K. *History of the Second Seminole War, 1835–1842.* Gainesville: University of Florida Press, 1967.

Maine Infantry, Eleventh Regiment. *The Story of One Regiment* [1861–66]. New York: J. J. Little, 1986.

Maloney, Walter C. *A Sketch of the History of Key West, Florida.* 1876. Reprint. Gainesville: University of Florida Press, 1968.

Mann, Albert W. *History of the Forty-fifth Regiment, Massachusetts Volunteer Militia, the Cadet Regiment.* Boston: W. Spooner, 1908.

Mann, Jesse T. "Fernandina: A City in Turmoil, 1863–1888." M.A. thesis, Florida State University, 1971.

Manucy, Albert. *Florida's Menéndez: Captain of the Ocean Sea.* St. Augustine: St. Augustine Historical Society, 1965.

———. *The History of Castillo de San Marcos and Fort Matanzas from Contemporary Narratives and Letters.* Washington, D.C.: U.S. Department of the Interior, National Park Service, 1959.

Marcy, Randolph B. *Border Reminiscences.* New York: Harper and Bros., 1872.

Marshall, Leonard. *Sacred Star; or, Union Collection of Church Music.* Boston: Oliver Ditson, 1861.

Martin, Sidney Walter. *Florida during the Territorial Days.* Athens: University of Georgia Press, 1944.

Mason, Lowell, ed. *The Boston Handel and Haydn Society Collection of Church Music.* Boston: Richardson and Lord, 1822.

Mason, Lowell, and George James Webb. *Cantica Laudis.* New York: Mason and Law, 1850.

Matter, Robert Allen. "The Spanish Missions of Florida: The Friars versus the Governors in the Golden Age, 1606–1690." Ph.D. diss., University of Washington, 1972.

Mattfield, Julius. *The Folk Music of the Western Hemisphere.* New York: New York Public Library, 1925. Reprint. New York: Arno Press, 1980.

Mattfield, Mary S. "Journey to the Wilderness: Two Travelers in Florida, 1696–1774." *Florida Historical Quarterly* 45, no. 4 (April 1967): 327–51.

Matthews, Donald G. *Religion in the Old South.* Chicago: University of Chicago Press, 1977.

Maxwell, Sir Herbert Eustace. "Regimental Music." In *The Lowland Scots Regiments,* pp. 331–39. Glasglow: J. Maclehose and Sons, 1918.

Mayo, James M. *Recollections, Reminiscences, Memories, and Dreams: A Diary, 1863–1864.* Jacksonville: Historical Records Survey, 1937.

Mellon, Knox, Jr., ed. "A Florida Soldier in the Army of Northern Virginia: The Hosford Letters." *Florida Historical Quarterly* 46, no. 3 (January 1968): 243–71.

The Middlesex Collection of Church Music. Boston: Manning and Loring, 1811.

Milanich, Jerald, and Samuel Proctor, eds. *Tacachale: Essays on the Indians of Florida and Southeastern Georgia during the Historic Period.* Gainesville: University Presses of Florida, 1978.

Milanich, Jerald T., and William C. Sturtevant. *Francisco Pareja's 1613 Confesionario.* Tallahassee: Florida Division of Archives, History and Records Management, 1972.

Miller, G. J. "Grenadier Music." *Tempo* 40 (Summer 1956): 29–30.

Miller, J. *Narrative of a Voyage to the Spanish Main in the Ship "Two Friends."* London: J. Miller, 1819.

Minstrel Songs Old and New. Boston: Oliver Ditson, 1882.

Mitchell, A. L. *Songs of the Confederacy and Plantation Melodies.* Cincinnati: George B. Jennings, 1901.

Montault de Monberaut, Henri. *Mémoire Justificatif: Indian Diplomacy in British West Florida, 1763–1765.* Translated by Milo B. Howard and Robert R. Rea. University: University of Alabama Press, 1965.

Moon, John C., Herbert E. Watson, and William I. White, comps. *Musick of the Fifes and Drums.* Williamsburg, Va.: Colonial Williamsburg Foundation, n.d. [c. 1976].

Moore, John Hammond. "A South Carolina Lawyer Visits St. Augustine, 1837." *Florida Historical Quarterly* 43, no. 4 (April 1965): 361–78.

Moore, Thomas. *Melodies, Songs, Sacred Songs, and National Airs Containing Several Never Before Published in America.* Exeter: J. and B. Williams, 1836.

———. *National Airs; and other Songs, now first collected.* London: Novello, n.d.

Morris, Allen, comp. *The Florida Handbook.* Tallahassee: Peninsular Publishing, 1947–87.

Morris, Allen Covington. *Florida Place Names.* Coral Gables: University of Miami Press, 1974.

Morris, Alton C. *Folksongs of Florida.* Gainesville: University of Florida Press, 1950.

Morris, Gouverneur. *The History of a Volunteer Regiment (Sixth New York Infantry).* New York: Veterans Volunteer Publishing, 1891.

Motte, Jacob Rhett. *Journey into Wilderness.* Edited by James F. Sunderman. Gainesville: University of Florida Press, 1953.

Mowat, Charles L. *East Florida as a British Province.* Berkeley: University of California Press, 1943. Reprint. Gainesville: University of Florida Press, 1964.

———. "St. Augustine under the British Flag, 1763–1775." *Florida Historical Quarterly* 20, no. 2 (October 1941): 131–68.

Mueller, Edward A. "East Coast Florida Steamboating, 1831–1861." *Florida Historical Quarterly* 40, no. 3 (January 1962): 241–60.

———. *Oklawaha River Steamboats.* Jacksonville: Mendelson Printing, 1983.

———. *Steamboating on the St. Johns.* Melbourne, Fla.: South Broward Historical Society, 1980.

Mueller, Edward A., and Barbara A. Purdy, eds. *The Steamboat Era in Florida.* Gainesville: University of Florida Press, 1984.

Murat, Prince Achille. *America and the Americans.* Translated by Henry J. Bradfield. New York: Wm. H. Graham, 1849.

———. "Florida." *American Quarterly Review* 1, no. 3 (September 1827): 232.

Murfin, James. *National Park Service Guide to Historic Places of the American Revolution.* Washington, D.C.: Government Printing Office, 1974.

The Musical Companion. London: T. T. and J. Tegg, 1833.

The Musical Entertainer. 2 vols. London: George Bickham, 1737–38.

Myers, John B. "Social life and Recreation in Tallahassee during Reconstruction, 1865–1877." *Apalachee* 7 (1968–70): 20–37.

Nance, Ellwood C. *The East Coast of Florida, 1500–1961.* Delray Beach, Fla.: Southern Publishing, 1962.

Nathan, Hans. *Dan Emmett and the Rise of Early Negro Minstrelsy.* Norman: University of Oklahoma Press, 1962.

Negro Melodies, Minstrels, and Songsters. Milkwood, N.Y.: Kraus-Thomson Organization, 1970.

Nettl, Paul. *National Anthems.* New York: Storm Publishers, 1952.

The New England Harmony; or, New England Repository of Sacred Music. Exeter: J. J. Williams, 1821.

The New Grove Dictionary of Music and Musicians. 20 vols. London: Macmillan, 1986.

Nichols, Richard Samuel. "Florida's Fighting Rebels: A Military History of Florida's Civil War Troops." M.A. thesis, Florida State University, 1967.

Nolan, Terence H. *History of Fort Clinch, Fernandina, Florida.* Tallahassee: Florida Department of State, 1974.

Nordhoff, Charles. *The Merchant Vessel.* New York: Dodd Mead, 1884.

———. *Nine Years a Sailor.* Cincinnati: Moore, Wilstach, Keys, 1857.

Norton, Herman. *Rebel Religion: The Story of the Confederate Chaplains.* St. Louis: Bethany Press, 1961.

Norton, O. W. *Army Letters, 1861–1865.* Chicago: O.L. Deming, 1903.

"Notes by the Way." Journal of a New York State monument manufacturer on a trip to Florida, November 6, 1855–January 29, 1856. Florida State University Archives.

Notices of East Florida, with an account of the Seminole Indians. By a Recent Traveller in the Provinces. Charleston, S.C.: By the author, 1822.

Núñez, Álvar. *Relation of Álvar Núñez.* Translated by Buckingham Smith, 1871. Readex Microprint.

Núñez Cabeza de Vaca, Álvar. *The Journey of Álvar Núñez Cabeza de Vaca.* Translated by Fanny Bandelier. Chicago: Rio Grande Press, 1964.

———. *The Narrative of Álvar Núñez Cabeza de Vaca.* Edited by Frederick W. Hodge. New York: C. Scribner's Sons, 1907.

———. "The Narrative of Álvar Núñez Cabeza de Vaca." In *Spanish Explorers in the Southern United States, 1528–43,* ed. F. N. Hodge. New York: Barnes and Noble, 1959.

———. *The Narrative of Álvar Núñez Cabeza de Vaca.*Translated by Fanny Bandelier. Barre, Mass.: Imprint Society, 1972.

Nutter, M. L. "Collection of Sheet Music." Vol. 1, 1830–51; vol. 2, n.d. Florida State University Music Library.

Ochse, Orpha. *The History of the Organ in the United States.* Bloomington: Indiana University Press, 1975.

O'Daniel, Victor Francis. *Dominicans in Early Florida.* New York: U.S. Catholic Historical Society, 1930.

Odell, George Clinton Densmore. *Annals of the New York Stage.* 15 vols. New York: Columbia University Press, 1927–49.

Ogasapian, John. *Henry Erben: Portrait of a Nineteenth-Century American Organ Builder.* Braintree, Mass. Organ Literature Foundation, 1980.

Ogilby, John. *America: Florida*. London: By the author, 1671.

Old Plantation Songster. Philadelphia: Fisher and Brother, 1850.

Olson, Kenneth E. *Music and Musket: Bands and Bandsmen of the American Civil War*. Westport, Conn.: Greenwood Press, 1981.

Oré, Luís Gerónimo de. *The Martyrs of Florida, 1513–1616*. Translated and edited by Maynard Geiger. New York: Joseph F. Wagner, 1936.

———. *Relación histórica de la Florida*. Edited by P. Atanasio López. Madrid: Ramona Velasco, 1931–33.

Ormond, James. *The Reminiscences of James Ormond*. Crawfordville, Fla.: Magnolia Monthly Press, 1966.

Orson [pseud.]. "Familiar Sketches of Life in Florida." *Knickerbocker* 8 (September 1836): 276–88; (November 1836): 555.

Osborn, George C. "A Religious Revival in Tallahassee in 1843 by the Rev. Dr. Nathan Hoyt." *Florida Historical Quarterly* 32, no. 4 (April 1954): 288–94.

Oswald, James. *A Collection of the Best Old Scotch and English Songs*. London, 1762.

———. *Fifty-Five Marches for the Militia*. London: By the author, 1765.

———. *Second Collection of Curious Scots Tunes*. London: Charles and Samuel Thompson, 1770.

Otaño, R. P. N., ed. *Toques de guerra*. Burgos: Radio Nacional de España, 1939.

Our War Songs North and South. Cleveland: S. Brainard, 1887.

Owens, Harry P. "Apalachicola before 1861." Ph.D. diss., Florida State University, 1966.

Paine, J. "Regimental Marches: English Regiments with Scottish, Irish, and Foreign Airs." *Army Quarterly* 27 (1934): 265–74.

Paisley, Clifton. *The Red Hills of Florida, 1528–1865*. Tuscaloosa: University of Alabama Press, 1989.

Parke, W. J. *Musical Memoirs: Comprising an Account of the General State of Music in England, from the First Commemoration of Handel in 1784 to the year 1830*. 2 vols. London: Henry Colburn and Richard Bentley, 1830. Reprint. New York: Da Capo Press, 1970.

Parker, Daisy. "The Inauguration of the First Governor of the State of Florida." *Apalachee* 2 (1946): 59.

Parkman, Francis. *Pioneers of France in the New World*. Boston: Little, Brown, 1865. Reprint. 1912.

Parsons, Elsie Clews. *Folk Tales of Andros Islands, Bahamas*. New York: American G. E. Stechert, 1918.

Parton, James. *Life of Andrew Jackson*. New York: Mason Brothers, 1860.

A Past Master. See *A Scottish Ritual of Freemasonry*.

Patrick, Rembert W. *Aristocrat in Uniform*. Gainesville: University of Florida Press, 1963.

Patterson, Cecil Lloyd. "A Different Drum: The Image of the Negro in the Nineteenth Century Popular Song Books." Ph.D. diss., University of Pennsylvania, 1961.

Patton, Abby Hutchinson. *Camp Meeting Songs of the Florida Freedman*. New York: William A. Pond, 1870.

Pearce, George P. *The U.S. Navy in Pensacola, 1825–1930*. Pensacola: University Presses of Florida, 1980.

Pedicord, H. W., and F. L. Bergmann, eds. *The Plays of David Garrick*. Vol. 1. Carbondale: Southern Illinois University Press, 1980.

Pennington, Edgar L. "The Church in Florida, 1763–1892." *Historical Magazine of the Protestant Episcopal Church* 7 (March 1938): 1–77.

Pennington, Edgar L., and Clark S. Northrup, eds. "An Early Poem on Florida." *Florida Historical Quarterly* 7, no. 1 (1928–29): 72–74.

Pete, Panhandle. "Singin' Men and Singin' Rails." *Florida's Panhandle Life*, May 1982.

Peters, Thelma. "The American Loyalists in the Bahama Islands: Who They Were." *Florida Historical Quarterly* 40, no. 3 (January 1962): 226–40.

Petre, F. Loraine. *History of the Norfolk Regiment, 1685–1918*. 2 vols. Norwich: Jarrold and Sons, 1924.

Phelps, John W. "Letters of Lieutenant John W. Phelps, U.S.A., 1837–1838. *Florida Historical Quarterly* 6 (1927): 67–84.

Phillips, Ulrich B. *Life and Labor in the Old South*. Boston: Little, Brown, 1929.

Pickell, John. "Brief Notes of the Campaign against the Seminole Indians in Florida in 1837." Edited by Frank L. White, Jr. *Florida Historical Quarterly* 38, no. 2 (October 1959): 115.

Pickman, Susan Lois. "Life on the Spanish-American Colonial Frontier: A Study in the Social and Economic History of Mid-Eighteenth Century St. Augustine, Florida." Ph.D. diss., State University of New York at Stony Brook, 1980.

Pidoux, Pierre. *Le psautier Huguenot du seizième siècle*. 2 vols. Bale: Baerenreiter, 1962.

"Pine Hill Plantation Papers" 1840–1895 and 1895–1909. Florida State University Archives.

Plymouth Collection of Hymns and Tunes. New York: Barnes and Burr, 1855.

Pope, John. *A Tour through the Southern and Western Territories of the United States of North America*. 1792. Reprint. Richmond, Va.: John Dixon, 1888; Gainesville: University of Florida Press, 1979.

Portier, Rt. Rev. Michael. "From Pensacola to St. Augustine in 1827, a Journey." *Florida Historical Quarterly* 26, no. 2 (October 1947): 135–60.

Potter, Woodburne. *The [Seminole] War in Florida, being an Exposition of its Causes and an Accurate History of the Campaigns of General Gaines, Clinch, and Scott*. Baltimore: Lewis and Coleman, 1836.

Prescott, W. H. *History of the Conquest of Mexico*. Philadelphia: J. B. Lippincott, 1873.

The Present State of the British Empire in Europe, America, Africa, and Asia. [Authorship attributed by Sabin to J. Goldsmith.] London: W. Griffin, 1768.

Price, Isaiah. *History of the Ninety-seventh Regiment, Pennsylvania Volunteer Infantry, during the War of the Rebellion, 1861–65.* Philadelphia: By the author, 1875.

Priest, Daniel. *American Sheet Music, 1775–1975.* Des Moines: Wallace-Homestead Book, 1978.

Priestley, Herbert Ingram. *The Luna Papers.* De Land: Florida State Historical Society, 1928.

———. *Tristán de Luna, Conquistador of the Old South.* Glendale, Calif.: Arthur H. Clark, 1936.

Proctor, Samuel. *Florida a Hundred Years Ago.* Coral Gables: Florida Civil War Centennial Commission, 1960.

———, ed. *Eighteenth-Century Florida: Life on the Frontier.* Gainesville: University Presses of Florida, 1976.

———, ed. *Eighteenth-Century Florida: The Impact of the American Revolution.* Gainesville: University Presses of Florida, 1978.

———, ed. *Eighteenth-Century Florida and Its Borderlands.* Gainesville: University Presses of Florida, 1975.

———, ed. *Eighteenth-Century Florida and the Caribbean.* Gainesville: University Presses of Florida, 1976.

———, ed. *Eighteenth-Century Florida and the Revolutionary South.* Gainesville: University Presses of Florida, 1978.

Program, Celebration of the Fourth of July, 1851, at Madison Court House, with the regular and volunteer toasts. Tallahassee: Florida Sentinel, 1851.

Purvis, Ann. "Sheet Music Collection." c. 1850. Florida State University Music Library.

Pyburn, Nita. *Documentary History of Education in Florida, 1822–1860.* Tallahassee: Florida State University, 1951.

Quinn, Jane. *Minorcans in Florida: Their History and Heritage.* St. Augustine: Mission Press, 1975.

Raney, E. L. "Sheet Music Collection." c. 1850s. Florida State University Music Library.

Rasico, Philip D. "The Spanish and Minorcan Linguistic Heritage of St. Augustine, Florida." *El Escribano,* no. 20 (1983): 1.

Rawick, George P. *The American Slave: A Composite Autobiography.* Westport, Conn.: Greenwood Press, 1979.

———. *Florida Writers' Project.* Works Progress Administration. Westport, Conn.: Greenwood Publishing, 1972.

Reaver, T. Russell. "Folk History from Northern Florida." *Southern Folklore Quarterly* 32, no. 1 (March 1968): 6–7.

The Rebellion Record, 1861–1868. 9 vols. New York: G. P. Putnam.

A Recent Traveller in the Provinces. See *Notices of East Florida.*

Recollections of a Checkered Life. By a Good Templar. Napanee: S. T. Hammond, 1868.

Reese, Gustave. *Music in the Renaissance.* New York: W. W. Norton, 1959.

Reid, John. [R. I., pseud.]. *A Set of Marches for two clarinets, hautboys, or German flutes, two horns, and a bassoon.* London: R. Bremner, 1770.

———. *A Set of Minuets and Marches.* London: R. Bremner, 1775.

Ribault, Jean. *The Whole and True Discoverye of Terra Florida.* London: Rowland Hall for Thomas Hacket, 1563. Reprint. De Land: Florida State Historical Society, 1927; Gainesville: University Presses of Florida, 1964.

Richardson, Joe M. "We Are Truly Doing Missionary Work: Letters from American Missionary Association Teachers in Florida, 1864–1874." *Florida Historical Quarterly* 54, no. 2 (October 1975): 178–95.

Richardson, Simon Peter. *The Lights and Shadows of Itinerant Life.* Nashville: Barbee and Smith, 1901.

Rickaby, Franz. *Ballads and Songs of the Shanty-boy.* Cambridge: Harvard University Press, 1926.

Ritson, Joseph. *A Select Collection of English Songs.* 3 vols. London: J. Johnson, 1783.

Roberts, Albert Hubbard. "The Dade Massacre." *Florida Historical Quarterly* 5, no. 3 (January 1927): 123–38.

Roberts, William. *An Account of the First Discovery and Natural History of Florida.* 1763. Reprint. Gainesville: University of Florida Press, 1963.

Robertson, Fred, comp. *Soldiers of Florida in the Seminole Indian, Civil, and Spanish-American Wars.* Live Oak, Fla.: Board of State Institutions, 1903.

Robinson, Ernest L. *History of Hillsborough County, Florida.* St. Augustine: Record, 1928.

Rodenbaugh, Theophilus F., ed. *From Everglade to Cañon with the Second Dragoons.* New York: D. VanNostrand, 1875.

Roe, Afred Seelge. *The Twenty-fourth Regiment, Massachusetts Volunteers, 1861–1866.* Worcester, Mass.: Twenty-fourth Veteran Assn., 1907.

Rogers, Seth. *Letters of Seth Rogers, 1862–1863.* Boston: J. Wilson and Son, 1910.

Rogers, William Warren. *Ante-bellum Thomas County, 1825–1861.* Tallahassee: Florida State University Research Council, 1963.

———, ed. "Florida on the Eve of the Civil War, as Seen by a Southern Reporter." *Florida Historical Quarterly* 39, no. 2 (October 1960): 145–58.

Romans, Bernard. *A Concise Natural History of East and West Florida.* 1775. Reprint. Gainesville: University of Florida Press, 1962.

Root, Deane L. *Music of Florida Historic Sites.* Tallahassee: Florida State University, School of Music, 1983.

Root, George F., ed. *The Bugle Call.* Chicago: Root and Cady, 1863.

The Rose-Bud Songster. New York: Richard Marsh, n.d.

Ross, Fitzgerald. *Cities and Camps of the Confederate States.* Edited by Richard B. Hartnell. Urbana: University of Illinois Press, 1958.

Rosser, John L. *A History of Florida Baptists.* Nashville: Broadman Press, 1949.

The Rough and Ready Songster, embellished with twenty-five splendid engravings, illustrative of the victories in Mexico. By an American officer. New York: Nafis and Cornish, 1848.

Rourke, Constance. *The Roots of American Culture and Other Essays*. New York: Harcourt, Brace, 1942.

Ruidiaz y Caravia, Eugenio. *La Florida: Su conquesta y colonización por Pedro Menéndez de Avilés*. 2 vols. Madrid: De los hijos de J. A. García, 1893.

Russell, Henry. *Cheer! Boys, Cheer! Memories of Men and Music*. London: J. MacQueen, 1895.

Rutherford's Compleat Collection of 112 of the most celebrated minuets, with their basses. 2 vols. London: 1775–80.

Rutherford's Compleat Collection of Two Hundred of the most celebrated Country Dances. 2 vols. London: 1756–60.

Sands, Mollie. "English Song Writers of the Eighteenth Century." *Monthly Music Record* 69 (1939): 228–33.

Scarborough, Rabun. *The Civil War Letters of Rabun Scarborough, Apalachicola, Florida, 1861–1862*. Edited by E. F. Smith. Crawfordville, Fla.: Magnolia Monthly Press, 1973.

Schene, Michael G. "Hopes, Dreams, and Promises: A History of Volusia County, Florida." Ph.D. diss., Florida State University, 1976.

Schmidt, Lewis G. *A Civil War History of the Forty-seventh Regiment of Pennsylvania Veteran Volunteers*. Allentown, Pa.: By the author, 1986.

Schoepf, Johann David. *Travels in the Confederation (1783–1784)*. 2 vols. Philadelphia: W. J. Campbell, 1911.

Scholes, Percy A. *The Oxford Companion to Music*. London: Oxford University Press, 1950.

Schwaab, Eugene L., ed. *Travels in the Old South*. Lexington: University of Kentucky Press, 1973.

Scott, Kenneth. "The City of Wreckers." *Florida Historical Quarterly* 25, no. 2 (October 1946): 193–201.

A Scottish Ritual of Freemasonry. By a Past Master. Dundee: David Winter, 1948.

Seay, Albert. *Transcriptions of Chansons for Keyboard Published by Pierre Attaingnant*. Dallas: American Institute of Musicology, 1961.

A Second Collection of Twenty-Four Favourite Marches in seven parts as they were performed by his Majesty's Foot and Horse Guards. London: C. and S. Thompson, 1771.

Sharp, Cecil J., *The Country Dance Book*. London: Novello, 1909–22.

Sharp, Cecil J., and Maud Karpeles. *English Folk Songs from the Southern Appalachian Mountains*. 2 vols. London: Oxford University Press, 1932.

Sharp, Elizabeth A. *Songs and Poems of the Sea*. London: W. Scott, 1888.

Shaw, Fred. *Fred Shaw's Dime Songster*. New York: Frederic A. Brady, n.d.

Shaw, Roderick Gaspero, and James Kirkpatrick. "Manuscripts, 1861–64." Florida State University Archives.

Shay, Frank. *American Sea Songs and Chanteys*. New York: W. W. Norton, 1948.

Shea, John D. G. *History of the Catholic Church in the United States*. 4 vols. New York: McBride, 1886–92.

Shippe, Lester B., ed. *Bishop Whipple's Southern Diary, 1843–1844*. Minneapolis: University of Minnesota Press, 1937.

Shofner, Jerrell H. *History of Jefferson County*. Tallahassee: Sentry Press, 1976.

Siebert, Wilbur H. *Loyalists in East Florida*. De Land: Florida State Historical Society, 1929.

———. "Slavery and White Servitude in East Florida, 1726–1776." *Florida Historical Quarterly* 10, no. 1 (July 1931): 3–23.

Silber, Irwin. *Songs of the Civil War*. New York: Columbia University Press, 1960.

———, ed. *Soldier Songs and Home Front Ballads of the Civil War*. New York: Oak Publications, 1964.

Silliman, Justus M. *A New Canaan Private in the Civil War*. New Canaan, Conn.: New Canaan Historical Society, 1984.

Simes, Thomas. *The Military Guide for Young Officers*. London: By the author, 1772.

———. *The Military Medley*. London: By the author, 1768.

Simmons, William Hayne. *Notices of East Florida*. Charleston, S.C.: A. E. Miller, 1822. Reprint. Gainesville: University of Florida Press, 1973.

"Sketches of East Florida." *Knickerbocker*, 1843–44, p. 566.

Smith, Buckingham. *Coleción de varios documentos para la historia de la Florida y tierras adyacentes*. London: Trubner, 1857.

———, trans. *Narratives of De Soto in the Conquest of Florida, as told by a gentleman of Elvas, and in a relation by Luys Hernández de Biedma*. Gainesville: Palmetto Books, 1968.

———, trans. *Relation of Álvar Núñez Cabeza de Vaca*. New York: J. Munsell for H. C. Murphy, 1871.

Smith, Elizabeth F. *Tom Brown's Tallahassee Days, 1825–1850*. Crawfordville, Fla.: Magnolia Monthly Press, 1971.

Smith, George G. *History of Methodism in Georgia and Florida from 1785 to 1865*. Macon, Ga.: John W. Burke, 1877.

Smith, Hale G. *Documentation concerning the First Christmas in the United States, Presented to the United States Postal Service Commemorative Stamp Committee*. Tallahassee: n.d. Reprint. Gainesville: Palmetto Books, 1968.

Smith, Jacob. *Camps and Campaigns of the 107th Regiment Ohio Volunteer Infantry from August 1862 to July 1865*. N.p. [c. 1910].

Smith, Josiah, Jr. "Diary, 1780–1781." *South Carolina Historical and Genealogical Magazine* 33, no. 1 (January 1932): 1–28.

Smith, Julia F. "The Plantation Belt in Middle Florida, 1850–1860." Ph.D. diss., Florida State University, 1964.

———. *Slavery and Plantation Growth in Antebellum Florida, 1821–1860*. Gainesville: University of Florida Press, 1973.

Smith, Mrs. Joseph Lee. "Journal, 1862–1863." Typescript. St. Augustine Historical Society.

Smith, Solomon Franklin. *The Theatrical Journey: Work and anecdotal recollections of Sol Smith*. Philadelphia: T. B. Peterson, 1854.

———. *Theatrical Management in the West and South for Thirty Years*. New York: Harper and Bros., 1868.

Smith, William B. *On Wheels and How I Came There*. New York: Hunt and Eaton, 1892.

Solís de Meras, Gonzalo. *Pedro Menéndez de Avilés*. Translated by Jeannette Thurber Connor. De Land: Florida State Historical Society, 1923.

Songs of Dixie. New York: S. Brainard's Sons, 1890.

"Songs of the Rebels." *Rebellion Record* 4 (1860–62): 51.

The Songster's Museum. Hartford: Silas Andrus, 1825; Henry Benton, 1835.

Southall, Geneva H. *Blind Tom: The Post Civil War Enslavement of a Black Musical Genius*. Minneapolis: Challenge Productions, 1979.

Spell, Lota. "The First Teacher of European Music in America." *Catholic Historical Quarterly*, n.s., 2 (1923): 372–78.

———. *Music in Texas*. Austin, Tex.: By the author, 1936.

———. "Music Teaching in New Mexico in the Seventeenth Century." *New Mexico Historical Review* 2, no. 1 (January 1927): 27–36.

Sprague, John T. "Macomb's Mission to the Seminoles." Edited by Frank F. White, Jr. *Florida Historical Quarterly* 35, no. 2 (October 1956): 130–93.

———. *The Origin, Progress, and Conclusion of the Florida War*. New York: D. Appleton, 1848.

Stakley, Charles E. "Introduction of the Negro into the United States." *Magazine of American History* 26 (1891): 358–63.

Stanley, J. Randall. *History of Gadsden County*. Quincy, Fla.: Gadsden County Historical Commission, 1948.

Stark, William. *An Account of East Florida*. London: W. Nicoll, 1766.

Starr, J. Barton. *Tories, Dons, and Rebels: The American Revolution of British West Florida, 1775–1783*. Gainesville: University of Florida Press, 1976.

The Stars and Stripes Songster. New York: Robert M. DeWitt, 1835.

Staudenraus, P. J., ed. "A [Union] War Correspondent's View of St. Augustine and Fernandina, 1863." [By Noah Brook.] *Florida Historical Quarterly* 41, no. 1 (July 1962): 60–62.

Steele, William O. *The Wilderness Tattoo: A Narrative of Juan Ortiz*. New York: Harcourt Brace Jovanovich, 1972.

Stern, Shepard, ed. *One Thousand Fiddle Tunes*. Chicago: M. M. Cole Publishing, 1940. Renewed, 1967.

Sternhold, Thomas, and John Hopkins. *The Whole Book of Psalms Collected in English Metre*. London: John Day, 1562.

Stevenson, Robert Murrell. "European Music in Sixteenth Century Guatemala." *Musical Quarterly* 50 (July 1964): 341–52.

———. *A Guide to Caribbean Music History*. Lima: Ediciones Cultura, 1975.

———. *Music in Aztec and Inca Territory*. Berkeley: University of California Press, 1968.

————. *Music in Mexico*. New York: Thomas Y. Crowell, 1952.

————. "Music Instruction in Inca Land." *Journal of Research in Music Education* 8, no. 2 (Fall 1960): 110–22.

————. *The Music of Peru: Aboriginal and Viceroyal Eras*. Washington, D.C.: Pan American Union, 1960.

————. *Patterns of Protestant Church Music in America*. Durham, N.C.: Duke University Press, 1953.

————. *Protestant Church Music in America*. New York: W. W. Norton, 1966.

————. *Renaissance and Baroque Musical Sources in the Americas*. Washington, D.C.: Organization of American States, General Secretariat, 1970.

————. *Spanish Cathedral Music in the Golden Age*. Berkeley: University of California Press, 1961.

Stillman, William James. *The Autobiography of a Journalist*. Boston: Houghton, Mifflin, 1901.

Stork, W. "An Account of East Florida." *American Quarterly Review* 2, no. 3 (September 1827): 214–37.

Stork, William. *An Account of East Florida, with Remarks on its Future Importance to Trade and Commerce*. London: W. Nicoll and G. Woodfall, 1766. Reprint. Fernandina, Fla.: Florida Mirror, 1881.

"The Story of Naval Stores." WPA Florida Writers' Program. *Florida Highways*, May 1943, p. 36.

Stowe, Harriet Beecher. *Palmetto Leaves*. 1873. Reprint. Gainesville: University of Florida Press, 1968.

Strickland, Alice. "Prince of the Wilderness," *Florida Speaks* 5, no. 2 (April 1953): 28–29.

Strutt, Joseph. *Sports and Pastimes of the People of England*. London: T. Tegg, 1845.

Stuart, Mary Frances. "The Uchee Valley Scots." M.A. thesis, Florida State University, 1956.

Stuart, Villiers. *Adventures amidst the equatorial forests and rivers of South America; Also in the West Indies and the Wilds of Florida*. London: J. Murray, 1891.

The Suffolk Collection of Church Music. Boston: Thomas and Andrew, 1807.

Swanton, John Reed. *Early History of the Creek Indians and Their Neighbors*. Washington, D.C.: Government Printing Office, 1922.

————. *The Indian Tribes of North America*. Washington, D.C.: Government Printing Office, 1952.

Swinson, Arthur. *A Register of the Regiments and Corps of the British Army*. London: Archive Press, 1972.

Swint, Henry L., ed. *Dear Ones at Home: Letters from Contraband Camps*. Nashville: Vanderbilt University Press, 1966.

Taillefer, Nugent. *Rondeaus of the British Volunteers*. London: Stanley Lucas, Weber, 1878.

Tanner, Helen Hornbeck. "The 1789 Saint Augustine Celebration." *Florida Historical Quarterly* 38, no. 4 (October 1959): 280–93.

————. "Vincent Manuel de Zespedes and the Restoration of Spanish Rule in East Florida, 1784–1790. Ph.D. diss., University of Michigan, 1961.

————. *Zespedes in East Florida, 1784–1790.* Coral Gables: University of Miami Press, 1963.

Tappan, John S. "Tallahassee and St. Marks, 1841." *Florida Historical Quarterly* 24, no. 2 (October 1945): 108–12.

Tate, Nahum, and Nicholas Brady. *A New Version of the Psalms of David.* London, 1696.

Tawa, Nicholas. *Sweet Songs for Gentle Americans.* Bowling Green, Ohio: Bowling Green University Popular Press, 1980.

Taylor, Matilda D. "Old Customs of the Early Days." *El Escribano,* no. 41 (October 1961): 7–8.

Tebeau, Charlton W. *A History of Florida.* Coral Gables: University of Miami Press, 1971.

Temperley, Nicholas. *The Music of the English Parish Church.* 2 vols. Cambridge: Cambridge University Press, 1979.

Tenney, John Francis. *Slavery, Secession, and Success: Memoirs of a Florida Prisoner.* San Antonio, Tex.: Southern Literary Institute, 1934.

TePaske, John Jay. "Funerals and Fiestas in Early Eighteenth Century St. Augustine." *Florida Historical Quarterly* 44, nos. 1–2 (July–October 1965): 97–104.

————. *The Governorship of Spanish Florida, 1700–1763.* Durham, N.C.: Duke University Press, 1964.

Ternaux-Compans, Henri. *Recueil de pièces sur la Floride.* Paris: A. Bertrand, 1841.

Thede, Marion. *The Fiddle Book.* New York: Oak Publications, 1967.

Thompson, Arthur W. "A Massachusetts Mechanic in Florida and Mexico in 1847." *Florida Historical Quarterly* 33, no. 2 (October 1954): 130–41.

————. "A Massachusetts Traveller on the Florida Frontier." *Florida Historical Quarterly* 38, no. 1 (October 1959): 129–41.

Thompson, Charles, and Samuel Thompson. *Thompson's Compleat Collection of Two Hundred Favourite Country Dances.* 4 vols. London: C. and S. Thompson, 1760. Reprint. 1770–80.

————. *Twenty-Four Favourite Marches in Five Parts, as they are performed by His Majesty's Foot and Horse Guards.* London: C. and S. Thompson, 1770.

————. *A Second Collection of Twenty-Four Marches in seven parts as they are perform'd by his Majesty's Foot and Horse Guards.* London: C. and S. Thompson, 1771.

Thompson, William. *Orpheus Caledonius; or, A Collection of Scots Songs set to music by W. Thompson.* 2 vols. London: By the author, 1733.

Thompson and Son. *The Compleat Tutor for the Fife.* London: By the authors, 1759.

Thouret, George, ed. *Musik am preussischen Hofe* (Music of the Prussian Court). Leipzig: Breitkopf and Hartel, 1896.

Till, Jacob E. "Pensacola during the Territorial Period, 1821–1845: Its Economic and Cultural Development." M.A. thesis, Florida State University, 1967.

Tinsley, Jim Bob. *He Was Singin' This Song*. Orlando: University Presses of Florida, 1981.

Tourtellotte, Jerome. *A History of Co. K of the Seventh Connecticut Volunteer Infantry in the Civil War*. N.P., 1910.

"Towns and Plantations." WPA. Corse Files no. 784. Jacksonville University Library.

Trend, J. B. *The Music of Spanish History to 1600*. New York: Oxford University Press, 1926.

Trumbull, Henry Clay. *War Memories of an Army Chaplain*. New York: Charles Scribner's Sons, 1898.

Trumpet of Freedom. Boston: Oliver Ditson, 1864.

Turnbull, Corrinne. "Sheet Music Collection, 1849–1880." Florida State University Music Library.

Tyler, James. "The Renaissance Guitar, 1500–1650." *Early Music* 3, no. 4 (1975): 142.

Uncle Ned Songster. Philadelphia, n.d., [c. 1852].

Van Brunt, Dorothy. "Father Hugon and the Early Catholic Church in Tallahassee." *Apalachee* 1 (1944): 62.

Van Campen, J. T. *St. Augustine, Capital of la Florida*. St. Augustine: J. T. Van Campen, 1959.

Vignoles, Charles B. *Observations upon Florida*. New York: E. Bliss and E. White, 1823.

Virginia Richly Valued. By a Gentleman of Elvas. London: F. Kyngston for M. Lownes, 1609. Reprint. Washington, D.C.: W. Q. Force, 1846.

Vocal Enchantress, presenting an Elegant Selection of the Most Favourite Hunting, Sea, Love, and Miscellaneous Songs. London: J. F. Fielding, 1783.

Walker, Jonathan. *The Trial and Imprisonment of Jonathan Walker*. Boston: Anti-Slavery Office, 1845. Reprint. Gainesville: University Presses of Florida, 1974.

Walkley, Stephen. *History of the Seventh Connecticut Volunteer Infantry, Hawley's Brigade, Terry's Division, Tenth Army Corps, 1861–1865*. Southington, Conn., 1905.

Warlike Musick. London: I. Walsh, 1760.

Warner, Thomas E. "European Musical Activites in North America before 1620." *Musical Quarterly* 70, no. 1 (Winter 1984): 77–95.

Watson, Robert. "His Confederate War Diary, 1861–1865." Florida State Archives.

Watts, Isaac. *Hymns and Spiritual Songs*. Exeter, N.H.: John I. Williams, 1822.
———. *The Psalms of David Imitated in the Language of the New Testament*. London, 1719.

Weaver, M. L. "Sheet Music Collection, 1827–1857." Florida State University Music Library.

Webster, Sarah E. "Sheet Music Collection, 1838–1864." Florida State University Music Library.

Wellman, Manley Wade, ed. *The Rebel Songster.* Charlotte, N.C.: Heritage, 1959.

Wenhold, Lucy L. "A Seventeenth Century Letter of Gabriel Diaz Vara Calderon, Bishop of Cuba, Describing the Indians and Indian Missions of Florida." In *Smithsonian Miscellaneous Collections,* vol. 95, no. 16. Washington, D.C.: Smithsonian Institution, 1936.

Wentworth, T. T., Jr. "Civil War Letters." Manuscript. University of West Florida Archives, Pensacola.

West, William Russell. "An Historical Study of Professional Theater Activities in Tallahassee, Florida, from January 1874 to November 1893." M.A. thesis, Florida State University, 1954.

Wharton, H. M. *War Songs and Poems of the Southern Confederacy, 1861–1865.* Philadelphia: W. E. Scull, 1984. (Includes diary excerpts.)

White, Benjamin Franklin, and E. J. King. *The Sacred Harp.* Nashville: Broadman Press, 1968.

White, Joseph. "Life in Florida." *Knickerbocker* 8 (August 1836): 150–55; (September 1836): 276–88; (November 1836): 553–59.

Williams, Edwin L., Jr. "Negro Slavery in Florida." *Florida Historical Quarterly* 28, no. 2 (October 1949): 93.

Williams, George W. *A History of the Negro Troops in the War of the Rebellion, 1861–1865.* New York: Negro University Press, 1969.

Williams, Grier Moffatt. "A History of Music in Jacksonville, Florida, 1822–1922." Ph.D. diss., Florida State University, 1961.

Williams, John Lee. *The Territory of Florida.* New York: A. T. Goodrich, 1837. Reprint. Gainesville: University of Florida Press, 1962.

———. *A View of West Florida.* Philadelphia: T. S. Tanner, 1827.

Williams, Linda K. "East Florida as a Loyalist Haven." *Florida Historical Quarterly* 54, no. 4 (April 1976): 425–42.

Williams, Robert. "Preservation of the Oral Tradition of Hymn Singing in Negro Religious Music." Ph.D. diss., Florida State University, 1973.

Willis, Etta Bell. "History of the Methodist Church of Quincy, Florida." Typescript. State Library of Florida.

Willson, Minnie Moore. *The Seminoles of Florida.* New York: Moffat, Yard, 1910.

Wilson, J. A. *Adventures of Alf. Wilson.* Toledo: Blade Printing, 1880.

Wilson, Joseph T. *The Black Phalanx.* Hartford, Conn.: American Publishing, 1890.

Winstock, Lewis. *Songs and Music of the Redcoats.* London: Leo Cooper, 1970.

Wisinewski, Jerome Joseph. *They Came and They Remained.* St. Leo, Fla.: Abbey Press, 1964.

Wolf, Edwin. *American Song Sheets, Slip Ballads, and Poetical Broadsides, 1850–1870: A Catalogue of the Collection of the Library Company of Philadelphia.* Philadelphia: Library Company, 1963.

Wolfe, Richard J. *Secular Music in America, 1801–1825.* 3 vols. New York: New York Public Library, 1964.

Woodward, Ashbel. *Life of General Nathaniel Lyon.* Hartford: Case, Lockwood, 1862.

Worcester, Donald E., trans. "Miranda's Diary of the Siege of Pensacola, 1781." *Florida Historical Quarterly* 29, no. 2 (January 1951): 163–96.

The WPA Guide to Florida. Written and complied by the Federal Writers' Project. New York: Pantheon Books, 1984. Reprint of *Florida,* New York: Oxford University Press, 1939.

Wright, J. Leitch. *Anglo-Spanish Rivalry in North America.* Athens: University of Georgia Press, 1971.

———. *Britain and the American Frontier, 1783–1815.* Athens: University of Georgia Press, 1975.

———. *British St. Augustine.* St. Augustine: Historic St. Augustine Preservation Board, 1975.

———. *Florida in the American Revolution.* Gainesville: University Presses of Florida, 1975.

———. *The Only Land They Knew.* New York: Free Press, 1981.

———. *William Augustus Bowles, Director-General of the Creek Nation.* Athens: University of Georgia Press, 1967.

Wroth, Warwick. *The London Pleasure Gardens of the Eighteenth Century.* London: Macmillan, 1896.

Wynne, John Huddlestone. *A General History of the British Empire in America.* London: W. Richardson and L. Urquhart, 1770.

Yonge, Julia J. *Christ Church Parish, Pensacola, 1827–1927.* Pensacola: Churchwardens and Vestrymen of Christ Church, 1956.

Young, Hugh. "A Topographical Memoir on East and West Florida, with Itineraries of General Jackson's Army, 1818." *Florida Historical Quarterly* 13, no. 1 (July 1934): 16–50; no. 2 (October 1934): 82–104; no. 3 (January 1935): 129–64.

Zabriski, George A. *Stephen Collins Foster.* Ormond Beach, Fla.: The Doldrums, 1941.

Zahendra, Peter. "Spanish West Florida, 1781–1821." Ph.D. diss., University of Michigan, 1976.

Zealley, Alfred E., and J. Ord Hume. *Famous Bands of the British Empire.* London: J. P. Hull, n.d.

ABOUT THE AUTHOR

Wiley L. Housewright, longtime Dean of the School of Music at Florida State University and Director of the University Singers, is Professor Emeritus of Music.